ENGLISH LAND & ENGLISH LANDLORDS

ENGLISH LAND

AND

ENGLISH LANDLORDS

An Enquiry into the Origin & Character of the

English Land System, with Proposals

for its Reform

BY

GEORGE C. BRODRICK

[1881]

DAVID & CHARLES: NEWTON ABBOT

7153 4267 3

First Edition 1881

(London: *Published for The Cobden Club by* Cassel,
Petter, Galpin & Company, 1881)

Reprinted 1968 by

AUGUSTUS M. KELLEY · PUBLISHERS

New York   New York   10010

Published in the United Kingdom by

DAVID & CHARLES (PUBLISHERS) LTD.

South Devon House   Newton Abbot   Devon

PRINTED IN THE UNITED STATES OF AMERICA
by SENTRY PRESS, NEW YORK, N. Y. 10019

ENGLISH LAND

AND

ENGLISH LANDLORDS.

ENGLISH LAND

AND

ENGLISH LANDLORDS.

*An Enquiry into the Origin and Character of the
English Land System, with Proposals
for its Reform.*

WITH AN INDEX.

BY

THE HON. GEORGE C. BRODRICK.

PUBLISHED FOR THE COBDEN CLUB BY

CASSELL, PETTER, GALPIN & CO.:

LONDON, PARIS & NEW YORK.

1881.

PREFACE.

THE present volume treats of the historical growth, the distinctive features, and the prospective development, of the English Land System. It does not purport to deal with the Scotch or Irish land systems, in so far as they differ from the English, except where these differences may be significant, for purposes of illustration. Nor does it purport to describe fully the land systems of foreign countries, though I have thought it well to introduce a concise review of the more important among these, in order to exhibit in stronger relief the unique character of the agrarian constitution established in England by the joint operation of Law and Custom. The peculiar essence of that constitution is to be found in the marked separation of the agricultural community into three classes—landlords, farmers, and labourers. Of these classes, the first is at once the most powerful, and the most typical product of the English Land System. I have, therefore, associated " English Land " with " English Landlords," in the title of a work chiefly designed to set forth the reciprocal influence of social and agricultural relations in the past, the present, and the future.

It has been my endeavour to bring the broader and

more characteristic aspects of the English Land System
within the comprehension of unlearned, and even of
foreign, readers. With this view, I have avoided
legal and agricultural details, as far as possible, and
have abstained from discussing questions outside the
main line of the enquiry. For example, while I have
indicated the extent of landed property held by corporations or trustees of charities, I have not touched
upon various schemes for its better management or
re-appropriation. Other topics connected with land
tenure in England have been omitted for similar
reasons; but I have not consciously shrunk from grap-
pling with any difficulties involved in the elucidation
or reform of the English Land System.

Though I have freely consulted other works, and
have derived much information from those of Mr.
Caird, in particular, I have adopted no conclusion as
my own without careful and independent research.
Since it would have been impossible to marshal the
whole evidence on which each statement is founded,
I have seldom cited authorities, unless for the sake
of acknowledging an obligation, or of noting an important conflict of opinion. To many personal friends
I am indebted for kind advice and criticism; but
my grateful thanks are specially due to Mr. John
Bateman, author of the "Great Landowners of the
United Kingdom," for his generous and valuable assistance in preparing the classification of landowners for
each county of England and Wales, appended to the
third chapter of Part II. I venture to believe that so

instructive an analysis of the official returns has never
before appeared, and that a careful study of it will
throw new light on the distribution of landed property
in this country.

In the first chapter of Part II., as well as in
other chapters of the same Part, I have not scrupled
to borrow liberally from Essays of my own, on the
"Law and Custom of Primogeniture," and "Local
Government in England," originally published by the
Cobden Club, and re-published in my "Political
Studies" (1879).

In laying before the public a comprehensive survey of the English Land System, with proposals for
its amendment, I am conscious of exposing myself to
a double charge of presumption. It may be thought, on
the one hand, that everything which can be said on that
system must already have been said in the numerous
books, pamphlets, and articles, which have lately been
put forth on the so-called Land Question. It may be
doubted, on the other hand, whether so vast and
complicated a theme can be adequately handled within
the compass of a single volume, or, perhaps, by any
writer who does not possess a very rare combination
of attainments. In reply to both these objections,
I can only plead that my task has not been undertaken without a full sense of its gravity, or without
a sincere desire to execute it impartially. It would
not have been undertaken at all, if any treatise already
published had appeared to supply the want of a
compendious work, at once historical, descriptive, and

suggestive, neither controversial in its spirit nor technical in its style. In prospect of early legislation on subjects closely affecting the Landed Interest, I have been induced and encouraged to attempt such a work. No one can be so conscious of its imperfections as the author, but if it shall in any degree serve to mark out the true course of constructive statesmanship by the light of past experience, I shall be amply rewarded.

GEORGE C. BRODRICK.

November, 1880.

CONTENTS.

—◦—

Part I.

Part II.

Part III.

Part IV.

PROPOSED REFORM OF THE ENGLISH LAND SYSTEM.

ENGLISH LAND

AND

ENGLISH LANDLORDS.

Part I.

HISTORICAL SKETCH OF THE ENGLISH LAND SYSTEM.

CHAPTER I.

Land Tenure and Agriculture in England from the Earliest Period to the Middle of the Fourteenth Century.

THE soil of England, though renowned for its fertility under the Romans, had been little disturbed by the plough before the invasion of Cæsar. Corn was already raised by settlers of Belgic race in the maritime districts which lay nearest to Gaul; but the interior was peopled by wild tribes, all but ignorant of husbandry, wandering from pasturage to pasturage with their stunted flocks or herds, and living chiefly on milk and flesh. Vast forests, parts of which have since been submerged, then overspread large tracts of the southern, western, and northern counties, serving as a bulwark against hostile incursions and as a natural division between different tribes. Fens and marshes of unknown extent covered much of the best wheat-growing land in the eastern counties, and many places now surrounded by waving corn-fields were then islands not yet made accessible by causeways. Half the roots and vegetables

now consumed as human food or as forage were unknown to the ancient Britons; even the beech-tree, on
whose fruit the Saxons fed their swine, had not been
introduced from the Continent, and no roads or means
of transport existed whereby the failure of a crop in
one district could be supplied by the plenty of another.
In such a state of society, the very idea of agriculture
was entirely wanting, and the only agrarian relation
that could exist was that of master and slave. If the
British chiefs possessed any separate property apart
from the hunting-grounds and clearings of their respective tribes, it was doubtless tilled by their families
and menials; but no rudiments of a land-system can
be discovered in the scanty and shadowy records of
pre-Roman Britain.

Though England was never fully subdued by the
Romans, and though, in the main, the rural districts
were governed by the conquerors from towns and military stations, yet the permanence of Roman influences
is truly remarkable. It was doubtless aided by the
paucity of the British population, which is estimated
to have been less than one million, while that of the
Roman settlers has been estimated at one hundred
thousand. The great roads which still remain after
seventeen or eighteen centuries as monuments of Roman
foresight; the sites of Roman camps which crown so
many commanding heights; the ruins of Roman towns,
with their walls and gateways, their amphitheatres and
public buildings; the basements of Roman villas, with
their baths and tesselated pavements; the enormous
relics of Roman potteries, ironworks, and mines—these
are the most familiar evidences of imperial rule and

domestic life among the Romans in Britain. But
there are also some traces of Roman agriculture on
land which afterwards relapsed into waste, and we have
the positive statement of the Emperor Julian that, in
the middle of the fourth century, a famine was averted
on the banks of the Rhine by the importation of corn
from Britain. The practice of agriculture was, indeed,
an instinct and a tradition among the bodies of settlers
who formed Roman colonies, nine of which at least
were established in Britain. How far they cultivated
the land with their own hands, and how far they employed the native population as bondmen, we have no
means of ascertaining. The condition of Roman "coloni"
is, indeed, involved in great obscurity, and even Savigny
could discover no historical connection between them
and the villeins of a later age; but it is at least probable that a servile class grew up under Roman dominion, which the Saxon invaders afterwards converted
into predial slaves.

It is, however, from the Anglo-Saxon age that we
must date the origin of that land-system, characteristic
of all Teutonic nations, which has been developed so
differently by England and by Germany. The organization of the German "Mark" has of late been so
elaborately analyzed and described that its leading
features now stand out in clear relief. It cannot be
asserted with confidence that it prevailed over the
whole of England, but there is good reason to believe
that it prevailed very widely, and furnished the primitive type upon which mediæval agriculture was moulded
in this country. The village-community thus constituted was a society of free proprietors, representing

either the first conquerors or their descendants. This society usually consisted of a clan or group of kindred families, each head of which is supposed to have received an allotment, though not perhaps an allotment of equal size with those of the chief or the more powerful members of the clan. Part of the district held by the village-community was owned jointly by the whole, and occupied as common pasturage, or common woodland; another part, near the inhabited "township" of the community, was divided into separate lots belonging to individual owners, but tilled, or reserved as meadow land, according to a fixed order of common husbandry, and thrown open for common pasturage after harvest; a third part, immediately surrounding the homesteads of the "township," comprised a number of little enclosures, in the nature of paddocks, gardens, or farm-yards, appropriated absolutely to different households. Careful research has gone far to prove that until the end of the last century, land in many English parishes was still cultivated on a system manifestly derived from that of the old village-communities; that "Lammas-fields" are nothing but fields which have remained subject to the old rights of joint pasturage over the fallows and stubbles of the arable "mark"; that enclosure of commons, mainly for the benefit of great landowners, is but the continuation of the process whereby demesne-land encroached upon the common pasture or "folkland"; and that lords of manors are legally, if not lineally, descended from the stronger members of Saxon townships, whose "properties" ultimately swallowed up the shares of their poorer neighbours in the *ager publicus* of the village.

In this antique form of agrarian partnership, there was no room for a tripartite division of burdens and profits between landlords, tenant-farmers, and farm-labourers. Every freeman was, in theory, his own landlord, his own farmer, and his own labourer, though we can hardly doubt that a simple form of co-operative agriculture had already been invented under the stress of necessity. The swine roaming the woods, or the sheep and cattle turned into the pasture of the village-community, would naturally be under the charge of common herdsmen or shepherds; the rude implements and vehicles then employed for ploughing and harrowing, getting in and housing the crops, would often be used in turn by more than one family; and the help still rendered to each other by French peasants and Irish farmers cannot have been wanting in the communistic infancy of husbandry. But it has yet to be shown that no man could own land in England without being a member of some village-community,[1] and analogy would lead us to suspect the concurrent existence of at least two systems which are conventionally treated as distinct stages in the history of land tenure. The manor, which fills so large a space in later jurisprudence, may have existed, and probably did exist, side by side with the "mark," or village-community. The homestead of a powerful chief must needs have overshadowed those of humbler freemen; and his share in the common field, even if originally the same, would soon become larger. Such a progressive inequality in the size of separate holdings would coincide with inequality in the skill of different

---

[1] Stubbs' "Constitutional History," vol. I., chap. v.

farmers, while both would tend directly to favour a progressive creation of separate ownership and the territorial aggrandizement of the chief. The first step would be the severance of his allotment from the common land, next would follow its enclosure; first, he would claim the lion's share of the waste, then he would acquire the power of treating it as his own property, subject to rights of pasturage and turf-cutting. The exact course of this remarkable transition has never been traced out, but it is tolerably certain that it was accomplished in most parts of England before the Norman Conquest. Whether by the solemn act of "commendation,"[1] or by less regular methods of submission, the peasant proprietors of Anglo-Saxon villages gradually transformed themselves into tenants of manors; and the greatest landowner of the village-community emerged into a lord of the manor, in everything but the name, which he did not acquire till a later period. The former were still freeholders, cultivating their lots of arable land as private estates more or less in accordance with the old rules of common husbandry, exercising the old common rights of wood and pasture over what now began to be called the lord's waste, and attending local courts for regulating common interests, such as the repair of cross-roads, the cleansing of streams, the preservation of fences, the removal of nuisances, and the decision of endless questions regarding stray cattle. But these courts were soon to be recognized, under various

---

[1] So highly was the protection of a superior prized by landholders, that an instance is given in which a man who had actually bought his land of the king commended himself, for greater security, to a lord.

names, as the lord's courts; for all who had "commended" themselves to a lord thereby placed themselves under his jurisdiction; and still ampler powers of jurisdiction over the lesser freeholders were often attached by express words to royal grants of land. Thus manorial influences waxed more and more paramount in these little village republics; and so generally had their inhabitants accepted or acquiesced in a state of vassalage that agrarian relations in most parts of England apparently underwent no violent change upon the introduction of feudal tenures.[1]

More than two centuries have elapsed since feudal tenures were abolished; yet the manorial land-system, which supplied the basis of them, is not yet extinct. However it may have been developed, and whether or not it embraced the whole country, that system was assuredly the germ of the modern English land-system, and resembled this in some respects more closely than it resembled certain phases of rural economy which intervened between the Norman times and our own. Through all the intricacies of tenure and custom which perplex legal antiquaries, we can still discern the simple features of village societies in England under the Henrys and the Edwards. The most central object was the parish church, next to which in dignity, and often closely adjoining it, rose the manor-house of the lord, with its great hall, in which Manor Courts were held, fines imposed,[2] homage received, and, perhaps, criminal

---

[1] See Maine's "Village Communities," pp. 140—6.

[2] Such petty offences as fraudulent adulteration, and the use of dishonest weights, seem to have been within the cognizance of the Manor Court.

justice administered under a special grant of jurisdiction. The best part of the cultivated land, ranging from one-quarter to one-half, formed the lord's private demesne, and was tilled under the bailiff either by villeins performing forced labour, or by free labourers working for hire. The rest of the cultivated land was divided between free tenants and villeins, each possessing the rights of pasturage, and often of turbary, over the waste. The 1,400 tenants-in-chief, and 7,871 *sub-feudarii*, who owned all the manors in England under the Conqueror, are the prototypes of the two or three thousand noblemen and squires who now own full half of England and Wales. The free tenants and higher orders of villeins are the prototypes of the modern tenant-farmer, being more dependent on the landlord for protection, though always enjoying fixity of tenure, when they did not hold under lease. The lower orders of villeins are the prototypes of the modern farm labourer, to whom they were inferior in so far as they were attached to the soil, but superior in so far as they had a proprietary interest in the soil, and could look down upon a slave class which still existed beneath them.

The survival of this slave class from the earliest ages is clearly established, though little is known of its actual condition. To diminish and mitigate slavery was among the most beneficent efforts of the Anglo-Saxon Church; yet we hear of English nobles breeding slaves for the market in the eleventh century, and of the Bristol slave trade being finally suppressed in the Conqueror's reign. More than 25,000 *servi* are registered in the Domesday census; and these, afterwards called " villeins in gross," were regarded as part of the live stock on a farm, with no right to migrate from it, yet with no interest in the soil, and liable to be transferred from one lord to another. It is no longer possible to interpret the exact distinctions between the various subdivisions of the class intermediate between slaves and freeholders—the 82,000 *bordarii*, the 7,000 *cotarii*, and the 110,000 *villani* of Domesday Book. Professor Stubbs identifies the *villani* with those freeholders of the old township or village-community who had degenerated into the customary tenants of the lord, and were the predecessors of the later copyholders. No doubt, this may have been the origin of many *villani*, but we cannot doubt that many others must have risen from the ranks of those landless serfs or slaves employed to cultivate the larger Anglo-Saxon domains, while many freeholders of the village-community are represented in Domesday not as *villani*, but as *socmanni*. The *cotarii* and *bordarii* are generally admitted to have been practically serfs holding cottages and small plots of land on condition of rendering compulsory services. The amount of these services became gradually defined by custom, and custom soon coupled with their due performance the enjoyment of such privileges as turning out a few cattle on the waste. The higher class of *villani* were only bound to aid in certain kinds of farm labour, and at certain seasons ; the lower class, with the serfs, were bound to work on the home farm throughout the year ; and the measure of their respective obligations was generally entered on the Court Roll.[1] As slavery became extinguished, and the condition of villeinage, in

---

[1] See Green's "History of the English People," chap. v. ; Nasse's "Agricultural Community of the Middle Ages," pp. 35—42.

all its forms, became elevated, the free peasant proprietor
was proportionately depressed in his relation to the
feudal hierarchy above him.   The higher class of villeins
and the lower class of freeholders insensibly passed into
each other, so that by the end of Henry III.'s reign
the best part of the rural population in England was
assimilated and absorbed into a new class of tenant-
farmers—a class which had begun to grow up much
earlier, but was then chiefly to be found upon ecclesiastical land.[1]   Some of these old English tenant-farmers
paid rent in money, some in kind, some in agricultural
services; but their rents were fixed, and their social position was that of yeomen rather than of villeins.   At the
same time, their legal status was materially strengthened
by a new writ, introduced in the reign of Henry
III., whereby a farmer holding under an ordinary
lease, even though not embodied in a deed, acquired a
right of property which could be enforced at law against
strangers, and even against his own lord.

There is no reason to believe that any material
progress was made in the art of agriculture between
the Roman age and the agrarian revolution of the
fourteenth century.   The actual extent of land under
cultivation in England during the Middle Ages was probably greater than is commonly supposed, for it is
certain that many thousands of acres then under the
plough were afterwards converted into parks and pas-
turages, or covered by the spread of towns.   But the
old "three-field husbandry" of the Anglo-Saxon
village-community, which has been perpetuated in the
midland counties down to our own times, seems to

[1] Rogers' "History of Prices," p. 3.

have prevailed generally during the whole of this period. Under that system, a crop of barley, oats, or beans, regularly followed a crop of wheat, and the field was left fallow every third year. The price of iron was so high as to make the wear and tear of agricultural implements a very serious consideration for the farmer, especially in dry weather. Manure was supplied, if at all, by turning out flocks of sheep on the fallow; ordinary farmyard manure was very scarce; stall feeding was little practised, and artificial manure was of course wholly unknown. The land was usually ploughed over twice, and, since the horses and oxen of those days were both underbred and underfed, a team consisted, as a rule, of eight draught cattle.[1] Yet the ploughing was, after all, but shallow, and two bushels of seed per acre yielded a return of no more than eight bushels, or one quarter, of wheat. During the century preceding the Black Death, the average price of a quarter was six shillings—equivalent to at least 120s. of our money—and the average corn wage paid to each labourer was about five quarters a year, on which he must be assumed to have kept his family.[2] Hay was produced exclusively from natural

---

[1] Nasse's "Agricultural Community of the Middle Ages," pp. 43, 44. Rogers speaks of four horses being attached to each plough. ("History of Prices," vol. I., p. 15.)

[2] In the rare tract of Bishop Fleetwood, entitled "Chronicon Pretiosum," and first published in 1705 or 1706, a large body of evidence is collected bearing on the cost of wheat and other commodities in the Middle Ages. From this it would appear that extremely violent fluctuations occurred in the market price of wheat during the twelfth and thirteenth centuries. In 1125, it is stated to have reached £1 per quarter, an almost incredible quotation, since it would be equivalent to about £20 of our present money. In 1270, however, a famine price of no less than

meadows, which, in the absence of artificial grasses and
winter roots, were extremely valuable.[1] Peas and
vetches, however, were grown in some parts of the
country.

Agricultural improvement was then confined to
very simple operations, such as hedging and ditching,
rough draining, marling, and liming.[2] Dairy produce
of all kinds was doubtless more abundant in country
villages than it now is; for the poorest serf was seldom
denied his " cow's grass," as it is still called in the
North, and there were no dealers to buy up milk for
great towns. Cheese and butter were made in the out-
buildings of manor-houses, and were cheap relatively
to bread of wheaten flour, which seems to have been
mainly consumed by the higher orders, as rye-bread
and oat-bread were by the poor. Butchers' meat was
then sold for about one farthing a pound, mutton
being somewhat cheaper than beef, notwithstanding
the want of winter food, which compelled farmers to
kill off a great part of their flocks at the end of the
autumn. Low as the price of mutton was, sheep-
farming was found to be very profitable, and for this
reason was generally retained in the lord's own hands.
Though a fleece of wool seldom weighed more than

£4 16s. per quarter is reported to have prevailed; whereas in years of
plenty, such as 1243, 1244, and 1288, wheat is said to have been sold for
2s. or even 1s. 6d. per quarter. In 1315—17 the price seems to have risen
again up to £2 and upwards per quarter. Some of these figures are so
astonishing as to suggest the suspicion that they represent maximum and
minimum prices in local markets, some taken just before, and some just
after, the harvest.
    [1] Rogers' "History of Prices," vol. I., p. 17.
    [2] Rogers' "History of Prices," vol. I., p. 19.

two pounds, and though enormous losses of sheep, as well as of cattle, were caused by frequent "murrains," yet the supply of wool seems to have been large enough, not only to meet the home demand, in days when clothes were chiefly woollen, but to leave a considerable and constant surplus for exportation. Thus, in 1354, the export of 32,000 sacks of wool, valued at £190,000, constituted nine-tenths of the whole export for the year, and this despite a duty of £80,000, or rather more than 40 per cent. A little later the exports are said by Robert of Avesbury to have amounted to 100,000 sacks.

It would appear, indeed, that in ordinary years the supply of most necessaries was abundant. If we read of local scarcity and famines, they may often be explained by the want of communication between different parts of the country. "Brewers in cities may well afford," says the statute of 1266, "to sell two gallons of ale for a penny, and out of cities three or four gallons for a penny." From these and similar facts we may gather that competition in production had not yet been followed by competition in transit throughout England; otherwise country brewers might surely have undersold their urban rivals. The violent fluctuations of price between different localities, and different seasons of the year, were probably aggravated by the very measures designed to remedy them. The statutes against "forestallers," and against "kidders or carriers of corn," purported to check the practice of keeping back grain with a view to enhance its price. But they really operated to suppress the trade of corn, thus compelling farmers to keep a great part of their produce locked up in granaries and stack-yards, instead of selling it off as quickly as possible, and letting it find its way to markets where it was most in demand.[1]

Later researches have confirmed the statement of Hume that neither carrots nor turnips nor other edible roots were cultivated in England before the sixteenth century, when they were introduced from Holland. The potato is known to have been imported from America in the reign of Elizabeth. Most of our kitchen vegetables were introduced at about the same date from Holland and Flanders, though onions and leeks, mustard and cresses, green peas and cabbage, were grown in English gardens long before the close of the Middle Ages. Apples and other fruits, which ripen easily without shelter in the open air, were more plentiful than vegetables ; and there is reason to believe that some of the vineyards planted by the Romans were still cultivated with success, especially in the vale of Gloucester.

---

[1] See "Wealth of Nations," book IV., chap. v.

CHAPTER II.

SUCH was the general condition of agriculture and the rural population, when England was visited by the most awful pestilence recorded in history. Advancing from the East by way of Cyprus, Italy, and France, the Black Death appeared in Dorsetshire on the 1st of August, 1348, and reached London by November. Its ravages, however, were greatest in the following year, and swept away, on the lowest computation, one-third of the two or three millions who then inhabited Great Britain. The great towns, with their crowded streets, naturally suffered most; but the country villages, with their squalid huts, and utter neglect of sanitary precautions, were scourged almost as fiercely. In the words of a living historian :[1] "The whole organization of labour was thrown out of gear. The scarcity of hands produced by the terrible mortality made it difficult for villeins to perform the services due for their lands, and only a temporary abandonment of half the rent by the landowners induced the farmers of their demesnes to refrain from the abandonment of their farms. For a time cultivation became impossible. The sheep and cattle strayed through the fields and corn, says a contemporary, and there were none left who could drive them. Even when the first burst of panic was over,

---

[1] Green's "History of the English People," vol. I., p. 429.

the sudden rise of wages, consequent on the enormous diminution in the supply of labour, though accompanied by a corresponding diminution in the supply of food, rudely disturbed the course of industrial employments. Harvests rotted on the ground, and fields were left untilled, not merely from scarcity of hands, but from the strife which now for the first time revealed itself between capital and labour." In spite of a Royal Ordinance forbidding peasants to go about begging in idleness, and requiring such persons to work at the rate of wages current before the Plague, labourers exacted a famine price for their services, and rents went down in proportion. To remedy this state of things, the Statute of Labourers was passed at the close of 1349, and, as this statute was the direct result of the Black Death, so the Peasant Revolt of 1381 was the direct, though remoter, consequence of this statute.

Had the policy of the Legislature prevailed, the effect would have been not merely to keep wages down while the price of food was going up, but to revive serfdom, which had already well-nigh died out. While the landless man was required to work for any employer willing to pay him the old rate of wages, villeins were forbidden to leave their parishes, and stewards of manors soon discovered flaws in the agreements whereby they had commuted forced service for money-payments. Such demands were more intolerable when pressed on men who had lately served in the French war, or who had sought a refuge from the burdens of serfdom in the rising industry of corporate towns.[1] The struggle

---

[1] It is difficult to reconcile the misery alleged to have been in existence at this period with the statement of William Longland in "Piers the

Land Tenure and Agriculture in England from the Middle of the Fourteenth to the End of the Sixteenth Century.

lasted for a whole generation, inflamed by religious excitement and political discontent, till it reached a head in the communistic rebellion which has derived its name from Wat Tyler. This rebellion was sternly crushed, the promises made to the insurgent peasants were violated, Parliament declared its resolution to uphold serfdom, and even petitioned the King to restrain villeins from sending their children to school in order to advance them in the world. A statute passed in 1388 forbade the labourer to migrate from the place of his settlement without a passport. Other statutes were passed to prevent villeins from seeking enfranchisement by becoming artisans, or to put down the growing practice of mendicancy. But these statutes were clearly ineffective against the operation of tendencies beyond the control of law. The growth of towns constantly increased the market for agricultural produce, and gave the owners of land the means of paying money wages to farm labourers. The same cause, as well as the depopulation of the country during the Plague, rendered farm labour scarce. The scarcity of farm labour paved the way for the general introduction of leases, inasmuch as the lords of manors could no longer rely on compulsory service. The system of leasing had already been adopted on college estates before the Peasant Revolt, in a form resembling the *métairie* of south-western Europe, the landlord providing the farm stock as well as undertaking every kind of permanent improvement. But it now received a very marked impulse ; and in the

Ploughman : "—"Labourers that have no land to live on but their hands disdain to live on penny ale or bacon, but demand fresh flesh or fish, fried or bake, and that hot or hotter for chilling of their maw."

fifteenth century a very large part of England was apparently farmed on lease, in small lots of five or ten acres, several of which were often held by the same tenant. Despite all legal obstacles, parcels of land often came into the market under the influence of the same causes, and the famous Election statute of 1430, limiting the county franchise to 40s. freeholders, and excluding those of less substance, is a sufficient proof of the importance attained by this great middle class in the fifteenth century.

That century may, indeed, be regarded as the golden age of the old English yeomanry, which then included the great body of tenant-farmers holding their lands on lease.[1] Never, perhaps, was the landscape of England so picturesque as it must have been during the Wars of the Roses, when inhabited castles still crowned many a rocky mound, when abbeys still nestled in many a secluded hollow by the banks of rivers, when forests still divided one district from another, when the beauties of cultivation were beginning to enliven desolate tracts of fen and moor, and when the snug homesteads of men farming their own lands were still thickly scattered over the country. It is a memorable remark of Philip de Comines that in England the miseries wrought by civil war fell solely upon its authors, and this remark might be extended to other social evils of the fifteenth century. While the great barons were fortifying their old ramparts

---

[1] Speaking of this century, Professor Thorold Rogers says :—" Crops were plentiful, prices were low, labour was relatively well paid, and the value of land rose rapidly, though rents were on the whole stationary." (" History of Rent in England," *Contemporary Review*, April, 1880.)

afresh, wasting their means on vast retinues with a barbarous profusion of entertainment, and ultimately destroying each other in a bootless war of succession, trade was steadily prospering in the boroughs, and the fragments of great estates were constantly passing into the hands of industrious yeomen. Many of the knights and squires, possessed by the military spirit, shared the fortunes and followed the example of the nobility, maintaining extravagant households, taking an active part in the politics of those perilous times, fighting under the Yorkist or Lancastrian banner for a cause which in no degree concerned the people of England, and paying the penalty of forfeiture when they chanced to be upon the losing side. It was the small proprietors and leasehold farmers, and especially the fortunate life-tenants of monastic lands, generally let at low rents, who profited most by the unthriftiness and ruin of the classes above them. In the reign of Henry VI., Fortescue was able to boast that in no country of Europe were small proprietors so numerous as in England. For many descendants of the old villeins had by this time become copyholders, and entered the ranks of the yeomanry, which now furnished the bone and sinew of the English commonalty.

The course of legislation was favourable to both classes. By statutes of 1449 and 1469 leaseholders were protected against disturbance by purchasers or creditors of the lord's estate ; by a judgment delivered in 1468 it was decided that a tenant in villeinage had a right to maintain an action of trespass against his lord. Meanwhile, taxation was more evenly distributed than it had been in the previous century, and the growing power of the Commons had mitigated the more intolerable abuses of royal " purveyance," which had formerly been extended from the compulsory purchase of goods at arbitrary prices to the compulsory impressment of workmen at arbitrary wages.   The general result was a degree of social equality such as has never since been witnessed, and a rural economy resembling that of modern Switzerland or Germany far more closely than that of modern England.   The necessaries of life were cheap and plentiful, the habits of life were simple; all the members of a yeoman's family were labourers on the farm; the women milked the cows, span the wool, and made up the garments; almost every article consumed was of home growth or home manufacture; and, if banking accounts were unknown, the practice of saving money and leaving it by will seems to have been habitual in this class.   Nor did the labourer, roused to a sense of independence by the democratic spirit of Lollardism, fail to partake in the general prosperity of the agricultural community.   The rate of wages, as compared with the price of food, was then so high that no man was cut off from the prospect of at least renting a plot of land ; for pestilence and war had proved but too complete a check on over-population, and the rise of craft guilds in towns offered an attractive outlet for surplus labour from country districts.

Under such conditions, it is reasonable to believe that subdivision of property would have been carried much further than it actually proceeded, but for the restrictions deliberately imposed upon it by law. During the four centuries which intervened between the Conquest and the accession of Henry VII., feudal rules of succession governed the descent of landed property, and feudal ideas of policy fostered the system of entailing. Under the Saxon laws, the freeholder had a full right to alienate his land by sale or gift, and to dispose of it by will,[1] in default of which it was equally divided among his children by the national custom of Gavelkind. This custom, which still prevails in Kent, is shown to be there co-extensive with socage tenure, and its maintenance in that county has been explained with much probability by the number and independence of the Kentish freeholders, by the vast possessions of the Church in Kent, and by its geographical position.[2] It is impossible to fix the precise year, or even the precise reign, in which Primogeniture was substituted for Gavelkind in the Common Law of England. Blackstone regards this feature of mature feudalism as introduced by the Conqueror; yet the Conqueror himself sanctions descent by Gavelkind in the charter which he granted to the City of London. Under the so-called Laws of Henry I., the eldest son had no pre-eminence beyond the right of appropriating the " capital fee," held by military tenure;[3] and, so late as the reign of Henry III., socage fees, the relic of the old

---

[1] It is said that in the wills of great nobles before the Conquest some preference for eldest sons was manifested. (Kenny's "Essay on Primogeniture.")

[2] See Elton on " Tenures of Kent," and Kenny's " Essay on Primogeniture."

[3] The current interpretation of this passage is disputed by Mr. Kenny. ("Essay on Primogeniture," p. 167.)

Saxon boc-land, continued to be partible among the
male children. Glanville, writing in 1187—9, speaks of
Primogeniture as if it were fully established on estates
held by knight service, and were spreading, though
only as a local custom, on socage estates. By the year
1200, however, the general presumption was held to be
in favour of Primogeniture ; and this rule of descent had
become almost universal, except in Kent, by the end of
the thirteenth century, by which time also the custom
of entailing, in its most ancient form, was already
established. Entails created in this form conferred no
indefeasible right of inheritance. When a fee was
granted to a man "and the heirs male of his body," it
was held that, upon the birth of a son, the grantee
might sell the land, or charge it with incumbrances, or
forfeit it by treason, so as to bar the interest of his own
issue. If he did none of these acts, however, it would
descend according to the express terms of the grant, for
he could not devise it by will. It has been doubted
whether tenants of the Crown ever possessed the full
liberty of selling, though others have considered this
liberty as characteristic of true feudalism, which denied
the son any vested right in the estate so acquired by
the father. According to this view, the famous
statute *De Donis* (13 Edward I., cap. 1), by which the
succession of the issue, and the ultimate reversion of the
donor on failure of issue, were secured against the risk of
being defeated by alienation, was a legislative encroachment on feudal principles, and a part of the same policy
which afterwards carried the statute *Quia Emptores*.
The entails made under *De Donis* created, in fact, a
perpetual series of life estates, and are stigmatised

in a well-known passage of "Blackstone's Commentaries:"—

"Children grew disobedient when they knew they could not be set aside; farmers were ousted of their leases made by tenants-in-tail . . . creditors were defrauded of their debts . . . innumerable latent entails were produced to deprive purchasers of lands which they had fairly bought . . . and treasons were encouraged, as estates-tail were not liable to forfeiture longer than for the tenant's life."

The fact of such consequences having resulted from indefeasible entails has never been disputed. It is significant that, when the absurd technical device of a "common recovery" was invented to break them, in the reign of Edward IV., Parliament took no steps to counteract it, and even expressly legalized disentailing by "fines."[1] Nevertheless, there is good reason to doubt whether the greater part of England was ever subject to entails under *De Donis*, and whether that system ever came into general use before the Civil Wars of the seventeenth century, soon after which the lawyers found means to defeat it. We must remember that wills of land, by which modern entails are often created, were not then permitted by Common Law, and that even devises of land, by means of "uses," which held good in equity, are believed to date from the early part of the fifteenth century. Entails must,

---

[1] " Taltarum's case," establishing the right of breaking an entail by a collusive action, was decided in 1472. By the statute 4 Henry VII., cap. 24, the alternative method of terminating entails by " fines " was legally sanctioned. By the statute 26 Hen. VIII., cap. 18, estates-tail were deprived of their immunity from forfeiture, on conviction for treason; by 32 Hen. VIII., cap. 18, tenants for life were enabled to grant leases, on reasonable terms, which would bind their issue-in-tail; by 33 Hen. VIII., cap. 39, all estates-tail were made liable to Crown-debts, secured by record or special contract.

therefore, have been created during the fourteenth century by deed, and, as the device of successive life estates followed by remainders in tail had not been invented, there was no recognised method whereby a landowner could entail an estate, and yet reserve to himself the possession of it. Indeed, the frequency of lawsuits concerning land in the fifteenth century is some proof of its frequently coming into the market. On the other hand, in days when personalty was extremely scarce, wills of land very rare, and settlements unknown, the law of Primogeniture, causing fee simple estates to descend like entailed estates, must have operated to an extent, and with a severity, which is happily difficult to conceive in the present age.

Many events concurred to make the sixteenth century a memorable era in the history of English land tenure, as well as of English agriculture. The destruction of the old feudal baronage in the Wars of the Roses, the invention of printing, the revival of letters, the opening of a New World to commerce, and the religious movement which gave birth to the Reformation, such were some of the great changes which marked the close of the Middle Ages in this country, and ushered in a new state of society. The impulse thus imparted to national energy soon made itself felt in rural economy, and it was here intensified by the action of special causes. The revival of trade with the Continent stimulated the production of wool and hides for exportation. The growth of a new plutocracy on the ruins of the old English nobility largely increased the application of capital to land, while it strengthened the operation of that commercial spirit which had early penetrated into the relations between English landlords and tenants. With the progress of settled government and the development of modern artillery, castles were replaced by castellated mansions, and these by Elizabethan dwelling-houses, while a multitude of armed retainers soon became an encumbrance. No longer requiring the military services of his free tenants, and having almost lost the customary services of his tenants in villeinage, the lord of the manor ceased to have a motive for encouraging small occupations, and began to consolidate his farms. Having gradually appropriated large tracts of the waste since the first sanction was given to encroachment by the Statute of Merton, he now realised that grazing land yields a larger rent to its proprietor than arable, though it may support a smaller population and contribute less to the national food supply.

Already, in the reign of Henry VII., complaints had been recorded in the preambles of statutes that country districts were being depopulated, that farm buildings were being pulled down, and that sheep or cattle were driving out Christian labourers. In the fourth year of that reign an Act was passed forbidding the demolition of any farmhouse having as much as twenty acres of tillage land annexed to it, whence it may be inferred that such was regarded as the minimum size of a yeoman's occupation.

A striking passage in Bacon's " History of Henry VII." contains an epitome of the objections

urged against the pasturage enclosures of this
period :—

"Inclosures at that time began to be more frequent, whereby
arable lands, which could not be manured without people and
families, were turned into pasture, which was easily rid by a
few herdsmen; and tenancies for years, lives, and at will,
whereupon much of the yeomanry lived, were turned into
demesnes. This bred a decay of people, and by consequence a
decay of towns, churches, tithes, and the like. The King like-
wise knew full well, and in no wise forgot, that there ensued
withall upon this a decay and diminution of subsidies and taxes;
for the more gentlemen, ever the lower book of subsidies."

He justifies the wisdom of the King and Parliament in legislating against this evil, and particularly describes the method adopted:— "Enclosures
they would not forbid, for that had been to forbid
the improvement of the patrimony of the kingdom;
nor tillage they would not compel, for that was to
strive with nature and utility; but they took a
course to take away depopulating enclosures, and depopulating pasturage," indirectly, by ordaining that
all farm-houses with twenty acres attached should be
kept up with "a competent proportion of land."
The houses must needs be inhabited, and "the proportion of land being kept up did of necessity enforce the dweller not to be a beggar or cottager,
but a man of some substance, that might keep hinds
and servants, and set the plough on going. This did
wonderfully concern the might and mannerhood of the
kingdom, to have farms as it were of a standard sufficient to maintain an able body out of penury, and
did in effect amortise a great part of the lands of

the kingdom unto the hold and occupation of the yeomanry or middle people, of a condition between gentlemen and cottagers or peasants." He proceeds to observe that, whereas the strength of armies consists in their infantry, "if a State run most to noblemen and gentlemen, and that the husbandmen and ploughmen be but as their workfolks and labourers, you may have a good cavalry, but never good stable bands of foot; like to coppice woods, that if you leave in them staddles too thick, they will run to bushes and briers, and have little clean underwood." Hence was it, in his opinion, that England, with a much smaller territory, produced more good soldiers than France or Italy.

In Henry VIII.'s reign, however, complaints against pasturage enclosures were redoubled, and statutable remedies were again provided. One Act (24 Hen. VIII., c. 24) directed that all farm-houses demolished since the fourth year of Henry VII. should be rebuilt, and that, in general, a dwelling-house in which a respectable man could live should be maintained on every plot of from thirty to fifty acres of land. An Act of the next year fixed 2,000 as the highest number of sheep that any man could possess, except on his own property, so as to check the practice of sheep-farming on a large scale.[1] The same policy dictated the provision in the Act granting monastic lands to the King, that each grantee of such lands should " keep on them an honest house and household," and plough the same number of acres which had been ploughed on an average of the last twenty years. Bishop Latimer, preaching before the Court of Edward

[1] See Nasse, " Agricultural Community of the Middle Ages," pp. 74–81.

VI., denounced the nobles as "enclosers, graziers, and rent-raisers." Other patriots of the same period raised equally indignant protests against the expulsion and impoverishment of the peasantry,[1] and evidence laid before a Commission appointed by the Protector Somerset fully confirms their allegations. Yet nothing resulted from the enquiry except a petition against throwing farms together and in favour of settling households on abbey lands. The abortive insurrection of 1549 in the eastern counties of England was directed, like that of the Irish Whiteboys, against the new fences and enclosures. This same grievance continued to be a fruitful source of agitation throughout the reign of Elizabeth, but no effectual attempt was made to redress it.

Prices and wages appear to have remained at nearly the same relative level, though subject to variation with the depreciation of coinage,[2] so that a labourer fortunate enough to get work may have been nearly as well off as before. But the repeated statutes against vagrancy are a conclusive proof that hundreds of thousands were

---

[1] Mr. Cliffe Leslie has collected several important passages on this subject from the works of Sir Thomas More, Bishop Gilpin, and Harrison. More complains that noblemen, gentlemen, and even abbots, in their eagerness to swell their revenues, "leave no ground for tillage; they enclose all into pasture; they throw down houses, they pluck down towns, and leave nothing standing." He declares that tenants were "got rid of by force or fraud, or tired out by repeated injuries into parting with their property." Mr. Cliffe Leslie shows that, in losing their rights of common, the peasantry often incurred the ultimate loss of their separate fields, since their husbandry was dependent on their stock. ("Land Systems of Ireland, England, and the Continent," p. 215.)

[2] Professor Rogers states, but without giving any authority, that prices were generally trebled in the course of about thirty years, 1530—1560. ("History of Rent in England," *Contemporary Review*, April, 1880.)

entirely thrown out of work, and even those in full employment must have felt the growing restrictions upon the old rights of common. Advocates of the new agriculture strove to show that enclosure was remunerative from an economical point of view, " that more was to be gained by ten acres in grass than by twenty under grain cultivation," and that " a poor man who possessed two acres of enclosed land was better off than if he had twenty in an unenclosed state." [1] All this might be true, but it brought little comfort to a poor man who lost his share in the open field or pasture, while his rich neighbour profited by the enclosure.

Scarcely less profound was the effect produced by the dissolution of monasteries on the whole rural economy of England. It has been estimated that about one-fifth of the soil was in the hands of the monastic societies, but that it brought in no more than one-tenth of the whole national rental, since it was usually let on beneficial leases with periodical fines on renewal.[2] The leasehold tenants of abbey lands were, in fact, the most enviable members of the agricultural class in the Middle Ages, and the monks set an example of agricultural improvement to all other landlords. Hospitality

---

[1] See authors quoted in Nasse's " Land Community of the Middle Ages," pp. 81—3. The enclosures of the sixteenth century do not appear to have been always made with a view of increasing the landlord's rental. Harrison complains that a vast number of parks had been formed only to be stocked with useless wild animals, and mentions that 100 parks were to be found in Essex alone.

[2] Mr. Pearson, in his " History of England during the Early and Middle Ages," gives reasons for estimating the whole annual value of Church property at three-tenths of the rental of the kingdom in the reign of William the Conqueror, and from one-third to one-half in the thirteenth century—the golden age of the mediæval Church in England.

and charity were practised on a vast scale, and some historians regard the regular distribution of alms at the convent door, or the dinner open to all comers in the refectory, as the mediæval substitute for the poor-law system. Considering how unequally the monasteries were scattered. over the surface of the country, such direct relief can only have been accessible to a small proportion of the rural poor, even where it was not capriciously bestowed; but the civilizing influences of monasteries doubtless extended far more widely, and were specially valuable in the North of England, where private estates were of enormous size, and where resident landowners were therefore few and far between. When merchants with a shrewd eye to business, and often living in London or other towns, succeeded the benevolent monks, as they were succeeding the free-handed nobles and knights, it must have fared ill at first with the weaker members of the labouring class. The dissolution of monasteries thus became a secondary cause of the great agrarian revolution which marked the sixteenth century, and which laid the foundations of the present English Land-system.[1]

This revolution was further aided by the constant migration of labourers from towns into the country, attested by contemporary writers, and due to several distinct tendencies. As life and property became more secure under the strong hand of Tudor government, boroughs ceased to be so necessary as an asylum for

---

[1] The North of England, where the monasteries had been almost the only centres of culture and improvement, appears to have suffered most by their dissolution, as the South gained most by the growth of London and the extension of intercourse with the Continent.

the oppressed, while the craft guilds were less and less willing to welcome strangers. Again, merchants and traders settling in the country sometimes located their own labourers in cottages around them, thus introducing an innovation upon the old system under which farm servants not holding land were generally lodged in the houses of their employers. Moreover, certain branches of industry hitherto confined to boroughs now began to spread into country districts, and ultimately gave birth to new country towns. Worcestershire now shared that woollen manufacture which derived its name from the city of Worcester; cloth-making sprang up in the villages of Somersetshire and Yorkshire; iron-smelting was carried on in many a woodland hamlet of the Sussex Weald, till Parliament interfered to check the wholesale destruction of the natural forests. All these disturbing agencies, though signs of social progress, helped to undermine the ancient status of the English peasant, and paved the way for the new order of things recognised, if not established, by the Poor Law of Elizabeth.

But the gradual divorce of the English peasant from the soil, which degraded him into the day-labourer, and was the manifest origin of pauperism, coincided with unabated and perhaps increasing prosperity in the higher orders of the agricultural community. The practice of breaking entails by means of " common recoveries " had already become well established, and must have brought many estates into the market. The same object was deliberately facilitated by the statute passed in the reign of Henry VII., which authorised a tenant-in-tail to bar his own issue by a simpler

proceeding known as a "fine." It has not been sufficiently realised that, during the period between the
introduction of these methods for disentailing and the
institution of family settlements in the seventeenth
century, the ownership of landed property in this
country was practically more absolute and the disposition of it less restricted than it had been for two
centuries before, or than it has since become. Each
successive tenant-in-tail, by levying a fine or suffering
a common recovery, was able to convert his estate into
a fee simple, and, as the use of life estates in tying up
land had not been discovered, the head of a family was
usually in this position. It is impossible not to connect the rapid growth and singular independence of
the English gentry under the Tudors and Stuarts with
the limitation of entails and freedom of alienation which
characterised this remarkable period. Many of the
humbler yeomen may have been crushed out or bought
out in the process of forming parks or turning arable
into pasture farms, and may ultimately have sunk into
the condition of the labourer. But the yeoman class,
as a whole, assuredly occupied a very much larger space
in country life, as country life was a far more important
element in national life than it is easy for the present
generation of Englishmen to conceive.

This class practically included a very large body of
copyholders, whom Coke describes as occupying a third
part of England at the beginning of the next century,
as well as the smaller freeholders of manors. A popular
description of yeomen is given in Harrison's description
of England under Elizabeth, prefixed to Holinshed's
" Chronicle ":—

"Yeomen are those who by our law are called *legales homines*, freemen born English, and may dispend of their own free land in yearly revenue to the sum of forty shillings, or six pounds as money goeth in our times."

He proceeds to describe their mode of life :—

"These commonly live wealthily, keep good houses, and travail to get riches. They are also, for the most part, farmers to gentlemen, or at the least, wise artificers, and with grazing, frequenting of markets, and keeping of servants—not idle servants, as the gentlemen do, but such as get both their own and part of their master's living—do come to great wealth, insomuch that many are able and do buy the lands of unthrifty gentlemen, and often setting of their sons to the schools, to the universities, and to the Inns of Court, or otherwise leaving them sufficient lands whereby they may live without labour, do make by those means to become gentlemen. *These were they that in times past made all France afraid.*"[1]

This passage is very interesting as exhibiting the exact process whereby a peasant, or at least a peasant's son, might rise through farming into the ranks of the landed gentry, and even into the Commission of the Peace, if he could improve his estate up to a value of £20 a year. In those days capital was extremely scarce, and, though land did not command a fancy price, there were very few who could afford either to buy or to stock a large arable farm. The hereditary owners of large estates were attracted to London by the increasing influence of metropolitan excitement and Court society, or carried off into foreign enterprise by the restless spirit of that adventurous age. As tenancy-at-will had scarcely been invented, they were glad to let their lands

---

[1] See Cliffe Leslie's "Land Systems of Ireland, England, and the Continent," p. 164.

on lease[1] in farms of that moderate size which, under like conditions, is still characteristic of Ireland. Meanwhile, the yeomen, born and bred in the country, were reinforced by a large influx of town manufacturers, who built what might now be called villas, but with large plots of land around them. These new-comers, with the other freeholders, copyholders, and leaseholders, were separated by no impassable barrier of caste either from the landed aristocracy or from the labourer. "County society" had not yet become an exclusive circle of families rich enough to frequent the London season; social prejudices had not yet been inflamed by sectarian jealousies; and the rural population was not yet stratified into the horizontal layers too familiar to modern observers. Whether or not England was ever the "merry England" of poets and chroniclers, it is certain that in the Elizabethan age the various classes of Englishmen had far more interests, ideas, sympathies, habits, and amusements, in common, than in the nineteenth century.

It is extremely difficult to compare the profits of farming in the Tudor period with any modern standard, not only because they were realised under wholly different conditions, but also because they were subject to more violent fluctuations. It is certain, however, that all classes of farmers must have profited by the general prosperity of the country and the immense demand, not only for English wool, but for English woollen

---

[1] It would appear, from a passage in Harrison, that it was usual to pay a premium on the renewal of farming leases. He says that a farmer would be ill content with his property if he had not saved up six or seven years' rent by the end of his lease to purchase a new one.

manufactures, on the Continent. Moreover, agriculture was rapidly becoming more scientific. Fitzherbert's treatises on Husbandry and Surveying, published in Henry VIII.'s reign, exhibit a thorough knowledge of practical farming, and prescribe a standard of industry, especially for the wives of farmers, which is not unworthy of study in the present day. They show that the value of manuring was even then fully appreciated, that draining was already common, and that artificial irrigation was occasionally employed. Fitzherbert points out that "an housbande cannot well thrive by his corne, without he have other cattell, or by his cattell without corne." He gives special directions for conducting each farming operation at the proper season, and he advises that, if ricks cannot be under cover, they should at least be raised by a scaffolding above the ground. Rollers were used to "role their barley grounds after a shower of rayne, to make ground even to mowe." Ploughs of various kinds were known; some adapted to hilly ground, which "wyll tourn the sheld bredith at every landsende, and plough all one way." In May the sheepfolds were set out, in June corn was weeded and meadows mown; the fallow, after three ploughings, was sown at Michaelmas; and, if the preparations against winter were inadequate, this may be referred to the absence of cultivated herbage and edible root crops rather than to any lack of foresight. Despite the tendency of the sixteenth century towards pasture farms, the advantage of keeping cattle on arable farms was beginning to be understood; and we learn from the "Book of Surveying" that the value set upon manure was such as to raise the

price of enclosed land to eightpence, where it had been
held at sixpence per acre before enclosure, " by reason of
the compostying and dongying of the cattell that shall
go and lie upon it both day and nighte." If, in the
face of these facts, the return of corn was but four
times the amount of seed sown,[1] it must be remembered that the proportion in Germany, Poland, and
Russia, has been no higher during the present century.

Perhaps the rent of land is one of the most stable
elements in any calculation of farming profits; but
during the sixteenth century rent bore no definite relation to annual value, though it may have averaged from
sixpence to a shilling per acre.[2]   We have the positive
statement of Latimer that, whereas his own father had
paid three or four pounds a year at most for a farm
which maintained six men out of its produce, besides
pasturage for 100 sheep and 30 milch kine, the succeeding tenant had to pay for the same farm sixteen
pounds a year or more.   If we look to the rate of
wages, so constantly regulated by law, we find less evidence of a progressive rise than we might expect.   By
a statute passed in the reign of Henry VI. (23
Hen. VI., cap. 12), the wages of a chief hind, carter,
or shepherd, had been fixed at twenty shillings a

---

[1] Holinshed states the average produce of wheat or rye as ranging from
16 to 20 bushels; that of barley he states at 36 bushels.   It is impossible
not to doubt the accuracy of these estimates, unless they are considered as
applying to soils of exceptional fertility.

[2] According to Professor Rogers, "the modern farmer's rent, that is,
the rent which rises and falls by competition between intending occupiers
of land, is first discovered in the reign of James I."   He considers that
in the fifteenth century the rental of land did not yield above five per
cent. on the purchase-money.   ("History of Rent in England," *Contemporary Review*, April, 1880.)

year, with four shillings for clothing, and those of a common farm labourer at fifteen shillings a year, with three shillings and fourpence for clothing, besides meat and drink. This gives a mean rate of about twenty-one shillings a year, or about fivepence a week, exclusive of rations, being more than double the rate prescribed for yearly wages by a statute of Richard II. passed in 1388. The same policy of regulating the maximum rate of wages in husbandry was carried out by later statutes, especially by the 11th of Henry VII., cap. 2, and the 6th of Henry VIII., cap. 3. Upon a comparison of the rates fixed by these statutes, passed respectively in 1495 and 1514, with those fixed by the Act of Henry VI., passed in 1444, we find that no material change had taken place in the maximum wages of agricultural labour. The Acts of Henry VII. and Henry VIII. allow common *day labourers* four-pence a day during the summer half of the year, and threepence during the winter half, with extra wages for harvest. About the same time, sixpence a day was the regular soldier's pay, being a little above the statutable wages of skilled artificers.[1] If a penny was then worth as much as a shilling now, even the common labourer's wages must be taken as at least equivalent to one pound a week; yet they did not represent the whole income of the labourer. It is tolerably certain that most labourers had at least the

---

[1] The regulation of wages by statute in the fourteenth, fifteenth, and sixteenth centuries is fully discussed by Sir G. Nicholl in his "History of the English Poor Law," vol. I., part i., chaps. ii. and iii. See also Bright's "English History," vol. II., p. 468; and the First Report of the Royal Commission on the Employment of Women and Children in Agriculture, secs. 245—7.

right of turning out a cow on the waste, and, as a statute passed in the 31st year of Elizabeth prohibited the erection of any cottage without an allotment of four acres, we may suppose that many of them increased their earnings or partially maintained their families by peasant-farming or market gardening. It is less easy to understand how farmers can have afforded to pay so high wages at a time when prices were comparatively so low except in years of famine. The Duke of Buckingham's Household Book shows that at the beginning of the century a calf sometimes fetched but half-a-crown, and a carcase of mutton little more than a shilling. The Duke of Northumberland's Household Book gives twentypence as the price of a sheep, eight shillings apiece as that of lean cattle, twopence as that of a lean capon, and threepence or fourpence as that of a pig. Yet Latimer, in Edward VI.'s reign, complained bitterly that all kinds of victuals had become exorbitantly dear, specially naming pigs, geese, fowls, and eggs, and predicting that before long pigs might be sold for a pound apiece. This rise in the price of butcher's meat was apparently maintained, for by a statute passed in the 24th year of Henry VIII. it was enacted that beef and pork should be sold for a halfpenny, and mutton for three-farthings, a pound. There is some ground for surmising that these were far above the fair market prices, and that in London itself meat was to be had for the poor at a much lower rate.[1] But even the maximum

[1] Froude's "History of England," vol. I., p. 21. Stowe tells us that " the butchers of London sold penny pieces of beef for the relief of the poor; every piece two pounds and a half; sometimes three pounds for a

of three-farthings a pound is only equivalent to nine-pence of our money; so that meat was then cheaper than it now is, while the labourer's wages were higher.

It is the price of wheat, however, which has always been considered as the chief measure of the farmer's gross receipts, since it is the crop to which he too often sacrifices other sources of profit, as it is also the main subsistence of the population. The price of wheat at various periods between 1350 and 1750 is fully discussed by Adam Smith in his elaborate " Digression concerning the Variations in the Value of Silver." His conclusion, which is adopted by more recent enquirers, is that " from the 25th of Edward III. to the beginning of the reign of Elizabeth, during the space of more than 200 years, six shillings and eight-pence had continued to be considered as what is called the moderate and reasonable—that is, the ordinary or average—price of wheat."[1] It was, in fact, enacted by repeated statutes of the fifteenth and sixteenth centuries that, whenever the quarter of wheat should reach this price, importation should be lawful, and that whenever it should fall below this price, exportation should be lawful. But, as the weight of silver in the shilling was constantly decreasing, the real value of this nominal sum was falling in proportion; and in the year 1562 the exportation of wheat from certain ports was allowed whenever the price of the quarter

penny." He adds, what may perhaps help to explain this apparent generosity, that at this time " foreign " butchers were first permitted to sell their meat in London.

[1] Bishop Fleetwood, in his " Chronicon Pretiosum " above cited, states that, although wheat rose to £1 per quarter in 1440, it never stood above 8s. for twenty years afterwards.

should not exceed ten shillings, which, according to Adam Smith, contained nearly as much silver as ten shillings of our present money. Supposing ten shillings to have been the average price of wheat at a period when the purchasing power of coin was twelve times as great as now, this price was equivalent to 120s. of our present money. The discovery of the American silver mines soon afterwards caused a prodigious depreciation of silver, and it appears from the accounts of Eton College that at the end of the sixteenth and the beginning of the seventeenth centuries wheat ranged in the Windsor market from thirty to fifty shillings a quarter.[1] Even the prices of 1562, being double the present average, appear at first sight highly remunerative; but we must remember not only how very high was the cost of labour, but how small was the average crop per acre, and how vastly greater must have been the difficulty and expense of carrying farm produce to market in days when not only railways but turnpike roads were unknown, and when parish roads were often impassable except to foot-passengers and pack-horses. That corn should have been exported at all from England under such conditions, while a population estimated at 4,000,000 or 5,000,000 was supported in a remarkable degree of physical vigour and comfort,

---

[1] Sir W. Raleigh, opposing the legislative encouragement of exportation in the House of Commons, is reported to have stated "that France had offered to serve Ireland with corn for 16s. a quarter." It appears from Bishop Fleetwood's "Chronicon Pretiosum" that violent fluctuations of price were still common. Stowe mentions that in 1557 wheat stood at £2 13s. 4d. per quarter before harvest and 5s. after harvest. In the twenty years beginning with 1574, it thrice rose above £2 per quarter, and in 1596 touched £4.

may fairly be cited as a striking proof of what English farmers can do under a system little resembling that of yearly tenancy without security for improvements. Upon the whole, farming was probably a more lucrative occupation in the England of Elizabeth than in the previous century ; and the landed interest, as distinct from the feudal aristocracy, had never been so powerful, especially as many provincial towns had decayed, and a manufacturing population was beginning to spring up in many agricultural districts.

CHAPTER III.

THE most important events in the history of the English Land-system during the seventeenth century were the introduction of modern family settlements and the abolition of military tenures. We have seen how, by the operation of recoveries and fines, the indefeasible entails of an earlier age had been rendered liable to be readily set aside, and the owner of land thus disentailed soon afterwards acquired the power of devising it freely under the Statute of Wills. In course of time, however, family pride, aided by lawyers, contrived new expedients for checking alienation by sale or subdivision by will, and placing the right of Primogeniture on a secure basis. The first of these expedients in logical, if not in chronological, order was the mere substitution of such words as "first son" or "eldest son" for "heir of his body" in entailing deeds. The legal effect of this was that, instead of the father taking an estate-tail under the settlement, which he might have forthwith converted into a fee simple, he took only a life-estate, and had no control over the remainder (whether for life or in tail) given by the same instrument to his eldest son. This idea was developed by conferring, as far as possible, life-estates instead of estates-tail on the whole first generation of persons included in a family settlement; so that, whereas a tenant-in-tail once in possession could not be deprived of his power to become master of the property, the acquisition of this power might be deferred to a second or even to a later generation. But, for reasons known to lawyers, that object could not have been accomplished effectually without a further expedient devised by Sir Orlando Bridgman and Sir Geoffrey Palmer during the Civil Wars, and generally adopted after the Restoration. This was the notable contrivance of " trustees to preserve contingent remainders," of which it is enough to say that it protected the interests of tenants-in-tail against the risk of being defeated by the wrongful act of preceding life-tenants. From this epoch, rather than from " Chudleigh's case " (1588), which is cited by Bacon, must be dated the modern type of settlement. Still, the principle was maintained that an entail might be cut off by a tenant-in-tail of full age, though it was technically necessary for him, unless in possession, to obtain the concurrence of the person (generally his own father) in whom the immediate freehold was vested.

The abolition of military tenures was finally effected by one of the first Acts passed by Charles II.'s first Parliament. Up to this period all tenures, except socage and copyhold tenures, were tenures " in chivalry," of which " knight service " was by far the commonest form. In theory, every person holding a knight's fee, the minimum value of which in the Norman era is stated to have been twenty pounds a year, was bound to serve in person, or to provide a fully-armed horseman, during forty days in the year. This service was due to the king, not only where the knight's fee was held imme-

diately from the Crown, but also where it was held from
a mesne lord, himself an immediate tenant of the Crown.
In the reign of Henry II., personal liability to military service was commuted into a liability to pay
scutage, and it is well known that the English armies
which invaded France under Edward III. and Henry V.
received military pay. Still the obligation remained
in theory, and many of those who fought around the
great nobles in the Wars of the Roses were animated
by a sense of feudal duty as tenants by knight service.
But the most onerous and practical burdens of tenure
by knight service were the incidents of " wardship "
and " marriage ;" and the profits of these were directly
reaped by the lord. The right of " wardship " accrued
when a tenant by knight service happened to be a
minor, and consisted in an absolute control over the
revenues of his lands during his minority, without the
necessity of rendering an account to him on his coming
of age. The right of " marriage " consisted in a like
control over the matrimonial alliances of heirs and
heiresses, being under age, of whose lands the lord might
dispose as his own property, either by negotiating an
eligible match for them in his own interest or by
exacting a heavy penalty for a marriage contracted without his consent. By the end of Henry VIII.'s reign
the king had acquired these rights as immediate
lord over a very large proportion of English estates,
together with certain other special perquisites which
belonged to no other lord. Probably they were seldom
fully exercised, but the deplorable picture which Blackstone draws[1] of the burdens legally imposed on a tenant

[1] Vol. II., p. 76.

in capite by knight service deserves to be kept in remembrance :—

> "The heir, on the death of his ancestor, if of full age, was plundered of the first emoluments arising from his inheritance by way of relief and primer seisin; and, if under age, of the whole of his estate during infancy. And then, as Sir Thomas Smith very feelingly complains, when he came to his own after he was out of wardship, his woods decayed, houses fallen down, stock wasted and gone, lands let forth and ploughed to be barren; to reduce him still farther, he was to pay half a year's profits as a fine for suing out livery, and also the price or value of his marriage. Add to this the untimely and expensive honour of knighthood, to make his poverty more completely splendid; and when by these deductions his fortune was so shattered and ruined that perhaps he was obliged to sell his patrimony, he had not even that poor privilege allowed him without paying an exorbitant fine for a *license of alienation.*"

At all events, the grievance was felt to be so real that, after an abortive attempt had been made to redress it in the reign of James I., it was swept away by an Act of the Long Parliament passed in 1656, and solemnly re-enacted after the Restoration. The famous statute, 12 Charles II., cap. 24, operating retrospectively, turned all military tenures into "free and common socage" from the 24th of February, 1645. Thenceforth freehold tenancy has been virtually equivalent to ownership, and the only restrictions to which it is subject are those which may be created by will or deed.[1] More than a century elapsed before land was emancipated from its feudal burdens in France, and this great reform was not accomplished in Prussia, Austria, Italy, or Russia, until a period within living memory. It is at least possible

---

[1] See Appendix I. and Digby's "History of the Law of Real Property," chap. ix.

that England may thus have obtained an advantage in agriculture over her foreign rivals which has not yet been fully exhausted.

The graphic pen of Macaulay has delineated the state of rural England at the close of the seventeenth century, and it seems to have differed but little from that which prevailed in the reign of Elizabeth. It has been computed that nearly 4,000,000, out of a population amounting to about 5,250,000, then lived in the country.[1] Adopting the result of Gregory King's and Davenant's statistical enquiries, Macaulay states that not less than 160,000 proprietors, representing, with their families, more than a seventh of the whole population, derived their subsistence from little freehold estates, and possessed an average income of between £60 and £70 apiece.[2] These yeomen, mostly of Puritan leanings, had constituted the strength of the Parliamentary cause during the Civil Wars, and are believed to have still outnumbered the body of tenant-farmers. Probably many of these yeomen were children of townspeople whose trade-earnings had been invested in land. Fynes Moryson, writing in the reign of James I., remarks that English gentlemen, disdaining traffic and thinking it proper to live in idleness on their revenues, " doe in this course daily sell their patrimonies, and the buyers (excepting lawyers) are for the most part citizens and vulgar men."[3]

The progress of agriculture during the seventeenth

---

[1] Macaulay's "History of England," vol. I., chap. iii.

[2] Professor Rogers states that in the last year of Queen Anne nearly 4,000 freeholders voted in a contested election for the county of Sussex.

[3] Moryson's "Itinerary," part III., bk. iii., chap. iii.

century appears to have been slow, and the chief improvement was the introduction of regular clover and turnip cultivation soon after the close of the Civil War. The whole annual yield of wheat, rye, barley, oats, and beans was estimated by Gregory King, in 1696, at somewhat less than 10,000,000 quarters; and that of wheat alone at less than 2,000,000 quarters.[1] As the consumption of grain per head of population may be roughly taken at nearly one quarter a year, it follows that less than one-half of the people then lived on wheaten bread. The price of wheat is computed by Arthur Young to have averaged 38s. 2d. for the whole century,[2] and this price must be considered very high if compared with the current rate of wages.[3] Nevertheless, so little did the crop then depend on the skill of the farmer, and so much on the caprice of the seasons, that violent fluctuations of price were constantly occurring. Pepys records a conversation at Lord Crewe's table on January 1, 1668, when " they did talk much of the present cheapness of corne, even to a miracle; so as their farmers can pay no rent, but do fling up

---

[1] Macaulay's " History," vol. I., chap. iii.

[2] Adam Smith's calculation, founded on the receipts of Eton College, gives nearly the same result.

[3] Arthur Young reckons the average rate of agricultural wages in the seventeenth century at 10¼d. a day.   It follows, as Malthus points out, that a labourer would be able to purchase with his day's earnings three-quarters of a peck of wheat; " whilst, during the first half of the eighteenth century, wages having risen and corn fallen, he would be able to purchase a whole peck ; " and it may be added that, at the present average rate of wages and prices, he would be able to purchase nearly one peck and a quarter. (See Sir G. Nicholl's " History of the Poor Laws," vol. II., chap. xi.)

their lands, and would pay in corne." The excess in this year's production was such that Pepys thought it could only be relieved by exportation, for he continues : "But (which I did observe to my lord, and he liked well of it) our gentry are grown so ignorant in everything of good husbandry that they know not how to bestowe this corne ; which, did they understand but a little trade, they would be able to joine together, and know what markets there are abroad, and send it thither, and thereby ease their tenants, and be able to pay themselves." A month later he speaks of so great a depreciation in land that estates with good titles, and houses upon them, might be had for sixteen years' purchase.

It is the less easy to understand the complaints recorded by Pepys because it appears from the "Eton Tables," preserved in the "Wealth of Nations," that in the previous year (1667) the price of the best wheat in the Windsor market was above three-fourths of the average price for the whole century. Twenty years later, however, it was little more than one-half of this average price, and, in the meantime, the Legislature, doubtless actuated by the same views as Pepys, virtually removed all checks on its exportation. In 1688 a further step was taken, and a bounty was actually granted on the exportation of corn, while that of wool remained prohibited. This bounty was to be payable until wheat should rise to 48s. a quarter, and was frequently renewed during the earlier part of the next century. It is stated by Adam Smith that no less than a million and a half was paid for bounty on

maintained an estimated population of 5,250,000 souls. In 1879 the whole area under crops or in pasture was about 27,000,000 acres, and the estimated population was about 25,000,000; but, since more than one-fourth of all the agricultural produce required by the population of the United Kingdom, including one-half the wheat, is now imported from abroad, we may reckon the number of persons in England and Wales fed on the agricultural produce of home growth at about 18,000,000. Since this number is maintained by an acreage less than one-third greater than that which is supposed to have maintained 5,250,000 in the seventeenth century, we must conclude that the soil of England and Wales is between twice and thrice as productive as it then was; unless, indeed, it be assumed that the average consumption per head of the population is now much lower than in a ruder state of society.[1]

The advance of agricultural improvement in the eighteenth century appears to have been steadily progressive. This advance was not so much due to any scientific discovery or legislative reform as to a constant and healthy growth both of population and of national prosperity. The more settled and constitutional government which prevailed under William III. and his successors, the long peace secured to England by the sober policy of Sir Robert Walpole, and the

acres in all, 2,000,000 of which he supposed to be covered by roads, rivers, sites of towns, royal forests, woods, commons, &c. He allotted, roughly, 16,000,000 acres to arable land, and 16,000,000 to grass. The total area of England alone, as stated in the Agricultural Returns, is 32,597,398 acres.

[1] See "Agricultural Returns for Great Britain," Tables 1 and 29; and Caird's "Landed Interest," p. 14.

more than eight million quarters of corn exported between 1741 and 1750; yet he also observes that, in spite of the bounty, the price of wheat ranged lower during the first sixty-four years of the eighteenth century than during the last sixty-four years of the seventeenth century.[1]

The price of meat in the seventeenth century appears to have been uniformly high;[2] and, but for the difficulty

[1] Fleetwood appends to his "Chronicon Pretiosum" an "Account of the true market-price of wheat and malt for sixty years last past"—that is, from 1646 to 1705. It hence appears that, during the first twenty years of this period, the "common price of wheat in London," being the mean between the Lady-day and Michaelmas prices, was £2 17s. 5¼d.; that, during the second twenty years, it was £2 6s. 3¼d.; and that, during the last twenty years, it was £2 5s. 9¼d. Allowing, however, for the probable excess of London over country prices, the author estimates that 40s. was the common price of wheat for the whole sixty years. The extraordinary inflation of prices in certain of the earlier years is a marked feature of these tables. For instance, wheat sold for £4 5s. per quarter in 1648, and £4 in 1649, and often ranged above £3 before 1675.

Several curious entries, throwing light upon the price of agricultural produce in Wiltshire, are preserved in a manuscript notebook kept by Nevill Maskelyne, of Purton, and now in the possession of N. S. Maskelyne, Esq., M.P. for Cricklade. It hence appears that, in 1639, four and a half acres were sown with ten bushels and one peck of wheat, at 5s. per bushel; three acres were sown with twelve and a half bushels and half a peck of barley, at 3s. 6d. per bushel; and seven acres were sown with twenty-four bushels and three pecks of beans, at 4s. per bushel. In 1640, however, seed-barley and seed-beans seem to have doubled in price. From another entry it appears that a breast of mutton then cost 10d.; a hind-quarter of lamb, 1s. 6d.; a shoulder of mutton, 1s.; and twenty-eight pounds of beef, 5s. 3d. But these were country prices, and it may be well to remember that in the same district milk is even now sold for little more than one-third of its London price.

This subject is fully discussed by Adam Smith in the "Wealth of Nations," book I., chap. xi. He arrives at the conclusion, largely based on statistics appended to Birch's "Life of Prince Henry," that at the beginning of the seventeenth century meat was dearer than it was a century later. These statistics are contained in an "Order for the

of maintaining cattle in the winter before root-crops were generally cultivated, the farmer ought to have realised large profits from this source. One important form which Protection then assumed was that of restrictions on the importation of cattle and beef from Ireland, and an Act passed with this object in 1664 is strongly condemned by Sir William Petty. But some deduction must be made from the ostensible profitableness of cattle-breeding, as measured by the market price of butcher's meat in London. In that age an ordinary ox or sheep weighed much less than half of the present average, and the cost of transporting beasts, as well as other farm produce, to a good market was proportionably far greater than it now is, not only because there were no railways and few tolerable roads, but also because towns with a large population of consumers were very thinly scattered over the country. Sheep-farming, which had been strongly recommended by Fitzherbert in the previous century, probably continued to be the most remunerative employment of farm-capital, and the repetition of statutes against the exportation of wool shows at least that it commanded what the Legislature thought an excessive price in the home market. Yet even in the middle of the seventeenth century Agricultural Free Trade was not without

Management of the Prince's Household," supposed to have been issued in December, 1610, and are here transcribed :—" The prices of flesh, as the Prince payeth, and the weight, as they are agreed for with the purveyors : An ox should weigh 600 lbs. the four quarters ; and commonly £9 10s., or thereabouts. A mutton should weigh 46 lbs., or 44 lbs., and they cost by the stone 2s. 3d., the stone being 8 lbs. Veals go not by weight, but by goodness only : their price is commonly 17s., or thereabouts. Lambs at 6s. 8d. the piece."

its advocates, for a treatise published in 1650[1] contains the startling doctrine that England might be none the worse if no land were ploughed at all, so long as enough wool were produced to buy the requisite amount of corn grown abroad.

It is needless to say that no such doctrine was likely to find acceptance with the Long Parliament. England was then, and for nearly two centuries later, a self-supporting country. If the imports of agricultural produce did not always balance the exports, decade by decade, under the old sliding-scale by which they were so long regulated, the difference never amounted to more than a small proportion of the national consumption. It may, therefore, be interesting to compare the productive capacity of the soil two centuries ago with its capacity in the present day. The whole area of England and Wales under crops or in pasture was then stated by Gregory King at 21,000,000 acres, of which he supposed 9,000,000 acres to be arable land, as distinct from meadow.[2] This area then

[1] Hartlib's " Legacy." Similar views were maintained by Davenant, who advocated the breeding and keeping of cattle as more profitable for the national interest than raising crops of corn.

[2] Macaulay probably relies on the authority of Gregory King in estimating the cultivated area as " not much more than half the kingdom." (" Hist. of Eng.," vol. I., ch. iii.) Such estimates, made by statisticians of the seventeenth century, must be received with some degree of caution. Gregory King reckoned the whole area of England and Wales at 39,000,000, whereas it is really 37,319,221 acres. Sir William Petty, in his " Political Arithmetic," reckoned the whole area of England and Wales, together with the lowlands of Scotland, at no more than 36,000,000 acres. It is curious that he also understates the area of Ireland by 4,000,000 acres. Even Arthur Young speaks of various estimates respecting the acreage of England (exclusive of Wales) as current in his own time. He adopts that of Harte, according to which England contained 34,000,000

consequent development of commerce and manufacturing industry, were the chief agencies which raised the landed interest of England from the state rapidly sketched by Macaulay to that minutely described by Arthur Young and Adam Smith. At the beginning of the century, the arable land still lay for the most part in open fields, at least throughout all the more backward districts.[1] It was still the custom to sow corn crops for several years in succession, and then to fallow the exhausted land till it had recovered fertility. Peas were often used as intermediate crops; but clover and turnips, though recommended for this purpose in the middle of the previous century,[2] were but seldom cultivated in fields; and regular "alternate husbandry," much more the rotation of crops, was still regarded as an agricultural experiment. Nevertheless, the production of wheat, stimulated by the bounty system, by the increasing facilities of locomotion, and by the immense increase of town markets, received a prodigious impulse in the reigns of Anne

---

[1] In Laurence's "New System of Agriculture" (1726) — one of several elaborate treatises on the subject produced in the first half of the eighteenth century — the question of enclosures is fully discussed. "It is believed," he says, "that almost one half part of the kingdom are commons;" and he proceeds to state with confidence that "a third of all the kingdom is what we call common-fields." Strongly recommending enclosure, he maintains that enclosed land will yield "seven, eight, or ten years crops successively, when the other has them but two years or three;" and that enclosed land will "produce more than twenty bushels to the acre." (Book I., chap. iv.) The common field-lands remaining open in 1879 were estimated at 264,000 acres.

[2] Blythe's "Improver Improved" (third edition, 1652). The first experiments in clover and turnip cultivation are attributed to Sir Richard Weston. Professor Rogers states that clover, saintfoin, and rye-grass were introduced from Holland in the early part of the eighteenth century.

and the first two Georges. In the year 1760 it was estimated by Charles Smith, author of the "Corn Law Tracts," that 3,750,000 of people in England and Wales then consumed wheaten bread, while about 2,250,000 lived on bread made of barley, rye, or oats. Though no less than 820,000 quarters were exported in 1763–4, it was then calculated that 4,000,000 quarters were consumed in England and Wales, the price being then 37s. 6d., or about 5s. above the average for the previous years of the century.[1]

To meet this ever-growing demand, the practice of enclosure was revived, but the enclosures of the eighteenth century were very different in their character and objects from the enclosures of the sixteenth century. Then, arable land was converted into pasture; now, waste land was to be reclaimed and brought under cultivation.[2] Many local Acts had been passed for this purpose since the reign of Elizabeth, in cases where the unanimous consent of all the parties interested in common rights could not be obtained.[3]

---

[1] M. de Lavergne, in his "Economie Rurale de l'Angleterre," makes the astounding statement that England, having doubled her population since the Stuart period, nevertheless became, in the last half of the last century, the granary of Europe. He adds:—"On a calculé que, dans la dernière moitié du dix-huitième siècle, elle vendit à ses voisins, et notamment à la France, pour un milliard de francs de céréales."

[2] Some of these enclosures were made for the purpose of planting. Bradley, whose treatise on "Planting and Gardening" appeared in 1731, proposes to show by statistics that an acre planted with oak "may produce the sum of £250 10s. 6d. in the space of twenty-five years, clear of all expenses of planting, and value of the land," with the prospect of a larger profit in future. (Part I., chap. v.)

[3] Elton "On the Law of Commons and Waste Lands," chap. ix. Under the Statute of Merton (2 Henry III., cap. 1) the lords of manors

Under such Acts large tracts of land in Bedfordshire and the West Riding of Yorkshire had been transformed from marshes or moors into fertile corn-fields. These improvements became more common under George II.; but it was not until the reign of George III. that enclosure became the settled policy of landed proprietors. Forty-seven Enclosure Bills were passed on the average in each year between 1760 and 1765; about 2,000, in all, had been passed before the General Enclosure Act of 1801, and about 2,000 more were passed between that Act and the General Enclosure Act of 1845. Macaulay, writing two or three years later, surmises that, since the accession of George II., a new area of more than 10,000 square miles, or 6,400,000 acres, had been added to the cultivated soil of England. Sir George Nicholls states more positively that an area of more than 2,500,000 acres was enclosed in thirty years, between 1769 and 1799. The estimate of Macaulay is remarkably confirmed by the authorities cited in the first "Report of the Royal Commission on the Employment of Women and Children in Agriculture," dated 1869. It is there stated that—

"According to the estimate made by the Select Committee of the House of Commons on Emigration in 1827, and the calculations of Mr. Porter in 1843, 7,175,520 statute acres had been enclosed in England and Wales since the first

first acquired the right of "approving," or improving, for their own benefit, by enclosing woods and pastures subject to common rights, so long as enough was left to satisfy the requirements of the commoners—a question left to be decided by a suit before the Judges of assize.

Enclosure Bill in the year 1710 up to the year 1843. To these, since 1843, have been added 484,893 acres, as appears by the 'Annual Report of the Enclosure Commissioners for 1867,' making together 7,660,413 statute acres added to the cultivated area of England and Wales since 1810, or about one-third part of the total of 25,451,626 acres in cultivation in 1867." [1]

But, as the more fertile parts of the island were doubtless the first occupied, and many enclosed plots are more suitable for timber than for crops, it cannot be inferred that a proportionate gain has accrued to English agriculture.

Nor must it be supposed that the number of landed proprietors was in any way increased by this process of enclosure. The area enclosed was divided among those, and those only, who already possessed common rights by virtue of their holding freeholds or copyholds, and the very idea of recognizing any public interest in open wastes or forests is entirely modern. [2] The lion's share was always reserved for the lord of the manor, and immense accessions of territory were thus secured by powerful landowners in days when the landed interest was paramount in the Legislature no less than in local administration. The chief sufferers

---

[1] See Cliffe Leslie's "Land Systems of Ireland, England, and the Continent," p. 214. The Commissioners proceed to remark that such enclosures, often made without any compensation to the smaller commoners, have deprived agricultural labourers of ancient rights over the waste, and disabled the occupants of new cottages from acquiring new rights.

[2] In St. John's treatise on the "Land Revenues of the Crown" (1787), the enclosure and cultivation of Royal forests is strongly recommended. The author treats enclosures of open land as pure gain, and the only serious opposition which he apprehends is on the part of great lords unwilling to lose their sporting rights.

were poor labourers, holding cottages at the will of
their landlords, who lost the privilege of turning out
pigs, geese, and fowls on the common, and for whom,
of course, no compensation was provided. The decay
of another class, little known to history, dates from
the same period. On the wild heaths which still
cover the borders of Surrey, Hampshire, and Sussex,
as well as in the great woods of the southern and
midland counties, there abode a race of " squatters,"
or "hutmen," which has since almost retired before
advancing civilization. Some few of them may have
established by prescription a claim to property in
their little tenements, and become peasant-farmers, but
the great majority were ousted as trespassers, with
the progress of enclosure, and must have passed into
the ranks as mere labourers, if they did not swell
those of poachers and other semi-criminal vagrants.
On the other hand, the Act of Elizabeth against the
multiplication of cottages was deliberately repealed in
1775,[1] as tending to check population, and as pressing hardly on the industrious poor.

It is worthy of observation that, while these
Enclosure Acts were applicable to " common fields,"
separate Acts were passed about the same period to
extinguish the primitive system of village husbandry
then still prevailing in many parts of England.[2] One
of these, passed in 1773, facilitated the division and
enclosure of these open fields. At the same time, it
gave a majority in number and value of the several
owners the power of regulating the course of husbandry
in fields which might remain unenclosed, notwithstand-

[1] 31 Elizabeth, cap. 7.   [2] See note 1, p. 53.

ing any custom to the contrary. From a purely agricultural point of view, such legislation was doubtless
wise ; but, since the weaker commoners are seldom able
to pay, or to assert their own claims before Committees
on Enclosure Bills, it is highly probable that enclosure
of common fields, like that of common pastures and
woods, helped to crush out the struggling peasant-
farmer.

The "Wealth of Nations" appeared in 1776, and
the various treatises of Arthur Young on British
agriculture were published at intervals between 1767
and 1808.   A careful digest of these treatises would
present a more complete picture of the English land-
system, in its practical working at the close of the
last century, than could be obtained from any other
source. Even in their present form, interpreted and supplemented by the contemporary work of the first great
English economist, they contain an invaluable repertory
of materials for the student of agrarian history.[1]

---

[1] Some of Arthur Young's general conclusions are of great interest, in
default of trustworthy statistics resting on official authority.

He estimates the whole population of England and Wales at 9,000,000 ;
and of these he supposes 2,800,000 to be immediately dependent on agriculture, exclusive of the landlords, the clergy, and the poor in receipt of
parish relief.   He values the rental of agricultural land at £16,000,000,
allowing £5,000,000 in addition for the rental of houses ; and he states the
capital-value of lands and houses, respectively, at £536,000,000 and
£100,000,000.   He estimates the "stock in husbandry," or farmers' capital,
at £110,000,000 ; the "product of the soil in husbandry," exclusive of
parks, woods, chaces, &c., at £83,237,691 ; the "expenditure of husbandry," including rent and wages, at £65,000,000 ; the farmers' profit,
at £18,237,691, or about two millions and a quarter above the landlords'
rental ; and the labourers' wages, at about £14,500,000.

He supposes about 3,000,000 acres to be laid down in wheat, producing
about three-quarters per acre, worth 38s. a quarter ; about 2,900,000 acres
to be laid down in barley, producing [about four quarters per acre, worth

In the first place, it is clear that, despite the recent improvements in agriculture, which appeared marvellous to Arthur Young and Adam Smith, the business of farming was carried on with far less capital, and that land yielded a far smaller rent, than is now the case, after the lapse of a century.[1] Arthur Young thinks it necessary to combat the common notion that a capital of thrice the rent will properly stock a farm, and complains that a great many farmers will take up land with a capital of only twice the rent, though such tenants must be ruined by a bad year, and cannot effect improvements in a good year. After ranging over 4,000 miles in three successive years, he states the average rent at thirteen shillings per acre; the

17s. a quarter; and about 2,300,000 acres to be laid down in oats, producing about four and a half quarters per acre, worth 15s. a quarter. He assigns above 4,000,000 acres to peas, beans, turnips, and clover; but he remarks that, although clover is a better preparation for wheat than fallow, the practice of growing it had not spread into all the English counties.

The annual "product of cows" for dairy purposes he reckons as worth £5 6s. 3d. on the average; the "profit on sheep" as averaging 10s. each; that on "fatting beasts" as averaging £7 each. He thinks a farmer should make a profit of £1 apiece on his young cattle, of 15s. on pigs, and of cent. per cent. on his poultry.

[1] Arthur Young often intimates the opinion that English farms are, for the most part, under-rented, that low rents make bad farmers, and that high rents are an undoubted spur to good husbandry. He considers the short-sighted ambition of farmers "not to farm well but much" as the chief weakness of English husbandry. "Nine out of ten," he observes, "had rather cultivate 500 acres in a slovenly manner, though constantly cramped for money, than 250 acres completely, though they would always have money in their pockets." (Compare "Northern Tour," vol. IV., pp. 344, 375, with "Farmer's Guide," book I., chap. xiv.) Professor Rogers disputes Arthur Young's statement that rents did not greatly increase in the first three-quarters of the eighteenth century, and believes them to have doubled within this period.

rents paid in the corn-growing eastern counties being, on the whole, the highest.   Nevertheless, he is of opinion that, where the soil is rich, grass-land is more profitable than arable land, requiring as it does less buildings and labour.   He remarks elsewhere that, although corn always fetches a higher price in Dorsetshire and Somersetshire than in the eastern counties, farmers never break up grass-land in the former, as they are eager to do in the latter; and he shrewdly points out that such eagerness only proves that a large profit may be reaped in the first years of cultivation by drawing unfairly on the permanent resources of the soil.   On the other hand, Adam Smith contends that, even after allowing for labour, an acre of arable land returns a larger surplus profit than an acre of grass-land; and this view soon became generally prevalent when tillage received an unhealthy impulse from the continuance of war prices.   The highest rents mentioned by Arthur Young are those paid on land specially adapted for growing carrots—a root-crop for which he exhibits a notable partiality.   He speaks of the very best carrot-growing soils as yielding a rent of £3 or £4 an acre, and yet returning an enormous profit to a tenant with plenty of capital.[1]   If the cultivation of carrots is now less remunerative, the explanation must be sought in the simple fact that, since Arthur Young's time, the supply has overtaken the demand, and that cattle are now fattened more rapidly on artificial food.

[1] He states that ten acres of carrots will produce a crop of 180 tons, worth about £180, and will keep eight horses, sixty sheep, and twelve oxen for a whole winter. In other parts of his works he estimates the annual profit of carrot-growing still higher. (Compare " Tour in the Eastern Counties," pp. 93, 105, with " Farmer's Guide," pp. 106—7.)

It is somewhat curious that a similar partiality for potatoes is evinced by Adam Smith in several passages of his great work. After observing that potatoes yield per acre six times as large a return as wheat, he goes on to predict that, if they should ever supersede wheat as the staple food of the people, in any part of Europe, population would increase, and rents would rise far above their former level—words destined to receive a disastrous verification in Ireland. He even compares potatoes very favourably with oatmeal, in respect of nutritive value, and adduces the superiority of Irishmen to Scotchmen in support of this marvellous paradox.[1]

The comparative advantages of large and small farms, as well as the reasons why gentlemen farmers rarely succeed, are discussed by Arthur Young with a practical sagacity which is by no means obsolete. No writer on agriculture has ever shown more clearly the supreme importance of personal attention to detail in the art of farming. According to him, the grand advantage which the small farmer has in competition with the large farmer, and, still more, the professional farmer with the gentleman, is that he brings the master's eye, and even the master's hand, to bear upon every department of his business. A farmer ploughing with his men will get 25 per cent. more work done in the day; a farmer who knows exactly what horses can do will get a full number of journeys performed by his team in the course of a week; a farmer who takes his meals with his men will feed them at half the cost that he must otherwise allow for their board, not to speak of the numberless ways in which his constant

[1] "Wealth of Nations," book I., chap. xi.

supervision will check waste. On the other hand, the small farmer has generally to pay a higher rent proportionably, because there are more applications for small farms ; he is apt to have a smaller capital proportionably, and he is seldom able or willing to carry out improvements. The disadvantages of small farming become greater the lower we descend in the scale ; for upon the smallest farm, as distinct from a market garden, two horses must be kept for ploughing, and the expense of keeping two horses will leave no margin for manures or other remunerative outgoings. The peasant-farmer of course possesses no sheep, which can only be reared profitably on a large acreage, and, having little or no stock, he grows little or no clover, but fallows his land, and exhausts it by too frequent wheat-crops. Meanwhile, he works harder, fares harder, and is really poorer than a day-labourer earning regular wages. In short, the management of very small farms, as practised in France, is simply British agriculture stripped of all the improvements which have caused it to flourish in Britain.[1]

Such are the main objections to small farming suggested to Arthur Young by a review of British agriculture a century ago. His conclusion is that, on the whole, farms of moderate extent—that is, from 100 to 200 acres—are most to be commended, and employ more labour than very large or very small holdings. It is singular that, in treating of the latter, he assumes that cultivation will be chiefly directed to produce grain, and takes little account of the *petite culture* to which labourers' allotments are best suited. He even observes

---

[1] "Notes in France," p. 410.

that the general public has little interest in the price of poultry, which the smallest Irish farmers breed and rear with so much success. Adam Smith appears to have shared these opinions, for he maintains that little profit can be made by market gardening, inasmuch as most of those who ought to be the best customers of market gardeners supply themselves with fruit and vegetables from gardens of their own. As for dairy-farming, Adam Smith regards it as " a business which, like the feeding of hogs and of poultry, is originally carried on as a save-all."[1] He adds that, in most parts of England, though not in Scotland, it had been generally stimulated by the rise of price, until some of the best lands in the country were appropriated to it; "and when the price has got to this height it cannot well go higher;" yet even in England "the dairy is not reckoned a more profitable employment of land than the raising of corn or the fattening of cattle." It is not surprising that neither Adam Smith nor Arthur Young was able to foresee the unlimited demand of modern London and other great towns for milk, butter, eggs, and other perishable kinds of farm produce, or the unlimited facility of locomotion about to result from the development of steam power. Both, however, refer to the influence of the London market on the price of meat even in remote counties, and record the opposition of provincial towns to an extension of turnpike roads ; but, while the one describes it as a protest of local consumers against the increasing dearness of

---

[1] The same contempt for poultry-breeding is exhibited in several passages of Marshall's " Review of the Reports to the Board of Agriculture," 1808; a work full of valuable information on the agriculture of that period.

provisions, the other describes it as a protest of landlords against a probable fall in the London price of
grass and corn, to be followed by a fall in rents.   The
former apprehension, as Adam Smith points out, was
amply verified by the experience of Scotland, where a
pound of meat had been as cheap as a pound of oatmeal, but trebled in price after the Union opened the
English markets to Highland cattle.

CHAPTER IV.

Recent History of Land Tenure in England.

THE century which has elapsed since the appearance of the "Wealth of Nations," though fruitful in agricultural reforms, has not been an eventful period in the history of English land-tenure. The system of family settlements has remained practically unchanged since the reign of Charles II., and the only material amendments introduced into it have been the creation of a simple machinery for barring entails, by the Act of William IV., for the abolition of Fines and Recoveries,[1] and the facilities given by later statutes for the sale and improvement of settled estates. The Act of William IV. is chiefly important as having set aside the old principle that an entail might be absolutely cut off by a tenant-in-tail of full age. This power was of no real value, inasmuch as, for technical reasons, it could not be exercised by a tenant-in-tail in reversion without the consent of the tenant-for-life in possession. Still, the principle was recognised by the law, until it was annulled by the Legislature by the statute which created, for the first time, a "protector of the settlement." Thenceforward it became a positive rule of law, and no longer a mere technical necessity, that when a tenant-in-tail under a settlement (not being in possession) wishes to bar the entail completely, he must obtain the consent of

[1] 3 and 4 Wm. IV. c. 74.

the "protector," that is, in legal phrase, of the person who has the first estate of freehold prior to his own estate-tail.

We are now, therefore, in a position to examine the mode whereby the objects of those perpetual entails which had been swept away four centuries ago are still practically secured in ordinary settlements of landed property, or, less frequently, in the wills of landed proprietors who have enjoyed an absolute power of disposition. This mode is thus explained in the standard work of Mr. Joshua Williams on the "Law of Real Property:"—

"In families where the estates are kept up from one generation to another, settlements are made every few years for this purpose; thus, in the event of a marriage, a life-estate merely is given to the husband; the wife has an allowance for pin-money during the marriage, and a rent-charge or annuity by way of jointure for her life, in case she should survive her husband. Subject to this jointure, and to the payment of such sums as may be agreed on for the portions of the daughters and younger sons of the marriage, *the eldest son who may be born of the marriage is made by the settlement tenant-in-tail.* In case of his decease without issue, it is provided that the second son, and then the third, should in like manner be tenant-in-tail; and so on to the others; and in default of sons, the estate is usually given to the daughters; not successively, however, but as 'tenants in common in tail,' with 'cross remainders' in tail. By this means the estate is tied up till some tenant-in-tail attains the age of twenty-one years; when he is able, with the consent of his father, who is tenant for life, to bar the entail with all the remainders. Dominion is thus again acquired over the property, which dominion is usually exercised in a re-settlement on the next generation; and thus the property is preserved in the family. Primogeniture, there-fore, as it obtains among the landed gentry of England, is a custom only, and not a right, though there can be no doubt that the custom has originated in the right which was enjoyed by the eldest son, as heir to his father, in those days when estates-tail could not be barred."

It should be remarked that a settlement of the kind described by Mr. Joshua Williams implies that full control has been acquired over the land before it is executed. For this purpose, most family properties are disentailed in each generation with a view to re-settlement by the joint act of the life-owner for the time being as "protector," and of his eldest son as tenant-in-tail in reversion. The former is actuated by a desire to perpetuate the entail by fresh limitations to a period as distant as the law permits; and often gains, in the process of re-settlement, the means of discharging his own debts, or making provision for those who have claims upon him. The son, on the other hand, taking a life-estate in lieu of his estate-tail, forfeits the prospect of becoming master of the property on his father's death; but, in consideration of this sacrifice, he usually receives an immediate rent-charge by way of allowance, and is placed in a position to marry early.

To complete this explanation, it should be added that almost all modern settlements contain a power of sale, enabling the trustees, with the consent of the tenant in possession, to sell portions or even the whole of the property, and to re-invest the purchase-money in other land, or to apply it in paying off mortgages and other charges on the property. Under these powers out-lying estates, or estates which may have come into the family collaterally, are very commonly sold off, and the produce is either applied in rounding off the central domain, or held upon trust for the same persons as would have received the income of the land, till it is sooner or later absorbed in paying charges which must otherwise have been raised upon the entire property.[1] In default of such powers being inserted in the settlement, the Court of Chancery may direct sales, with the consent of the parties interested, for the purpose of paying off charges, or of buying other landed property to be held on the same trusts as that sold.[2]   It may, therefore, be asserted that, with the exception of a very few domains inalienably settled, like Blenheim, on a particular family, no estate in England is literally unsaleable.   But the Settled Estates Act of 1856, as well as the amending Acts of 1858 and 1864, while they purport to render all settled property capable of sale, are encumbered by elaborate precautions for the protection of every interest, both actual and contingent. Moreover, the powers which they confer are not to be exercised, even by the Court of Chancery, " in any case where an express declaration or manifest intention that they shall not be exercised is contained in the settlement, or may reasonably be inferred therefrom, or from extrinsic circumstances or evidence."   These Acts, therefore, are doubly permissive, and can seldom operate except where powers of sale have been omitted in a settlement out of pure inadvertence.

By the same Act of 1856, life-tenants, who had pre-

---

[1] It is stated by Mr. George Shaw Lefevre, M.P., in an interesting paper on the " Limitation of Entails and Settlements," that old settlements, or settlements made under wills, or those drawn by country practitioners, seldom contain these powers, and that very few settlements authorise the investment of money realised by sales in the permanent improvement of the rent of the property.

[2] 19 & 20 Vict., c. 120.

viously been disabled from granting leases which would hold good against a reversioner, were empowered to grant binding leases for twenty-one years. The Act also enables the Court of Chancery to authorise building and mining, as well as agricultural, leases, on settled estates; but here, again, the powers conferred on the life tenant and the Court may be defeated by express words in the settlement, or even by an inferential construction of it. In the meantime, special powers of borrowing money for agricultural improvements were conceded to landowners, under the control of the Enclosure Commissioners. This system originated in State loans granted for purposes of drainage and reclamation, after the repeal of the Corn Laws and the Irish famine. After the sums thus voted by Parliament were exhausted, Land Improvement Companies were formed to advance money for the same objects, as well as for the erection of farm houses and labourers' cottages. Such loans are secured by a first charge on the inheritance, sanctioned by the certificate of the Enclosure Commissioners, which is willingly accepted by the prior creditors as an adequate safeguard for their claims. We learn from the Report of the House of Lords Committee on the Improvement of Land (1873) that "the interest at which the land companies lend is usually $4\frac{1}{2}$ per cent. The sinking fund calculated to repay the loan in twenty-five years, together with the interest and sinking fund on the preliminary expenses,[1]

---

[1] Evidence was given before the Committee, showing that the preliminary expenses for small loans sometimes amounted to upwards of 15 per cent. on the capital borrowed, the average being 7 per cent. (Report, paragraph 9, subsection 3.)

bring up the average payment on the effective outlay to a little more than 7 per cent." It was stated by Mr. James Caird, one of the Enclosure Commissioners, in 1878, that some £12,000,000 had then been charged on the land of Great Britain, besides £3,000,000 on the land of Ireland, during the previous thirty years, part of it having been advanced by the State and part by private companies. The principle adopted is that of periodical redemption within twenty-five or at most thirty years, so that each generation may, as a rule, bear the charge of its own improvements.

This principle has been vigorously impugned in the interest of agriculture, on the ground that landowners will not readily undertake so heavy a charge as 7 per cent. and upwards, and that a tenant-for-life should be enabled to create a permanent mortgage for the benefit of the property on the same terms as a proprietor in fee simple. The question here involved really turns upon the policy of family settlements, the object of which would evidently be defeated if successive tenants-for-life could burden the estate for ever. For the present, however, we must regard guaranteed loans for agricultural improvement, even though subject to redemption within twenty-five or thirty years, as an important extension of limited ownership. It is satisfactory to know that about two-thirds of the whole amount borrowed has been spent on drainage, the most remunerative of all investments on land. It is still more satisfactory to learn, on high authority, that a much larger sum has been laid out by landowners on improvements out of their own resources, for which purpose statutory powers of charging the inheritance have been provided by the Act of 1864.[1] This policy has been carried still further by the Agricultural Holdings Act of 1875. Under that Act, hereafter to be noticed, tenants are encouraged to make improvements of a permanent character by the assurance of legal compensation on a prescribed scale, with the previous consent in writing of the landlord or his agent. But it is to be observed that an important distinction is drawn between tenants of absolute owners and tenants of "limited" owners under settlements. The former are entitled to receive back, at any time within a period of twenty years, the cost of the improvement, subject to a deduction for every year in which they have enjoyed the benefit of it. The latter are only entitled to receive compensation at the expiration of their tenancy, if and so far as the letting value has been increased by the improvement. The amount to be received under these different principles of compensation respectively may or may not be the same, but the fact of different principles having been adopted shows how deeply the system of family settlements is rooted in the English law of Real Property.

It would be easy to enumerate secondary reforms in that law, and especially in the practice of conveyancing, which have been founded directly or indirectly on the exhaustive Reports of the Real Property Commissioners (1829-33). Such are the abolition of antiquated suits for the recovery of rights in land; the extended liability of real estates to debts, and especially to mortgage debts, which used, by a most iniquitous rule, to be charged on personalty; the statutable importation of

<hr/>

[1] Caird's "Landed Interest," p. 87.

certain powers into settlements, mortgages, and wills ; and the facilities provided for effecting exchanges through the Enclosure Commissioners without deeds or investigation of title.[1] But all these amendments, however useful, leave untouched the organic framework of Real Property law, and avail but little to encourage or to cheapen the ordinary transfer of land, which, though effected by means of secret deeds, is often as expensive and troublesome as a lawsuit in open court.[2]

It would be no less vain than wearisome to dwell minutely on the all but fruitless attempts to simplify Land Transfer without simplifying the law of Real Property which have been made within living memory. This question is far older than is generally supposed. Not only has the mystery and the expense attending all dealings with land in England been recognised by the greatest English lawyers, but more than one treatise in favour of registration as a remedy for these evils was published at the beginning of the last century. In 1857, when the Commission on Registration of Title published its Report, it was stated that no less than twenty Bills dealing with the subject had been introduced within twenty years. In 1859 a Bill for the Registration of Title was introduced by Lord Cairns, then Sir Hugh Cairns, on behalf

---

[1] For a more complete enumeration of such measures, see the Address of Mr. N. Tertius Lawrence to the Incorporated Law Society at Cambridge, on October 7, 1879.

[2] It has been well pointed out by Mr. Wren-Hoskyns, in his Essay on the English Land-System, that the Statute of Uses, passed in the 27th year of Henry VIII., and five years before the Statute of Wills, first legalised the system of conveying land by secret deed, without publicity or registration.

of the Government, but was defeated by the opposition of the legal profession. In 1862 Lord Westbury's Transfer of Land Act actually became law. Under this Act, provision was made for the registration of fee-simple estates, with an indefeasible title. Such registration was only to be obtained after a full official investigation of all the interests affecting the estate, which interests were to be duly recorded in the register. The register was thenceforward to contain a complete and conclusive history of all transfers, charges, and incumbrances to which the estate might be subjected, no unregistered conveyance or mortgage being allowed to prevail against a registered interest. The object, of course, was to create a new starting-point beyond which it would be needless for an intending purchaser or mortgagee to carry back his enquiries; but the necessity of registering all future interests that might affect the estate, whether equitable or legal, was found to involve a considerable increase of expense, with little increase of security. In fact, Lord Westbury's Act virtually established an optional registration of deeds, similar to the compulsory registration of deeds which had existed in Middlesex and Yorkshire since the reign of Queen Anne. Now, the Middlesex and Yorkshire system of registration had been emphatically condemned by a Royal Commission, which reported in 1857, because it did not and could not operate by itself to simplify either title or the forms of conveyancing. The Commissioners pointed out that retrospective investigations and abstracts of title would not be curtailed, however they might be facilitated, by a mere registration of deeds, while " the technicalities and anomalies of the law of Real Property would be confirmed rather than lessened or relieved." The same view was adopted by another Royal Commission, appointed eleven years later, and was, on the whole, justified by experience. The number of titles registered under Lord Westbury's Act gradually dwindled, and had not reached 400 in all within a period of twelve years. In the year 1875, after Lord Selborne had vainly attempted to effect a more comprehensive reform, a second Land Transfer Act, based on a different principle, was introduced and carried by Lord Cairns.[1] Unlike Lord Westbury's Transfer of Land Act, Lord Cairns' Act provided for a registration of title alone, and not for a registration of assurances. Its object was not to preserve a record of all the interests affecting an estate; on the contrary, "it recognised for the purposes of actual registration only the proprietors of certain defined interests in the land,"[2] leaving all other interests to be protected by caveats and inhibitions. Moreover, it authorised the registration not only of "absolute" and "qualified" titles, but even of mere "possessory" titles, which it was hoped might ultimately ripen, in the absence of hostile claims, into indefeasible titles.

It is the less necessary to describe further the distinctions between Lord Westbury's and Lord Cairns' Act, because the latter, being equally permissive, proved still more abortive in its operation.

---

[1] In the meantime, important reforms had been initiated by the Vendors and Purchasers Act, and the Real Property Limitations Act of 1874.

[2] "Report of the Select Committee on Land Titles and Transfer," 1879.

The Select Committee of the House of Commons which reported in June, 1879, found that, down to the date of the last return, only forty-eight titles had been registered under it, of which but a small proportion were possessory titles. Various causes were assigned by Lord Cairns and other witnesses for this deplorable failure, such as the reluctance of English landowners to part with their title-deeds and to incur immediate trouble and expense for the sake of a remote benefit, the inveterate prejudice of the legal profession against a new course of procedure, and the discredit reflected on any scheme of registration by the ill success of Lord Westbury's experiment. The Committee, however, without ignoring these adverse influences, were driven to conclude that, practically, the main obstacle to an effectual registration of title is the hopeless difficulty of reconciling that system with the complexities of the English law of Real Property. They forcibly observe that, "From the very moment that the ownership of any given plot of land is split up amongst different persons, every scheme for the registration of title necessitates one of two things; either the interests carved out of the original fee must be themselves placed on the Register—a process which would defeat the first object of such a registration, simplicity of title for the purpose of disposition—or an owner, *pro hac vice*, so to speak, must be created for the purpose of registration, while all remaining interests, being kept off the register, must (as in the analogous case of copyholds) become the subject of a second record of title outside the register. But this is not all. In exact proportion as the registered owner is left free and unfettered to deal with the land, the owners of unregistered property are exposed to the risk of having their property dealt with behind their backs, and are left to protect themselves as best they can by a system of cautions and inhibitions."

Upon these and like grounds, the Committee reported unfavourably upon the system of registering titles, and recommended, in effect, a recurrence to the alternative principle of registering deeds. At the same time, they suggested various improvements in the machinery provided by Lord Westbury's Act, the compulsory use of brief statutory forms, the reduction of mortgages to a simple charge upon land, the extension to real property of the control already entrusted to executors over personal property, the repeal of the Statute of Uses, and other salutary amendments in the procedure of land-transfer. What they could not advocate, without exceeding their powers, was such a reform of English land tenure as would make the difference between registration of deeds and registration of title a matter of little moment. Nor did they venture to advocate, in express terms, compulsory registration in this country. In Australia, as they pointed out, registration works smoothly and regularly enough, because there "every landowner has a perfect root of title to his property, and a trustworthy key to its identity." Therefore, although registration is only compulsory in the case of Crown grants, there is every inducement for its general adoption. Why it should be hopeless for landowners in the mother country to realise the same advantages is by no means self-evident, and is not explained in the Report of the Committee.[1]

In the meantime, a series of attempts has been made to assimilate the devolution of real to personal property on intestacy, and thus to abolish the law, as distinct from the custom, of Primogeniture. In 1836, and again in 1837, Mr. Ewart moved for leave to introduce a bill with this object, whereby undevised realty would have vested, like personalty, in the executor or administrator; but was defeated on both occasions.[2] The struggle was renewed again and again by Mr. Locke King from 1850 to 1869, in which year he actually obtained a majority in favour of a bill providing that where any person beneficially entitled to any real estate shall die without a will, that estate shall pass to his executor or administrator, and shall be either divided or sold, exactly as if it were per-

---

[1] This point is fully discussed in an able pamphlet on "Land Law Reform in England," by Mr. G. Osborne Morgan, M.P., Chairman of the Select Committee. Mr. Morgan combats the notion that land can be made as transferable as stock, on the ground "that land is a concrete and stock an abstraction; that stock possesses no boundaries, conceals no minerals, supports no game, pays no tithes, admits of no easements, is let to no tenant, and hampered with no adjoining owner;" moreover, that, since one £1 of stock is as good as another, no difficulty can arise in its partition. He compares the registry established under Lord Westbury's Act to "an old palimpsest, in which a dozen different titles met and intersected each other at every turn." He maintains that Lord Cairns' Act failed, because it imported the South Australian system into English law, without clearing the ground for it; because it was "an attempt to transplant into a soil choked by the weedy and tangled growth of centuries of feudalism and pedantry, the product of a democratic community, without a history, without ancestors, and without lawyers." His conclusion is "that the first step towards making a register of titles practicable is to make a clean sweep of our present Real Property Laws."

[2] See Kenny's "Essay on Primogeniture," p. 66, and Laurence's "Essay on Primogeniture," pp. 146—9.

sonalty, for the benefit of creditors and the next of kin. A "Real Estate Succession Bill" of the same general character was announced in the Speech from the Throne, and introduced by the Government in the Session of 1870; but that bill, unlike Mr. Locke King's, was intended to cover legal as well as equitable estates, while it included various saving clauses more or less open to criticism. It was not pressed beyond the first stage, and the promise given to re-introduce it was not redeemed. Another bill, introduced by Mr. Locke King and Mr. Hinde Palmer in the Session of 1873, after providing against certain technical difficulties, embraced within its definition of real estate every kind of property which is not personal estate. This bill never even came on for discussion. The Real Estate Intestacy Bill, introduced by Mr. T. B. Potter in 1876, and rejected on the second reading by 210 to 175, was based on the original bill of Mr. Locke King. Not one of these bills went the length of vesting in any legal representative of the intestate realty passing by devise, in the same manner as personalty, including leaseholds passing by bequest, vests in the executor under the existing law. Nor did any provide that real estate passing by descent or devise, shall cease to be exempt from the probate duty imposed on personalty. Still less did any interfere with the rule under which a person succeeding to real estate, though he may inherit in fee simple, is charged with succession duty on his life interest only, and is permitted to pay this duty by instalments—a rule which amounts to a legislative protection of landed property against a salutary liability to dispersion.

CHAPTER V.

Recent Progress of Agriculture in England.

THE progress of agriculture in the present century has probably been more rapid than during any similar period. It has been shown by Mr. Porter[1] that, while the population of the United Kingdom increased by 10,700,000 between 1801 and 1841, and while the number of persons employed in agriculture began to decline relatively to other classes after 1811, the production of corn almost kept pace with the growing consumption, until shortly before the repeal of the Corn Laws. In the first forty years of the century, only 25,000,000 quarters of wheat were imported, so that the home supply fell short of the demand by little more than half a million of quarters annually. This result was due to a constant extension of enclosure and drainage, as well as to successive improvements in the practice of agriculture. Not the least important of such improvements was the demolition of useless fences and straggling hedgerows, the multiplication and irregular outlines of which had long characterised old-fashioned English farming. Under the impulse of temporary war prices, many an ancient pasture was recklessly broken up, and though once more covered with greensward, has never recovered its original fertility. Happily, the use of crushed bones

[1] " Progress of the Nation," sect. II., chap. i.

for manure was introduced in 1800, and has been followed by a far more general application of chemical science to raising crops. Still more remarkable has been the effect of mechanical science in the development of new agricultural implements, such as reaping, mowing, and threshing machines, steam ploughs, and other inventions, which not only economise labour but enable the farmer to save precious time at the most critical seasons of the year. The encouragement given by the Royal Agricultural Society, and provincial institutions founded on the same principle, has produced a like revolution in the breeding of stock, with especial regard to early maturity. But for the advantage thus obtained, it would have been impossible for the soil of England to have so nearly maintained its population before the ports were freely thrown open to foreign competition, and, even with this advantage, it ultimately failed to do so.

It is often assumed that, under the influence of Protection, wheat commanded something like a famine price, even in ordinary years. This assumption is not fully borne out by statistics, nor was the importance of cheapening the food of the people altogether neglected by Parliament during the French war. So far back as the year 1793, a Select Committee of the House of Commons was appointed to take into consideration "the present high price of corn," and in 1794 a Select Committee of the Privy Council took evidence on the harvest of that year, the stock of grain then existing in the country, and the means of obtaining supplies from abroad. It is true that little resulted from the labours of these Committees, and in the year 1812 the price of wheat reached its maximum of 126s. 6d. per quarter.[1] In 1815 the British farmer was practically guaranteed a monopoly of the home market so long as the price did not exceed 80s. per quarter, but, in fact, it never reached that standard except twice (in 1817 and 1818) during the next twenty years.[2] In 1833, and again in 1836, Committees of the House of Commons were appointed to enquire into the state of Agriculture and the causes of the distress affecting the farming interest. Strange to say, the immediate occasion. for the second enquiry was the occurrence of three magnificent harvests in succession, which brought down the average price of wheat in 1833 to 52s. 11d., in 1834 to 46s. 2d., and in 1835 to 39s. 4d.[3] It was stated before the Committee of 1836, by the Comptroller of Corn Returns, that in the period between 1814 and 1834 the quantity of home-grown wheat fell short of the consumption, on the average, by about a million of quarters a year, of which at least half was

[1] See the tables given in McCulloch's "Essay on the Corn Laws and Corn Trade," appended to Adam Smith's "Wealth of Nations," note 10, Part II. The price here given (126s. 6d.) was the "average price" of British wheat for that year, as ascertained by the Receiver of Corn Returns. The price of middling wheat in Windsor market was 128s. for the same year.

In Appendix V. will be found tables showing the average Gazette prices of British wheat, barley, and oats, from 1790 to 1879. From these tables it appears that, during the period 1800 to 1848, the average price of British wheat was £3 10s. 3d., and that during the period 1849 to 1879 it was £2 11s. 10d. The corresponding decrease in the price of barley and oats has scarcely exceeded 2s.

[2] It is said to have touched 120s. in 1817. ("Minutes of Evidence taken· before the Committee of 1836," paragraph 8494.)

[3] "First Report of the Select Committee on the State of Agriculture." 1836, appendix 1.]

contributed by Ireland. The average price for this period was about 60s. a quarter; but, as we have seen, an excess of production in the years 1833-5 had the immediate effect of reducing the average to about 46s.

In default of agricultural statistics, which were first officially collected in 1867, it is impossible to say what area was then devoted to growing wheat. Inasmuch, however, as that area almost sufficed to feed an estimated population of fourteen millions and a 'half, whereas the area now devoted to wheat crops, with a larger yield per acre, certainly feeds a smaller population, it may safely be inferred that far more land was then under wheat crops than at present.[1] Since the year 1836, when the Committee on Agricultural Distress published its evidence without making a report, the average price of wheat has been about 54s. a quarter, and since 1849, when the Repeal of the Corn Laws took full effect, the average has been 51s. 10d. In the first six years of this period it averaged 48s. 3d.; in the second, 56s. 10½d.; in the third, 47s. 11d.; in the fourth, 56s. 2d.; and in the last seven, 50s. 5d. But it is important to observe how little can be learned from these figures without taking into account the average produce per acre in each year, how sensible an effect this last element exercised upon the price for many years after the free

---

[1] Mr. Caird estimates the yield per acre at 26¼ bushels in 1850, and at 28 bushels in 1878. The population maintained by home-grown or foreign wheat cannot be estimated accurately, since the diet of the Scotch and Irish peasantry mainly consists of oatmeal. But, if Mr. Caird's estimate of the acreable yield be accepted, the Agricultural Statistics for 1879 clearly show that, of the wheat now consumed in the United Kingdom, little more than two-fifths is of home growth.

admission of foreign competition, and how trifling an effect it now exercises.[1] For instance, it has been calculated that in 1863, when the harvest was far above the average standard, but the price fell below 41s. a quarter, the farmer would not have realised more than £10 0s. 6d. per acre upon his wheat crop, exclusive of the straw. On the other hand, after the harvest of 1867, which proved the worst in the whole period, the farmer was partially compensated by a rise of price, and might have realised above £8 per acre. Whereas in 1873 "we observe a marked change in this relation between quantity and price." In that year, and the five which followed it, the harvests were 13 per cent. below the average; yet the average price of wheat, instead of rising to meet the deficiency, fell to 51s. 6d. a quarter, or nearly five shillings below the average of the six years 1867–72. The result is that for the years 1873–8 the farmer would only realise about £7 12s. per acre, and his average receipts for the last four years of the six must have been even lower. "In the memory of living men there has been no such concurrence of bad seasons," that of 1879 being probably the most disas-

---

[1] See an able review of the facts relating to home-grown wheat during the period 1849—1878, in the address of Mr. George Shaw Lefevre, M.P., to the Statistical Section of the British Association in 1879. The average produce per acre is calculated by Mr. Shaw Lefevre from a table in Mr. Caird's "Landed Interest," which exhibits the comparative yield of wheat crops in the United Kingdom for each of the last thirty years. The average prices for 1863, 1867, and 1873, given in Mr. Shaw Lefevre's address, differ considerably from the average Gazette prices given on official authority in the Appendix and followed in the text, but not sufficiently to affect the value of the argument

trous of all, and prices ceased to move upwards with a deficiency of home produce.[1]

The steady rise in the value, and even in the rental, of agricultural land, under such conditions, needs some explanation. About thirty years ago Mr. Porter estimated that, " with scarcely any exception, the revenue

[1] A Parliamentary Return, issued on August 13, 1879, contains valuable statistics on the importation of grain and flour between 1820 and 1878, as well as on the average prices of corn, butcher's meat, and other agricultural produce, during this period. From this return it appears that until 1849 the importation of foreign wheat had never exceeded 12,000,000 cwt., but that from that date it increased rapidly until it reached 54,000,000 cwt. in 1877, and nearly 50,000,000 cwt. in 1878. The price of wheat is shown to have fluctuated between 40s. and 102s. per quarter (in 1847), but was on the whole as high in the later years of the period as in the earlier. The price of meat, on the contrary, ranged upwards at the Metropolitan Cattle Market, from 2s. per stone in the earlier years to 6s. per stone in the later; though in 1827 that of beef reached 5s. 4d.

More complete Tables, showing the relative amounts of Farm Produce imported into, and exported from, the United Kingdom during the present century, will be found in Appendix IV. Table I. A gives the quantity of wheat, barley, and oats imported from 1800 onwards. The import returns of other articles included in that Table, as well as the import returns of live animals, and other provisions included in Table I. B, commence with 1820. The export returns of corn and similar articles raised in the United Kingdom and included in Table II. A commence with 1828; those of animals and other provisions raised in the United Kingdom and included in Table II. B, commence at various periods from 1827 onwards. The export returns of corn and similar articles of Foreign and Colonial Farm Produce included in Table III. A, commence at various periods from 1800 onwards; those of Foreign and Colonial " provisions " commence at various periods from 1820 onwards.

Table IV., giving approximately the percentage of agricultural Exports to Imports from 1828 onwards, exhibits, as might be expected, a continuous decrease in the former. Thus, if we compare the twenty years before 1848 with the decennial period 1869—1878, we find that the percentage of exported to imported wheat had declined from 6·4 to 3·3, that of wheat flour from 12·6 to 3·8; that of barley from 5·0 to 0·8; that of oats from 23·6 to 3·0; and that of butter and cheese from 18·3 to 4·4.

drawn in the form of rent has been at least doubled in every part of Great Britain since 1790." According to Mr. Caird's estimate, which purports to be founded on "authentic sources and parliamentary returns," the rent of cultivated land per acre, which in 1770 had averaged but 13s., reached an average of 27s. in 1850, and of 30s. in 1878. We are led to a similar conclusion by the income-tax returns for the fifteen years 1863-77, which distinguish the gross annual value of "land" from that of houses, mines, ironworks, railways, and similar kinds of property. From these it appears that, whereas the "land" of England and Wales had been assessed at £44,611,281 in 1863, it was assessed at £51,811,324 in 1877.[1] Some allowance must doubtless be made for possible variations in the official standard of assessment, but it is well known that income tax returns are more trustworthy, because framed on more uniform principles, than local estimates of rateable value. Upon the whole, it may be taken as certain that a progressive and continuous rise in the rental of land has taken place within the last twenty or thirty years, though it was checked in 1878-9 by the effect of bad seasons. This rise may be dated, approximately, from the Crimean War (1854-56), when the price of wheat

---

[1] "Statistical Abstract" for 1864-78 (Table 12). It appears from the Appendix to Mr. Goschen's "Report on Local Taxation" (Part II., Table 2) that the aggregate annual value of real property in England and Wales under the old Schedule A of the Income Tax Assessment, which included railways, canals, mines, gasworks, waterworks, &c., rose from £53,495,000 in 1815 to £143,872,000 in 1868. In 1877, the assessed value of land and houses alone amounted to £142,388,539, and that of all real property formerly included in Schedule A to about £190,000,000. The annual value of lands alone is stated in Table 11 of the same Appendix (Part II.) to have been £37,063,152 in 1814, and £47,766,763 in 1868.

averaged above 72s. per quarter, and much land destined by nature for sheepwalks was again brought under the plough, as it had been fifty years earlier. On many estates all the farms were revalued, and the growing prosperity of landowners showed itself in the growing luxury of metropolitan society. In Scotland, where rents have long been more directly regulated by competition, and where the national rental had almost trebled itself in twenty years between 1795 and 1815,[1] the recent increase has been still greater proportionably than in any other part of the United Kingdom. But the capital value of the increase in England and Wales alone between 1857 and 1875 is stated by Mr. Caird at £268,440,000, being thirty years' purchase of £8,948,000 increase on gross annual value in the income tax returns.

Mr. Caird accounts for this extraordinary result partly by the enormous expenditure on agricultural improvements out of public loans and private capital, but mainly by the great advance in the consumption and value of meat and dairy produce. Whatever increase of rental may be due to improvements carried out at the landlord's cost is, of course, in the nature of interest on a commercial investment, the benefit of which is shared by the rest of the community. It is otherwise with that increase of rental which may be due to a rise in the general value of agricultural produce, notwithstanding the late fall in the price of wheat. This increment may properly be called "unearned," since it has been won by

---

[1] "Report of the Highland Society on the Agriculture of Scotland," 1878, p. 26.

no foresight or skill on the landlord's part, but springs
naturally out of the growing numbers and prosperity of
the community, each member of which indirectly helps
to swell the landlord's rental by paying more for almost
every article of food produced by the farmer.

Still more emphatically is this true of the increase
in the selling value of land, which, though it cannot
be exactly ascertained, must have been relatively far
greater than any increase in the letting value for purposes of agriculture. Land is bought not only to be
let out in farms, but also to be covered with buildings,
with railways, with docks, or with reservoirs. Moreover, it is bought with a view not only to immediate,
but also to future gain, and experience has more than
justified the speculative enhancement of its ostensible
value. The landed interest of England is estimated to
have received a sum exceeding the national revenue
from railway companies alone over and above the
market price of the land thus sold. But this extra
price by no means represents the whole profit of the
landowners on such a sale. We must add to it the
increased value of the land adjoining the line, and
the increased facilities of transport afforded to all the
farms within reach of a station—an advantage sure to
make itself felt, sooner or later, in an increased rent.
The extension of towns, with their water-works, gasworks, and public institutions spreading far into the
country, the development of mines, the opening of
quarries—in short, each successive expansion of population or industry—inevitably contributes to raise the
selling value of land. One nobleman is known to have
received three-quarters of a million sterling for the

mere site of docks constructed by the enterprise of others: The soil of England may have little more than doubled its agricultural rental in a century, but it must assuredly be worth many times its value in the days of our great-grandfathers, if we include in the calculation all the land which then sold by the acre and now sells by the yard.   Moreover, a very large proportion of the purely agricultural land now possesses a value entirely independent of its rent-producing capacity.   It has been purchased at a fancy price, not for the sake of the interest which it may yield, but for the sake of the social position, territorial influence, and legal privileges, which attach to ownership of land in this country, and the competition for which seems to be ever on the increase.   When all this is considered, it will cease to be thought marvellous that money should be invested in land at two or three per cent., and that its price should be scarcely affected by a temporary diminution of rental.

Part II.

CHAPTER I.

The Law and Custom of Primogeniture.

THE most distinctive features of the English Land-system, as it now exists, are the Law and Custom of Primogeniture governing the ownership of land; the peculiar character of family settlements, which convert the nominal owner of land into a tenant-for-life, with very limited power over the estate; the consequent distribution of landed property and territorial influence among a comparatively small and constantly decreasing number of families; the direction of cultivation by a class of tenant farmers usually holding from year to year without the security of a lease; and the dependent condition of the agricultural labourers, who are mostly hired by the day or week, and have seldom any interest in the soil. This Land-system has been described by an eminent authority " as the gradual growth of experience in a country of moderate extent where land is all occupied, where capital is abundant and constantly seeking investment in land; and where other industries than agriculture are always demanding recruits from the children of the agricultural labourer, who find, besides, a ready

outlet in those British colonies where the soil and
climate are not much different from that which they
leave, and where their own language is spoken."[1]   Yet
the same writer justly characterizes it as wholly exceptional in Europe, and we have already seen reason to
doubt whether artificial restrictions have not contributed
more than natural tendencies or economical experience
to establish it in Great Britain.   We know that Primogeniture was introduced with feudal tenures by Norman
lawyers ; that landed property was far more subdivided
than it now is during the two centuries when the
operation of entails was suspended ; that family settlements were a contrivance of lawyers under the Commonwealth and Restored Monarchy ; that leasehold
occupancy was once the rule in England, as it still is
in Scotland, but was discouraged by the inability of
life-owners to grant leases binding on their successors ;
and that agricultural labourers were too often ousted
of their little tenements by Enclosure, as well as pauperised by the operation of the old Poor Law.   We
also know that, not merely in America and our own
colonies, but in countries of smaller extent, and with
a more crowded population than our own, where the
price of land is equally high, and where towns compete
quite as actively with the country for labour, a Land-
system of an entirely different type is maintained with
equal tenacity and an equally firm belief in its beneficial
effects.   With these facts before us, we cannot regard
the agrarian constitution of England as a spontaneous
or necessary development of our soil, our climate, our
geographical position, or our national character.   In

---

[1] Caird's " Landed Interest," chap. v.

studying its distinctive features, we shall find much to admire as well as something to condemn, but we shall not be justified in assuming that it is impossible to eliminate the one without sacrificing the other.

The Law of Primogeniture, in its strictest form, has now determined the descent of land on intestacy in this country for more than six centuries. It has been shown that not long after the Norman Conquest the right of an eldest son to inherit his father's estate, if held by knight service, was fully recognised, and had been extended by the end of the thirteenth century to socage tenures. It has also been shown how this right has survived all recent attempts to abolish it, so that, while all personalty is divided, on the death of an intestate, between his widow and children, all realty still devolves, by common law, on the eldest male descendant of the eldest line. The Custom of Primogeniture, under which landed property is usually settled by deed or will upon the eldest male descendant of the eldest line, is of less ancient origin, as we have seen, but has prevailed with little variation for the last two centuries. It will be remembered that, since the modern system of family settlement was completed by the invention of "trustees to preserve contingent remainders," in the reign of Charles II., an additional refinement has been imported into it. This is the institution of the "protector,"[1] who is nearly always the life-tenant in possession, and whose consent must be obtained by the first tenant-in-tail in order to cut off the entail and to bar all the remainders effectually. This is usually done with a view to resettle the pro-

---

[1] By the statute of 3 and 4 William IV., cap. 74.

perty in the manner already described,[1] failing which,
it would descend, under the settlement, upon the first
tenant-in-tail, who may instantly transform himself, on
acquiring possession, into an owner in fee simple. The
possible duration of such a family settlement is limited,
it is true, by the legal doctrine long since established,
that no entail can be made on the unborn child of an
unborn child. But since an unborn child may be
made, as he usually is, the first tenant-in-tail, and since
any number of life-estates may be interposed to precede
his interest, it is not impossible that some eighty years,
or nearly three generations, may elapse before he attains
his majority—in other words, before any one becomes
free to dispose of the property, or deal with it as an
owner.[2]

In reviewing the actual operation of Primogeniture
in this country, whether by virtue of the law prescrib-
ing the course of descent or intestacy, or under the
express terms of settlements or wills, we encounter a
difficulty but too characteristic of the English Land-
system. Among our Anglo-Saxon forefathers, the
practice was to enrol all transfers of land in the shire-
book, after proclamation openly made in the shire-mote,
or county court[3]—a primitive but effective substitute

---

[1] See above, pp. 65—67.

[2] In Kenny's " Essay on Primogeniture," chap. iii., a succinct review
is given of the " successive safeguards of primogeniture," showing historically how the heir's expectancy was protected by restrictions on alienation,
in the form of laws for the direct benefit of the heir, of laws for the direct
benefit of the lord, of entails, and of settlements preserving contingent
remainders.

[3] Gurdon " On Courts-Baron," quoted by Wren Hoskyns, in " Systems
of Land Tenure."

for a modern registry of title or assurances. For centuries after the Conquest, the publicity of "feoffments,"
and the "inquisitiones post mortem" taken on the
death of all tenants holding by knight service from the
Crown, kept alive evidence of conveyances or succession for a very large proportion of English properties,
which might have been embodied in periodical revisions of
Domesday Book.[1] It was not until private and unregistered deeds, couched in the jargon of legal pedantry, had
finally superseded the old simplicity of land-transfer
and land-succession, that "real property" became the
stronghold of conveyancing mystery, and transactions
relating to land ceased to be the subject of public
notoriety or interest. At this moment the statistical
materials requisite for a record of English land tenure,
as affected by the Law and Custom of Primogeniture,
are still very imperfect. No register of settlements,
conveyances, or mortgages, exists as yet for any part of
England, except Middlesex and Yorkshire, though such
a register has existed in Scotland a century and a half,
and is admitted to answer its purpose admirably.
Accordingly, very conflicting estimates have been formed
of the proportion which settled bears to unsettled
estates, though many settlements, and those not the
least unjust or capricious, are made by will. Wills, it
is true, are preserved, but they do not show the extent
of land devised by them; nor is there any means of
ascertaining, with any approach to accuracy, how far
they are employed to aggravate, and how far to mitigate, the inequality arising from the custom of settling

[1] The compilation of Domesday Book itself is supposed to have been
facilitated by reference to the books of the Anglo-Saxon county courts.

landed estates upon eldest sons. It might have been expected, however, that a complete record of the land devolving annually under the Common Law rule of descent would be kept for State purposes and public information. Instead of this, no distinction appears to be drawn between land which passes by will and land which passes by settlement, being equally charge-able with succession duty; while, for a like reason, no separate account is published of land transmitted to heirs by the law of intestate succession. We are, therefore, thrown back on secondary evidence, such as the facts and professional opinions collected by Royal Commissions or Parliamentary Committees, for the means of estimating the dominion of Primogeniture over the land-system and social life of England.

It has frequently been asserted, and is widely believed, that a mere fraction of the land which yearly changes hands on death is governed by the law of intestate succession. There are no adequate means of verifying or disproving this assertion, but there are good reasons for distrusting it. There is scarcely a wealthy or noble family of any considerable antiquity in which the estates have not at some time descended to an heir or coparceners by the effect of this law. Such an event, however, is far more likely to happen in families less habitually guided by the advice of solicitors, and accustomed to dispense with marriage-settlements. The savings of shopkeepers in country towns are very often invested in the purchase of villas or small plots of land, and such persons very often omit to make a will, being perfectly satisfied with the distribution of personalty on intestacy, and never having realised the responsibilities of a land-owner. What is really true is that landowners con-scious of these responsibilities seldom deliberately intend to die intestate, and that most descents by operation of law are the result of negligence or misadventure. It is not every layman who can be expected to know that, whilst most shares in railways and canals are per-sonalty in the eye of the law, New River shares are invested with the character of real property; or that, while a lease for 999 years is personalty, a lease for life, though it be the life of another, is realty.[1] But it is not only through ignorance of the Common Law rule that land is left to descend upon a single legal "heir." A man, perhaps, makes several contradictory wills, all of which prove to be void for want of proper attestation, or by reason of his incompetence; or he makes a good will so worded that it does not cover the whole of his real property, including that which he may have contracted to buy; or, having recently purchased a small freehold, he is just about to devise it, when he is suddenly cut off. Moreover, intestacies may easily escape public observation, even when they occur in wealthy families. The known wishes of an intestate may be carried into effect by arrange-ment within the family, or an amicable suit in equity, without the public becoming aware of the fact, especially if those wishes should nearly coincide with the course of descent at common law. Several notable examples of the contrary kind, where the known wishes of the intestate, and the plain requirements of justice,

---

[1] See Laurence's "Essay on Primogeniture," sect. vi.

were flagrantly violated by the law of intestate succession, have been cited by Mr. Locke King and others in Parliamentary debates.[1]

Upon the whole, then, we may conclude, with Mr. Joshua Williams,[2] that "the property which descends to heirs under intestacies, though large in the aggregate, is generally small in individual cases," where, however, it often works grievous hardship. Those who suffer by it are usually persons for whom no other provision has been made, and members of a class to which the idea of making an eldest son, and beggaring the rest of the family, would be utterly repulsive. The direct effect of the Law of Primogeniture in keeping together great estates, and aggrandising the heads of great families, is probably not very considerable. Its indirect effect on the minds of testators and settlors cannot be measured by any definite test, but reason and analogy would certainly lead us to believe that it has been a most powerful agent in moulding the sentiment of the class by which the Custom of Primogeniture is maintained. From this point of view, it is certainly a significant fact that no sooner was the Law of Primogeniture swept away in the United States than equal partibility became the almost universal custom, notwithstanding that American landowners are by no means destitute of family pride, and enjoy very nearly

---

[1] In one of these cases, a man in humble circumstances, having no children, had employed the fortune of his wife, with her full concurrence, to buy the house in which they lived; after which he died intestate, a nephew claimed and obtained the property, and his widow, left destitute, was reduced to work as a menial servant.

[2] "Personal Property," p. 402.

the same liberty of devising or settling their estates as an English proprietor.[1]

It is still more instructive to observe that personal property in this country, being exempt from the Law of Primogeniture, is little affected by the Custom, save when it is thought necessary to accumulate the lion's share of it on the eldest son, that he may the better keep up the dignity of a family place. On the contrary, ordinary wills of personalty closely follow the Statutes of Distributions, under which the "next of kin" are placed in the same position as "the heir" under the Law of Primogeniture. Rich capitalists, who do not invest in land, or aspire to found a county family, seldom make an eldest son, and of those who do indulge in this ambition, some prefer to buy a moderate estate for each of their sons. Still more habitually is equal division recognized as the dictate of natural equity by the great body of merchants, tradespeople, and professional men, as well as by the labouring classes throughout Great Britain and Ireland; in short, by the middle and lower orders of society, divorced from the soil in this country, and by the landless members of the upper orders. Nor must it be forgotten that, by English law, ordinary leaseholds, whether they consist of lands or houses, count as personalty, and are distributed as such on intestacy; whereas money in trust for investment in land counts as realty, and falls under the same rule of inheritance. Vast lease-

[1] See Kenny's "Essay on Primogeniture," pp. 64–5; and Mr. Ford's "Report on Land Tenure in the United States," presented to Parliament, with similar reports from other countries, in 1869–70.

hold interests are constantly included in settlements
of personalty; and few of these settlements, whether
made on the marriage of a duke's younger son or
on the marriage of a shopkeeper, exhibit any bias
towards Primogeniture. In most instances, the funds
are directed to be invested for the benefit of all the
sons and daughters of the marriage equally, though
a power is usually reserved to the parents of modifying this distribution by " appointment," at their own
discretion. The same course is generally followed by
testators possessed of small landed estates purchased
with their own earnings, who, for the most part,
devise their land to trustees for sale, and direct the
proceeds to be divided among their children. In families
of the yeoman class, the ordinary practice appears to
be that hereditary property should go to the eldest
son, but that, in accordance with the Scotch rule of
legitim, younger children should be compensated, so
far as possible, for their disinherison, and that, if
burdened with mortgages, the land should be sold
for the equal benefit of all. Even the rude wills and
settlements drawn up by priests or schoolmasters for
Irish peasant-farmers, among whom the instincts of
proprietorship are cherished in their intensest form,
embody the principle of Gavelkind and not of Primogeniture. Though often destitute of any legal validity,
and purporting to dispose of an interest which has no
existence in law, they usually disclose a clear intention
to place the younger children on a tolerably equal
footing with the eldest son, either by the subdivisions
of which Irish landlords complain so much, or by
heavy charges on the tenant-right.

It may, therefore, be safely affirmed that Primogeniture, as it prevails in England, has not its root in popular sentiment, or in the sentiment of any large class, except the landed aristocracy and those who are struggling to enter its ranks. By the great majority of this class, embracing the whole nobility, the squires of England, the lairds of Scotland, and the Irish gentry of every degree, Primogeniture is accepted almost as a fundamental law of nature, to which the practice of entails only gives a convenient and effectual expression. Adam Smith remarks that " in Scotland more than one-fifth, perhaps more than one-third, part of the whole lands of the country are at present supposed to be under strict entail "—that is, entailed under a system, introduced in 1685, which barred alienation far more inexorably than was permitted by the English rule against perpetuities. Mr. McCulloch, writing in 1847, calculated that at least half Scotland was then entailed; but an Act passed in the following year facilitated disentailing by provisions borrowed from the English law.[1] In England, where so much land is in the hands of corporations or trustees for public objects, and where almost all deeds relating to land

---

[1] See Laurence's " Essay on Primogeniture, pp. 67-8." By the Act of 1848 (11 and 12 Vict., cap. 36) tenants in possession were enabled to bar entails with the consent of all the remaindermen, if less than three, or of the three remaindermen next in succession. Under a subsequent Act (38 and 39 Vict., cap. 61, sec. 5), on an application to the Scotch Court to disentail an estate held by tailzie, dated prior to August 1, 1848, the Court may dispense with any consent thus required by the former Act, except that of the immediate heir, or first remainderman. But it was provided that the value in money of their expectancies or interests in the entailed estate should be ascertained, and paid into Court or duly secured. See Appendix VII.

are in private custody, we cannot venture to speak with so much confidence on this point. Considering, however, that in most counties large estates predominate over small, and that large estates, by the general testimony of the legal profession, are almost always entailed either by will or settlement, while small estates, if hereditary, are very often entailed, there is no rashness in concluding, in accordance with the evidence given before Mr. Pusey's Committee, that a much larger area is under settlement than at the free disposal of individual landlords.[1]

It is well known that in families which maintain the practice of entailing, the disparity of fortune between the eldest son and younger children is almost invariably prodigious. The charge for the portions of younger children, when created by a marriage settlement, is created at a time when it is quite uncertain how many such children there will be. It is rarely double of the annual rental, and often does not exceed the annual rental; indeed, in the case of very large estates, it may fall very far short of it. In other words, supposing there to be six children, the income of each younger brother or sister from a family property of £5,000 a year will consist of the interest on a sum of £1,000, or, at the utmost, of £2,000 ; and, even if there were but one such younger child, his income from the property would probably not be more than one-twentieth or one-thirtieth of his elder brother's rental. Nor does this represent the whole difference between their respec-

---

[1] The estimates given before that Committee represented the estates then under settlement as exceeding two-thirds of the kingdom. Others have stated the proportion at three-fourths and upwards.

tive shares of the family endowment; for the eldest son, who pays no probate duty, finds a residence and garden at his disposal, which he may either occupy rent-free or let for his own private advantage. Of course, where a father possesses a large amount of personalty, he may partially redress the balance; and there are exceptionally conscientious landowners who feel it a duty to save out of their own life incomes for younger children. But it is to be feared that accumulations in the Funds are too often employed, not exclusively nor mainly to increase the pittances allotted for portions, but on the principle of "To him that hath shall be given," to relieve the land of some outstanding incumbrance, and to aid the eldest son in conforming to a conventional standard of dignity.

It is, indeed, wholly delusive to contrast the Law with the Custom of Primogeniture, as if the harsh operation of the former were habitually mitigated by the latter. The contrary tendency is assuredly far more prevalent in the higher ranks of the landed aristocracy; and the younger members of families in this class would generally have reason to congratulate themselves if the law alone were allowed free scope, instead of being aggravated by the effects of the custom. For instance, in the case last supposed, if a family estate of £5,000 a year were charged with no portions for younger children, but left to descend under the law of intestate succession, each of five younger children would lose £1,000, or, at the utmost, £2,000. But then, if the last owner were possessed of £90,000 in personalty, and this also were left to be divided among the children under the Statute of Distributions, each child would receive a share of £15,000. Suppose, however—and it is no improbable supposition—that portions have been charged for younger children, but that one-third of the personalty, or £30,000, is bequeathed to the head of the family to keep up the place, the fortune of each younger child will be reduced to £12,000, so that he would lose £3,000, and would gain no more than £1,000 or £2,000. But it is not very often that a landowner with a rental of £5,000 a year has £90,000 to leave among his children. The same imaginary obligation to preserve that degree of state and luxury which is expected of country gentlemen with a certain status and acreage offers an obstacle to saving which the majority find insuperable. Besides, nine out of ten men who inherit their estates burdened with charges for their father's widow and younger children would think it Quixotic to lay by out of their available income, as men of business would do, for the benefit of their own younger children. Hence the proverbial slenderness of a younger son's fortune in families which have a " place," and especially in those which have a title, to be kept up. As for the daughters, their rank is apt to be reckoned as a substantive part of their fortunes ; and not only are their marriage portions infinitely smaller than would be considered proper in families of equal affluence in the mercantile class, but it is not unfrequently provided that, unless they have children, their property shall ultimately revert to their eldest brother.

It remains to consider how far the institution of Primogeniture, which has so profoundly influenced the land system and social life of England, deserves to be upheld in future, whether by virtue of its intrinsic merits or by reason of its having become incorporated into our national character. That it was not inherited from our Saxon forefathers, that it was gradually introduced under the pressure of military expediency and Norman jurisprudence, that it was perpetuated and stereotyped into its present form by legal ingenuity rather than by legislative policy, are historical facts which cannot be altogether overlooked in an enquiry of this nature. A review of foreign laws and customs regulating the devolution and settlement of land strongly confirms the conclusion that it is, in fact, an unique survival of English feudalism, modified by the exigencies of a commercial age. As such, it must be studied by itself; and we must beware of confounding its direct and inevitable effects with other features of the English Land system indirectly connected with it, such as the prevalence of limited ownership and tenancy at will.

In approaching this study, we must resolutely put aside two lines of reasoning which have done much to obscure it. The first of these is that which starts from the idea that younger sons have certain natural rights of which they are deprived by the Law and Custom of Primogeniture. Now, it is impossible to form any definite conception of rights in this sense, except as arising from the personal exertions of those who claim them; or, at least, from expectations fostered by the law, or the parent, as the case may be. If the Code Napoléon had been introduced into England, and if the existing rule of descent by Primogeniture were afterwards substituted for it, the generation of younger sons affected by the change would have good cause for complaint unless their interests were expressly reserved. Again, if a father had led his children to count upon an equal division of his property, and were then to accumulate all upon the eldest son, a palpable wrong would be done to all the rest. But the supposed grievance of existing younger sons who receive the small fortunes to which they were born, and have always looked forward, will not bear a very close investigation. It is not, in its essence, more real than the grievance of those who are born to no fortune at all, and look wistfully at the inherited wealth of the richer classes. Indeed, the cadets of territorial families who are disposed to regard themselves as the victims of injustice may well reflect that, but for the institution of Primogeniture, those families might perhaps have little or no territory in their possession, but might long since have been merged in the mass of the community. Except where the law steps in, on intestacy, to defeat the known intentions of a father, or a father disappoints the hopes encouraged by himself to aggrandise an eldest son, it can hardly be said that Primogeniture involves personal injustice to younger children. Whatever injustice it may involve is sustained by society at large; and, though society consists of individual members, those of its members who ultimately suffer most by the operation of Primogeniture are certainly not to be found in families which owe their social existence to it.

Still more irrelevant are the attacks which have recently been made on Primogeniture from a communistic point of view. Communistic theories of property, if valid at all, are valid not against any particular rule of succession, but against individual proprietorship as such, or against the ample and peculiar rights of English landlords—rights of which no proprietary class is more tenacious than new purchasers. No doubt, it is a perfectly intelligible proposition that all the land in the kingdom ought to be "nationalised" and placed under public management, because individual owners cannot be trusted with full dominion over that part of the earth's surface by which and upon which all natives of England must live, unless they choose to emigrate. It is evident that, apart from all other objections, this doctrine is the very negation of the belief in peasant-proprietorship and "the magic of property," being, in fact, an essentially urban sentiment, and inevitably destructive to all independence of rural life. Nor can it be said that our experience of corporate administration, in the case of lands held by collegiate, ecclesiastical, and municipal bodies, as well as by trustees of charities, is such as to recommend the substitution of public for private ownership on a much grander scale. At the same time, it is incontestable that land has actually been treated by all governments, not excluding our own, as more within State control, for many purposes, than other kinds of property; and it is possible to conceive circumstances under which it might be expedient to extend State control much further over the soil of these islands. But what has all this to do with the right of Primogeniture? and what consistency is there in a programme which couples the abolition of that right and the adoption of Free Trade in Land with provisions designed to withdraw from the market and consolidate into large municipal domains more and more of the properties which are already supposed to be too few? This is not the place to discuss the moral or economical aspects of these provisions; suffice it to point out that, except so far as they are aimed at overgrown private estates, they have nothing in common with the policy of reforming the Law and Custom of Primogeniture. This policy assumes the maintenance of private property, and is directed to its more equitable distribution among individuals, without contemplating a return to a communal system of ownership, which, if accepted, would supersede all laws of inheritance and powers of disposition. It is the more necessary to insist on this point, because the cause of Primogeniture has been strengthened, and the efforts of its opponents weakened, by the unfounded impression that it cannot be touched without reconstructing our whole law of property, whereas no more is demanded or required than an amendment of one single chapter.

The most familiar as well as the strongest arguments in favour of Primogeniture, as it exists in England, are derived from considerations which must be called, in the largest sense, political. It was as a powerful bulwark of our landed aristocracy that Burke defended it in his "Appeal from the New to the Old Whigs," emphatically declaring that "without question it has a tendency (I think a most happy tendency) to preserve a character of consequence, weight *and prevalent influence over others*, in the whole body of the landed interest." The Real Property Commissioners appointed in 1828 fully endorsed this opinion in their first Report, which contains a laudation of the settlements then in use as the best means of "preserving families," and as investing the ostensible lord of the soil "with exactly the dominion and the power of disposition over it required for the public good." The English law of intestacy is regarded by the Commissioners with equal approbation, since it "appears far better adapted to the constitution and habits of this kingdom than the opposite law of equal partibility, which, in a few generations, would break down the aristocracy of the country, and, by the endless subdivision of the soil, must ultimately be unfavourable to agriculture, and injurious to the best interests of the State." Very similar opinions are expressed by Mr. McCulloch, in combating the well-known *dictum* of Adam Smith, that "nothing can be more contrary to the real interest of a numerous family than a right which, in order to enrich one, beggars all the rest of the family." Mr. McCulloch indeed, though he condemns the old indestructible Scotch entails, since abolished by law, treats it as a characteristic merit of English Primogeniture that it sustains a high standard of luxury among country gentlemen of which the example is not lost upon the mercantile classes.

If we analyse this plea for Primogeniture somewhat more closely, it will be found to resolve itself into several distinct lines of reasoning. In the first place, it is alleged, or rather suggested, that without Primogeniture it would be impossible to maintain an hereditary peerage. This argument will hardly be accepted as conclusive by those who regard the principle of an hereditary peerage as not less vulnerable than Primogeniture itself.   From an opposite point of view, it is, perhaps, a sufficient reply that an hereditary peerage may be kept up, and is kept up in some Continental States, either by means of *majorats* specially created, or by making certain estates " run " with the titles derived from them, without any general Law or Custom of Primogeniture.[1]   Moreover, unless Primogeniture be defensible on other grounds, as beneficial to the whole community, it would surely be monstrous that it should be imposed, in case of intestacy, on the families of some hundred thousand free-holders—not to speak of those who may be rendered landless by its indirect operation—for the sake of the few hundred families composing the hereditary nobility.   In fact, Burke himself, with all his aristocratic bias, was careful not to rest the case on so narrow a ground ; and few admirers of Primogeniture would now venture to advocate it in the interest of the Upper House as distinct from that of the nation at large.   It may be granted that a peer of the realm has a stronger motive than an ordinary landowner for making an eldest son, inasmuch as that son, if he survives him, will succeed to a seat in the House of Lords, and will be the more capable of rendering public service in

---

[1] Mr. Kenny, in his " Essay on Primogeniture," advocates " a distinct law of inheritance " for all estates, " which otherwise would descend un-severed, to support the rank of independence of a peer of England."   Mr. Laurence argues that, even if the English Peerage were deprived of their legislative power, the custom of primogeniture would still be necessary to maintain the dignity and influence properly belonging to patents of nobility. But he proceeds to admit that it would probably work more harm than good if " devoted to the maintenance of a wealthy and unprivileged class, without political power and devoid of all conception of social duties correlative to their rights."

that capacity, if he is a man of independent fortune. But an exclusive law of intestate succession, and a privilege of forming a settlement to last for two or three generations, are not required to give him this power, of which nothing but a law of compulsory partition could deprive him.

But, secondly, it is urged, and not without great force, that Primogeniture is actually productive of greater benefits, political and social, to English society as a whole than could be expected from a system of more equal partibility. It is better, we are told, for rural England, at least, to be paternally governed by a comparatively limited hierarchy of eldest sons, whose successors are usually designated long beforehand, than for estates to become subject to division once in each generation, with the risk of passing into the hands of new purchasers having no ancestral connection with land. The ideal owner of an hereditary property, having been thoroughly instructed in all the manifold duties of property during his father's lifetime, and conscious that a large body of tenants and dependents look to him for guidance and example, enters upon the management of his estate in a spirit altogether superior to commercial self-interest, prepared to do for it what no mere land speculator would think of doing, and no small proprietor could afford to do. If he is a religious man, he builds churches in neglected hamlets; if he is an agriculturist, he sinks more in drainage and farm buildings than he will ever live to receive back in rent, if he is a social reformer, he erects model cottages, carries out sanitary improvements, patronises schools, or devotes himself to bringing forward the most promising youths in the parishes of which he is lord. In all these enterprises, as well as in the unpaid services which he renders on the magisterial bench, on local boards, and in the varied spheres of influence open to resident landlords, he is actuated by no hope of pecuniary reward or even of personal gratification, but rather by that peculiar sense of honour, compounded of public spirit and family pride, which has played so large a part in the history of England. His character, thus developed, exhibits a marked individuality, but it is by no means a one-sided individuality. With education enough to understand the economical and legal questions which he is daily called upon to settle in practice; with leisure enough to follow the course of affairs both at home and abroad; with refinement enough to appreciate art and literature; with energy enough to enjoy a life of constant activity, in which " county business" is relieved by field sports and a laborious summer holiday; with independence enough to smile at official favours or displeasure : the model English country gentleman represents a species which has never been developed in any other country, and the absence of which goes far to account for the failure of local self-government in France. Is it, we are asked, a legitimate object of State policy to promote the gradual extinction of this class, and meanwhile to disorganise the whole structure of family life within it, for the sake of any doubtful advantage that may be gained by a wider distribution of proprietary rights ?

Such a landlord as has been described may be taken as the embodiment of the English landed aristocracy, *as it should be,* from the political and social point of view. Possibly, an equally attractive and not less faithful picture might be drawn of a landed democracy, *as it should be,* illustrated by Swiss and American experience. We have not, however, to deal with ideals, but with realities; not with exceptions, however numerous, but with general tendencies. Let it be granted, once more, that a high standard of political and social responsibility is recognised by a very large number of English country gentlemen—the special products, *ex hypothesi,* of Primogeniture; and, further, that an institution so bound up with much that is admirable should not be lightly disturbed. Still, we are bound to inquire whether these results have not been purchased too dear; whether the continued maintenance of Primogeniture in its integrity involves no countervailing evils, and whether a nearer approximation to ancient usage and foreign codes of land-tenure might not conduce to greater stability and greater unity in our body politic.

It is certainly impossible to ignore the grave political danger involved in the simple fact that nearly all the soil of Great Britain, the value of which is so incalculable and progressively advancing, should belong to a section of the population relatively small and progressively dwindling. We have already seen[1] that the income-tax assessment of real property has trebled itself in the last sixty-five years, and the Commissioners of Inland Revenue give reasons for believing the real advance in its annual value to have been much greater. If all the windfalls of which the landowner has reaped the exclusive benefit during this period could be added to the increment of rent, the fallacy of describing land

[1] P. 85, note 1.

as an "article of luxury" would at once become apparent; while the fact that shrewd men are still as eager as ever to invest in it at a low present rate of interest is the best proof either that a further increase in its annual value is expected, or that its annual value is no measure of its real worth to a purchaser. In short, the man who buys land buys not only what may pay him so much per cent., but what may give him social position, and power over his tenants and neighbours. It is precisely this which renders the undue concentration of landed property so detrimental to public interest in quiet times, and so perilous to its possessors in times of revolution. We shall hereafter see that, whether the aggregate number of English landowners be swelled to nearly a million by including the very smallest properties, or reduced to a few thousands by a narrower definition, a few hundreds of them possess more land than all the rest together, having dominion, moreover, over the greater part of London itself, and many of our provincial capitals. Had the legal rights actually possessed by such metropolitan proprietors as the Dukes of Westminster, Bedford, and Portland, been strained to the utmost, instead of being exercised for the most part with forbearance and discretion, legislative interference would assuredly have been needed to avert a revolutionary solution of the English land question. In the midland and northern counties less public spirit has, on the whole, been shown by great landowners. The result has been not only the exclusion of manufacturing industry from sites naturally adapted to it, but its excessive concentration on sites artificially limited, with the consequent evils of overcrowding in towns and depopulation in some country districts. Other serious issues have already arisen in England upon which the interests of rural landowners have been ostensibly in antagonism with those of the commercial and industrial classes. Still more serious risks of collision between town and country are foreshadowed by recent events in France, where the millions of peasant proprietors constitute the one great barrier against communism. Were it possible to imagine a similar crisis occurring in England, it is to be feared that no similar barrier could be presented by the handful of great proprietors, however powerful their existing influence, who have profited so enormously, and with so little effort of their own, by the growing prosperity of the country during the present century.

In the next place, we cannot and must not ignore the less favourable aspect of Primogeniture in its relation to public life and national energy. An unfriendly critic has spoken of their tendency " to establish in the centre of each family a magnificently fed and coloured drone, the incarnation of wealth and social dignity, the visible end of human endeavour, a sort of great Final Cause, immanent in every family." Without adopting this somewhat invidious conception of the system, we may well ask ourselves whether it is, on the whole, for the public good to encourage the development of a class wholly dependent on birth, and independent of merit, for the command of all that makes life desirable. Berkeley asks, " What right hath an eldest son to the worst education ? " and Bacon, after describing a new expedient for defeating the recent legislation against entails, touches in a pregnant sentence the very bottom of this question :—

"Therefore, it is worthy of good consideration, whether it be better for the subject and sovereign to have lands secured to men's names and blood by perpetuities, with all the inconveniences above-mentioned, or to be free, with hazard of undoing his house by unthrifty posterity."

It is too often forgotten that Primogeniture, as secured by modern settlements, compels many a territorial family to support, not one "drone" only, but two, with separate establishments yielding no agricultural return. The head of the family, however, is usually a man of mature age, and, feeling the weight of actual responsibility, may well be impelled by the salutary influence of public opinion, as well as by the dictates of his own conscience, to set a good example. But can this be said with equal truth of the eldest son, upon whom no such responsibility is cast, whose right to succeed is indefeasible, for whom a present income has been reserved out of the rental upon resettlement, and whose power of raising money on his expectations is unlimited? It is contended, indeed, that an heir born to a great position, and trained from his earliest years to make himself worthy of it, will acquire habits and will be fortified by motives which are powerful securities for his future virtue and capacity. No doubt it may be so, and it would be easy to cite instances of landowners, especially in the higher ranks of the nobility, who devoted themselves in youth to laborious preparation for territorial duties, as others do to a lucrative profession. These instances must be duly taken into account, nor must it be lightly assumed that the choicest results of English Primogeniture could be produced under an opposite system. But are these instances common enough to be treated as typical? Would it be difficult to cite a larger number of instances where the heirs of ancestral estates have been spoiled and demoralized by their great expectations, even if they are afterwards reformed by the effect of realizing these expectations? Would not the senseless frivolities and reckless extravagance of the London season, the scandals of turf speculation, the restless passion for amusement, and the ignoble race of social competition, be sensibly checked by the withdrawal of this *jeunesse dorée* from English society, and especially from those circles in which match-making is the supreme end of human ambition? Would the army be less efficient if it should lose the services of a few officers in the Household Brigade and cavalry regiments, who take up with military life as a gentlemanlike pastime, and have no intention of continuing it for more than a few years? Would the wisdom of Parliament be diminished if the number of young county members were lessened by the subtraction of those who owe their seats to mere acreage and family names? These are questions which cannot be answered by reference to statistics, but on which a knowledge of the world may throw some light, and which must be faced by those who imagine that Primogeniture is maintained at the cost of younger sons alone, and not also at the cost of the country. It may be too much to assert that family settlements induce unprincipled or careless landowners to neglect the education of their eldest sons, knowing that, however worthless or dissipated they may prove, neither the estate nor the social estimation of the family can be diminished; or that family settlements "*often* set up in influential positions as examples to society men of luxurious and idle habits, depraved tastes, and corrupted morals."[1]   But they assuredly guarantee wealth and power to men who may be utterly unworthy of either, yet whose conduct and manners are too apt to become a standard for imitation in their own class, and even in the classes below them.   If the general effect of such a provision be indeed as beneficial as it is represented to be, we must suppose the ordinary laws of human nature to be reversed for the purpose of justifying the English Law and Custom of Primogeniture.

One thing is certain, that eldest sons, with an indefeasible right of succession to great estates, are exposed to special temptations on the part of money-lenders, and often fall into their hands.   It has been shown by Mr. Lefevre[2] how ruinous are the terms on which accommodation is obtained by needy reversioners on post-obit bonds.   According to his statement, the immediate value of the reversion to a property of £10,000 a year is but £15,000, if the father should be aged forty-five and the son twenty-one when the loan is made; so that an advance of £5,000 would swallow up one-third of the son's prospective rental for the rest of his life.   If the secrets of re-settlements could be disclosed, it would probably be found that liabilities of this kind, postponed for a generation, had contributed far more than portions for younger children or

[1] Kay's "Free Trade in Land," letter iv.
[2] Paper on the "Limitation of Entails and Settlements," in the sessional proceedings of the Social Science Association, April 7th, 1877.

jointures for widows to encumber family properties. The eloquent passage in which Mr. Cliffe Leslie describes the circumstances under which these re-settlements are usually made cannot be too often quoted. It is all the more impressive, if we clearly realize that in the process of breaking or renewing entails an hereditary estate may be, and constantly is, burdened again and again by private arrangement between the present and the expectant head of the family, not to provide for any other members of it, nor to make improvements on the land, but to satisfy debts incurred by the father when he was himself "an eldest son"—it may be in gambling speculations, or in some other form of self-indulgence:—

"It is commonly supposed that the son acts with his eyes open, and with a special eye to the contingencies of the future and of family life. But what are the real facts of the case? Before the future owner of the land has come into possession; before he has any experience of his property, or what is best to do, or what he can do in regard to it; before the exigencies of the future or his own real position are known to him; before the character, number, and wants of his children are learned, or the claims of parental affection and duty can make themselves felt, and while still very much at the mercy of a predecessor desirous of posthumous greatness and power, he enters into an irrevocable disposition by which he parts with the rights of a proprietor over his future property for ever, and settles its devolution, burdened with charges, upon an unknown heir."

When it is justly claimed for Primogeniture that it creates a "leisure class," we cannot but ask ourselves whether the creation of a leisure class is a legitimate object of State policy, or an unmixed benefit in itself. "Leisure" may be essential to æsthetic and intellectual culture, but it is the leisure earned

by honourable exertion or guaranteed by a discrimi-
nating use of endowments, not the leisure inherited
as a right attaching to private property. It would
be difficult, indeed, to show that our Peerage and landed
aristocracy, with all their overwhelming advantages,
have contributed one-half so much to science, literature,
or art, as the rest of the community who have been
thrown upon their own labour for the means of making
their bread. The laudable energy and public spirit of
English noblemen and country gentlemen in the discharge of unpaid public services can hardly be adduced
as an argument in favour of Primogeniture; for it is
certain that equal vigour and independence were displayed by Saxon freeholders before Primogeniture was
introduced, as they are still displayed on thousands
of Boards and Committees whose members owe nothing
to Primogeniture. Even in politics, where eldest sons
long enjoyed a precedence that might easily have
proved exclusive, younger sons and men of no family
at all have more than equalled them in the attain-
ment of great eminence; and it is no absurd opinion
that England would have produced a larger number
of really illustrious men if she had abandoned Primogeniture long ago. Were the inheritance of a great
name and fortune a security for public virtue, we
should expect to find the standard highest of all
among Princes of Royal blood, and far higher in the
most exalted orders of our own nobility than among
Peers of inferior rank, still more than among commoners. Is such the result of experience? No doubt
the cases in which an illustrious name is disgraced
are exceptions, but they are by no means rare excep-

tions. They are exceptions, moreover, of which Primogeniture must bear the whole discredit, for they are the direct result of settling princely territories upon unborn heirs of whose capacity and character there is not the smallest presumption. On the other hand, the whole credit of instances, happily more numerous, in which a noble estate is nobly administered, cannot fairly be assigned to Primogeniture. Before we can be assured that society is a clear gainer by the existence of a great landowner combining every perfection of his type, we must be satisfied that he does more good than all the yeomen whom he displaces, and more than he would have done himself, if compelled to win his own position in the world, perhaps struggling, like Warren Hastings, for the redemption of a lost patrimony.

Indeed, the merits so freely claimed for Primogeniture, from this point of view, only appear irresistible so long as we leave out of sight those which may be claimed for the alternative. When, for instance, it is urged that no incentive to honourable ambition is so potent as the prospect of founding a family, it is forgotten that, whatever be the force of this incentive, it is exhausted by one individual to the detriment of his descendants. The first bearer of a title may have rendered important services to the State in the attempt to achieve success; but no sooner is success achieved than an indefinite series of male successors is placed above the operation of the very motives which inspired and ennobled the exertions of their ancestor. Again, when it is contended that Primogeniture keeps up the local settlement of families, which is assumed to be an unmixed benefit, it is entirely forgotten that, while it roots the elder branch for the time being in the soil, it uproots all the others. The eldest male in each generation is selected to occupy the family mansion and estates, but the other members of the family are by the same act divorced from the place of their birth, and scattered abroad to seek their living in other parts of England, in the metropolis, or in the colonies. This dispersion of families, which does not equally prevail in any other class, or in any other country, is, in fact, often represented as one of the blessings incident to Primogeniture. It is by no means uncommon to hear eloquent discourses on the happiness of younger sons in having to start in life without a competence, and especially without a competence in land, by persons to whom it never occurs that, if the heritage of poverty be so enviable, it would not be difficult to devise means whereby it might be shared by eldest sons also.

Equally delusive is the notion that Primogeniture has saved England from an aristocratic caste, like the old *noblesse* in France and some other Continental nations. True it is that our Peerage is not an exclusive order of nobility in the foreign sense. As Mr. Freeman has well remarked, " it is not only a rank to which any man may rise, but it is a rank from which the descendants of the hereditary holders must as a matter of course come down." But these results are not due to the English Law and Custom of Primogeniture. It is perfectly consistent with an exclusive inheritance of landed property by the eldest son that younger children should inherit their father's rank. The younger sons of German Counts were Counts before the principles of the Code Napoléon were adopted in Germany. The younger sons of an English Sovereign are as much Princes as their eldest brother, though his exclusive right of succession is secured by the strictest rule of Primogeniture. Even the younger sons of English Dukes and Marquises bear the courtesy title of "Lord," while that of "Lady" is extended, by an anomaly of etiquette, to the daughters of Earls. The non-inheritance of titles by the cadets of noble families, therefore, is by no means a necessary incident of Primogeniture, while it is obvious that a commoner might equally be ennobled, as a reward of merit, whether or not his younger sons were destined to inherit his title. The refusal of this privilege to the younger sons of English Peers is more properly to be explained by the fact that Peers are hereditary legislators, and that only one son can be permitted to represent the family in the House of Lords.

In the meantime, Primogeniture has developed and consolidated a landed aristocracy, of which the Peerage itself is but the most influential section. There is little meaning in the allegation that it operates as a democratic solvent on this aristocracy, inasmuch as younger sons, who might otherwise form part of it, are thus constantly thrust down into the plebeian class. This argument is not easily reconciled with another often used to reinforce it—that, if the landed aristocracy were swelled by the accession of younger sons, it would cease in a few generations to be an aristocracy at all, and would be merged in the vulgar mass of the people. What is certain is that, while intermarriages between the nobility and middle classes are more frequent in England than on the Continent, the want of social unity is among the greatest of our national weaknesses, strongly contrasting with that political unity which is a main source of our national strength. It does not follow that a law of equal partition would remedy this; and it is notorious that in Germany, where titles descend to younger sons, the utmost insolence of family pride is often manifested by the poorest scions of nobility. On the other hand, it is certainly Primogeniture which has narrowed the landed gentry of England into a privileged, though not an exclusive, order, and the strongest line of demarcation in English society is that between those connected with this privileged order and the rest of the community. The younger sons of noblemen and great landowners mostly retain, for good and for evil, the spirit and ideas of their caste, and a true caste it still is, though admission to it may be purchased with wealth - as well as inherited by gentle birth. For, after all, men's habits and bearing are governed rather by early training than by future prospects; and a youth brought up in one of our ducal palaces, though destined to be cut off with a beggarly fortune, is more likely to be an aristocrat in character than if brought up in a frugal home with great expectations.

But these are not the only or the main fallacies which beset the social argument in favour of Primogeniture. That argument rests upon the further assumption that entails and settlements are at least effectual to give us a resident proprietary capable of discharging in person the manifold duties attached to landed property in a country where landed property is the basis of social power. This assumption will scarcely bear examination by the light of every-day experience. Instead of Primogeniture creating a wealthy resident proprietary, it is certain that it produces, and almost demonstrable that it must produce, the very opposite effect. Formerly, there was a resident squire, and often more than one squire, besides one or two yeomen, in each parish; but this state of things has long passed away. A comparison of the number of persons owning half England and Wales with the number of parishes in England and Wales shows that each of their estates covers an area equal to four or five parishes. Out of three English proprietors owning above 100,000 acres each, two have properties scattered respectively over eleven counties. Most of our great aristocratic houses possess more than one family place. It is impossible for the head of the family to reside continuously at each; during the whole London season he is nominally in attendance on the House of Lords, and, unless he is exceptionally conscientious, he easily satisfies himself with a flying visit once a year to his less favoured estates, in which the agent really fills the landlord's place. In short, absenteeism is the inevitable consequence of a system which concentrates landed property in few hands, and, where absenteeism exists, the *raison d'être* of Primogeniture is materially weakened. But this is not all. Entails and settlements provide an ample security against landed property being divided according to the

dictates of natural affection, but they provide no
adequate security against its remaining practically
without a responsible owner during a whole lifetime,
or even against its ultimately passing into the hands of
strangers. If a duke ruins himself by gambling, and is
declared bankrupt, his domains may be managed for the
sole benefit of his assignees during half a century, unless
he can make up his own mind, and can obtain the concurrence of his eldest son, to sell them outright. In
this case, the whole inheritance of a family may be
converted into money at a stroke by collusion between
two of its members, for the exclusive profit of themselves or their creditors, without the semblance of
consent on the part of the younger children and
junior branches, who are supposed to have a moral,
if not a legal, interest in the land thus alienated. It is
true that where such things happen—and such things
do happen—the farmers and cottagers on the estate
usually change masters for the better, and profit by an
act which nevertheless cuts the ground from under the
whole argument for Primogeniture as a safeguard for
the maintenance of territorial families.

This brings us back to what may be called the
domestic aspect of Primogeniture ; that is, to its influence upon the happiness and welfare of the households
immediately affected by it. Apart from the question
whether upon other grounds it is expedient, in the
interest of the State, to perpetuate a landed aristocracy,
we have to consider the question whether the English
institution of Primogeniture conduces to family peace
and dutiful conduct within that aristocracy. This is a
question which has been very fully discussed by Mr.

Locke King and Mr. Neate, the latter of whom specially insists on the humiliating and unbecoming position in which the father as life-tenant is placed towards the eldest son as tenant-in-tail in remainder. "It is a hard thing," he says, "for a father to have to confess and excuse his extravagance to a son, or to justify his desire for a second wife. It is a worse thing for a son to judge of his father's excuses, or to decide virtually, as head of the family, whether it is right that his father should be allowed to marry again." Yet this is but one of the forms in which our system of entails operates to sow discord and undutiful feeling in families. Long before the heir to a great estate emerges from boyhood, he is made aware that his fortune does not depend on his father's will or his own deserts. He soon learns to consider the estate as his, subject only to his father's life-interest, and expects to receive an allowance enabling him to live in idleness. As the father grows older, and the son's expectation of succeeding becomes nearer and nearer, painful jealousies are very apt to spring up between them, till at last, perhaps, not a lease can be granted or a fall of timber authorised, lest it may prejudice or be represented as prejudicing the reversion. Of course, there are many examples of families owning settled estates, where the father and eldest son work together in harmony, both looking upon themselves as trustees not only for the rest of the family, but for all placed under their control. But it is self-evident that an indefeasible right of succession vested in the eldest son must tend to weaken parental authority, and to facilitate borrowing money upon the security of reversionary interests.

We have already seen that it is fallacious to speak generally of Primogeniture as inflicting injustice upon younger children. It is, however, equally fallacious to describe it as securing to younger children, regarded individually, a full equivalent for an equal share of the family heritage upon the father's death. In what does this imaginary equivalent consist? Certainly not in anything capable of being reduced to a definite conception, unless it be the enjoyment of a rank partly determined by that of their elder brother, and of a claim on his influence for their advancement in life, as well as the maintenance at his expense of a country seat where they are welcome and honoured guests. Of these privileges, the two last depend entirely on their remaining on good terms with the head of the family, whose interest naturally centres in his own children rather than in his father's children, and whose residence, however freely thrown open to them, cannot after all be treated as their home. As for the first privilege, it may well be doubted whether rank or status out of proportion to a man's pecuniary means be not an encumbrance rather than a boon. To have acquired, under a parent's roof, habits, tastes, and ideas of style which cannot be gratified in maturer years without running into debt, has been the ruin of many a promising career. To this cause more than any other is traceable the self-imposed celibacy too prevalent among younger sons of good family in the metropolis, and inevitably prejudicial not to morality only, but to steadiness and earnestness in practical work. By this cause more than any other was fostered the shameful jobbery of former days, when the Church, the Army, and the Civil Service were refuges for the privileged destitute, and junior members of the aristocracy were said to rely on the Budget for their " ways and means." Now that patronage has been most properly restricted, that capital and mercantile connection is almost essential for success in business, and that even the Bar is becoming more and more dependent on the lower branch of the legal profession, it is very doubtful whether younger sons of county families stand a fair chance in the race of life against young men of the middle class with larger fortunes, more active backing, less sensitive feelings, and a more utilitarian education. If they have no right to complain of a lot which appears very enviable to most of their countrymen, and which only needs exceptional energy to make it so, yet they owe no gratitude to a system which inverts the natural order of human life, accustoming them to ease and luxury in youth, but offering them no adequate provision either for an early settlement or for an early retirement.

From every point of view, then, we are led to an adverse judgment on the extreme development of Primogeniture established in England by the joint operation of law and custom. It must be condemned, politically, as aggravating the perilous dualism of town and country ; as affording the very minimum of constitutional stability to be derived from the conservative instincts of proprietorship ; and as giving a very limited body of landlords a preponderance in the State none the less unreasonable and obnoxious because it is defended on the untenable ground that it is bound up with the existence of the Upper House. It must be condemned, socially, because it helps to stereotype the caste-like organisation of English classes "in horizontal layers," setting up in thousands of country parishes a territorial autocracy which, however benevolently exercised, keeps the farming and labouring population in an abnormal state of dependence on a single landowner, often non-resident, while the rural districts have gradually been deserted by the lesser gentry who helped to bridge over the chasm between rich and poor in ancient times. It must be condemned, economically, because it cramps the free play of economical laws in dealings with land, multiplies the difficulties and cost of transfer, and discourages a far-sighted application of capital to agriculture, either by the landlord, who is usually a mere life-owner, or by the tenant, who seldom holds a lease. It must be condemned, morally, because it holds out to almost every eldest son, in what must still be regarded as the governing class, the assurance of wealth and power, whether he be worthy of it or not, and subject to no condition but that of surviving his father. Lastly, it must be condemned, in the interest of family government, because it fatally weakens the authority of parents over eldest sons, and introduces a degree of inequality into the relations of children brought up together which often mars the cordiality of their intercourse in after life.

CHAPTER II.

Family Settlements and Limited Ownership.

THE economical objections to family settlements of landed property deserve separate consideration, because, grave as they are, they apply to the Custom and not to the Law of Primogeniture—to its incidental effects, and not to its principle. It is the system of limited ownership adopted in all modern settlements which is specially open to such objections. This system practically vests the control of property not in a series of hereditary landowners, but in a series of hereditary life-tenants, without the full rights and sense of proprietorship, sometimes heavily embarrassed, and almost always with a standard of unproductive expenditure more than commensurate with their means. Now, whenever the Law of Primogeniture operates directly, it operates in a contrary direction. It hands over all the land of an intestate landowner, undivided, and often unencumbered, to a single "heir," who takes it, not as a tenant-for-life or as a tenant-in-tail, but as a tenant in fee-simple. The Law of Primogeniture, therefore, cannot be held directly responsible for the evils of limited ownership. Nor are the evils of limited ownership inseparably connected with the Custom of Primogeniture. That custom existed for centuries, in forms now obsolete, before the present system of limited ownership was devised, and it would of course be possible to maintain the integrity of family estates by means of this system, without giving an habitual preference to eldest sons. At the same time, it would be idle to ignore the fact that limited ownership, complicated by the addition of contingent remainders in tail, is the familiar substitute for perpetual entails, and, like them, has been developed for the express purpose of keeping together family estates in the interest of successive eldest sons, to the extreme limit permitted by law.

In order to understand clearly the nature and operation of limited ownership, it may be convenient to commence our review of it at the most critical moment in the history of a family estate—the moment of re-settlement. In most families, re-settlements take place once in each generation, and the few minutes which may elapse between the execution of the disentailing deed and the execution of the new entailing deed are literally the only periods during which many a noble property comes into the possession of an absolute owner from century to century. Let us now suppose the ordinary case of a father (A) and eldest son (B) concurring to bar the entail and to re-settle the estate. Hitherto the father has been a life-tenant, while the eldest son has been tenant-in-tail in reversion. There are probably a number of charges on the estate, imposed at the last settlement or under powers contained in it. For instance, there may be mortgages for debts incurred before the last re-settlement, as well as charges for the portions of A's brothers and sisters, and A may already have exercised the right then given him of charging the estate for a pension to his widow (if any), and for the portions of his younger children, the brothers and sisters of B. These mortgages and charges, of course, take precedence of A's and B's interest, and cannot be prejudiced by anything which they may do. Subject to these, the estate is at the free disposal of A and B, who settle it again upon A for life, with remainder to B, not in tail as hitherto, but for life, with remainder to the first and other unborn sons of B in tail, with remainder to B's next brother (C) for life, with remainder to his first and other sons in tail, and so forth.

Before making this re-settlement, however, it is necessary for A and B to agree with each other respecting the means of paying off existing charges, and the amount of future charges which the estate may be able to bear. Let us suppose it to have a gross rental of £10,000 a year, but to be already burdened with a charge of £1,000 a year for interest on the portions of A's younger brothers and sisters, which have not yet been paid off. Let us suppose, further, that it is mortgaged to the extent of £40,000 or £50,000, to cover the cost of election contests, or land purchases, or building schemes, incurred in past times, and fastened on the estate by previous settlements. Let us suppose, lastly, that a jointure of £1,500 a year has been secured to A's wife during widowhood by the last settlement, and that under powers therein reserved to him A has charged, or intends to charge, the estate with £20,000 for the portions of his own younger children.

The estate, then, is already paying interest amounting to about £3,000 a year on existing charges and mortgages, and will have, moreover, to bear a temporary charge of £1,500 in case of A's wife surviving him, besides the capital sum of £20,000 required to be raised for the portions of A's younger children. How are these charges to be met? Of course, if A had been living very much within his income, as any prudent merchant or professional man would do, he would have saved enough to relieve the estate of the charge for his own younger brothers and sisters. But these, unhappily, are exceptional cases. Few life-tenants leave a large margin between their ostensible rental and their expenditure, and most consider themselves fortunate if they have succeeded by the end of their lives in clearing off family charges inherited from their predecessors. For the present, therefore, we must suppose that £3,000 a year will have to be deducted from the income of the estate, though it is possible that A may now be prepared to insure his life heavily, so as to cancel at his death the £1,000 a year payable on the portions of his own brothers and sisters. In the meantime, his gross income is £7,000 a year, but he must forthwith secure in the re-settlement a proper allowance for B, his eldest son. Let us suppose this allowance to be no more than £1,000 a year; A will then have a gross residuary income of £6,000 a year, subject to all the deductions incident to an income derived from a landed property of £10,000. As for the portions of his younger children, it is very unlikely that he will be disposed to spare the estate from providing them, in addition to paying off his brothers and sisters.[1] Accordingly, a prospective

---

[1] Mr. Arnold White, a solicitor of great experience, stated before the Lords' Committee on the Improvement of Land that no one ever thought

charge of £1,000 a year, payable at A's death, will be substituted for the charge of £1,000 a year payable during his life, to which must be added, prospectively, a possible charge of £1,500 a year for the jointure of A's wife, B's mother. The prospective income of B, in which his own allowance will be merged, would not therefore exceed £5,500, if his mother should happen to survive his father. But provision must be made in the re-settlement for B's marriage,—if, indeed, that is not the occasion of the re-settlement,—for the jointure of his prospective wife, and for the portions of his prospective younger children. Unless B is prepared to insure his life with a view to these contingencies, and to save the premiums out of his income, it will be necessary—and it is almost invariably thought necessary—to confer on him new powers of charging the estate for these purposes. And, unless he takes care to lay by, in one form or another, enough to pay off his brothers and sisters, the inevitable result will be that, on his death, two generations of younger children will be drawing revenue from the estate, which may also have to support two dowagers at the same time.

We may now realize without difficulty how it is that successive life-tenants, miscalled owners, of landed property, find themselves almost passive links in a chain of destiny forged by custom, it is true, and not by law, yet so cleverly strengthened by legal and moral sanctions that no ordinary force of will can break it. For

of paying off younger children's portions out of rental, and that he, consequently, always recommended insuring the eldest son's life on re-settlement, so as to relieve the estate from the burden of his younger children's portions.

instance, if B should refuse to concur with A in breaking the entail and tying up the estate afresh, he would
not only have to brave his father's displeasure, but
might be left entirely without an allowance for thirty
or forty years, and without the means of making a
settlement on his marriage, except by the ruinous expedient of post-obit bonds; for his reversion, though
absolutely secure in the event of his surviving his
father, is absolutely dependent on that event. Having
concurred in making the re-settlement, he thenceforth
becomes a prospective life-tenant instead of a prospective owner,[1] and, when his time comes, is probably as
anxious as A was to deprive his successor of the capacity
to deal freely with the estate, the settlement of which
may be complicated with a far greater variety of claims
and conditions than has in this case been supposed.

In comparing the position of a life-tenant, or
"limited owner," thus situated, with that of an
absolute owner, we have not merely to consider the
legal power which they may respectively possess, but
also the motives which may be expected to influence
them respectively in the use of these powers. The
legal powers vested in limited owners by most settlements are greater than is commonly known, and have
been largely extended by recent legislation. Formerly,
a tenant-for-life could make no lease to endure beyond

---

[1] Lord St. Leonards states that attempts made by eldest sons to set
aside re-settlements, on the ground of parental influence or the want of
sufficient consideration, have rarely proved successful, as "the inclination
of the Court is to support such a transaction." On the other hand, he
thinks it more than doubtful whether Courts of Equity should assume
the right to restrict the powers of tenants-for-life in respect of "waste."
("Handy Book of Property Law," pp. 112—125.)

his own life, unless specially empowered to do so. Hence it became customary to confer on him such a power by settlement, and where no such power was contained in the settlement, recourse was often had to private Acts of Parliament, 700 of which are said to have been procured in the early part of this century for the relief of limited owners. At last, in 1856, a general Act was passed for the same purpose, and it is now provided by the Settled Estates Act of 1877[1] that every tenant-for-life may grant agricultural leases for twenty-one years, unless the settlement contains an express declaration to the contrary, and that, with the same reservation, mining and building leases of far greater length may be granted by tenants-for-life under the authority of the Court of Chancery. We have already noticed the Acts under which tenants for life can borrow money for drainage and other improvements of land under the authority of the Enclosure Commissioners,[2] provision being made for the repayment of such advances with yearly interest by a rent charge on the property, usually amounting to more than 7 per cent. for a term of twenty-five years, or somewhat less for a term of thirty years.[3] Upon a similar principle, tenants-for-life are enabled by the Agricultural Holdings Act of 1875 to charge the inheritance, within certain limits, with the cost of improvements made by the occupier and not by the landlord, though it has already been shown that occupiers under tenants-for-life have less

---

[1] 40 and 41 Vic., cap 18. [2] See pp. 69—71.
[3] For a summary of these Acts, see "Williams' Real Property" (Ed. 1877), pp. 30—2.

encouragement to improve than occupiers under absolute owners.[1]   Even the sale of settled estates is not so
impossible or rare an event as it is sometimes represented to be.   In the ordinary form of family settlements, clauses are inserted empowering the trustees,
upon the request of the tenant-for-life, to sell land,
and to apply the proceeds either in the purchase of
other land, to be settled in the same way, or in discharging any mortgage or other incumbrance affecting
any part of the property.   Where no power of this
kind is given by the settlement, but where the settlement contains no express declaration to the contrary,
the Court of Chancery, being satisfied that it is for
the interest of all parties entitled, may direct a settled
estate to be sold.   The proceeds may be applied as
under the common form of settlements.   In one case,
at least, the Court of Chancery went so far as to
sanction the expenditure of a large sum out of a trust
fund produced by the sale of a settled estate in the
improvement of another estate purchased with the rest
of the trust fund, instead of insisting on the whole
fund being reinvested in the purchase of land.[2]   In
many cases, a trust fund, representing the price of a
settled estate, is allowed to remain invested for a long
period in Government securities, being impressed, as
the saying is, with the character of realty, while the
interest is applied exactly in the same manner, and for
the benefit of the same persons, as if it were actually
the rent of land.

[1] See p. 71.
[2] See the evidence of Mr. Arnold White before the Lords' Committee on
the Improvement of Land.

But it may be asserted broadly that powers are scarcely ever inserted in settlements, or exercised by the Court of Chancery, for the purpose of enabling the whole of a settled estate to be sold with a view to a permanent investment of the proceeds in personalty, or of enabling part to be sold with a view to a thorough improvement of the remainder. Even where the powers vested in the Court were invoked and exercised, the proceedings were of a very cumbrous and dilatory nature. In the language of Lord Cairns, "the petition had first to be presented to the Court, then advertisements had to be inserted in newspapers, then notice had to be given to all persons concerned, and then, when publicity had been secured, and every person is represented before it, the Court proceeded to decide whether the power of leasing or selling could be given to a particular person with reference to a particular estate before the Court. If there was to be a sale, the sale took place under the Court, and not as a sale out of doors, and the conveyances had to be settled by the Court." With slight modifications, this system is still in force, and represents a sensible advance in the law applicable to settlements. But no system thus complicated by obstructions and formalities, notices and consents, for the protection of reversioners, can possibly be a substitute for the freedom of real ownership. Most settled estates pay a handsome percentage on their income to family lawyers, whose services are continually in requisition, if not to conduct suits, friendly or otherwise, between the parties interested, yet to give advice and prepare deeds which under a system of undivided ownership would be wholly needless.

Moreover, it is quite possible so to settle land by deed or will that it may remain altogether *extra commercium* for as much as two generations after his own death, and in the meantime to regulate its management by the most capricious and short-sighted directions. For the Court of Chancery will not overrule an express declaration in the deed or will, however preposterous, unless it be contrary to some established principle of policy.

The most vigorous attempt hitherto made to reconcile the right of settling with Free Trade in Land is embodied in the Settled Land Bill, and two supplementary measures, introduced by Lord Cairns, in February, 1880. The Settled Land Bill was entitled " A Bill for facilitating sales, leases, and other dispositions of settled land, and for promoting the execution of improvements thereon." It was founded on the broad principle that settlements of real property are not to be regarded as mere family compacts, but as acts essentially affecting national interests. It therefore purported to confer on a limited owner all the powers which a prudent owner in fee-simple would exercise, subject only to checks designed to protect the objects of the settlement. These powers, being the same as those hitherto vested in the Court of Chancery for the benefit of limited owners, it gave directly, as an incident of ownership, not to trustees, but to the tenant-for-life, not by way of boon or exception, but as part and parcel of his estate. The future tenant-for-life would thus have been enabled—in spite of any restrictions imposed on him by the settlement—to sell, to exchange, and to grant not only agricultural leases,

but mining and building leases, either with the concurrence of his trustees, or even without their concurrence, if their objections should be overruled by the
Court. The tenant-for-life under existing settlements
would have been compelled, in all cases, to obtain the
sanction of the Court for the exercise of these new
powers. The purposes to which the purchase-money
received on a sale might be applied under the Bill
were as various as could be desired—the discharge of
incumbrances and redemption of the land-tax, the
adjustment of partitions or exchanges, the enfranchise-
ments of copyholds, the purchase of the reversion to
leaseholds, the purchase of freeholds, mines or minerals,
the satisfaction of any legitimate claim on the land or
any charges arising out of transactions authorised by
the Bill itself, and, above all, the execution of any
improvements authorised by the Bill itself. These
improvements were enumerated in a subsequent clause,
and comprised almost every operation which can increase the value of an estate for agricultural, manufacturing, building, or mining purposes. The erection
of labourers' cottages, the construction of water-works,
the laying out of free public gardens on building-
estates, and the opening of trial pits for mines, were
expressly specified as within the scope of the Bill; and
it was provided that money derived from any one part
of the settled land might be employed in improvements on any other part of it. A certificate from the
Enclosure Commissioners was, however, to be required
for expenditure of trust-moneys on improvements; and,
even after they should have approved a scheme, it was
only to be carried out with the sanction of the trustees

or the Court, and under the superintendence of the commissioners. Moreover, it was specially ordained that no family mansion-house, nor any park or domain land usually occupied therewith, should be either sold or leased without the consent of the trustees or an order of the Court. It is perhaps needless to add that no power was given to retain the proceeds of a sale in the form of money upon the trusts declared by the settlement; for such a power, if widely exercised, would destroy the very *raison d'être* of Primogeniture, as a territorial institution, and would surely lead to its abolition.

The other Bills introduced at the same time by Lord Cairns dealt, respectively, with the practice of conveyancing and the remuneration of solicitors. The first provided that certain ordinary conditions of sale should be imported by implication of law into contracts for the purchase of land; that official certificates of search for incumbrances should be made legal evidence; that the doctrine of constructive notice should be confined within just limits; that covenants for the production of title-deeds should "run with the land;" and that an accidental breach of covenants in leases should no longer involve the right of re-entry or the penalty of forfeiture; besides giving effect to a number of minor reforms, some technical, but some of great practical importance, long demanded by the common sense of the legal profession. The second Bill struck at the root of all conveyancing abuses, by empowering the Courts to fix a reasonable scale of cost for settlements and other deeds relating to Real Property, under which a fair rate of commission or percentage should be charged "without regard to length." If these Bills, together with the Settled Land Bill, should ever become law, they would doubtless go far to simplify the form of family-settlements, and to diminish the legal disabilities of limited owners. But they would do nothing, and were deliberately framed to do nothing, towards curtailing the right of settling. The power of crippling ownership would be maintained, though artificial limbs would be amply provided to aid the life-tenant in moving. The grasp of the dead hand would be as powerful as ever for the purpose of regulating the relative interests of the unborn, and the living head of the family as powerless as ever, except for the purpose of improving the family property, of which he would remain a mere life-tenant.

It is often alleged, indeed, that an ordinary settlement does no more than is necessary to preserve the capital of the family property, and gives a tenant-for-life every power that he can desire, except that of mortgaging the fee and granting wasteful leases.[1] Lord St. Leonards, the highest of all authorities on the law of Real Property, even maintains that "for all purposes of reasonable enjoyment he would be ignorant, were he not otherwise aware of the fact, that his rights of ownership are curtailed."[2] Let it be granted, for the sake of argument only, that all this is true in a

---

[1] See the Address of Mr. W. T. Lawrence to the Incorporated Law Society, delivered at Cambridge, Oct. 7, 1879.

[2] "Handybook of Property Law," p. 121. "He is enabled," continues Lord St. Leonards, "to make every disposition of the estate which tends to ameliorate it; he has every capacity of an owner in fee to benefit the estate and himself, as the temporary owner of it, in common with remainder-men, but none to injure it."

purely legal sense, and that, all other conditions being equal, a limited owner, without exceeding his legal powers, might do as full justice to an estate as an owner in fee simple. But it does not follow that all other conditions are equal, or that men placed under entirely different influences and circumstances will act alike, merely because they are permitted by law to do so. The efficacy of institutions consists not merely in their compulsory operation, but in the spirit which they engender. A limited owner is essentially the creature of a system elaborated for the sole and single purpose of keeping great family estates undivided in the possession of the eldest male representative, and, if he should be ever so impatient of that system, he cannot make himself wholly independent of it.

In the first place, having been designated long beforehand as tenant-in-tail, probably by the decree of a grandfather, and owing his right of succession to no merit or qualification of his own, he grows up with the idea that family estates were made for heirs, and not heirs for family estates. He may have laid to heart the maxim that property has its duties as well as its rights, but the duties to which he has looked forward, and for which he may have striven to educate himself, are social and political, rather than agricultural, duties—the occupations and amusements of an English country-place, not the practical details of estate management. He commences life with an act which appears to him one of self-abnegation, not always deliberate or quite disinterested, but eminently calculated to relieve his conscience from a sense of the responsibility which rests on a landowner, as distinct from the head of a family.

By surrendering his reversion in tail, and accepting a reversion for life only, in consideration of a fixed allowance, he escapes at once the effort of bracing himself up to a profession, and that of considering what use he will make of the property when he shall become master of it. Thenceforward, he regards himself not as a future landowner, but as the future trustee of a family estate, which he ought not to waste or burden unduly, but which no one can expect him to develop, as an enterprising purchaser might develop it. Perhaps, he sees his father struggling, under the weight of old encumbrances, to keep up a grand house and ornamental park, with costly gardens and game preserves, in the style prescribed by the example of some ancestor four times as wealthy, and sacrificing to this object all prospect of carrying out long-needed repairs of farm buildings, or saving for the fortunes of younger children. When he succeeds, he finds himself entangled in the same web of social necessity, and equally unable to improve the estate, unless he can bring himself to let the family mansion for a time, and afterwards to re-occupy it with an establishment on a reduced scale. No doubt, like his father, he can borrow money at 7 per cent. and upwards, if he will, and charge it on the inheritance. But this rate of interest is nearly 3 per cent. more than an absolute owner need pay on mortgage, or than his tenants will probably be willing to repay in increased rent. Moreover, he can only obtain such a loan by invoking the vexatious interference of the Enclosure Commissioners, and must keep down the interest on it by diminishing *pro tanto* his power of laying by during his own lifetime for his younger children. In the absence of windfalls, or of casual accessions to family capital through matrimonial alliances, he must, in the natural course of things, be crippled in the race of agricultural improvement. For the inevitable tendency of " limited ownership " under family settlements is to minimise the fund which might otherwise be thus appropriated. The law may not prohibit a limited owner from having a large capital in proportion to acreage, and may even offer special facilities to him for increasing the inheritance of his eldest son, mainly at the expense of himself and his younger children. But the law cannot supply adequate motives for the adoption of these facilities by the great body of limited owners; and a very simple illustration will show why, as compared with a fee-simple owner, a limited owner is likely to have a small capital in proportion to acreage.

Let us suppose that a capitalist purchases a landed estate of 10,000 acres, with a rental of £10,000 a year, having besides a personal estate of £100,000. If he were to make no settlement, but to divide both the land and the personalty among five sons, either in equal or in unequal shares, it is. to be presumed that he would proportion the one to the other, so that each would have £2,000 a year in land and £20,000 in personalty, or, it may be, that the eldest would have £4,000 a year in land with £40,000 in personalty, while the rest had but £1,500 a year in land and £15,000 in personalty. In either case, there would be a landlord's capital of £10 per acre. But, if he were to settle all the land in the ordinary way on his eldest son and the male issue of that eldest son, this proportion could not be maintained without utterly beggaring all the rest of the family.

Even if he were to leave the eldest son as much as £40,000, charging the estate with only £10,000 for younger children, (or £30,000, without so charging the estate), the limited owner's capital would only be £3 per acre instead of £10 per acre. In short, a system under which the landed property of a family is constantly settled upon one member, but laid under a constant subsidy for the benefit of others, while the funded property is shared among all, must needs tend directly to impoverish the collective resources of landowners for purposes of improvement. It may, and does, aggrandise individual heads of landowning families, who are far richer, on the average, in this country than in any other, by virtue of their enormous acreage. But, if their average wealth is great, it is only because their number is small, and the larger the surface over which their spare capital is spread, the less benefit will each acre derive from it. Of course, there is one obvious method by which this result of the system might be gradually counteracted, but that is a method which has not yet received the sanction of the Legislature, and is scarcely consistent with the objects of settlements. If every limited owner were empowered to provide for legitimate claims upon him by selling off portions of the estate at his own discretion, instead of by charging it, his capital in proportion to acreage might be indefinitely increased, the portions sold off would profit by the application of new capital, and the fortunes of younger children might not only be enlarged, but would cease to be a tax upon land. This is what a fee-simple owner would naturally do; and until the limited owner is allowed the same liberty of alienation, it is perfectly idle to contend that he is, or can be, as capable of doing justice to his land, even if he could break loose from the moral fetters of custom and tradition which forbid him to part with an acre of the family property. As the expense, delay, and annoyance involved in an application to the Enclosure Commissioners too often deter him from borrowing for improvement, so the difficulty of obtaining the consent of trustees, and a vague fear of family opinion, too often deter him even from resorting to the powers of sale, for purposes of re-investment, usually inserted in settlements.

It may be conceded that somewhat undue stress has been laid on these aspects of the question by some opponents of limited ownership, who measure its economical defects by the whole difference between the actual produce of England and that which might be realized, if the whole area of the country, including the waste lands, were brought into the very highest state of cultivation. In judging of the system, we must not dwell exclusively on those embarrassed tenants for life, cursed with a splendid place and a meagre rental, who might well be glad to seek relief from an Encumbered Estates Court, if such an institution existed in England. We must also remember those limited owners of ancient lineage, honourably represented in the highest rank of the Peerage, who take a leading part in agricultural reforms, bringing to bear on estate-management an administrative ability scarcely to be expected of the yeoman or the squire, and a reserve of ready money, drawn from ground rents of town properties, which few owners in fee simple possess.

It should be further conceded that ancestral con-

nection may count for something against a superior
command of capital available for agricultural improvements; that rents are seldom excessive on settled
estates; and that, until the labourers in country
districts can be raised to greater independence, they
might often suffer by the substitution of strictly commercial relations for their present semi-feudal con-
nexion with the family on whose property they are
settled. A limited owner of a good old stock, and
belonging to the good old type of country gentleman,
may be too obstinate or too short of cash to spend
much in remunerative improvements, yet liberal in his
support of the church and school, the village clothing
club, and the cottage hospital, equally welcome at the
coverside and at the quarter sessions, respected by his
tenants, and beloved among the poor. The aggregate
amount of good done by such a landlord, though he be
a limited owner, may outweigh his shortcomings from
an economical point of view, and reflect credit on a
system which, nevertheless, is indefensible as a whole.

For the vices of limited ownership are peculiar to it
and inherent in it, whereas the virtues which it may
appear to foster have really no connection with it and
must be attributed to other causes. The character of
the English gentry and aristocracy was formed in ages
before limited ownership was known, and when estates
descended from father to son either in fee simple or
in fee tail—a tenure which after 1472 might be immediately converted into fee simple. In those days,
the continuity of succession and territorial ownership
was placed under the guardianship of the family itself,
and not under the protection of conveyancers; and the

nation was content that great estates, coming into the possession of degenerate heirs, should be sometimes broken up and purchased by worthier competitors. There is nothing to show that a law of natural selection, by which many of our modern properties have been formed, and to which many a noble house owes its origin, has now ceased to have a salutary effect, and ought to be arrested by legal artifices. On the contrary, the general opinion of persons conversant with the sale of land [1] amply confirms the inference deducible from the laws of political economy—viz., that, in the majority of instances, when land comes into the market, it passes from worse into better hands, and that, consequently, so far as limited ownership artificially obstructs Free Trade in Land, and saves the estates of spendthrifts from partition, it works a substantial injury to society. The new purchaser may be comparatively ignorant of country life, but he is not encumbered by rent-charges of indefinite duration, by mortgages contracted to pay off his father's debts, by dynastic traditions of estate-management, by the silly family pride which must needs emulate the state of some richer predecessor, by the passion for political dictation to which the refusal of leases is so frequently due, or by the supposed necessity of satisfying the supposed expectations of the neighbourhood. Having no liabilities of a past generation to discharge, he can make a liberal provision for younger children out of his rental, by way of life insurance or otherwise; and, if this should not suffice with such addition as he may be able to make from

---

[1] See especially the evidence on this subject taken by the Lords' Committee on the Improvement of Land, 1873.

invested funds, there is nothing to prevent his leaving them portions of the estate or directing portions to be sold for their benefit. Meanwhile, he is master of his own property, and free to develop its resources without feeling that he is either compromising or unjustly enriching an eldest son. These advantages make themselves felt, even when the new purchaser is surrounded by great settled estates, and strongly influenced by the example of their possessors. But they might be expected to make themselves far more conspicuously felt, if all landowners enjoyed the same freedom of disposition.

It has been urged, indeed, and not without a certain force, that a limited owner has, at all events, less power of mortgaging than an owner in fee simple, and that settled estates ought consequently to enjoy a comparative immunity from this form of encumbrance. But here, again, we must distinguish between legal powers and moral tendencies. No doubt, a limited owner, as such, can mortgage nothing but his own life-interest; but a time usually comes in the course of his lifetime when the entail is broken for the purpose of settlement, and he acquires, with the concurrence of his eldest son, the same powers as an owner in fee-simple. These powers, as has been already explained, are constantly exercised by mortgaging the estate, or granting rent charges upon it, as a security for debts incurred by father or son. On the other hand, a fee-simple owner, though his power of mortgaging is unlimited, has not the same motive for exercising it, inasmuch as he is perfectly free to sell as much land as will produce the sum that he requires. In most cases, he will find

it far more profitable to adopt this alternative. It has
been calculated that, if an estate of £1,000 a year were
mortgaged for £10,000, the owner would have little
more than £350 to live upon, after paying interest at
4½ per cent., and deducting 20 per cent. for rates,
taxes, repairs, and cost of maintenance for the whole
property. But, if he were to sell a third of the property, at 30 years' purchase, he might obtain £10,000
free of interest, and would retain a gross income of
£660, upon the remaining two-thirds, subject only to a
deduction of 20 per cent., or £132,—that is, a net
income of £528.[1] It may be added that a great landowner, reducing his estate by a third, might effect an
almost proportionate reduction in the cost of agency,
as well as in those moral claims for subscriptions and
subventions, both charitable and religious, which go
far to make land an unprofitable investment in the
hands of a conscientious purchaser. The legal incapacity of a tenant-for-life to meet his liabilities
in this way without the consent of his successor, who is naturally reluctant to sanction a diminution of the family property, constitutes just one
of the peculiar disabilities which beset limited ownership, and causes settled estates to be practically more
encumbered then unsettled estates. As they are rarely
sold, they can only be made to yield the necessary

---

[1] See an article by Mr. J. Boyd Kinnear, on "The Coming Land
Question," in the *Fortnightly Review* of September, 1879. Mr. Kinnear
advocates the entire abolition of the mortgaging power, on the ground that
land should not be permitted to be specially pledged for one particular
debt, but should be equally liable with the rest of a debtor's property for
all his liabilities. Whatever may be thought of this doctrine, the simple
calculation in the text is entirely independent of it.

capital by mortgaging them, and it must be admitted that a mortgaged estate is not likely to be well managed. The landlord, with a curtailed income, has to meet all the risk of bad seasons, insolvent tenants, and other losses, while the mortgagee, like the incumbrancers, pockets a fixed share of the rental without feeling the least responsibility or making the smallest return.

CHAPTER III.

To say that a land system founded on the Law of Primogeniture and guarded by strict family settlements has a direct tendency to prevent the dispersion of land, is only to say that it fulfils the purpose for which it was instituted. It is hardly less evident that it must have the further effect of promoting the aggregation of land in a small and constantly decreasing number of hands. The periodical renewal of entails is intended to secure, and does secure, ancestral properties against the risk of being broken up; and, practically, they very seldom come into the market, except as a consequence of scandalous waste or gambling on the part of successive life-owners. The typical English family estate is that which, like Sir Roger de Coverley's, neither waxes nor wanes in the course of generations, and there are still many such estates in counties remote from London. But there is nothing to check the cumulative augmentation of ancestral properties by new purchases of land, which is the darling passion of so many proprietors. There is always some *angulus iste* to be annexed and brought within the park palings or the ring-fence on the first good opportunity; and scarcely a day passes without some yeoman of ancient lineage being erased from the roll of landowners by the competition of his more powerful neighbour. Not that any tyranny or unfair dealing is involved in this process of aggrandisement, which is the consequence of economical laws quite as simple as that of natural selection in the animal creation. The yeoman sells his patrimony either because he has ruined himself by drinking or improvidence, or because he finds that by turning it into money he can largely improve his income and the future expectations of his family. The nobleman or squire buys it at a price which is not commercially remunerative, either to prevent its being covered with buildings, or because it lies conveniently for his own agricultural designs, or because he wants to extend his influence in the county ; for one or all of which reasons, it is worth more to him than to any one else. It is known in some parts of the country that it is utterly vain to bid against the great territorial lord of the district, whose agent is instructed to buy up all properties for sale, regardless of expense. In other parts of the country, men who have made their fortunes in trade are equally covetous of land, which for them is the one sure passport to social consideration, and equally anxious to keep it together by entails. Thus by the normal operation of supply and demand large estates are perpetually swallowing up small estates, while, by a suspension of that operation through the Law and Custom of Primogeniture, they are themselves preserved, to a great extent, from dissolution.

On the other hand, it must not be forgotten that a counter-tendency, no less natural and legitimate, partly neutralizes this gravitation of smaller towards larger aggregates of land. The enormous rise in the value of all sites within easy reach of great towns or railway stations sometimes offers to great landowners an inducement to sell which they cannot resist. In this way, under the powers of sales already mentioned, distant and detached portions of great estates are frequently passing in large blocks into the hands of new landlords, generally of the mercantile class, or are bought up by land-jobbers and sold in petty blocks to retired tradesmen. The villa-residences of such immigrants from towns, fronting the road in unsightly rows, with an acre or two of freehold land at the back of each, are a characteristic feature of many country villages, and have been too much overlooked in popular descriptions of rural England. They may be regarded as the modern counterpart of the ruder but more picturesque village homesteads in which, as we have seen, thousands of townspeople invested their savings and sometimes carried on their handicrafts in the fifteenth or sixteenth centuries. But this class, though of great importance to election agents, fills a very small place in the agricultural economy, or even in the social life of an English county, since the members of it seldom regard their villas as a home, or take an active part in county interests, while their sons are generally absorbed into the urban population. At the same time, the acquisition of minute plots by the working classes has been facilitated of late by the agency of freehold land societies originally established for political objects. It would doubtless prevail to a much greater extent but for the exorbitance of law charges on small purchases of land,[1] and may hereafter be developed into a modified form of peasant proprietorship.

In the meantime, a considerable impulse has been given to subdivision of landed property by the operations of the Enclosure Commissioners. It appears by their Thirty-Second Annual Report that, between 1845, when the General Enclosure Act was passed, and 1877, nearly 600,000 acres of common and commonable land had been partitioned among 26,000 separate owners, in an average proportion of forty-four and a half acres to each lord of the manor, twenty-four acres to each owner of common rights, and ten acres to each purchaser of lands sold to cover part of the expenses, where they were not wholly raised by rates. Of course, the allotments received by lords of manors, 620 in number, mostly contributed to swell the acreage of large estates, and even those received by commoners would often form appendages to existing freeholds. But it may fairly be presumed that, of the 3,500 purchasers among whom the residue of 35,450 acres was distributed, chiefly in small lots, a large proportion became landowners for the first time, and this presumption is confirmed by the

---

[1] Mr. Wren Hoskyns, in his Essay on the English Land-System, published in " Systems of Land-Tenure," cites Tables laid before the Registration of Titles Commission, which show that a purchaser's expenses, irrespective of stamp duty, and also irrespective of all expenses incurred by the vendor, average about six per cent. on properties under £1,000 in value, or twelve times the *ad valorem* stamp duty, while on properties of larger value they average about 2½ per cent. The disadvantage to which the owners of small properties are subjected in borrowing for purposes of improvement are still more prohibitive. It appears from the evidence taken before the House of Lords' Committee on the Improvement of Land that, in such cases, the preliminary charges for loans under the Acts may practically amount to fifteen per cent.

classification of allottees and purchasers which the Commissioners subjoin as approximately accurate. This classification is as follows :—

" Yeomen and farmers, 4,736 ; shopkeepers and tradesmen, 3,456 ; labourers and miners, 3,168 ; esquires, 2,624 ; widows, 2,016 ; gentlemen, 1,984 ; clergymen, 1,280 ; artizans, 1,067 ; spinsters, 800 ; charity trustees, 704 ; peers, baronets, and sons of peers, 576 ; professional men, 512 ; besides about 3,000 others comprising nearly every quality of calling, from the Crown to the mechanic, quarryman, and domestic servant."

The words in which the Commissioners sum up the results of this process of *morcellement* deserve to be quoted in full :—

" Thus, in the course of one generation, an extent of land equal to that of a county has been redeemed from common and waste, and has been divided among a far larger and more varied body of land-owners than that of any county in England. Valuable public roads of great extent have been constructed, opening up for business and pleasure many otherwise inaccessible localities, and at no cost to the public. The area of production and employment has been increased, and in the same proportion that of public and local taxation has been extended. A great number of small landed properties have been created, and labourers' field-gardens in the rural districts have been afforded in larger proportion to the extent of the land than appear by the Agricultural Returns to exist elsewhere in England."

In default of authoritative statistics, the loosest conjectures were long current respecting the distribution of ownership caused by these divergent tendencies towards aggregation and subdivision. It was confidently stated, for instance, that, whereas in the latter part of the last century this country was divided among 200,000 landowners, it had come to be divided among no more than 30,000. No proof was thought necessary to support the former assertion; the latter was supported by a proof, which, on examination, turned out to be perfectly worthless. In the Occupation Returns of the Census for 1861, only 30,766 persons described themselves as land-proprietors, and these figures were most persistently quoted as official evidence on the subject, in the face of the patent fact that above half of the whole number were females. The probable explanation of this circumstance is that women owning land feel a pride in recording their ownership; whereas thousands of male landowners returned themselves as peers, members of Parliament, bankers, merchants, or private gentlemen. At all events, the mere existence of so palpable a flaw in the return utterly destroyed its value for the purposes of statistical argument. Equally reckless assertions were made in support of the contrary opinion, and until the year 1875 it was regarded as open to doubt whether the whole body of English landowners, properly so called, amounted to 30,000 or 300,000.

The appearance of the "New Domesday Book," as it was called, was the first step towards a thorough investigation of this question, which it ought to have set finally at rest. It purported to show that England and Wales, exclusive of the metropolis, were divided in 1874-5 among 972,836 proprietors in all, owning 33,013,514 acres, with a " gross estimated rental " of £99,352,301. Of these proprietors, however, no less than 703,289, owning 151,171 acres, with a gross estimated rental of £29,127,679, were returned as possessors of less than one acre each. The aggregate acreage and gross estimated rental of the 269,547 proprietors owning one acre and upwards were stated as follows :

	No.	Extent of Lands.			Gross Estimated Rental.	
		A.	R.	P.	£	s.
Total No. of Owners of						
1 acre and under 10 acres ...	121,983	478,679	2	27	6,438,324	15
10 acres ,, 50 ,, ...	72,640	1,750,079	3	38	6,509,289	18
50 ,, ,, 100 ,, ...	25,839	1,791,605	2	23	4,302,002	12
100 ,, ,, 500 ,, ...	32,317	6,827,346	3	11	13,680,759	16
500 ,, ,, 1,000 ,, ...	4,799	3,317,678	0	11	6,427,552	4
1,000 ,, ,, 2,000 ,, ...	2,719	3,799,307	0	28	7,914,371	10
2,000 ,, ,, 5,000 ,, ...	1,815	5,529,190	0	13	9,579,311	13
5,000 ,, ,, 10,000 ,, ...	581	3,974,724	3	24	5,522,610	6
10,000 ,, ,, 20,000 ,, ...	223	3,098,674	2	30	4,337,023	4
20,000 ,, ,, 50,000 ,, ...	66	1,917,076	1	31	2,331,302	12
50,000 ,, ,,100,000 ,, ...	3	194,938	3	36	188,746	12
100,000 ,, and upwards	1	181,616	2	38	161,874	9
No areas	6,448	—			2,831,452	13
No rentals	113	1,423	2	28	—	

This Return, prepared by the Local Government Board, was represented as no more than " proximately accurate," and a very cursory inspection sufficed to disclose errors of detail so numerous and important as to cast suspicion even upon its proximate accuracy. Further analysis of its contents has amply confirmed this suspicion, and although the New Domesday Book contains a mine of precious materials for an exhaustive treatise on the distribution of landed property in England and Wales, the actual figures given in it cannot be accepted, without large corrections, as the basis of any sound conclusions on that subject.

In the first place, it is evident on the face of the Return itself, and we are expressly informed in the Explanatory Statement prefixed to it, that it does not include any property except that assessed to rates. Now, at the date of its compilation (1874-5) all woods, except saleable underwoods, were exempt from rates, and are therefore excluded from the return. Waste and common lands, being equally exempt from rates, were equally ignored in the rate-books from which these statistics are borrowed, although a very rough and untrustworthy estimate of the area covered by them was appended in a separate column. The result is that whereas the whole area of England and Wales amounts to 37,319,221 acres, only 34,538,158 acres are recognised at all in the New Domesday Book. Of these, 33,013,514 acres are assigned to landowners great and small, while the "estimated extent of commons and waste lands" accounts for 1,524,648 acres. The remaining 2,781,063 acres comprehend "waste lands the area of which could not be ascertained, woods other than saleable underwoods, rivers and roads, Crown property not let, and churchyards and other lands not rateable." A very large proportion of these woods and plantations—not to speak of manorial rights over commons—must belong to great landowners, the real extent of whose estates is therefore very much understated, by virtue of this omission alone.

In the second place, the exclusion of the whole metropolis, vast districts of which are owned by wealthy peers and commoners, makes the rental of such "ground-landlords" appear much smaller than it really is, as compared with that of less fortunate proprietors. The gross estimated rental of the metropolis, according to a Return of 1873, was nearly £25,000,000, and if to this be added the profits derived by the landlords of England and Wales as a body, from docks, harbours, bridges, and other forms of property ignored in the New Domesday Book, it will easily be understood how largely their gross income exceeds the £99,352,301 with which they are credited.   Again, no distinction is drawn between house property and agricultural land, or between copyholds and freeholds, or even between either of these and property held on lease for terms of above 99 years.   The effect of this indiscriminate classification is of course mainly felt in the illusory multiplication of small estates, the vast majority of persons returned as " *owners* of less than one acre " were probably the possessors—and, most of them, mere leaseholders—of house-property in towns or suburbs of towns.   If proof were needed of this infer- ence, it is supplied by the fact that whereas the average rental of these petty estates, as stated in the Return, is nearly £200 per acre, the average rental of all the estates ranging from one acre upwards does not greatly exceed £2 per acre.   A very considerable deduction should be made, on this account, even from the 121,983 estates ranging between one and ten acres, among which must be included a large number of business premises, gardens, and pleasure grounds, destitute of any agricultural value or character.   The absurdity of reckoning among land- owners the purchasers of such little plots is sufficiently manifest, but, as Mr. Kay has shown,[1] it is scarcely less misleading to dignify the greater leaseholders with such a title.   It is not only that leaseholds are ultimately returned into the hands of the ground-landlords with all the improvements resulting from the lessee's expenditure, but also that they are subject to an infinite variety of covenants, wholly inconsistent with the sense or reality of proprietorship.   No rate-books or parochial returns, however, could effectually distinguish between leaseholds and freeholds.   As the overseers and rate-collectors

" Free Trade in Land," p. 123.

were often compelled to act on hearsay evidence, and as neither owners nor occupiers of land are apt to be communicative respecting the nature of their interest, the probability is that many lessees are improperly entered as owners, especially in the East of England, where leases are more common.

But far graver and more prolific sources of error remain to be considered. We are warned in the official preface that glebe lands and estates known to be the property of corporations or charities are printed in italics; but that names of individuals have often been inserted, by mistake, instead of the public bodies or offices which they represent. Now, there are 14,367 entries of estates belonging to church benefices, charities, and other public authorities in England and Wales, comprising in all 1,449,008 acres. The further deduction to be made from the number of apparent landowners, by reason of the official blunders thus acknowledged, is far greater than might be supposed at first sight. Mr. Arthur Arnold's estimate of 10,000 parcels of glebe land in the 15,000 parishes of England and Wales may probably be excessive, but he certainly quotes very significant facts in support of his conclusion that parochial clergymen own, *virtute officii*, a much larger acreage than is indicated in the New Domesday Book. Having selected casually, by way of sample, the Domesday Returns for the counties of Buckingham, Hertford, and Lancaster, he found, in the first, only five parcels of glebe land marked in italics, but 235 "owners" with the prefix of " Reverend ;" in the second, only three parcels of glebe land so marked, but 159 " owners " with that prefix; and in the third, only seven parcels of glebe land, but 186 " owners " with the clerical

title.[1]   The inference is irresistible that most of these
680 " reverend " gentlemen should be deducted from
the list of individual " owners " as being merely in
official possession of Church property.

But it is also important to observe that most bearers
of a clerical title figure in the Returns as " owners " of
small estates, and thus swell the apparent number of
yeomen and petty squires, as distinct from great landowners.   Let us take, for the sake of illustration, the
seven English counties which stand first in alphabetical
order.   In Bedfordshire there are 15 clergymen returned
as " owners " of estates between 300 and 1,000 acres;
and 28 clergymen returned as owners of between 100
and 300 acres.   In Berkshire there are 19 clergymen
returned in the former class, and 21 in the latter; in
Buckinghamshire 28 and 54, respectively; in Cambridgeshire 23 and 48, respectively; in Cheshire 11 and
12, respectively; in Cornwall 22 and 52, respectively;
and in Cumberland 19 and 33, respectively.[2]   It follows
that not only the original enumeration of English landowners, but also the official classification subsequently
founded on it,[3] is vitiated, to a serious extent, by the
intrusion of heterogeneous elements.   It is at least doubtful whether official representatives of the Church, as well
as trustees of charities, hospitals, colleges, and railway
companies, ought to be included in a list of " owners "
at all; but it is self-evident that, if included, they should
be properly identified, and placed in a separate category.

[1] Arthur Arnold's " Free Land," pp. 8, 9.

[2] For these figures I am indebted to the kindness of Mr. John Bateman,
F.R.G.S., author of " Great Landowners of Great Britain and Ireland."

[3] " Summary of Returns of Owners of Land in England and Wales,"
ordered by the House of Commons to be printed, 4th July, 1876.

The effect of double entries on the apparent number of landed proprietors is still more deceptive. No attempt, indeed, was, made to group together all the estates owned by the same proprietor in different counties, and it seems to have depended on the efficiency of the local compilers whether the estates of one proprietor in one county were entered under one name or several. The consequence of this slovenly and hap-hazard registration is that, instead of being a perfect record of "owners," the New Domesday Book is, at best, an imperfect record of estates, many of which, as we have seen, belong to public bodies, and many others of which are mere fragments of great properties owned by a single individual. It has been ascertained by Mr. Arthur Arnold that twenty-eight dukes own 158 separate estates within the United Kingdom, comprehending 3,991,811 acres; that thirty-three marquises own 121 separate estates, comprehending 1,567,227 acres; that 194 earls own 634 separate estates, comprehending 5,862,118 acres; and that 270 viscounts and barons own 680 separate estates, comprehending 3,780,009 acres. In other words, the names of dukes are repeated 5·6 times, those of marquises 3·7 times, those of earls 3·3 times, and those of viscounts and barons 2·5 times. The Duke of Buccleuch alone counts as fourteen landowners, in respect of as many separate estates in England and Scotland, and four other peers are multiplied in like manner by eleven, figuring, perhaps, as small yeomen in counties where they happen to own but a few acres. Altogether, the 525 members of the peerage stand for upwards of 1,500 "owners" in the New Domesday Book. Mr. Arnold calculates that if all the landed gentry have been multiplied in the same ratio, four-fifths of the soil of the whole United Kingdom must be in the possession of less than 4,000 persons. But, allowing for the fact that few of the lesser gentry can have estates scattered over more than one county, he arrives at the conclusion that four-fifths of the United Kingdom belongs to a body of owners numbering about 7,000.

Before we can accept this conclusion as a safe guide to the distribution of landed property in England and Wales, we are bound to remember how much greater is the average size of properties in the other parts of the United Kingdom. Even if our present inquiry embraced the whole United Kingdom, it might well be contended that, from an agricultural point of view, the vast moors of the Highlands, with the desolate bogs of Ireland, may as legitimately be excluded from the account as the few acres of ornamental ground surrounding a suburban villa. However this may be, we possess sounder, as well as far more instructive, evidence of the proportion in which England and Wales are divided between various classes of landowners, in the Parliamentary return of 1876, and Mr. Bateman's admirable analysis of the New Domesday Book. From the former it would appear that 5,408 persons are entered as owning estates of 1,000 acres and upwards in England and Wales, " without reference to the fact that some of such owners hold property in more counties than one." From Mr. Bateman's revised list of English Landowners it would appear that the New Domesday Book contains entries of some 1,688 individuals in England and Wales owning estates of 3,000 acres and upwards, with a rental of at least £3,000 a year ; and of some 2,529 individuals owning between 1,000 and 3,000 acres each, or deriving a rental of less than £3,000 from estates exceeding 3,000 acres. It follows that the New Domesday Book exaggerates the number of owners above 1,000 acres, at least in the proportion of 5,408 to 4,017. The result of an independent analysis shows that owners of 2,000 acres and upwards are there repeated about 1·7 times, by reason of their having estates in more counties than one. There is good reason to believe that a further deduction of at least 8 per cent. should be made for the names of persons entered twice in the same English county, and a much larger deduction for the names of persons entered twice in the same Welsh county.[1] At all events, it is certain that not more than 4,000 persons, and probable that considerably less than 4,000 persons, owning estates of 1,000 acres and upwards, possess in the aggregate an extent of nearly 19,000,000 acres, or about four-sevenths of the whole area included in the Domesday Book Returns. If we now subtract the owners of between 1,000 and 2,000 acres, who ostensibly number 2,719, and must really number as much as 1,750, we find that a landed aristocracy consisting of about 2,250 persons own together nearly half the enclosed land in England and Wales.[2] The residue of owners between one acre and 2,000 ostensibly

---

[1] See the tables and explanatory note which conclude this chapter, by Mr. John Bateman, author of the " Great Landowners." See also the Statement in Appendix VI.

[2] Mr. Kay, in his " Free Trade in Land " (Letter I.), states that " a body of men which does not probably exceed 4,500 own more than 17,498,000 acres, or more than one-half of all England and Wales." He

number 249,996, but may be reduced by a proportionate allowance for double entries to 147,657.[1] This would give a net total of about 150,000 owners above one acre in England and Wales, or less than $\frac{1}{110}$ of the population—a result which corresponds somewhat closely with Mr. Shaw-Lefevre's conclusion that the whole number of landowners, properly so called, in England and Wales, certainly does not exceed 166,000. But since about 15,000,000 acres out of 33,000,000 are owned by about 2,250 proprietors, it may be truly affirmed that nearly half the enclosed land in England and Wales belongs to a body numbering but $1\frac{1}{2}$ per cent. of all the landowners, even excluding those below one acre.

A close investigation of the returns for single counties fully bears out these inferences, and places the inequalities of landed proprietorship in a still more striking light. Take, for instance, Northumberland and Nottinghamshire, which stand next to each other in alphabetical order, but differ widely from each other both in agricultural features and in the character of their population. According to the official returns, which are subject, as we know, to a large discount, the number of owners below one acre in Northumberland is 10,036; but they own no more than 1,424 acres

adds that 710 persons own more than one-fourth, that 523 persons own one-fifth, and that less than 280 persons own nearly one-sixth; that 100 persons own 3,917,641 acres, and that sixty-six persons own 1,917,076. These estimates probably err on the side of moderation, no allowance being apparently made for double entries.

[1] It is true that comparatively few owners of very small estates would appear as owners in more than one county, but, on the other hand, a greater proportion of such owners would probably be entered more than once in the same county.

between them, so that each possesses, on an average, less than one-seventh of an acre. In Nottinghamshire 9,891 petty landowners rule over 1,266 acres between them, possessing, on an average, one-eighth of an acre apiece. Little more than a fourth of Northumberland, and much less than half of Nottinghamshire, is in the hands of owners possessing less than 2,000 acres. If we now look at the higher end of the scale the contrast is striking. Above three-fifths of Northumberland is in the hands of forty-four proprietors, nearly half is in the hands of twenty-six, and far more than one-seventh is in the hands of one proprietor, the Duke of Northumberland, who has also landed estates in other counties. In Nottinghamshire two-fifths of the whole acreage belongs to fifteen proprietors, and one-fourth to five proprietors. If the division of landed property over England and Wales corresponded with the division of landed property in Northumberland and Nottinghamshire, one-half of the whole country would be in the hands of about 1,000 proprietors; and these proprietors, by virtue of their family connections and social ascendancy, would exercise a power far more than commensurate with their acreage.

It would be highly interesting, were it possible, to extract from the New Domesday Book the exact amount of land held by the various classes of society, and, in particular, the amount held by the class of yeomen whose gradual extinction is so often deplored. Unfortunately, the returns furnish no adequate material for an exhaustive classification of this kind, and the apparent owner of a "yeoman's" estate may be either a mere leaseholder or the lord of a great territory in some other county. The careful researches of Mr. John Bateman, however, enable us to apportion the area of each county, with at least "proximate accuracy," among various orders of landowners, if not among various classes of society. For this purpose he distributes the landowning hierarchy into eight divisions, the first and last of which—Peers and Public Bodies—are defined sufficiently by their mere designation, without reference to acreage. The second division consists of "great landowners" owning above 3,000 acres; the third, of "squires," owning between 1,000 and 3,000 acres; the fourth, of "greater yeomen," owning between 300 and 1,000 acres; the fifth, of "lesser yeomen," owning between 100 and 300 acres; the sixth, of "small proprietors," owning between 1 and 100 acres; the seventh, of "cottagers," owning less than one acre. Of course these descriptions must be accepted in the most general sense, and with many qualifications; but they may serve to denote roughly the several grades of land-ownership, and to afford an useful basis for a comparison of one county with another.

For instance, if we take, as before, the seven counties which stand first alphabetically—Bedfordshire, Berkshire, Buckinghamshire, Cambridgeshire, Cheshire, Cornwall, and Cumberland—we find very marked differences in the proportionate acreage held by the various divisions of landowners. More than one-fourth of Cheshire, and nearly one-fifth of Bedfordshire, is owned by peers; whereas only one-ninth of Cambridgeshire, and little more than one-tenth of Cornwall, belongs to members of the same class. Less than one-hundredth part of Cornwall, and little more than one-fortieth of Cumberland, is assigned to public bodies, while nearly one-eighth of Cambridgeshire is corporate, and much of this collegiate, property. Coupling together both classes of yeomen, we observe that one-third of all Cumberland, and something like two-fifths of all Cambridgeshire, are in the hands of this class, which, in Cheshire, owns but from one-fifth to one-sixth only of the entire area.

Cambridgeshire, again, stands first in the number of its "small proprietors," between one and 100 acres; but Cheshire far surpasses all the other six counties in the number of its cottagers, who represent nearly three-fourths of its whole proprietary, though possessing less than $\frac{1}{150}$ of its total acreage. The pre-eminence of Cambridgeshire and Cumberland in the proportion of "yeoman" properties might have been anticipated, since the former county offered little attraction to great landowners in early times, and the latter, with the bordering districts of Westmoreland and Yorkshire, is well known as the last stronghold of the primitive statesmen. But it is a significant fact that even in Cambridgeshire estates of all kinds below 1,000 acres occupy but 59·4 per cent. of the whole returned acreage, and in Cumberland but 57·2. It may be added that in Essex they occupy 55·1 per cent., in Somersetshire about 53·, in Lincolnshire 45·8, and in Cornwall 45·1. But the most extreme diversity in the percentage of estates below 1,000 acres is presented by the counties of Middlesex (exclusive of the metropolis) and Northumberland. In the former of these counties, no less than 114,439 out of 143,013 acres are occupied by estates of this class; in the latter, no more than 196,000 acres out of 1,190,043. Such figures speak for themselves, and sufficiently indicate the nature of the causes which promote or prevent the multiplication of small properties in modern times. One of these causes has already been fully considered. It has been shown that Primogeniture, operating for many generations, has directly contributed to reduce the landed aristocracy of England and Wales to a body even smaller than had been commonly supposed, but that in those classes which do not maintain the custom of Primogeniture landed property is naturally broken up into a multitude of small parcels. The owners of such parcels are, for the most part, not yeomen, but shopkeepers and artisans, too humble, and too dependent for their livelihood on urban trade and industry, to fill any perceptible place in the rural economy of this country.

It may perhaps surprise many to discover that less than one million and a half of acres in England and Wales belong to " Public Bodies," in the very widest sense of that elastic term, which includes the Crown itself with the pettiest mercantile company. If we had equally trustworthy statistics of lands held in mortmain during the Middle Ages, the contrast would be most startling, and it is certainly a remarkable proof of the extent to which individual ownership has since established its predominance, that little more than 5 per cent. of English soil now remains under corporate or public management. It would be still more instructive if we had the means of comparing this management with that of individual owners, in its effect upon agriculture, and the welfare of the classes dependent upon the land. Probably it might be found that, while Crown property is managed with a strict regard to economy, the lessees and tenants of College property enjoy more independence, and are usually treated with more indulgence, than if they rented under a resident landlord. Whether agricultural labourers derive equal benefit from absenteeism is more than doubtful, and, since Colleges have adopted the system of running out beneficial leases, the semi-proprietary interests which in some degree compensated for absenteeism are, of course, in process of extinction. Upon the whole it must be evident that a threefold agricultural community of landlords, farmers, and labourers can hardly reach its highest ideal where the landlord is so nearly a dormant partner. The sale of corporate estates may be open to grave objections on grounds of general policy, and would be the exact antithesis to a "nationalisation of land." But it could not fail to be ultimately beneficial, in an agricultural sense, especially if it were so conducted as to give improving tenants a fair opportunity of purchasing their own farms.

It is extremely difficult to compare the distribution of ownership disclosed by these returns with that recorded in the original Domesday Book. This marvellous survey includes neither the Welsh Counties nor the Northern Counties of Northumberland, Cumberland, Westmoreland, and Durham, the collective area of which is about one-fifth of all England and Wales; nor is it possible to identify with certainty those who can properly be called land*owners* among the various classes of land*holders* therein enumerated. According to the analysis of Sir Henry Ellis, which is adopted by the compilers of the New Domesday Book, the whole number of genuine freeholders, registered under various titles, amounted to 54,813, including 1,000 *presbyteri*. After making a moderate deduction for ecclesiastical estates, as well as for the omitted counties, we may conclude that about two-thirds of England and Wales was then shared between upwards of 53,000 lay freeholders, together with 7,968 *burgenses*, and 108,407 *villani*. Both these classes, however, had an essentially proprietary interest in the lands which they occupied, and the greater part of them may fairly be taken as corresponding with the owners of between one and ten acres registered in the New Domesday Book. If this be granted, it follows that in the reign of William the Conqueror the soil of England was divided among a larger body of land-owners than it is at present. The force of this inference is prodigiously strengthened by the fact that forests, wastes, and fens then covered the greater part of whole counties. Were these excluded from the calculation, and nothing taken into account but cultivated land, the proportion of landowners to acreage would of course be vastly increased, and the average extent of each landowner's rateable property in the eleventh century would be equally reduced. But even supposing the number of landowners to have been then no larger, and the area of cultivation no less, than it now is, the distribution of ownership relatively to population might well startle admirers of the existing English land-system. For England is estimated to have contained little more than 2,000,000 inhabitants at the Conquest, so that if the actual number of landowners was the same then as now, the proportion of land-owning to landless heads of families must have been at least tenfold greater.

TABLES SHOWING THE LANDOWNERS DIVIDED INTO EIGHT CLASSES
ACCORDING TO ACREAGE—WITH NUMBER OF OWNERS IN EACH
CLASS ; AND EXTENT OF THEIR LANDS.

" Peers " include Peeresses and Peers' eldest sons.

" Great Landowners " include all estates held by commoners owning at least
3,000 acres, if the rental reaches £3,000 per annum.

" Squires " include estates of between 1,000 acres and 3,000, and such
estates as would be included in the previous class if their rental reached £3,000,
averaged at 1,700 acres.

" Greater Yeomen " include estates of between 300 acres and 1,000,
averaged at 500 acres.

" Lesser Yeomen " include estates of between 100 acres and 300, averaged
at 170 acres.

" Small Proprietors " include lands of over 1 acre and under 100 acres.

" Cottagers " include all holdings of under 1 acre.

" Public Bodies " include all holdings printed in italics in the " Government
Return of Landowners, 1876," and a few more that should have been so printed,
being obviously Public properties.

" Peers " and " Great Landowners " are assigned to those counties in which
their principal estates are situated, and are never entered in more than one
county. The column recording their numbers in each county must be taken
with this qualification, but the acreage of all the " Peers " or " Great Landowners " in each county is correctly given, and their aggregate number, as well
as their aggregate acreage, may be learned from the summary.

ENGLISH COUNTIES.

BEDFORD.			BERKS.		
No. of Owners.	Class.	Acres.	No. of Owners.	Class.	Acres.
3	Peers	53,789	*6	Peers	48,849
14	Great Landowners	60,127	20	Great Landowners	119,604
27	Squires	45,900	40	Squires	68,000
74	Greater Yeomen	37,000	153	Greater Yeomen	76,500
195	Lesser Yeomen ...	33,150	244	Lesser Yeomen ...	41,480
1,825	Small Proprietors	38,906	2,315	Small Proprietors	42,376
5,302	Cottagers	824	4,172	Cottagers	1,000
244	Public Bodies ...	16,380	290	Public Bodies ...	33,940
	Waste...	1,127		Waste...	2,114
7,684—Total.		287,203	7,240—Total.		433,863

* Inclusive of the Queen.

BUCKS.			CAMBRIDGE.		
No. of Owners.	Class.	Acres.	No. of Owners.	Class.	Acres.
5	Peers	87,954	1	Peers	57,783
17	Great Landowners	118,036	13	Great Landowners	70,097
29	Squires	49,300	39	Squires	*57,000
132	Greater Yeomen	66,000	216	Greater Yeomen	†99,360
357	Lesser Yeomen ...	60,690	505	Lesser Yeomen ...	85,850
2,672	Small Proprietors	49,339	5,373	Small Proprietors	86,793
6,420	Cottagers	1,153	6,677	Cottagers	1,193
276	Public Bodies ...	23,737	350	Public Bodies ...	63,851
	Waste...	2,942		Waste...	2,554
9,708—Total.		459,151	13,174—Total.		524,481

CHESTER.			CORNWALL.		
No. of Owners.	Class.	Acres.	No. of Owners.	Class.	Acres.
13	Peers	160,655	6	Peers	85,549
27	Great Landowners	157,451	29	Great Landowners	246,216
39	Squires	66,300	48	Squires	81,600
122	Greater Yeomen	61,000	224	Greater Yeomen	112,000
309	Lesser Yeomen ...	52,530	699	Lesser Yeomen ...	118,830
5,296	Small Proprietors	77,922	4,028	Small Proprietors	105,295
17,691	Cottagers	4,664	8,717	Cottagers	1,186
223	Public Bodies ...	21,696	115	Public Bodies ...	8,285
	Waste...	6,707		Waste...	70,968
23,720—Total.		608,922	13,866—Total.		829,929

* Actual extent.　　　　　† Average only 460 acres.

CUMBERLAND.			DERBY.		
No. of Owners.	Class.	Acres.	No. of Owners.	Class.	Acres.
4	Peers	97,027	6	Peers	182,337
18	Great Landowners	120,418	21	Great Landowners	120,640
51	Squires	86,700	38	Squires	64,600
242	Greater Yeomen	121,000	144	Greater Yeomen	72,000
943	Lesser Yeomen ...	160,310	384	Lesser Yeomen ...	65,280
4,497	Small Proprietors	120,903	6,017	Small Proprietors	95,240
9,617	Cottagers	1,957	12,874	Cottagers	1,597
141	Public Bodies ...	22,496	382	Public Bodies ...	19,262
	Waste	114,025		Waste	11,655
15,513—Total.		844,836	19,866—Total.		632,611

DEVON.			DORSET.		
No. of Owners.	Class.	Acres.	No. of Owners.	Class.	Acres.
17	Peers	217,088	10	Peers	122,625
50	Great Landowners	364,566	24	Great Landowners	192,847
108	Squires	183,600	59	Squires	100,300
496	Greater Yeomen	248,000	131	Greater Yeomen	65,500
1,557	Lesser Yeomen ...	264,690	229	Lesser Yeomen ...	38,930
7,509	Small Proprietors	204,687	2,794	Small Proprietors	39,179
21,647	Cottagers	2,981	7,694	Cottagers	1,631
425	Public Bodies ...	31,372	162	Public Bodies ...	12,377
	Waste	77,868		Waste	13,751
31,809—Total.		1,594,852	10,903—Total.		587,140

DURHAM.			ESSEX.		
No. of Owners.	Class.	Acres.	No. of Owners.	Class.	Acres.
5	Peers	129,659	5	Peers	68,328
11	Great Landowners	83,670	39	Great Landowners	202,445
33	Squires	56,100	87	Squires	147,900
141	Greater Yeomen	70,500	387	Greater Yeomen	193,500
351	Lesser Yeomen ...	59,670	953	Lesser Yeomen ...	162,010
2,376	Small Proprietors	58,566	5,476	Small Proprietors	96,172
31,205	Cottagers	4,773	14,833	Cottagers	4,033
195	Public Bodies ...	57,582	525	Public Bodies ...	76,046
	Waste	47,388		Waste	6,896
34,317—Total.		567,908	22,305—Total.		957,330

GLOUCESTER.			HEREFORD.		
No. of Owners.	Class.	Acres.	No. of Owners.	Class.	Acres.
7	Peers	110,125	4	Peers	26,454
34	Great Landowners	165,068	26	Great Landowners	158,918
55	Squires	93,500	49	Squires	83,300
251	Greater Yeomen	125,500	177	Greater Yeomen	8,500
597	Lesser Yeomen ...	101,490	448	Lesser Yeomen ...	76,160
7,107	Small Proprietors	97,482	3,781	Small Proprietors	50,615
29,280	Cottagers	6,030	9,085	Cottagers	1,301
374	Public Bodies ...	34,446	161	Public Bodies ...	21,312
	Waste	7,429		Waste	10,073
37,705—Total.		741,070	73,731—Total.		516,633

HERTS.			HUNTINGDON.		
No. of Owners.	Class.	Acres.	No. of Owners.	Class.	Acres.
10	Peers	82,682	6	Peers	38,214
15	Great Landowners	74,862	11	Great Landowners	61,797
39	Squires	66,300	8	Squires	13,600
138	Greater Yeomen	69,000	64	Greater Yeomen	32,000
237	Lesser Yeomen ...	40,290	179	Lesser Yeomen ...	30,430
2,184	Small Proprietors	34,196	1,612	Small Proprietors	27,400
9,556	Cottagers	2,339	1,816	Cottagers	399
208	Public Bodies ...	15,139	207	Public Bodies ...	21,323
	Waste...	5,302		Waste...	795
12,387—Total.		390,110	3,903—Total.		225,958

KENT.*			LANCASTER.		
No. of Owners.	Class.	Acres.	No. of Owners.	Class.	Acres.
18	Peers	122,571	10	Peers	135,322
36	Great Landowners	193,741	36	Great Landowners	218,570
75	Squires	127,500	79	Squires	134,300
356	Greater Yeomen	178,000	257	Greater Yeomen	128,500
788	Lesser Yeomen ...	133,160	692	Lesser Yeomen ...	117,640
6,062	Small Proprietors	119,790	10,845	Small Proprietors	168,100
26,925	Cottagers	8,128	76,177	Cottagers	14,811
423	Public Bodies ...	67,717	639	Public Bodies ...	30,221
	Waste...	5,302		Waste...	64,305
34,683—Total.		955,909	88,735—Total.		1,011,769

* Exclusive of what lies within the Metropolitan area.

LEICESTER.			LINCOLN.		
No. of Owners.	Class.	Acres.	No. of Owners.	Class.	Acres.
7	Peers	98,132	12	Peers	253,606
17	Great Landowners	99,398	56	Great Landowners	418,886
38	Squires	64,600	91	Squires	154,700
164	Greater Yeomen	82,000	497	Greater Yeomen	248,500
487	Lesser Yeomen ...	82,790	1,205	Lesser Yeomen ...	204,850
3,823	Small Proprietors	71,730	14,118	Small Proprietors	222,586
8,921	Cottagers	1,742	13,768	Cottagers	2,824
391	Public Bodies ...	18,834	750	Public Bodies ...	100,591
	Waste	298		Waste	5,762
13,848—Total.		519,524	30,497—Total.		1,612,305

MIDDLESEX.*			MONMOUTH.		
No. of Owners.	Class.	Acres.	No. of Owners.	Class.	Acres.
5	Peers	13,789	5	Peers	61,632
4	Great Landowners	9,640	8	Great Landowners	62,417
5	Squires	8,500	14	Squires	23,800
41	Greater Yeomen	20,500	71	Greater Yeomen	35,500
168	Lesser Yeomen ...	28,560	256	Lesser Yeomen ...	43,520
2,433	Small Proprietors	34,295	2,366	Small Proprietors	46,963
9,006	Cottagers	6,574	4,970	Cottagers	1,082
219	Public Bodies ...	21,156	121	Public Bodies ...	14,283
	Waste	2,591		Waste	7,594
11,881—Total.		145,605	7,811—Total.		296,791

* Exclusive of London.

NORFOLK.			NORTHAMPTON.		
No. of Owners.	Class.	Acres.	No. of Owners.	Class.	Acres.
15	Peers	194,331	13	Peers	148,236
55	Great Landowners	322,939	23	Great Landowners	132,120
113	Squires	192,100	31	Squires	52,700
341	Greater Yeomen	170,500	156	Greater Yeomen	78,000
824	Lesser Yeomen ...	140,080	444	Lesser Yeomen ...	75,480
7,936	Small Proprietors	152,446	3,287	Small Proprietors	67,053
16,552	Cottagers	2,468	10,010	Cottagers	3,022
812	Public Bodies ...	60,020	501	Public Bodies ...	36,161
	Waste	12,869		Waste	254
26,648—Total.		1,247,753	14,465—Total.		593,026

NORTHUMBERLAND.			NOTTS.		
No. of Owners.	Class.	Acres.	No. of Owners.	Class.	Acres.
9	Peers	322,722	9	Peers	156,754
53	Great Landowners	471,523	21	Great Landowners	123,313
84	Squires	*173,000	25	Squires	42,500
181	Greater Yeomen	90,500	109	Greater Yeomen	54,500
289	Lesser Yeomen ...	49,130	282	Lesser Yeomen ...	47,940
1,531	Small Proprietors	42,456	3,838	Small Proprietors	61,108
10,036	Cottagers	1,424	9,891	Cottagers	1,266
76	Public Bodies ...	39,288	344	Public Bodies ...	19,956
	Waste	30,286		Waste	1,449
12,257—Total.		1,220,329	14,519—Total.		508,786

* The Squire class in this county averages about 2,055 acres instead of 1,700.

OXFORD.			RUTLAND.		
No. of Owners.	Class.	Acres.	No. of Owners.	Class.	Acres.
9	Peers	82,503	1	Peers	42,500
17	Great Landowners	84,057	5	Great Landowners	23,794
40	Squires	68,000	*5	Squires	7,471
126	Greater Yeomen	63,000	10	Greater Yeomen	4,577
342	Lesser Yeomen ...	58,140	32	Lesser Yeomen ...	5,440
2,493	Small Proprietors	45,876	458	Small Proprietors	6,782
6,833	Cottagers	876	861	Cottagers	132
317	Public Bodies ...	46,831	53	Public Bodies ...	2,392
	Waste	2,949		Waste	401
10,177—Total.		452,232	1,425—Total.		93,479

SALOP.			SOMERSET.		
No. of Owners.	Class.	Acres.	No. of Owners.	Class.	Acres.
8	Peers	195,276	10	Peers	120,519
44	Great Landowners	223,429	31	Great Landowners	217,352
65	Squires	110,500	67	Squires	113,900
222	Greater Yeomen	111,000	270	Greater Yeomen	135,000
447	Lesser Yeomen ...	75,990	882	Lesser Yeomen ...	149,940
3,841	Small Proprietors	57,738	10,831	Small Proprietors	173,918
7,281	Cottagers	4,544	20,370	Cottagers	5,227
211	Public Bodies ...	13,464	304	Public Bodies ...	24,627
	Waste	19,674		Waste	31,246
12,119—Total.		811,615	32,765—Total.		971,729

* This and the two following classes are given the actual extent of their holdings ; Rutland being too small to average fairly.

SOUTHAMPTON.			STAFFORD.		
No. of Owners.	Class.	Acres.	No. of Owners.	Class.	Acres.
13	Peers	122,091	10	Peers	164,506
55	Great Landowners	279,286	23	Great Landowners	148,100
78	Squires	132,600	37	Squires	57,400*
281	Greater Yeomen	140,500	137	Greater Yeomen	68,500
452	Lesser Yeomen ...	76,840	414	Lesser Yeomen ...	65,412†
5,102	Small Proprietors	80,756	8,617	Small Proprietors	105,283
21,236	Cottagers	5,749	33,672	Cottagers	4,287
255	Public Bodies ...	46,827	641	Public Bodies ...	24,595
	Waste...	78,843		Waste...	7,808
27,472—Total.		963,492	43,371—Total.		645,893

SUFFOLK.			SURREY.		
No. of Owners.	Class.	Acres.	No. of Owners.	Class.	Acres.
10	Peers	132,385	12	Peers	47,946
36	Great Landowners	233,263	11	Great Landowners	60,290
65	Squires	110,500	41	Squires	69,700
297	Greater Yeomen	148,500	174	Greater Yeomen	87,000
798	Lesser Yeomen ...	135,660	318	Lesser Yeomen ...	54,060
4,965	Small Proprietors	102,770	3,813	Small Proprietors	49,569
12,511	Cottagers	3,673	12,712	Cottagers	2,860
594	Public Bodies ...	45,686	212	Public Bodies ...	27,322
	Waste...	7,831		Waste...	40,036
19,276—Total.		920,268	17,293—Total.		438,783

* As worked out. See Preface.
† At what is the real average for Staffs., viz., 158 acres instead of 170.

SUSSEX.			WARWICK.		
No. of Owners.	Class.	Acres.	No. of Owners.	Class.	Acres.
19	Peers	195,016	9	Peers	111,223
40	Great Landowners	185,374	19	Great Landowners	119,043
86	Squires	146,200	32	Squires	54,400
280	Greater Yeomen	140,000	143	Greater Yeomen	71,500
537	Lesser Yeomen ...	91,290	507	Lesser Yeomen ...	86,190
3,915	Small Proprietors	82,024	3,519	Small Proprietors	62,191
14,675	Cottagers	3,950	46,894	Cottagers	5,883
182	Public Bodies ...	25,569	393	Public Bodies ...	30,592
	Waste...	23,738		Waste...	1,833
19,734—Total.		893,161	51,516—Total.		542,855

WESTMORELAND.			WILTS.		
No. of Owners.	Class.	Acres.	No. of Owners.	Class.	Acres.
2	Peers	54,366	16	Peers	239,708
11	Great Landowners	74,064	28	Great Landowners	225,893
20	Squires	34,000	61	Squires	103,700
109	Greater Yeomen	54,500	209	Greater Yeomen	104,500
352	Lesser Yeomen ...	59,840	335	Lesser Yeomen ...	56,950
2,055	Small Proprietors	53,205	3,485	Small Proprietors	54,759
1,714	Cottagers	326	9,635	Cottagers	1,519
113	Public Bodies ...	4,849	244	Public Bodies ...	41,920
	Waste...	114,282		Waste...	1,930
4,376—Total.		449,442	14,013—Total.		830,879

No. of Owners.	WORCESTER. Class.	Acres.	No. of Owners.	YORK, N.R. Class.	Acres.
7	Peers	77,480	11	Peers	200,656
18	Great Landowners	87,753	39	Great Landowners	302,319
25	Squires	42,500	80	Squires	136,000
130	Greater Yeomen	65,000	230	Greater Yeomen	115,000
475	Lesser Yeomen ...	80,750	618	Lesser Yeomen ...	105,060
4,803	Small Proprietors	65,265	4,991	Small Proprietors	133,340
16,008	Cottagers	4,733	10,115	Cottagers	2,113
338	Public Bodies ...	17,580	229	Public Bodies ...	36,988
	Waste	3,415		Waste	247,408
21,804—Total.		444,476	16,313—Total.		1,278,884

No. of Owners.	YORK, E.R. Class.	Acres.	No. of Owners.	YORK, W.R. Class.	Acres.
6	Peers	134,619	19	Peers	236,181
27	Great Landowners	221,635	66	Great Landowners	442,031
44	Squires	74,800	101	Squires	171,700
183	Greater Yeomen	91,500	366	Greater Yeomen	183,000
486	Lesser Yeomen ...	82,620	1,119	Lesser Yeomen ...	190,230
3,602	Small Proprietors	60,601	14,735	Small Proprietors	228,025
15,012	Cottagers	5,398	59,496	Cottagers	13,226
216	Public Bodies ...	35,511	1,011	Public Bodies ...	67,953
	Waste	4,049		Waste	99,912
19,576—Total.		710,733	76,913—Total.		1,632,258

WELSH COUNTIES.

ANGLESEA.			BRECON.		
No. of Owners.	Class.	Acres.	No. of Owners.	Class.	Acres.
3	Peers	31,339	1	Peers	21,722
8	Great Landowners	66,175	10	Great Landowners	106,029
*6	Squires	10,200	†34	Squires	57,800
31	Greater Yeomen	15,500	97	Greater Yeomen	48,500
86	Lesser Yeomen ...	14,620	237	Lesser Yeomen ...	40,290
955	Small Proprietors	20,421	796	Small Proprietors	25,001
3,015	Cottagers	234	1,195	Cottagers	248
37	Public Bodies ...	3,447	44	Public Bodies ...	2,648
	Waste...	5,678		Waste...	115,106
4,141—Total.		167,614	2,414—Total.		417,344

CARDIGAN.			CARMARTHEN.		
No. of Owners.	Class.	Acres.	No. of Owners.	Class.	Acres.
1	Peers	42,890	2	Peers	48,745
§	Great Landowners	96,909	13	Great Landowners	124,830
‡48	Squires	81,600	§50	Squires	85,000
110	Greater Yeomen	55,000	198	Greater Yeomen	99,000
304	Lesser Yeomen ...	51,680	497	Lesser Yeomen ...	84,490
1,553	Small Proprietors	61,290	2,093	Small Proprietors	62,689
1,278	Cottagers	287	5,168	Cottagers	2,286
14	Public Bodies ...	2,030	45	Public Bodies ...	3,534
	Waste...	6,971		Waste...	18,077
3,316—Total.		398,657	8,066—Total.		528,651

* Inclusive of two virtual yeomen whose rents are respectively under £1,000 p. a., and under £200.
† Inclusive of twenty-five persons whose rentals are under £1,000, one having as little as £83 for 1,255 acres.
‡ Nineteen of these have less than £1,000 rental, one with 1,443 acres having but £15 p. a.
§ Inclusive of sixteen rentals under £1,000.

No. of Owners.	CARNARVON. Class.	Acres.	No. of Owners.	DENBIGH. Class.	Acres.
4	Peers	102,470	0	Peers	20,812
10	Great Landowners	100,861	16	Great Landowners	130,165
*19	Squires	32,300	†38	Squires	64,600
42	Greater Yeomen	21,000	106	Greater Yeomen	53,000
96	Lesser Yeomen ...	16,320	254	Lesser Yeomen ...	43,180
1,407	Small Proprietors	23,527	1,773	Small Proprietors	31,436
4,610	Cottagers	373	3,436	Cottagers	721
52	Public Bodies ...	4,382	85	Public Bodies ...	4,503
	Waste	14,563		Waste	18,812
6,240 —Total.		315,796	5,708—Total.		367,229

No. of Owners.	FLINT. Class.	Acres.	No. of Owners.	GLAMORGAN. Class.	Acres.
3	Peers	25,416	6	Peers	84,549
5	Great Landowners	39,113‡	19	Great Landowners	149,830
9	Squires	15,300	§36	Squires	61,200
44	Greater Yeomen	22,000	106	Greater Yeomen	53,000
111	Lesser Yeomen ...	18,870	210	Lesser Yeomen ...	35,700
1,225	Small Proprietors	15,179	1,373	Small Proprietors	29,184
2,048	Cottagers	562	6,570	Cottagers	685
65	Public Bodies ...	5,847	106	Public Bodies ...	14,238
	Waste	4,312		Waste	47,018
3,510—Total.		146,599	8,426—Total.		475,404

* Only six of these have over £1,000 rental.   † Sixteen of these have less than £1,000 p. a.
‡ Over a quarter of these belong to Mr. Gladstone.   § Nine have under £1,000 rental.

MERIONETH.			MONTGOMERY.		
No. of Owners.	Class.	Acres.	No. of Owners.	Class.	Acres.
	Peers	16,684	2	Peers	61,070
12	Great Landowners	128,593	9	Great Landowners	86,587
*37	Squires	†68,800	‡42	Squires	71,400
96	Greater Yeomen	48,000	128	Greater Yeomen	64,000
135	Lesser Yeomen ...	22,950	280	Lesser Yeomen ...	47,600
346	Small Proprietors	14,244	1,418	Small Proprietors	43,956
1,044	Cottagers	212	1,314	Cottagers	262
25	Public Bodies ...	3,174	48	Public Bodies ...	5,510
	Waste...	416		Waste...	6,956
1,695—Total.		303,073	3,241—Total.		387,341

PEMBROKE.			RADNOR.		
No. of Owners.	Class.	Acres.	No. of Owners.	Class.	Acres.
2	Peers	24,522	2	Peers	15,572
19	Great Landowners	109,495	11	Great Landowners	62,119
§41	Squires	69,700	‖18	Squires	30,600
130	Greater Yeomen	65,000	65	Greater Yeomen	32,500
263	Lesser Yeomen ...	44,710	203	Lesser Yeomen ...	34,510
1,134	Small Proprietors	29,483	850	Small Proprietors	28,446
492	Cottagers	278	452	Cottagers	90
40	Public Bodies ...	12,511	41	Public Bodies ...	3,557
	Waste...	12,260		Waste...	77,799
3,121—Total.		367,95	1,642—Total.		285,193

* Including 28 rentals under £1,000.   † Average 1,860 acres instead of 1,700.
‡ Including 16 rentals under £1,000 p. a.   § Including 11 rentals under £1,000.
‖ Including 12 rentals under £1,000.

SUMMARY TABLE OF ENGLAND AND WALES.

No. of Owners.	Class.		Extent in Acres.
400	Peers and Peeresses		5,728,979
1,288	Great Landowners		8,497,699
2,529	Squires		4,319,271
9,585	Greater Yeomen		4,782,627
24,412	Lesser Yeomen		4,144,272
217,049	Small Proprietors		3,931,806
703,289	Cottagers		151,148
14,459	Public Bodies.	The Crown, Barracks, Convict Prisons, Lighthouses, &c.	165,427
		Religious, Educational, Philanthropic, &c.	947,655
		Commercial and Miscellaneous	330,466
	Waste		1,524,624
973,011—Total.			34,523,974

These figures are compiled from those at the foot of each County in the Return of 1873. They do not harmonise exactly with the summary at the beginning of the Blue Book, but that summary itself varies from the County summaries in many instances—in Durham, for instance, by some 2,800 acres.

NOTES ON THE FOREGOING TABLES BY THE COMPILER.

" 'THE Government Return of Landowners, 1873,' dispelled the absurd illusion that some 30,000 persons owned all England and Wales, and raised the aggregate number of English and Welsh landowners to something like a million. Still, it was evident that useful as this compilation might be, it was marred by several serious blots : such as the non-entry of the metropolitan area, the omission, in some counties at least, of the woods, which in 1873 were still unrated, and the occasional double entry of one and the same man; specially where he was blessed with a double-barrelled name, such as Knatchbull-Hugessen or Cowper-Temple, to say nothing of grosser cases, where some four surnames are strung together, rope of onion fashion, like Butler-Clarke-Southwell-Wandesforde. A study of the blue-book convinced me that something like 2 per cent., if not more, of the landowners thus appeared more than once, and, when compiling 'The Great Landowners of Great Britain,' I wrote to every large owner, begging a correction. The answers proved that my surmise was perfectly right. Two instances may be given, in each of which cases the landowner is one and the same man.

CASE OF CAPT. EDWARDS-HEATHCOTE, COPIED VERBATIM FROM THE RETURN
(HIS REAL INITIALS BEING J. H.).

Staffs.	Name of Owner.	Address of Owner.	Extent of Lands.			Gross estimated Rental.	
			A.	R.	P.	£	s.
Page 19, line 19	Edwards, H. T. H.	Apedale Hall	962	3	0	1,587	12
—— 27 ,, 42	Heathcote, Capt. E.	Audley	—			9,703	16
——ᴵ ,, 44	Heathcote, J. E.	Newcastle, Stafford	44	0	20	154	0
—— ,, 45	Heatchcote, J. H. E.	Apedale Hall	—			1,097	0

Capt. Heathcote's real acreage is much over the amount with which the return credits him. The property lies in at least four parishes, principally in Audley, in which I believe Apedale Hall stands ; and Newcastle is his post town.

CASE OF MR. ROBERT CHICHESTER OF HALL. (COPIED VERBATIM.)

Devon.	Name of Owner.	Address of Owner.	Extent of Lands.			Gross estimated Rental.	
			A.	R.	P.	£	s.
Page 12, line 38	Chichester, Robert	Bishop's Tawton	3,906	3	20	4,153	12
—— ,, 37	Chichester, Richard	Drewsteignton	440	1	30	374	0
Cornwall.							
Page 6, line 25	Chichester, R.	Bishop's Tawton	402	2	9	188	15
—— ,, 26	Chichester, R.	Hall, Barnstaple	846	0	30	223	15
—— ,, 27	Chichester, Robert	St. Day, ,,	24	3	24	525	10

Bishop's Tawton, Drewsteignton, and St. Day are places in which Mr. Chichester has property ; " Hall " being his seat, and Barnstaple his post town.

" Having considerably weeded out these double, treble, and multiple entries before compiling the ' Great Landowners,' I have used that work as well as the Government returns in compiling the foregoing tables, adopting such corrections as had been sent up to Christmas, 1877, but none of later date. Curiously enough, a few corrections more or less scarcely alter the totals in each column ; because the cases of over-estimation in the Return are very nearly balanced by others which tell in an opposite way.

" The third class (squires), and the fourth and fifth (greater and lesser yeomen) are averaged on the scales of 1,700, 500, and 170 acres, in all cases but Cambridge, Northumberland, Rutland, Stafford, and Merioneth. In these counties, if the usual averages had been strictly adhered to, the result would have been misleading. For instance, I worked out the actual extent of the lands held by the 'squires' on Tyneside, which proved them to hold 355 acres apiece more than their fellow squires nearer the metropolis.

" As to Staffordshire, a county very familiar to me, the staggering fact came out, after totalising the lands proper to each class, that the sixth-class landowner in Staffordshire was the lowest specimen of his race, being a holder of only 11 acres, while a semi-Cockney of the same class in Surrey, which county most nearly approached him, held 13 acres of the soil. The explanation of this fact appears to be that Staffordshire is pre-eminently a land of colliers, and that among the Staffordshire colliers, as among the small farmers of Cheshire, a man's worth and respectability are apt to be gauged by the number of cows which he milks. To my certain knowledge there are hundreds, nay thousands, of colliers who hold from $4\frac{1}{2}$ to $7\frac{1}{2}$ acres, milk two or at most three cows (a mark of high rank), and will actually slave in the pits or ironworks to provide the rent, in case they are tenants, or the interest on the mortgage, which is nearly inevitable, in case they are freeholders.

" The prevalence of this mania for cow-milking as the badge of respectability in Mercia, as contrasted with the counter-mania for the same badge in the form of keeping a servant-girl or one-horse chaise in Middlesex, leads to the large number and small extent of the Mercian sixth-class holdings.

" Rutlandshire supplies a tempting text for statistical sermons on the distribution of landed property in England—and the more so, as the Government return of Rutlandshire landowners is but $4\frac{1}{4}$ pages long, as compared with 185 pages allotted to Yorkshire. Unfortunately for the preachers, this little county signally illustrates the proverbial fallacy of statistics. It so happens that thousands upon thousands of its glorious fields, the delight of fox-hunters, belong to proprietors residing in other counties. For instance, among foreigners owning their soil are the following :—

Adderley, Sir Charles (now Lord Norton, a Warwickshire man).
Aveland, Lord (who is classed as a Lincolnshire Peer, his principal property being there).
Belgrave, Mr., of Maydwell, in Northamptonshire.
Brooke, Sir W. de C., Bart., also of Northamptonshire.
Hankey, Mr., of Balcombe, Sussex.
Lonsdale, Lord, from the North Country.
Northwick, Lord, a Worcestershire Peer.
Richards, Mr. Westley, of Birmingham.
Exeter, Lord (who is classed as a Northamptonshire Peer).
Pochin, Mr., of Edmondthorpe, Leicestershire.
Pierrepoint, Mr., of Chippenham, Wilts.
Rutland, Duke of, a Leicestershire Peer.
Kennedy, Mr., " of London " (a somewhat vague address).
De Stafford, Mr., a Northamptonshire man.
Blake, Mr., of Welwyn, in Herts.
Laxton, Mr., from Huntingdonshire.

" These sixteen persons among them own nearly 37,000 acres, or two-fifths of the whole county.

"Again, the unwary statistician who can only succeed in finding five persons ranging from 1,000 acres to 5,000 might be misled by supposing that ' *Mr. Fludyer*,' who figures for 1,100 acres, and ' *Mr. Hudyer*,' who owns 1,500, are two separate persons; whereas Sir John Fludyer tells me that he is the person aimed at in the returns of 1873, under both the letters F and H.

"Where landowners only reach 5 in the third class, a mistake of one is serious, and any generalisation therefore based on Rutlandshire alone would affect England as judged thereby to the extent of one-fifth at the least.

"Merioneth deserves special distinction as exemplifying class six in its highest stage of ownership; yet a walk through two counties would bring a traveller from this paradise of small proprietors into Staffordshire, its lowest type of degradation. A glimpse at the column devoted to ' waste,' will show the reason why—a reason in itself sufficient to prove that the parochial authorities who compiled the crude materials for the return had many curious eccentricities. ' Waste' figures for only 416 acres in Merionethshire, certainly a most bucolic part of the Queen's dominions, if not exactly (as may be said of Connaught or Ross-shire) ' west of the law.' I have no doubt that I could pick a dozen spots on its wild mountain ranges where no policeman could be found within half-a-dozen miles. Contrast this with the neighbouring counties of Brecon, Denbigh, Montgomery, and Radnor, where the waste reaches a total of 215,000 acres, or say 53,000 acres each. Yet Merioneth is a wilder county than any of the four. The obvious moral is that in Merioneth all *joint* lands have been equally divided in the rate-books among the participants, while in the four neighbouring counties they figure not as *joint*, but as *waste* lands. As to waste, though no uniform system of excision from other lands has been adopted in the Return, it may be roughly taken as a fact, that generally (but by no means always) they include, in the southern counties, heaths, charts, unfenced land, and, in some cases, salt marshes; and, in the northern ones, all such land as is entered in the valuable agricultural returns published of late years annually as ' Mountain Pasture' and ' Barren Heath.' But on what principle can one reconcile figures like the following :— Kent—waste, five thousand odd acres. Surrey—forty thousand? Kent is more than twice the size of Surrey, and as a fact contains, though perhaps in smaller proportion to its area, quite as much ' heath,' ' common,' and ' chart' as Surrey. We must guess that in the rate-books of Kent these wastes swell the estates of the local Lords of the Manor.

" The northern counties contain vast areas of ' waste.' Much of this is ' waste' only in name, being unfenced, heathery-furzy-ferny-swampy-rocky pasture, much of it at a level of some 1,000 to 2,000 feet over sea-level, and affording fair pasturage to the hardy local sheep and cattle, though useless as nourishment to a 3,000 guinea shorthorn. These ' wastes' are locally divided into what are called *cattle-gates*, each *gate* representing sufficient summer feed for one beast. In Kendal, Hexham, or Carlisle such cattle-gates are as saleable as an ' eligible building plot' is in Kennington, Highgate, or Clapham; in no sense are they waste, but a rough survival of the Russian Communal land system. Let the south-country agrarian agitator try the experiment of

settling himself as a virtuous and contented agriculturist
on a five-acre plot, carved out of the braes of Skiddaw,
treeless, undrained, exposed to all the winds, and hand-
somely fenced with rough posts and rotten colliery-rope.
I fear the contentment would vanish, whether or not
the virtue should remain.   Meanwhile, let him bear in
mind a few simple facts : that in the northern counties
he may have to rear his family without such aids to
digestion as onions, gooseberries, strawberries, rasp-
berries, or other berries, apples, cherries, cabbages, and
peas, none of which flourish in Northumbria over the
1,000 feet level, besides combining all trades in his
own proper person—such as stonemason, waller, butcher,
plasterer, shoemaker, painter, glazier, and possibly accou-
cheur.   The case of the southern wastes is equally un-
promising in a money-making or self-supporting point
of view.   Many a Kentish ' chart,' if parcelled out
into fifteen-acre freeholds, would hardly support a full-
grown man with a healthy appetite on each of them.
Their only advantage over the northern moors is their
much larger allowance of bright sunshine, a commodity
of which the supply is now regularly registered in the
daily weather reports.

   " The climate of these islands, I fear, is not suitable
for what the French call ' the small culture.'   No man
on an average British plot of $2\frac{1}{2}$ acres can raise and
support a healthy family.   I would put the smallest
desirable peasant-holding at from $4\frac{1}{2}$ to 6 acres, and
these only in the eastern—i.e., the drier—half of England.   In the western counties, where the bulk of the
land is under permanent pasture, and corn-growing is a
secondary interest, the minimum should be raised to

what would keep four cows; and this minimum would vary much in different counties, say from 9 acres in the vale of Evesham, to 45 or 50 in north-western Devonshire. Desirable as it is in every way to encourage the subdivision of the soil on political grounds, specially from the moderate Tory point of view, it cannot be too strongly urged that if a man buys a small freehold (as we all hope he may one day be able to do), that man should have some other trade or means of livelihood than the tillage of the soil. 217,000 of these men are already in our midst—'small proprietors,' who own some twenty acres apiece—and it will be well for England when the number is quadrupled. Beyond that point it would so far do harm as to (I believe) materially reduce the amount of food grown on the fair face of Old England. In face of the terrible competition of American produce, large capital, open-handed use of all manures, close-fistedness in bargaining, and money enough to avoid having to sell at bad prices, combined with a largish area to work on, and much knowledge of his business, are the only conditions under which the British farmer can hold his own. Men of this stamp are far too wise to aspire to the ownership of the lands they till.

" When divided by the number of small proprietors in Class VI., the four million acres they hold shows the following approximate average size of holding in each county :—

Staffs., 12⅕

Flint, 12⅓

Surrey, 13

Hereford, 13⅓

Worcester, 13⅗

Gloucester, 13⅝

Dorset, 14

Middlesex, 14 1/10

Cheshire, 14⅔

Rutland, 14¾

Salop, 15

Lancashire, 15½

York (W.R.), 15½

Herts, 15⅔

Wilts, 15⅔

Lincoln, 15⅚

Hampshire, 15⅘

Derby, 15⅚

Somerset, 16	Norfolk, $19\frac{1}{4}$	Pembroke, 26
Cambs., $16\frac{1}{6}$	Kent, $19\frac{3}{4}$	Cornwall, $26\frac{1}{3}$
Carnarvon, $16\frac{2}{3}$	Monmouth, $19\frac{5}{6}$	York (N.R.), $26\frac{3}{4}$
Notts., $16\frac{2}{3}$	Bucks, 20	Devon, $27\frac{1}{4}$
York (E.R.), $16\frac{3}{4}$	Sussex, $20\frac{1}{10}$	Northumberland, $27\frac{2}{3}$
Huntingdon, 17	Northampton, $20\frac{1}{3}$	Cumberland, 29
Essex, $17\frac{1}{2}$	Glamorgan, $21\frac{1}{4}$	Carmarthen, $29\frac{9}{10}$
Warwick, $17\frac{2}{3}$	Anglesea, $21\frac{1}{3}$	Montgomery, $31\frac{1}{10}$
Denbigh, $17\frac{3}{4}$	Beds., $21\frac{1}{2}$	Brecon, $31\frac{2}{5}$
Oxon, $18\frac{1}{4}$	Suffolk, $22\frac{3}{4}$	Radnor, $33\frac{1}{2}$
Berks, $18\frac{1}{3}$	Durham, $24\frac{3}{5}$	Cardigan, $39\frac{1}{2}$
Leicester, $18\frac{3}{4}$	Westmoreland, $25\frac{1}{2}$	Merioneth, $41\frac{1}{6}$

It may be noted how closely the averages of many neighbouring counties run—the four northern counties and their neighbour the North Riding; the three cider-making counties of Gloucester, Hereford, and Worcester; Lancaster and the West Riding; Kent and Sussex; and, though divided by the 'silvery Thames,' it is hard to raise a distinction between a small holding in Oxon and its fellow in Berks.[1]

"The two classes of yeomen show also a few curious facts; notably, the very large proportion of them who have the prefix 'Rev.' to their names. Of course, it may so happen that in some parts of the country the rate-collectors, following the example of high ecclesiastical authorities, refuse this prefix to our nonconforming clerics, and thus simplify my labour of 'cleric extraction' from the ranks of the yeomen; but I take it that, as a rule, not only 'Church parsons,' but their nonconforming, and even their Roman Catholic, brethren are entered as 'Rev.' Their total number is 3,185, out of a total landed yeomanry of 33,998; in other words, not

---

[1] Appendix IX. shows the average extent of land held by "small proprietors," between 1 and 100 acres, in groups of counties, arranged geographically.

far short of ten per cent. Names with the clerical prefix are thickest in Northampton, Leicester, and Rutland, where about one in five of my yeomen is a cleric. This, of course, means that the glebe-land has not been entered as the Local Government Board directed, as the property of 'The vicar of Blank,' but in the vicar's name, as 'Rev. J. Smith.'

" After all, 'yeomen' is but a makeshift title for the holders of between 100 and 1,000 acres. If we could imagine all the members of this class to be called out for a yeomanry drill, we must be prepared to see an Ambassador, an ex-Cabinet Minister, a popular Dean, and a well-known Leicestershire M. F. H. dressed in line with the Poet Laureate; for all these swell the numbers of the 'yeomen' in the preceding tables. Yet it would not be easy to suggest a better designation for the great majority of the class.

" It is much to be hoped that, if ever a revision of the Great Return of 1873 is made, a separate volume will be given to all town properties; as it is essentially absurd to mix the rental (say £10,000) derived from a row of warehouses in Bristol, covering three acres, with £50 more derived from fifty acres of Gloucestershire clay. This is always done in the present Return; thus—

Extent, 53 acres; *Rental*, £10,050.

Let us hope that ere another edition is produced our rulers, eschewing revolutionary legislation, will go so far as to shatter the hopeless legal bonds which fetter and prevent the free sale of land; and the extension thereby of Class VI., a class which, multiplied fourfold, would greatly add stability to our country and its institutions.

" JOHN BATEMAN.

" *Carlton Club, Oct.*, 1880."

CHAPTER IV.

"THE great bulk of the land in the United Kingdom is not cultivated by the owner, but by tenant-occupiers. Of these there are 561,000 in Great Britain[1] and 600,000 in Ireland," the average of cultivated land in each farm being fifty-six acres in Great Britain and only twenty-five acres in Ireland.[2] Such is Mr. Caird's succinct account[3] of a feature in the English land system not less singular in Europe than the Law and Custom of Primogeniture. In the great majority of European countries, and especially in the most highly civilized, the land is chiefly tilled by the owners, who thus constitute a real peasantry of a class well nigh extinct in

[1] It is curious that Arthur Young (in his "Northern Tour") estimates the number of farms in England at no more than 111,498.

[2] On a very extensive property, scattered over several counties, and distributed into 278 farms, 140 of these farms (or more than one-half) are between 100 and 300 acres, 62 farms are between 50 and 100 acres, and 59 are between 300 and 500 acres, while three only exceed 1,000 acres.

It is hardly possible to ascertain the average size of farms in other countries of Europe, owing to a frequent confusion between holdings and properties. Much valuable information on the subject is, however, collected in Mr. James Howard's "Treatise on Continental Farming and Peasantry." The report of the Indian Famine Commission shows that in the Punjaub the average holding of a tenant is about 6 acres ; in the North-West Provinces, about 4½ ; in Oude and Bengal, little more than 3 acres. In the Central Provinces the holdings appear to range from 14 to 20 acres.

[3] "Landed Interest," pp. 46, 47. According to the Agricultural Statistics of 1880, there are 553,739 " holdings " in Great Britain.

England, though represented in Ireland by small
farmers holding under the custom of tenant-right.
In France, it is true, the number of tenant-farmers
is no less than 830,000, exceeding by nearly one-half
the number in Great Britain.   The cultivated area
of France, however, is thrice as great as the cultivated area of Great Britain ;   more than half of
this is cultivated by the owner himself on the *Faire-
valoir-direct* system ;   and, since the farms so cultivated are on the average much smaller, seventy per
cent. of the farmers in France are peasant-owners.
Even in Ireland it was found in 1870 that 20,000
holdings were then occupied by owners in fee, and a
considerable number of farms have since been purchased by their occupiers under the Irish Church
Act.   In this country, there are no trustworthy statistics enabling us to compare the number of proprietor-
farmers with that of tenant-farmers, though it is
certain that the former is quite insignificant.   The
most important part of the former class is composed,
not of yeomen, but of country gentlemen, who retain a home farm nominally under their own management, but really under that of a bailiff, for the purpose
of breeding pedigree-stock, conducting agricultural experiments, or otherwise setting a good example to
their neighbours.   It may surprise many people to
learn that fifty-eight acres is the average size of a
farm in Great Britain, and that, owing to the preponderance of small farms in Ireland, seventy per
cent. of the holdings in the whole United Kingdom
are of less extent than fifty acres.   But, of the
small farms in Great Britain, a very large number

are mere appendages to villa-residences, or little plots tenanted by persons who have other means of livelihood, the result being that less than one-sixth of the land in Great Britain is occupied by farms of less than fifteen acres each. The most important and typical class of English farms ranges from 100 to 400 acres ; and though farms on a much grander scale are associated with most foreign conceptions of English agriculture, since they figure more prominently in agricultural exhibitions, the fact is that in England alone there were in 1880 but 4,095 farms between 500 and 1,000 acres, and 500 only exceeding 1,000 acres.[1]

The causes which have divorced rights of property from the cultivation of the soil, and created a separate class of tenant-farmers, are common to England and Scotland; but the prevalence of yearly tenancy, without the security of lease, is specially characteristic of England. The origin of leasehold tenure is not easily traced. Adam Smith explains the gradual introduction of long agricultural leases in the latter part of the Middle Ages by the increase of personal extravagance among the great proprietors. In earlier times, he thinks, a baron was content to maintain an army of retainers in coarse plenty on the produce of his own demesnes ; but when his successors acquired more luxurious tastes and habits, they were driven to extract a full rent from their lands, which could only be done by letting them on lease. On the other hand, the inability of individual landowners, under the old system of strict entails, to grant leases binding on their

[1] Agricultural Statistics for 1880. Table 8. See Appendix X.

successors, drove the most enterprising farmers to seek
tenancies under monastic houses ; and it was to im-
provement-leases granted by monastic houses that
England owed the first great experiments in drainage.
For ecclesiastical corporations and colleges, like the
great barons, found it too burdensome to superintend
personally the cultivation of their enormous estates,
and their members were seldom unwilling to profit by
the fines taken on the creation and renewal of a beneficial lease. The practice of letting on lease must also
have been encouraged by the Statute *Quia Emptores,*
which rendered it impossible to create a subordinate
tenure in fee simple. After this statute, if a lord
desired to retain all the feudal rights of a seigniory
over the estate, and yet to relieve himself of its
agricultural management, his simplest course was to
demise it for his own life at least, and perhaps for
that of his tenant. The Act of Henry VI. which
created the 40s. county franchise introduced a new
motive for letting farms on lease which has not
received sufficient attention. It was held that a lease
for life constituted a freehold, which, if above the
value of 40s., carried with it a vote for the county. As
English tenants have always been wont to follow the
politics of their landlords, the multiplication of such
freeholds because a ready source of political influence.
We have the emphatic assurance of Adam Smith that a
great part of the " yeomanry," under which term he
expressly includes tenant-farmers, had freeholds of this
kind in his time ; and he adds that, by virtue of the
independence thus secured to so many, " the whole
order become respectable to their landlords." An exact

parallel is supplied by the contemporary history of Ireland, where similar leases were granted with reckless profusion to middlemen, with similar objects, after the 40s. franchise was extended to Roman Catholics in 1793. In some counties, and notably in the West of England, the custom of granting leases for lives became firmly established, and a few of these leases, constantly renewed, are still in force on Devonshire and Somersetshire estates.

But the greater certainty of occupation under leases for definite periods must always have rendered this a more eligible form of tenure for a prudent farmer. The recent investigations of Professor Thorold Rogers have shown that short leases, extending from seven to ten years, were not uncommon in the fourteenth century, and that, under such leases, the stock, both live and dead, was usually let with the land, at an additional rent, while all the repairs were executed by the landlord. From the general prevalence of farming leases for terms of years in the fifteenth century, he justly infers that entails of great estates must have been rare. For, as we have seen, a lease granted by a tenant-in-tail would not have been valid against his successor until the statute of 32 Henry VIII., c. 28, which partially removed this disability. The frequent legislation on the subject of leases in the succeeding age clearly proves how large a space they occupied in the agricultural economy of our Elizabethan ancestors,[1] and how

---

[1] The earliest statutes of importance on the subject of leases are the statute of 32 Henry VIII., cap. 27, regulating the leasing powers of ecclesiastical corporations and the incumbents of benefices, and that of 32 Henry VIII., cap. 28, enabling tenants in tail to demise lands which

strange it would then have been thought that English
yeomen should be generally displaced, not by leaseholders, but by tenants-at-will, or tenants from year
to year.

It has been confidently asserted that English farms
were commonly held under lease until the period of the
French war at the end of the eighteenth century. No
positive evidence exists by which such an assertion can
be established, but the presumption is certainly in its
favour, and it is supported by the indirect testimony of
Adam Smith and Arthur Young. The prevalence of
leases for terms of years may probably be one reason
why no other form of security for unexhausted improvements was then demanded by tenants, and Arthur
Young, complaining that "some landlords will not
grant leases at all," evidently regards them as a per-
verse minority. "If a man really means to be a
good farmer," he says, "it can never answer to him
to enter a farm with a shorter lease than twenty-
one years; nor can it ever be for the advantage
of the landlord to let his farms on shorter. I am
now speaking of rich soils. As to poor ones, to be
inclosed, or marled, or chalked, &c. &c., *it is at once
apparent that no man will hire without a long lease.*[1] Still
more significant is his statement that landlords spend
much less money than tenants in agricultural improvements ;[2] for, whatever may have been the practice
in Ireland, it is absurd to suppose that English farmers

had been usually let for agricultural purposes, but not so as to bind
remaindermen or reversioners.

[1] "Farmer's Guide," Book I., chap. xii.
[2] "Northern Tour," Vol. IV., p. 370.

would lay out large sums without the security of a
lease.   At the same time, he admits " that farms are
often very well managed by men that have no leases,"
where tenancies have virtually become hereditary on
hereditary estates ; and Adam Smith remarks that
England is the only country in which a tenant will
build on his land, without a lease, relying on the
landlord's honour.[1]

We may safely assume that tenancy-at-will existed
in every stage of our agricultural history, but it doubtless became more and more prevalent with the gradual
extinction of serfdom.   Those villeins whose right of
occupancy was not sufficiently well established to be
developed into copyhold, and those free labourers who
ultimately superseded villeins, must have formed a class
of tenants-at-will paying a fixed rent for their cottages
and plots of ground, but liable to be turned out at the
pleasure of the lord.   At a very early period, however,
the common law gave a tenant-at-will, under the name
of "emblements," the property in crops actually sown
by him, but not yet reaped, when he might be thus
evicted.   In the sixteenth century this right was so
far extended by the courts of law that a tenant-at-will,
having entered and paid rent, was held to be in effect a
tenant from year to year, and entitled to a six months'
notice to quit.   The qualified security thereby obtained,
and fortified in some counties by local customs of
tenant - right protecting unexhausted improvements,
gradually developed into a tenancy from year to year,
so long as both parties should please, and this form of

---

[1] " Wealth of Nations," Book II., chap. iii.

tenancy gradually superseded the older and sounder practice of leasehold tenure.

Two causes largely contributed to accelerate this transition within the last hundred years. The extraordinary rise of agricultural prices during the Great War rendered most landlords very unwilling to part with the immediate control of their properties, except in consideration of an exorbitant rent. On the other hand, the extraordinary fluctuation of these prices may well have deterred prudent tenants from "hanging a lease round their necks," as the saying is, and undertaking to pay an exorbitant rent for a long term of years. After the war came to an end, these motives ceased to operate, but a new and powerful motive for refusing leases was created by the Reform Act of 1832. Under the so-called "Chandos clause," or section 20, of that Act, every tenant of a farm, paying a rent of £50 or upwards, for the first time acquired the county franchise. Thenceforward the political influence of landlords was multiplied by the votes of their farm tenants, and, in order to maintain that influence, it was thought necessary to keep farm-tenants in a state of dependence by letting farms only from year to year. Doubtless, the confidence inspired by the liberal management of many great hereditary properties, as well as a wholesome dread of periodical valuations incident to a system of leases, have done much to make English farmers content with a tenure under which Adam Smith declares that it would be absurd to expect an occupier to improve, and which Scotch farmers have long since declined. The importance attached to rights of sporting in England often induces landlords to accept.

low rents from non-improving tenants, who can be
turned out at short notice if they meddle with the
game; and the power of distress enables them to dispense with too strict inquiries into a tenant's skill and
capital.   By the operation of these and other causes, it
is tolerably certain that yearly tenancy has become the
rule, and leasehold tenure the exception, in most
English counties.[1]   The recent agricultural depression
has aggravated this retrograde tendency by inclining
landlords to keep farms at their own disposal rather
than let them for a considerable period at a minimum
rent, and by inclining farmers to rely on the forbearance
of landlords under a yearly tenancy rather than accept
the onerous responsibilities of a lease.   Even the Agricultural Holdings Act of 1875, though it indirectly
discouraged mere verbal agreements and honourable
understandings, did not, like the Irish Land Act, offer
any premium to landlords for granting leases, and does
not seem to have produced any appreciable effect in
promoting their adoption.

This Act, which has been said to mark a new
point of departure in English agriculture, is really
little more than a statutory recognition of tenant-
right, already established in many parts of the
country, and closely bound up with the system of
yearly tenancy.   It, in fact, presupposes the general
prevalence of that system, and proceeds to lay down

---

[1] See the article on the English Land Law in the Memoir prepared by
the Royal Agricultural Society of England for the Paris Exhibition of
1878. See also the Appendix to Mr. B. Samuelson's speech on the Agricultural Holdings Act (March 25, 1879), printed by Cassell, Petter, &
Galpin. From the evidence there given, it would appear that leases do not
prevail widely in one-fourth of the English counties.

rules which, under a system of leasehold tenure, would
be for the most part superfluous. It divides improvements made by tenants into three classes, assigning
to each a distinct standard of compensation. Drainage
and other permanent improvements of the first class
are presumed to continue for a maximum period of
twenty years. For such improvements an outgoing
tenant, if he be fortunate enough to hold under an
absolute owner, is entitled to compensation upon the
basis of their cost price *minus* a proportionate deduction for each year already expired since the improvement was made. But he must always have obtained
beforehand the written consent of the landlord or his
agent, and the landlord may always limit the sum to
be spent or the period over which compensation may
be claimed, and the amount of compensation will, after
all, be dependent not merely on the efflux of time, but
also on the unexhausted value of the improvement, as
ascertained by valuers. Moreover, as we have already
seen, the compensation to be paid by a limited owner
will depend, further, on the degree in which the letting
value of the holding shall have been increased by the
improvement. Chalking, liming, and other durable
improvements of the second class are presumed to continue for a maximum period of seven years, subject
to like conditions with improvements of the first class.
They may be made, however, without the previous
written consent of the landlord ; but, on the other
hand, notice must be given to the landlord, who may
inspect the work, and dispute the claim to compensation for any sum not proved to have been " properly
laid out." The application of purchased manures and

other temporary improvements are presumed to continue for two years, subject to special conditions of a technical character, and the amount of compensation will not exceed such proportion of the sum "properly laid out" by the outgoing tenant as "fairly represents" the value of the improvement to an incoming tenant.   In all cases of improvements, the landlord is entitled to make a counter claim for rates, taxes, and tithe rent-charge, for rent, for allowances made in consideration of the improvement, for waste, or for breach of covenant.

A like principle governs the clauses of the Act relating to "fixtures," the sole property in which had formerly been vested in the landlord by the old rule of *Quicquid plantatur solo, solo cedit.*   This maxim was established by the Statute of Gloucester in the sixth year of Edward I., and has ever since had a grievous effect in discouraging tenants' improvements.   Engines, machinery, and some other fixtures erected by an outgoing tenant, may now in general be removed by him, after one month's previous notice to the landlord, to whom is reserved the right of purchasing them, and subject to his claim for rent, as well to an obligation of making good any damage caused by the removal. But, whereas other engines may be put up without the landlord's consent, steam-engines are expressly excluded from this provision, and the landlord's objection will bar the tenant's right to remove such engines under the Act.   Nor does the Act go so far as to reverse the old maxim in the tenant's favour.   A barn erected by a tenant would still belong, in law, to his landlord; fruit-trees planted by a tenant could neither be transplanted nor cut down without express permission; and the broad recognition of tenant-right in fixtures introduced into the Irish Land Act has been studiously excluded.

It would be absurd to regard a statute guarded by so many exceptions and limitations as calculated to work a revolution in the English land-system, even had its operation been compulsory. But its operation, as is well known, is strictly permissive. Not only may a landlord and tenant "contract themselves out of it" by entering into a special agreement providing for the same objects, but it may be set aside by a mere stroke of the pen in any agreement, however contrary to its spirit. The consequence is that, with a very few exceptions, the whole body of English landlords have negatived its application to their own estates, both in respect of pre-existing tenancies and in respect of tenancies afterwards created.[1] So far, it is almost a dead letter; but there is reason to believe that its principles, if not its express terms of compensation, have been imported into many agreements between landlord and tenant, while the salutary clause substituting twelve months' for six months' notice to quit has been very widely adopted. Indirectly, therefore, it may be said to have exercised a considerable influence on agricultural relations, and to have supplied a statutory definition of tenant-right which may gradually mature itself into an universal custom of which

---

[1] See the abstract of answers returned to circulars issued by the Farmer's Club, in the article on the English Land Law, "Journal of the Royal Agricultural Society," 1878. See also the Appendix to Mr. Samuelson's speech on the Agricultural Holdings' Act, March 25th, 1879.

courts of law must take cognizance.   In the meantime, it cannot be regarded as a step towards a restoration of leasehold tenure in English agriculture, but
rather as an expedient for stereotyping, in a more
liberal form, the unstable system of yearly tenancy.

CHAPTER V.

Dependent Condition of Agricultural Labourers.

THE Poor Law of Elizabeth may be regarded as the grand turning-point in the history of the English peasantry, and as the proximate origin of the English agricultural labourer. In the rude times immediately before or immediately after the Norman Conquest, the actual cultivators of the soil were for the most part serfs or villeins, indeed, but still peasants, with the security, and not without the pride, of proprietorship.[1] In their personal relation to their lords they were little removed from predial bondsmen; yet they were freemen in relation to all others, occupied homesteads of their own, and enjoyed imperfect rights of property which ultimately elevated many of their descendants into copyholders. The class of free labourers which gradually succeeded them possessed greater independence with less fixity of tenure, working for hire

---

[1] Professor Thorold Rogers, in an article on the History of Rent in England (*Contemporary Review*, April, 1880), thus states the result of his researches into original documents of the mediæval period:—"I have never seen any single instance, even in the earliest times, of the slave proper—*i.e.*, of a person whose services could be demanded at the pleasure of his owner, and who received a bare subsistence as the equivalent of his labour." He points out that a serf could not be ejected from his land, except by the judgment of the manor-court, in which the freeholders sat as jurymen. He elsewhere states that, in studying many thousands of mediæval accounts, he never found any evidence of villeins, or even of their services, being transferred to third parties.

instead of rendering forced services, and holding their little plots of land at will, instead of by a customary title, when they were not, as they often were, boarded and lodged by their employers. The steady rise of wages originally caused by the Black Death was hardly checked by the various Statutes of Labourers; and the Peasant Revolt, though quenched for the moment in blood, ushered in a century of prosperity for the masses in country districts, only terminated by the pasturage-enclosures of the Tudor period. The growth of a large export trade in wool, the revolution in rural life which followed on the demolition of feudal castles, the encroachments of commercial upon patriarchal land-lordism, the final suppression of monasteries, the contraction of common rights over woods and wastes, and the sudden rise of prices in the middle of the sixteenth century, produced or fostered that destitution and vagrancy which a long series of cruel enactments inevitably failed to extinguish. This failure, at last recognised by the Legislature, had prepared the way, by the end of the sixteenth century, for the Poor Law of Elizabeth, passed in 1601. Another cause, hitherto little recognised, contributed to strengthen the necessity for such legislation. However ineffective may have been the earlier statutes fixing a maximum rate of wages, that of Elizabeth, placing the regulation of wages in the hands of the justices, seems to have been stringently carried out, thus artificially restricting the wage-fund out of which the whole body of labourers had to be maintained. By mitigating the consequences, otherwise intolerable, of this restriction, the first Poor Law was an indirect method of cheapening labour, and its operation in keeping down the rate of agricultural wages has been sensibly felt ever since.[1]

Compared with the older Statutes of Labourers, however, it was a humane and even statesmanlike enactment. The extreme severity which had prevented the execution of those laws was now wisely avoided; it was provided that able-bodied paupers should be set to work, and the impotent properly relieved; while a parochial assessment of all inhabitants was substituted for the precarious humanity of relations and the voluntary alms of religious houses or charitable neighbours. Power was also given to erect houses for the poor on waste lands, and this power was extended to parochial town lands by a later statute of Charles II. Whatever may be the defects of the first Poor Law from an economical point of view, it had certainly more effect in restoring order than scourging or branding sturdy beggars, and all the other penalties of earlier legislation. We hear no more of bands of lawless men, who defied the inefficient constabulary of those days, and who formed the nucleus of every local rebellion. Robbers were no longer hung up by the score, and life in the country was comparatively secure, notwithstanding the survival of highwaymen on the great roads up to a much later age. Since unemployed labourers were now entitled to fall back on the rates in the last resort, it became the interest of all ratepayers to find work for those willing to serve; and the same object was promoted by the law which restricted monastic lands

---

[1] The Statute of Elizabeth, requiring four acres of land to be attached to each new cottage, may be regarded as another attempt to mitigate the consequences resulting from an effective regulation of wages.

from being turned into pasture by their new proprietors.

As a measure of police, therefore, and as a means of
organising a regular system of agricultural labour, the
first Poor Law was highly successful. At the same
time it was this law, with the disastrous amendments
engrafted upon it, which accustomed the peasantry of
England, no longer worthy of the name, to rely for
their support entirely upon daily wages, supplemented
by public relief in old age or times of scarcity ; rendering it easy to live without the possession of land, and
utterly extinguishing the very desire of acquiring property. The pauperising effects of this important
change did not make themselves seriously felt until
nearly two centuries later. Population increased very
slowly under the Stuart dynasty, and, notwithstanding
the depreciation of silver, the experiment was conducted
under very favourable conditions. Improvements in
the manufacture of linen and woollen cloth enabled a
labourer to clothe himself better and more cheaply than
at any former period. The development of trade, carefully excluded from Ireland and the colonies, opened a
vast amount of industrial employment in manufacturing
towns, while the more enterprising members of the
working classes were learning to better themselves by
emigration to America. It was not until the last forty
years of the eighteenth century that the home demand
for labour was overtaken by the supply, or that the
burden of poor-relief began to press heavily on the
ratepayers. Malthus estimated that, in 1720, the
wages of a labourer commanded more than at any
previous or subsequent time ; but from that date until

1770 they continued to rise in nominal amount, if not in purchasing power.[1] In the Report of a recent Commission, the advantages of his position during that period are forcibly summed up:—" Previous to 1775, the agricultural labourer was in a most prosperous condition. His wages gave him a great command over the necessaries of life: his rent was lower, his wearing apparel cheaper, his shoes cheaper, his living cheaper, than formerly; and he had on the common and wastes liberty of cutting furze for fuel, with the chance of getting a little land, and, in time, a small farm."[2]

But if the lot of agricultural labourers in the eighteenth century was in many respects enviable, their social habits and their standard of civilisation were deplorably low. The Legislature, which showed a sort of barbaric generosity in its treatment of questions affecting the physical comfort of the masses, did not even attempt to diffuse education among them. Accordingly, agricultural labourers were then sunk in an ignorance hardly to be equalled by that of the French peasants groaning under the corvées—an ignorance extending to the simplest rules of decency, cleanliness, and the nurture

---

[1] Arthur Young estimated the average wages of labourers in the seventeenth century at 10¼d. a day, and for the first sixty-six years of the eighteenth century at 1s. a day. The last occasion on which the justices seem to have fixed wages under the old statutes was in 1725, when the magistrates of Lancashire established a scale, under which a labourer working by the week was to receive from 9d. to 1s. a day, without meat and drink. The average price of wheat for that year in Windsor market was 43s. per quarter, whence Sir George Nicholl infers that Malthus' estimate of the agricultural labourer's condition at that period was too favourable. ("History of the English Poor Law," Vol. II., chap. xi.) But the value of a labourer's wages is not to be measured by the price of bread alone.

[2] First Report of the Women and Children's Employment Commission (1868), paragraph 251.

of children. The mortality of English labourers' children in the last century is known to have been enormous, as it continued to be in Scotland until a very recent period, and in both cases the overcrowding of cottages was doubtless one of its principal causes. The hard-drinking squires who then ruled the country villages naturally despised and discouraged a book-learning in which they were themselves too often deficient; the clergy were generally retainers of the squire, and far less alive to their responsibilities than in the present day; neither philanthropists nor educationists had yet arisen to study the condition of the people; the Press was almost silent on such topics; and Parliament regarded them as matters of local concern. There was, therefore, no quarter from which a higher civilisation might proceed, and village-life in England was probably little more refined than it had been in the Middle Ages. In the meantime the stringency of the Poor Law was gradually becoming relaxed. Though a high average rate of wages prevailed, it did not rise, as it naturally should, with the price of provisions, and in bad years the labourer found it hard to support his family. On such occasions the magistrates forbore to enforce the Poor Law strictly, and gave a premium to idleness and improvidence by making labourers allowances out of the poor rate in proportion to the size of their families. This practice, which is said to have begun about 1763, especially in the metropolitan districts, shortly bore the fruit that might have been expected. The population increased by 2,000,000 between 1760 and 1800,[1] and before 1782 the number

---

[1] Arthur Young estimated it at 9,000,000 in 1771, but this estimate was certainly too high, since it had only reached 9,172,931 in 1800.

of able-bodied paupers had become so large that it was thought necessary to provide afresh for their employment. By Gilbert's Act of that year, under which Poor Law Unions and guardians of the poor were first established, the wasteful and demoralising system of out-door relief was directly sanctioned. Hitherto the workhouse-test, introduced in 1723, had operated as a powerful check upon pauperism, and the labour exacted in return for maintenance had been irksome enough to be more or less deterrent. It was now enacted that guardians should find work for applicants near their own homes, and might eke out insufficient wages by money payments out of the rates. The spirit of independence was thus effectually sapped among English labourers, and the least respectable of them, relieved of the necessity to procure and keep work by good conduct, were virtually guaranteed short intervals of debauchery between spells of enforced labour.

The consequence of this short-sighted policy fell heavily on the farmers, who, however, were only too willing parties to it—failing to see that, in the end, the competition of the parish must be ruinous to individual employers, unless the parish be made the harder taskmaster and worse paymaster of the two. This is exactly what Gilbert's Act omitted to secure, and the evil which it engendered propagated itself, under various forms, in various parts of the country. In the decade between 1785 and 1795 we find traces of a system, long since forgotten, under which labourers out of work were hired out, as it were, under the name of " roundsmen," to one farmer after another, who gave sixpence a day

in wages, besides victuals, while the parish added a
subsidy of fourpence.[1] In the following year (1786)
Pitt delivered a remarkable speech against the abuses
of the old Poor Law, showing a comprehensive grasp of
the whole question far in advance of the opinions then
current; but the bill which he soon afterwards introduced was conceived in a less enlightened spirit, and
failed to effect its object. The poor-rates, which are
not supposed to have exceeded £1,000,000 at the beginning of the eighteenth century, had risen to upwards
of £2,000,000 at the end of the American War, and to
upwards of £4,000,000 in 1801. By the census of that
year, the population of England and Wales was ascertained to be 9,172,980, and the price of corn, which
had reached 134s. per quarter in the previous June,
mounted up to 156s. 2d. in the spring of 1801,
though it fell to 75s. 6d. by the end of the year.[2] Still
the disease continued to be aggravated by remedies
unskilfully applied. Three-quarters of a century had
elapsed since wages had been regularly fixed by justices
of the peace, but the magistrates of Berkshire and some
other southern counties now issued tables defining the
normal rate of wages, according to a sliding scale varying with the size of a labourer's family, and the price
of bread. They further directed the parish officers,
where the wages should fall short of this standard, to
make up the deficit out of the rates.[3] At last, in 1815,

----

[1] Sir G. Nicholl's "History of the Poor Law," Vol. II., p. 123.

[2] Nicholl's "History of the Poor Law," Vol. II., p. 135. The
average gazette price of wheat, in 1800, was 113s. 10d., and, in 1801,
119s. 6d.

[3] McCulloch's Essay on the Poor Laws. Note XXII. to his edition of
"The Wealth of Nations."

justices of the peace were expressly empowered by the Legislature to give out-door relief, even to able-bodied paupers, not merely during a time of temporary destitution, but for a period varying from three to nine months.

A less demoralising, but still mischievous, form of parish relief was introduced by the institution of parochial farms. In the year 1817, Sturges Bourne's Committee reported in favour of this plan for giving employment to labourers out of work, and the Select Vestry Act (59 George III., cap. 12) regulated its adoption. By sect. 12 of that Act, churchwardens and overseers were authorised, with the consent of the vestry, to purchase or hire, on account of the parish, "any suitable portion or portions of land, within or near to such parish, not exceeding twenty acres on the whole," and to employ thereupon, at reasonable wages, any person who might be set to work, under the poor laws. By a later statute (1 and 2 Wm. IV., cap. 42) this power was extended to purchasing, hiring, or enclosing, out of common land, as much as fifty acres for the same purpose. The discretion thus given was largely used, and parochial farms became common in most parts of England, being treated, like the public works during the Irish famine, as a convenient refuge for the destitute in the winter months. The practice, however, was condemned by the Poor Law Inquiry Commissioners a year or two later, and has since fallen into general disuse.[1]

It was the crushing weight of poor rates resulting

[1] See "Nicholl's "History of the Poor Laws," Vol. II., pp. 186 and 216–7.

from this ruinous policy, coupled with the violent
fluctuations of price resulting from the Corn Laws,
which depressed agriculture during the half century
preceding the Poor Law Amendment Act of 1834.
No wonder that at this period the small farmer is said
to have "lived harder, worked longer, and fared worse"
than the labourers in his employ. The condition of
these would, indeed, have been comparatively prosperous but for their unduly rapid multiplication. The
researches of Arthur Young disclose much less striking
variations in the standard of wages than in that of
rents. Possibly the levelling effect of poor-law allowances may have contributed, with other causes, to
maintain a tolerably uniform rate of wages in all parts
of the kingdom, although considerable variations in
the mode of payment were established by local custom.
In 1780 it would probably have been impossible to find
cases, such as Mr. Caird noted in 1850, in which the
wages paid by Northern farmers were double those
paid by Southern farmers for the same hours of work;
but the amount of work expected of the labourer differed greatly in different localities. Thus, in Dorsetshire, less than one shilling a day was paid for about
six hours' work indifferently performed ; while, in the
North, labourers earned nine shillings a week by working about eight hours a day. In 1796 the Dorsetshire
wages had so far advanced, that Sir Francis Eden
quotes them as ranging about 8s. a week, and fifty
years later Mr. Caird found exactly the same rate still
prevailing.[1] As a general rule, the highest wages, as

[1] See Mr. Little's Treatise on "The Agricultural Labourer," in the
Journal of the Royal Agricultural Society for 1878.

well as the highest rents, seem to have been paid upon
the best lands; perhaps because the worst lands had
usually been on the verge of the waste, and the wages
there paid had originally been supplemented by common-
rights now extinguished in the process of enclosure.
The average rate in Arthur Young's time may be taken
at 7s. or 8s. a week, and this, with extra wages at
harvest time, he considered to be ample for the support
of a family, with bread at 2d. a pound, butter at 6½d.,
cheese at 3½d., and meat at 4d.[1] In reviewing these
prices, he significantly remarks that "if bread were to
be 6d. a pound, meat 1s., and cheese 9d., labour must
rise greatly, or the poor starve ; *but cases which can have
no existence ought not to occasion such arguments.*" Yet in
some parts of the country, and notably in Wiltshire,
prices were much higher in 1850 than in 1770, while
the rate of wages had actually receded. It is no less
curious to study, by the light of modern experience,
his comment on the fact that, within a radius of fifty
miles round London, wages averaged almost 9s. a week.
" The vast population of London and its neighbourhood
ought to lower the price of labour, and, did not the
debauched life of its inhabitants occasion them to be
more idle than in the country, it would have that
effect."

The Poor Law Amendment Act of 1834 was among
the greatest achievements of the reformed Parliament,
and, though irregularly carried out, has worked a gradual improvement in the character and prospects of the

---

[1] Adam Smith remarks that in almost every part of Great Britain one
pound of the best butchers' meat costs somewhat more than two pounds of
the best white bread.

agricultural labourer. The startling rise of poor rates
until they reached a total of between £8,000,000 and
£9,000,000,[1] the gross abuses of out-door relief in aid
of wages, the notorious prevalence of jobbery in the
management of poor-houses, and the entire lack of
uniformity in Poor Law administration for want of
guidance from a central office, had been forced upon
public attention by the report of the Poor Law Inquiry
Commission, until the conscience of the nation was
thoroughly roused. It was at last realised how utterly
the virtues of prudence, thrift, and self-respect had been
undermined among the labouring classes by indiscriminate relief. In some cases rent had actually been
paid by the parish ; in others, the whole rateable income
of the parish was absorbed in grants of " bread money "
to half-paid labourers, or in pensions to sturdy vaga-
bonds, as they would have been called in earlier days,
who never worked at all. It was proved that during
the year 1832, out of £7,000,000 collected for poor

---

[1] This was in 1830. The following Table, abridged from that given in
Nicholl's " History of the Poor Law," Vol. II., p. 303, shows the pressure
of poor rates, relatively to population and the price of wheat, at various
epochs within a period of forty years :—

Estimated Population.	Years ending Lady Day.	Price of Wheat.	Amount Expended on Relief and Maintenance of Poor.	Rate per Head of Population.
10,505,800	1813	108/9	£6,656,106	12/8
11,876,200	1818	84/1	7,870,801	13/3
12,517,900	1824	62/-	5,736,900	9/2
14,105,600	1832	63/4	7,036,969	10/-
14,372,000	1834	51/11	6,317,255	8/9½
17,504,000	1848	64/6	6,180,765	7/1¾
17,928,000	1852	39/4	4,897,685	5/5½

The prices here given differ considerably from the " Average Gazette Prices " given in
Appendix V.

rates, only about £350,000, or one-twentieth, was paid
for actual work performed.   Yet so uneven was the
distribution of this wholesale relief, that paupers might
be pampered in one parish and harshly stinted in the
next.   For instance, it was found that in ninety-three
parishes, with a population of 113,000, the expenditure
was at the rate of 14s. 5d. a head; whereas in eighty
neighbouring parishes, with nearly the same population, the expenditure was at the rate of only 5s. 9d.
a head.   Nevertheless, the law of " settlement," though
denounced by Pitt, continued to prohibit migration
from parish to parish.

The new Poor Law re-organised the entire administrative machinery on a sound footing, and gave the
central Board a power of checking out-door relief, which,
on the whole, has been wisely and firmly exercised.
Thenceforward, wages ceased to be paid in part out of
the rates; each labourer depended for his earnings on
his own industry; pauper-marriages, and even bastardy,
were no longer encouraged by parochial authority;
crime was sensibly diminished; and the impotent poor
were in every respect the gainers.   But it was impossible for any administrative reform to provide adequately
for the surplus population which the old system had
brought into the world.   Every influence had been
recklessly employed to stimulate improvident marriages,
and to place the childless labourer at a disadvantage as
compared with the father of a family.   After the first
two children, the sum of half-a-crown, or one-third of a
labourer's whole earnings, was allowed for each additional child, with a further allowance during pregnancy.
A labourer marrying at eighteen might thus find him-

self at twenty-three with his income doubled, and, being comparatively independent of wages, might shift from one employment to another out of pure caprice. The single labourer, though forced to subsist on his own earnings, was liable to be dismissed in favour of a married neighbour, whose family might otherwise become "chargeable." All these superfluous hands were now thrown upon the open labour-market, and the agricultural interest profited directly by the change. For the first time, farms were now worked up to something like their full value, with an unlimited supply of cheap labour. Not merely was the rate of wages for able-bodied labourers fully one-third lower than at present, but half the work of a farm was then done by those whose labour could be had for little more than the bare cost of their subsistence. As compulsory education was then unknown, boys could be obtained in any number for 2s. 6d. or 3s. a week, with a dinner, the amount of work performed by them varying more or less with the quality of their food. Indoor servants in farm-houses at the same period were content with £3 or £4 a year and their board. It appears from the books of a Norfolk farmer, whose experience extends over nearly half a century, that, for some years after 1835, he employed a dairymaid, housemaid, and groom, at money-wages amounting altogether to no more than £10 yearly. In several other respects the expenses of a farmer were then singularly low. Cart-horses, in particular, were so cheap, that in many districts £100 would buy two serviceable teams.[1]

---

[1] Arthur Young, in reckoning up the expenses of stocking a farm of sixteen acres, assumes that two horses might be bought for £16.

Yet the complaints of agricultural distress so constantly renewed between the Poor Law Amendment Act and the repeal of the Corn Laws, proceeded from the farmers, and not from the labourers, whose interests, it must be confessed, were little regarded by the Legislature. Probably their condition had never been so low, relatively to other classes and the general progress of civilisation, since the close of the Middle Ages. The old Poor Law, concurring with other causes, had crushed out within them all the instincts of property and of home, attaching them indeed to the soil, but giving them no interest in it, and offering them, in lieu thereof, a claim to parish doles, with a final refuge in the workhouse—a fit asylum for worn-out slaves.[1] The new Poor Law emancipated them, it is true, from a servile reliance on out-door relief, but it could not restore their manhood or elevate them once more into free peasantry. Having once "got off the rates," the most vigorous and intelligent of the rural labourers soon became eager to "get off the land," either by migrating into the manufacturing districts, or by emigrating to America and Australia. Those who remained behind were, for the most part, men of inferior physique or energy, and it is certain that, notwithstanding the improvement of his diet and lodging, the agricultural labourer of the present day is too often a degenerate specimen of his ancestral type.

The growing scarcity of agricultural làbour after the repeal of the Corn Laws, and the extension of the

---

[1] See an article on "Pauperism and Territorialism," by the Rev. F. Barham Zincke, in the *Fortnightly Review* of June, 1879.

railway system, naturally produced a rise of wages.
We have seen that in the North, where agriculture had long competed with manufactures, and the
labourers were virtually a picked class, the rate of
wages had already been almost doubled between 1790
and 1850. In the South, where it had scarcely risen
at all on the average during that period, it rose
about 2s. a week between 1850 and 1870—seldom,
however, exceeding 12s. or 13s. Such a disparity, in
days when locomotion was easy and knowledge widely
diffused, is an economical paradox which needs some
explanation. In the first place, it must be remembered
that good labourers in the southern counties were
always able to increase their ordinary earnings very
largely by harvest wages and piecework. Some very
interesting statistics on this subject were recently published by the Royal Agricultural Society,[1] from which
it appears that on a farm in the east of England nearly
£30 was earned by one family, consisting of six persons
(four below seventeen years of age), in the five harvest
weeks of 1877. These earnings were realised by reaping
and tying, carting, thatching, gleaning, and so forth, in
spite, or rather in consequence, of the use of machinery.
The same family was found to have earned above £97
in the year, though only the father and one boy of
fourteen were constantly at work. In the second place,
it must not be forgotten that, as low wages had long
been supplemented by parish allowances, so they have
since been often supplemented by a variety of perquisites and privileges which, in the aggregate, amount to

[1] See Mr. Little's Treatise on "The Agricultural Labourer" in the
Journal of the Royal Agricultural Society for 1878.

a considerable sum. A man who pays but a shilling a week for a cottage, with a garden of half an acre, may be really better off, with twelve shillings a week. than his fellow whose actual wages are four shillings higher, but who pays a full rent of three or four shillings for a cottage without land. Many a labourer, too, gets an allowance of cider, or presents of firewood, or "the grass of a cow," or the free use of potato-ground ready ploughed and manured, over and above his regular wages, as part of an unwritten agreement between him and his employer. Where the highest wages are paid, such indulgences are, of course, less common. Labourers' cottages are built to pay; the roadside strip on which a stray cow or pig might feed is carefully enclosed, and fields are cut too close for the encroachment of a cottage-garden. Moreover, what may be called "outside" wages are paid only during a labourer's best years. If he fall sick, he must recover speedily, on pain of losing his place; when he grows old, he must fall back upon savings or the bounty of relations, or, in the last resort, upon the workhouse. The kindly attempts of an old-world farmer to find employment for decrepit or incompetent labourers cannot be imitated, if they are not ridiculed, by men cultivating 800 acres, at a rent of 45s. an acre, and paying wages of 18s. or 20s. a week. Nor must it be concealed that a stricter administration of the Poor Law has inevitably impaired, in some degree, the domestic relations of the labourer. The system of out-door relief, with all its abuses, had the advantage of maintaining the concentration of a family round its head up to the very last. The present system, coupled with the more general scattering of families in search of work, has perhaps diminished the aged labourer's enjoyment of life. A man past work, living upon the surplus earnings of his children, is too apt to be treated as a burden; and, if he is driven to enter the workhouse, he may too pro-bably be left to die without the consolations of family affection. In fact, the very provision which compels a pauper's family to contribute towards his maintenance affords a pretext for withholding all other proofs of family interest, and is often treated as a discharge in full of all filial obligations.

It was not to be expected that education, facility of transit, and other influences resulting from the great social movement of our age, should fail to disturb the simplicity of the old semi-feudal association between farmers and labourers. But these influences doubtless received a powerful impulse from the formation of the Agricultural Labourers' Union in 1871—four years after householders in country villages had been deli-berately excluded from the franchise conferred on house-holders in towns, solely because their political education was not considered to be sufficiently advanced. Since that period, strikes and lock-outs have ceased to be unknown evils in agricultural districts, and wages have been raised by one or two shillings a week in most parts of the country.[1] On the other hand, labour-saving machines have been largely introduced, and greater efforts have been made by farmers to reduce the number

[1] Professor Rogers estimates that the money-wages of agricultural labourers may have risen about forty per cent. in the last forty years. Mr. Caird, writing in 1850, estimated the rise in money-wages since Arthur Young's time to have been no more than fourteen per cent. Probably the purchasing power of a given sum paid in wages is on the whole as great as

of their labourers to a minimum. The average rate of wages for common day-labourers was stated in the *Journal of the Royal Agricultural Society* for 1878 to vary from about 13s. in the South, to 18s. in the North-east, and even 20s. or 21s. in the extreme North.[1] Such differences in the price of labour correspond nearly to differences in its efficiency. It is well known that a given quantity of agricultural piecework costs about the same in the North as in the South, though it may require more labourers to do it in Hampshire than in Northumberland. It is also well known that labourers assisted to migrate northwards in quest of higher wages have frequently been compelled to return from inability to give the day's work required to earn those wages. But violent fluctuations in the rate of wages paid in

---

it was forty years ago. The rent of cottages, as well as the price of fresh meat and butter, has doubtless increased, but, on the other hand, the price of bread, cheese, bacon, and clothing has been considerably reduced, especially within the last few years.

[1] In some parts of the Scottish Lowlands wages have been doubled within the last thirty years. Mr. Bailey Denton, writing in 1869, esti-mated the mean nominal money-wages of able-bodied men throughout England at 12s. 6d. a week, and the mean time-wages at nearly £1 a week for the whole year. The difference he considers to be made up by the extra earnings of hay and corn harvest, allowances of beer and cider, profits of occasional piecework, and value of cottages and gardens above the rent paid for them. This rent is seldom regulated by the law of supply and demand, or by the ordinary rate of interest on capital, except where cot-tages are built by speculators. In some counties, and in many parishes, it is as high as 4s. a week, or above £10 a year. In others, it is as low as 1s. a week, or £2 12s. a year. On Lord Tollemache's estates, in Cheshire and Suffolk, the rent of each cottage, with three bedrooms, and a small flower-garden, is £3 10s. a year; and this may be taken as a fair specimen of the rent charged by very benevolent landlords. As such cottages now cost £150 to build, a rent of £3 10s. certainly does not represent above half their real value.

the same part of the country, or under like conditions, are no longer possible, and a fall of 2s. or 3s. a week could not occur in one county, if the demand for labour remained steady in another.

If we exclude from view his absolute dependence on a landlord and an employer, the present lot of an English agricultural labourer is by no means an unattractive one.   Bred in a cottage which, humble as it is, might well excite the envy of a town artisan, he is protected by the Legislature against premature labour on the farm, and gets his schooling for a fraction of the cost price at the joint expense of taxpayers and ratepayers, or perhaps voluntary subscribers.   During boyhood, he easily finds leisure for the manly amusements which his class—happily for England—shares freely with the gentry.[1]   As a young farm-labourer, he can have no difficulty in living within his income, either under his parent's roof or in lodgings, which he can procure for less than 2s. a week.   In some parishes the excellent practice of attaching sleeping accommodation to the village-club enables unattached labourers to live decently and cheaply without being driven by sheer discomfort into early marriage.   If he will delay this step for some five or six years after he begins to earn man's wages, he ought to have a small deposit in the savings' bank, and may yet save more

---

[1] The English day-labourer enjoys a great advantage over those of some other countries, in drawing wages regularly for six working days in the week, instead of having his work interrupted and his wages suspended by the irregular occurrence of holidays. This was noticed, three centuries ago, as one reason why Protestant farms prospered better than Roman Catholic farms in Ireland.

against the period of heaviest strain. This will come upon him if he should have three or four children of school age at the same time, with others too young for school—neither his wife nor any member of his family being able to supplement his earnings. Soon after passing this stage, a good labourer will probably have attained promotion from the lowest agricultural ranks. As a shepherd, a herdsman, a carter, or a foreman superintending the work of others, he may be occupying a cottage and garden rent-free, with some extra allowances, even if he cannot aspire to fill the higher post of farm-bailiff. The butcher's cart will now be seen oftener at his door, while he will be planting out his children in some business which, though it may bring in little at first, will enable them to rise in the world. With good health, a good character, and moderately good fortune, he may hope to retain his place up to an advanced age, and to become dependent on his club or the contributions of his children for a very few years only. Such a career and such prospects may excite the compassion of those who imagine that every man is capable of winning a prize in life, but they do not compare unfavourably with the lot of other industrial classes, at home or abroad, so far as physical comfort is concerned. The clever artisan has a better chance of raising himself by his skill, and ultimately becoming a capitalist, but he pays a heavy price for it in health and in the quiet enjoyment of existence. The French peasant-farmer has more self-respect and independence, but his life is one of unceasing toil and anxiety; he is liable to conscription in youth, he is heavily taxed, and his ambition, no less than his ideas, is generally confined within the bounds of his own commune or arrondissement. The English agricultural labourer has much to learn from the one in culture and intelligence, as well as from the other in thrift and courtesy; but it may well be doubted whether he is not, in his own way, a happier being than either.[1]

Still, the fact remains that he scarcely ever becomes the owner of land, and seldom rents enough to call forth his full energies, or to serve as a stepping-stone from the occupation of a cottage to the occupation of a farm. The want of such a link between the two working orders of the agricultural community has long been recognised as a radical defect in our rural economy. In many parishes, an useful but very inadequate substitute for it has been provided by the allotment system, the extension of which has been constantly recommended by Parliamentary Committees, and even encouraged by the Legislature, within the last hundred years. As early as 1795, a Select Committee of the House of Commons took evidence on the subject, and reported very favourably of the system. It was shown that, in 1770, the lord of a manor near Tewkesbury, remarking the exceptionally good character of families holding plots of reclaimed land, set apart some twenty-five acres for cottagers' allotments, and had the satisfaction of seeing the poor-rates reduced in two years to fourpence in the pound, while they stood at 2s. 6d. in the surrounding parishes. The Select Vestry Act of 1819, which authorised the institution of parish farms, also encouraged the formation of

---

[1] The Essay of Mr. Little, already cited above, contains an admirable and graphic picture of the early life, daily work, recreation, and last years, of a typical agricultural labourer in the midland or southern counties.

parish allotments. By section 13, the churchwardens and overseers were empowered, "for the promotion of industry among the poor," to let any portion of parish land "to any poor or industrious inhabitant of the parish," to be cultivated by him, on his own account, at a reasonable rent, and for a term to be fixed by the vestry. The later Act of 1 and 2 William IV., cap. 42, enabled the parish authorities to hire, purchase, or enclose out of common land as much as fifty acres for poor-allotments, in lieu of a parochial farm, if they should think proper; and another Act of the same year (1 & 2 William IV., cap. 59) facilitated the enclosure of Crown land for the same purpose. An Act of the following year (2 William IV., cap. 42) provided for the letting of allotments in parishes enclosed under Acts of Parliament, and the application of the rents to a distribution of fuel among the poor.[1] It does not appear how far these powers were exercised by the parish authorities; but occasional experiments of the same kind were tried by individual proprietors, with marked success, in the dark age preceding the Poor Law Amendment Act. In one instance, cited in the First Report of the Women and Children's Employment Commission,[2] the largest occupier in a parish of 650 inhabitants had been driven to give up his farm by the pressure of rates amounting to nearly sixteen shillings in the pound. A considerable part of it was then let out to labourers, in parcels varying from one to five or even ten acres, and this division was followed by a very sensible reduction

[1] Nicholl's "History of the English Poor Law," Vol. II.
[2] Page 141.

of rates, which, however, was partly attributable to other causes. Meanwhile, the Board of Agriculture, so prematurely dissolved, had offered a medal for the best cottages with a plot of land attached to each sufficient to maintain a cow and a hog. The utility of such allotments was, again, emphatically recognised by a Select Committee of the House of Commons in 1843. In the report of this Committee it was urged that "the tenancy of land under the garden allotment system is a powerful means of bettering the condition of those classes who depend for their livelihood on manual labour, and the benefits are obtained without corresponding disadvantages."

Notwithstanding all this weight of testimony in favour of allotments, the Women and Children's Employment Commission of 1868 found that a very sparing use had been made of the facilities granted by the Legislature, and that only 2,119 acres out of more than 7,000,000 enclosed since 1760 were believed to have been thus appropriated.[1] Of course, a very much larger area is covered by cottage-gardens or other allotments, held of individual landlords, or, not unfrequently, carved out of glebe-land by parochial incumbents. Still, the Commissioners felt themselves bound to advocate a more general adoption of the system, and to lay down the main conditions of its success, as tested by experience. One of these was, in their opinion, that no allotment should be too large for a man to cultivate with his family in spare hours, so that labourers should not become "catch-

---

[1] First Report, paragraph 196.

men." If the allotment was near home, they considered half an acre to be a proper limit. But, even where the allotment was no more than a quarter of an acre, its value was estimated by one witness at £4 a year on bad land, and £5 on good land; by another, at thirteen weeks' consumption of a large family; and by a third, at two shillings a week. Evidence was also given that allotment rents were paid with almost invariable punctuality, and that allotment-tenants would put on the land a quantity of manure, averaging from fourteen to seventeen cartloads per acre.[1] With such *data* before them, the Commissioners proceeded to indicate the amount of land which ought to be set apart for labourers' allotments. Now, the whole number of agricultural labourers, above 20, as enumerated under the Census of 1861, was 746,000. Reckoning one-fourth of these as capable of cultivating half-acre allotments, and assigning quarter-acre allotments to the remainder, they found that some 233,117 acres would be required to provide for all. Assuming, further, on the authority of competent witnesses, that allotments were actually worth £16 an acre to cottagers, over and above the ordinary farm rent, they arrived at the startling conclusion that "the total net annual value given to those 233,117 acres, in gardens and allotments would be (233,117 × 16 =) £3,729,872."[2]

[1] First Report, paragraphs 162, 188, 190-1, 200. The evidence to which the Commissioners here refer was taken before the Allotments Committee of 1843.

[2] Report, page xliii. According to the Census of 1871, there were then but 620,000 agricultural labourers above the age of 20 in England

It is now generally acknowledged that allotments of moderate extent have a beneficial effect on the character of the labourer, and this principle has lately been sanctioned by the Legislature. A special provision in the Agricultural Holdings' Act enables the landlord to resume possession of land occupied by a tenant, for the purpose of granting labourers' allotments, as well as for the erection of cottages, and other objects of public importance. Nevertheless it cannot be said that allotments are accessible to most English labourers, even at accommodation-rents; and peasant-farms of the class so common in Ireland are still extremely rare in England. The owners of a few acres who occupy a very large space in the New Domesday Book are for the most part not agricultural owners at all. They are occupants of freehold villas within reach of London or other great towns, and "their land is bestowed in lawns, in gardens, in shrubberies, in paddocks, producing nothing but perhaps a portion of the fodder required for saddle and carriage horses." [1] The few peasant-farmers scattered among them are generally to be found in the northern counties, and are more often men who have accumulated a little capital in

and Wales. The Registrar-General states the number of allotment gardens below a quarter of an acre at 250,000, and that of allotments between a quarter of an acre and five acres at 160,000. Too much stress must not be laid on these figures, since the General Report on the Census admits the difficulty of distinguishing farm labourers from other labourers, while the difficulty of distinguishing their allotments from those of other classes must be almost insuperable. The migration of labourers from the agricultural counties is clearly shown by the census returns to have been general, and not confined to districts in which low wages prevailed.

[1] See Mr. Arthur Arnold's "Free Land," Chapter I.

business, than labourers who have saved enough out of their wages to stock and rent a farm.

Here and there, however, the experiment of graduating farms down to a size not altogether beyond the ambition of a thrifty labourer has been tried with very encouraging results. Some forty years ago a system of this kind was established on the Annandale estate, in Dumfries-shire, and continued for many years, under the care of an admirable factor, to bear remarkable fruits. Leases of twenty-one years were offered, at ordinary farm-rents, ·to deserving labourers, carefully selected for their character, who built their own cottages at a cost to themselves varying from £21 to £40, exclusive of labour, while the landlord supplied timber, stone, and so forth, at a cost of about £22. These houses were not grouped in villages, but chiefly situated along roads, with plots of from two to six acres attached to each, or the addition of grass for a cow. All the work on these little farms was done at by-hours, and by members of the family, the cottager buying roots from the farmer, and producing in return milk, butter, and pork, besides rearing calves. Among such peasant-farmers pauperism soon ceased to exist, and many of them soon bettered themselves in life. It was also particularly observed that habits of marketing, and the constant demands on thrift and forethought, brought out new virtues and powers in the wives. In fact, the moral effects of the system in fostering industry, sobriety, and contentment, were described as no less satisfactory than its economical success. On the same estate there was a regular graduation of larger farms, ranging from those of " one plough," or some sixty acres, up to holdings of £400 a year. When a farm of £100 a year fell vacant, out of eleven eligible offers for it, four came from promoted labourers.[1]

Unhappily, the deplorable failure of the cotter-system in Ireland, under wholly different conditions, has brought discredit on peasant-farming in all parts of the United Kingdom. Because a swarming population of Celtic race, and of the Roman Catholic religion, depending for their subsistence on potato-gardens, and mainly holding under middlemen, without security of tenure yet without the kindly supervision of a resident landlord, perished by thousands in the worst European famine of modern times, it has been far too hastily assumed that even the most exemplary Scotch or English labourers are unworthy of being elevated into peasant-farmers; or, if so elevated, would be unable to maintain themselves in that position. Capitalist-farmers are perhaps naturally jealous of such competition; land-agents studiously discourage a multiplication of small tenancies which might increase their own trouble; and landlords are easily persuaded that, although peasant-farmers would undertake to pay a comparatively high rent, they would be constantly behindhand, and liable to break down in bad seasons. Thus it is that a rigid division between the status of a farmer and that of a labourer has come to be a distinctive feature of

---

[1] See a remarkable article in the *North British Review*, Vol. XXXIV. (February, 1861), entitled "Large Farms and the Peasantry of the Scottish Lowlands." The result of more or less similar experiments in other parts of Great Britain shows how much depends on the selection of the peasant farmers, and on the intelligent supervision of the landlord.

English agriculture, and is defended by many English economists as if its necessity were a self-evident axiom of rural economy. In vain is it demonstrated that in the most progressive countries of Europe, in France, Germany, Holland, Belgium, Denmark, Switzerland, and Lombardy—not to speak of America and the Colonies—no such division prevails, and the great majority of agricultural labourers are occupiers of land at least, if they are not landowners. In vain is history invoked to show that England herself flourished during many ages under a wholly different agrarian constitution, or that a landless and homeless class of agricultural labourers has been the slow growth of three centuries, dating from the earliest Poor Laws. All such appeals to foreign experience or ancient custom are supposed to be silenced by the allegation that a free labourer at high wages can earn more in the year than he could make by farming without capital; that, if he were a proprietor, he might lose the whole of his savings in one or two bad seasons; that he would therefore do wisely to prefer any other form of investment; and that, after all, English agriculture is able to yield larger returns, *with fewer labourers*, from a given surface of land, than any system of husbandry conducted by peasant-farmers or peasant-owners. It is admitted, indeed, by many admirers of the English system that an opposite system might work very well if the spirit necessary to make it succeed existed among English labourers; and it is even admitted that such a spirit has actually taken root in Ireland. But they do not seem to perceive that a spirit of proprietorship can only be called forth in any class by enabling it to obtain property; and that, if English labourers no longer regarded it as hopeless to get possession of a small farm, they might possibly develop, like their fellows in other countries, the qualifications for cultivating it efficiently.

Part III.

CHAPTER I.

The Peculiar Burdens and Privileges of Landed Property in England.

THE incidence of Taxation, as affecting the agricultural interest, has long been a favourite battle-ground of political and financial controversy. It is alleged, on the one hand, that land, and especially agricultural land, has been unjustly relieved from its fair share of the national burdens by the paramount influence of the landlord party in the State; and, moreover, that if emancipated from the disabilities which now oppress the soil, it could well bear an additional charge of several millions. It is alleged, on the other hand, that landlords and farm-tenants are far more highly taxed upon their real incomes than other members of the upper and middle classes, and that charges now exclusively thrown upon land ought to be spread over other forms of property. In the discussion of such questions a remarkable confusion of thought may often be detected, and the economical issue is apt to be obscured by the introduction of perfectly irrelevant considerations. For instance, it is one thing to show that in the Middle Ages, when the possession of land was the sole foundation of civil rights as well as the grand source of wealth, the whole pressure of Imperial and local taxation rested upon land; it is another thing to show that a similar principle should be maintained in the present day, when incomes derived from personalty are sevenfold greater than incomes derived from land, and a landless capitalist may outweigh a duke in political influence. Again, it does not follow that because a past generation of landowners may have selfishly abused their power by undertaxing themselves, their sins are to be visited on their descendants in the form of excessive rates, whether or not it be for the interest of the nation at large. Equally absurd were it to personify "the land," as if it could possibly be the subject of any claims or liabilities apart from those of the persons connected with it, as owners, farmers, labourers, or otherwise; and as if a rational statesman could possibly entertain sentiments of tenderness or hostility towards Real Property in itself, as distinct from personalty, or towards agricultural land, as distinct from house property. Taxes are paid, not by property, but by persons in respect of property. If it so happened that all the members of a State derived their incomes, however unequal in amount, from land, or trade, or professional industry, or all together in equal proportions, there could be no inequality in laying taxation exclusively on one of these sources. It might be more convenient to take the money out of one pocket than out of another, but, as between classes or individuals, it could make no difference which pocket might be selected.

Nor can much light be thrown upon the best modes of adjusting taxation between various kinds of property, by proving that landowners are now contributing more or less to Imperial or local taxation than when they purchased or inherited their estates. Every man who purchases or inherits an estate takes it for better or worse, and it would be just as reasonable to mulct him of the additional value which may be imparted to it by a possible reduction of rates, as to guarantee him against a possible increase of rates. At the same time, any sudden or violent disturbance in the distribution of taxation between different classes of society would inevitably cause great hardship to individuals, as well as a general sense of insecurity; and, from this point of view, it is highly important to distinguish between taxes of old standing and those of recent origin. When land has been inherited or purchased subject to certain taxes, its owner is virtually trustee for the locality or the State of a rent-charge sufficient to satisfy this liability. When new taxes are imposed, he may fairly ask why other classes should not contribute equally with himself. Bearing these distinctions in mind, let us consider simply whether the agricultural interest is actually taxed more heavily, for Imperial or local purposes, than other sections of the community; and, if so, how far this inequality is to be justified by sound reasons of financial policy.

It is scarcely contended by those who condemn the "peculiar burdens" on landed property, that it bears, on the whole, a disproportionate share of Imperial taxation; but it is often stated, and still more often implies, that both Tithes and Land-tax form an integral part of this share. If this notion be true at all, it is true only in a sense which has no bearing on the present inquiry.

Tithes represent a reservation from the landed rental of the country made a thousand years ago for ecclesiastical purposes. Such a reservation might have been made by an equivalent allotment of land in every parish, and its character is in no degree altered by the fact of its having been made out of the produce, and not out of the soil itself. Formerly the tenant was the paymaster, and since the amount payable fluctuated year by year, he was led to imagine that tithes were an addition to his rent. Now the landlord pays tithes, in the form of a rent-charge, but they do not, therefore, come, in reality, out of the landlord's pocket, or constitute a deduction, by way of tax, from the income of the landed interest. On the contrary, tithe-owners are themselves members of the landed interest and partners with the landlords, many of them, indeed, being laymen, and holding their own lands tithe-free. If there be any grievance in respect of tithes, it is certainly not that modern landlords are too heavily charged for the benefit of the Church, but rather that, under the Act for the commutation of tithes, passed in the reign of William IV., the Church has received far less than its due. The reason of this is that, whereas a tithe was formerly a tenth of the gross produce, and far more than a tenth of the rent, in the case of arable land, it is now assessed yearly by reference to septennial averages of agricultural prices, without regard to any increase of gross produce or of rental upon the valuation fixed in 1836. " Up to that time," says Mr. Caird, " the income of the Church increased with the increased value yielded by the land, the original object, that the Church should progress in material resources in equal proportion with the land, being thus maintained. From 1836 that increment was stopped. Since that time the land rental of England has risen fifty per cent., and all that portion of the increase which, previous to 1836, would have gone to the Church, has gone to the landowners." Indeed, Mr. Caird estimates that, but for this measure, aggravated by changes in the mode of assessment, the annual income of the Church would now have been two millions greater than it is, and points out that "under the operation of a law intended simply to encourage agricultural improvement, the community, represented by the Church, are gradually losing a part of their natural inheritance."[1] Of course, this process is occasionally checked in years of agricultural depression, when tithe-rent charges, calculated on the average receipts of the preceding seven years, are high in proportion to landlords' rental; but such checks are temporary, and, unless there should be a permanent diminution in gross produce or fall in rental, the advantage will still remain with land-owners as against tithe-owners.

The case of the Land Tax obviously stands on a different footing.[2] It was originally introduced into the fiscal system of this country in lieu of the ancient "subsidies," and established as a regular source of revenue by an Act passed in 1692. Though landed property had always been the chief subject of taxation,

---

[1] Caird's "Landed Interest," chap. x.

[2] In Appendix I. will be found a Memorandum on the abolition of Feudal Tenures and the Land Tax. The substance of this memorandum has been contributed by Mr. A. C. Humphreys-Owen, of Glansevern, Montgomeryshire.

yet personalty, too, was liable to contribution under votes of "subsidies," and this liability was maintained under the first Land Tax Act, which, in fact, purported to impose a general property or income tax. It set out by laying a duty of four shillings in the pound on the assumed yearly interest of ready money and other personal estate, as well as on the salaries of offices and other profitable employments ; after which it charged landed property of all descriptions with a like duty upon its "full yearly value." The original liability of personalty, or "stock," to Land Tax is fully recognised by Adam Smith, who remarks that "if the greater part of the lands of England are not rated to the Land Tax at half their actual value, the greater part of the stock of England is, perhaps, scarce rated at the fiftieth part of its actual value." ("Wealth of Nations," Book V., chap. ii.) Personalty may or may not have been subjected under the new Land Tax to a larger proportion of the national burdens than it had theretofore borne under the old votes of subsidies, and it may or may not have been just to substitute excise duties, mostly paid by the people, for the feudal dues, entirely paid by that class of landlords who held in chivalry. But the fact that personalty was originally liable to Land Tax cannot be ignored in an historical review of the question, nor must we forget that, if land now contributes but a fractional part of the quota then assigned to it, personalty was formally exempted from the operation of the Land Tax in 1833. It would appear, indeed, from the language of the Assessments Act passed in 1697, that in that year it was the intention of the Legislature to obtain as much as possible by taxation of personalty, leaving real property to make up any deficiency in the required supply. But it is equally clear that in 1692 the Legislature intended land to be assessed, " according to the full true yearly value thereof," upon the basis of a rack-rent valuation, which of course would naturally rise with every increase of rental. This intention was notoriously defeated just as the pressure of " subsidies " had been evaded, by continuing for centuries to assess them upon a valuation made in the reign of Edward I. For a century after its first imposition, the Land Tax was renewed, by annual Acts, at various rates in the pound, " though not always without murmurs from the country gentlemen,"[1] notwithstanding that it was invariably assessed upon the original valuation. At last Mr. Pitt, in 1798, fixed it at a perpetual charge of 4s. in the pound, and gave a power of redemption, under which more than £800,000 has already been cleared off, leaving the present yield no more than £1,100,000. The landowners of the present day, therefore, pay infinitely less under this head than their predecessors in the early part of the last century; " the constancy of the valuation," as Adam Smith observed, being " advantageous to the landlord and hurtful to the sovereign." They also pay infinitely less than land-owners in most foreign countries; and what they do pay, having been practically fixed nearly two centuries ago, has long ceased to be felt as a burden, though its remission might be welcomed as an unearned bonus of nearly £30,000,000 by the landowners of England. The Land Tax, therefore, is not in the nature of an income-tax on land-

---

[1] Macaulay's " History of England," Vol. IV., chap. xix.

owners. It cannot, however, be said with strict accuracy of the Land Tax, as of Tithes, that it is not a tax upon land at all, but a mere reservation of income from land; nor should the landowners, who have escaped so lightly from this impost, be invidiously compared with owners of personal estate, who have escaped from it altogether.

The Inhabited House Duty may doubtless be regarded as a special charge on Real Property, since, in theory, it should come out of rent, and not out of the occupier's income. In fact, however, the increasing demand for house accommodation, owing to the growth of population, has been such as to raise the rent of houses far more than any house-duty or window-tax could sink them, and economists have found good reason to doubt whether, in the metropolis and other populous towns at least, the house-duty, as well as the local rates, is not really paid by the occupying tenant. It is not unworthy of remark that farm-houses are placed in the same category of "inhabited houses" with shops, and charged with a lower rate of duty.

There are very few other branches of Imperial taxation which can be supposed to press either too lightly or too heavily on Real Property in general, or on agricultural land in particular, as compared with personal estate of all kinds. No inequality is alleged to exist in respect of Stamp Duties, the receipts from which must obviously depend on the number and nature of the deeds executed. The Railway Duty, though sometimes loosely included among taxes on land, is really a tax on locomotion, and assuredly comes, in the long run, out of the pockets of passengers and shareholders, who are not usually classed with landowners. Indirect taxes on articles of consumption, whether in the form of Customs Duties or Excise Duties, affect all classes equally, and vary only with the amount of expenditure. It is otherwise with Income Tax, Probate Duty, and Succession Duty, in respect of which important dis- tinctions have been drawn between Realty and Per- sonalty, which deserve separate examination.

Though incomes derived from landed property are nominally charged at the same poundage rate with professional and trade incomes, there can be little doubt that, in reality, they contribute a much larger quota proportionally. Not merely is it certain that profits made in business are often fraudulently understated, and seldom very strictly assessed, but deductions are allowed in the one case which are not allowed in the other. The exact acreage of an estate is a matter of public notoriety, and it is easy to ascertain the gross rent, upon which the Income Tax is assessed under Schedule A, without abatement for necessary outgoings, such as agency and the repair of farm-buildings. Trade- incomes, on the contrary, are debited with "the average repairs of all premises, implements, and utensils em- ployed in business, for bad and even doubtful debts, for parochial rates, for wages, clerks, shopmen or assistants, for stationery and the other petty outlays."[1] It has been estimated that, in consequence of this difference in the mode of assessment, the net income which pays Income Tax under Schedule A is at least ten per cent. below the gross income upon which the poundage rate is charged. The incomes of tenant-farmers, however,

[1] See the article by Captain Craigie on "Taxation as affecting the Agri- cultural Interest," in the *Journal of the Royal Agricultural Society*, 1878.

are treated with far greater leniency, being taken at one-half the rental, and subjected to exemptions and abatements, which practically reduce the aggregate produce of Schedule B for the whole United Kingdom to little more than one-tenth of the sum produced by Schedule A.

The history of the Succession Duty has been described, not without some reason, as " a scandal of class legislation." It is certainly impossible to justify the partiality for landed property, which left the inheritance of it untaxed for seventy-three years after Pitt's Legacy Act of 1780 had imposed a duty upon the inheritance of personalty. Even under Mr. Gladstone's Act of 1853, whereby successions to landed property were first made liable to duty, a notable deviation from the rule applicable to personalty was made in their favour. When legacies of money are given by way of annuity, the value of the annuity is calculated by certain official tables, and duty paid upon that value, instead of upon the capital fund; but when they are given in the form of a capital fund, the whole fund is of course subject to duty. Yet it is expressly enacted that the interest of every successor to land—though he may succeed in fee simple—is to be reckoned as representing, not the capital value of the land, but an annuity equal in amount to its nett annual value, after making certain allowances for necessary outgoings. This annuity is to be valued, with reference to age, by the same rules as an annuity of money, and the duty on it is to be paid, not at once, but in eight half-yearly instalments.[1]

---

[1] As it is the custom on many properties for rents to be paid some months after they are legally due, and as rents legally due fall into the

By the same Act, successions to personalty *under settlements*, which had formerly been exempt from duty, were deprived of this exemption; but a person thus becoming absolutely entitled to a sum of money, unlike a person becoming absolutely entitled to a landed estate, must pay duty on the whole capital value, and not only on his life-interest. This inequality is greatly aggravated by the entire exemption of landed property from Probate Duty, which is exclusively levied on personalty, and brings in a revenue exceeding two millions and a quarter annually.

It is the less necessary to dwell minutely on other items of Imperial taxation, as affecting Real Property and "land" respectively, because the general result, ascertained by different methods of investigation, admits of little dispute. The official tables appended to Mr. Goschen's Report on Local Taxation (1870) show that, in the previous year, the proportion of Imperial taxation falling on Real Property in England and Wales was £5,677,000 out of £46,652,949, or 12·17 per cent.; while the proportion falling on land only was £2,537,529, or 5·44 per cent.[1] The calculations made on behalf of the Royal Agricultural Society in 1878 give £3,315,000 as the share of Imperial taxes on property or income "specially affecting agricultural incomes" in the whole United Kingdom,[2] while the amount of Imperial taxation on "lands" in the whole

personal estate, the first instalment may sometimes have to be paid out of borrowed money.

[1] See Appendix to Mr. Goschen's Report on Local Taxation, Part III., Tables XIII.—XVII.

[2] See Captain Craigie's article on "Taxation as affecting the Agricultural Interest" in the *Journal of the Royal Agricultural Society*, 1878.

United Kingdom was roundly stated by Mr. Goschen, in 1870, as £3,000,000.

These estimates do not materially differ, when the minor items which they include or exclude respectively are set off against each other; and little is to be gained by any further attempt to apportion the pressure of Imperial taxation between the several classes engaged in agriculture or other employments. It matters little, for instance, whether agricultural labourers, drinking less spirits than artisans in towns, but perhaps smoking more tobacco, contribute equally towards customs and excise duties. The broad fact appears to be that about one-eighth of the total Imperial taxation falls upon owners of lands, houses, and other "hereditaments," while farmers contribute somewhat less than tradespeople with equal incomes. Considering that capital in every form is more heavily taxed for Imperial purposes than earnings, the proportion charged upon landowners corresponds nearly with that charged upon other owners of realised property.[1] It is well known that in other

---

[1] The instructive article of Captain Craigie, already cited, on "Taxation as affecting the Agricultural Interest," is too largely founded on conjectural data to be accepted as a conclusive statement. According to his computation, "upper and middle class incomes" generally contribute at the rate of somewhat less than three per cent., and "agricultural incomes" at the rate of somewhat more than three per cent., towards Imperial taxation. But the aggregate of upper and middle class incomes is composed, to a great extent, of trade profits and professional receipts.

Captain Craigie accepts the Income-tax valuation of the landlord's rental for the United Kingdom (£67,000,000), and the Income-tax estimate of tenant's income at half the landlord's rental (£33,500,000), though Scotch and Irish farmers enjoy the privilege of being assessed at one-third only of the rental. Adding an estimated labourer's income of £58,000,000, he states the aggregate income of the agricultural classes in the United Kingdom at about £158,000,000, or about one-seventh of the

countries land bears a far larger per-centage of the whole Imperial taxation. Speaking of Imperial burdens in 1871, Mr. Goschen stated that "the amount paid by land alone in England is $5\frac{1}{2}$ per cent.; in Holland, land alone pays $9\frac{1}{2}$ per cent.; in Austria, $17\frac{1}{2}$ per cent.; in France, $18\frac{1}{2}$ per cent.; in Belgium, $20\frac{1}{2}$ per cent.; and in Hungary, $32\frac{1}{2}$ per cent." But these statistics are not, in themselves, sufficient to prove that land is far more lightly burdened in England than in any other European State, for purposes of Imperial taxation. In order to justify that conclusion, we must further ascertain the value of land relatively to other kinds of realised property in the various States compared with each other; and though in Belgium the relative value might not be very different from that ascertained for England, it is certain that in Hungary it must be very much higher.

But the real stress of the argument respecting the alleged over-taxation of the agricultural interest turns upon the incidence, not of Imperial, but of local imposts. In approaching this part of the subject, it, is specially necessary to guard against a frequent source of misapprehension, indicated by Mr. Goschen. When it is found that a very large proportion of local taxation falls on Real Property, it is often loosely assumed that it falls

whole national income. Half of this agricultural income of £158,000,000 he reckons to be derived from capital, and to be in the nature of interest, and half to be derived from earnings, in return for labour and superintendence. After comparing the estimated amount of capital invested in land with that of capital invested in other enterprises, he concludes that "the income returned by the combined capital of the landowner and the farmer (say £80,000,000) is no more than $3\frac{1}{2}$ per cent., in contrast with the average of $4\frac{1}{2}$ per cent. yielded by all descriptions of British capital."

on the class popularly known as "land-owners." This assumption is doubly erroneous. "Real Property" includes not only land but houses, and not only houses but railways, canals, and other works, legally classed with realty only because they must needs be planted on the soil. Again, rates on Real Property are not exclusively paid by the owners thereof, but in many cases are mainly, if not wholly, paid by the occupiers. As Mr. Goschen has well remarked,[1] "If a comparison were drawn between persons deriving an income from Real Property and persons deriving income from other sources, the case would be by no means identical with that which is made out when 'taxes on Real Property' are spoken of generally, instead of taxes on income from Real Property." This qualification, which applies also to Imperial taxation, is of the greater importance in proportion as houses contribute more to rates than lands, because the proportion of rates paid · by the occupiers of houses greatly exceeds that paid by farm-tenants. It is also of peculiar importance in relation to England, because the relative aggregate value of houses, as compared with lands, is infinitely greater in England than in foreign countries.[2] Supposing a new rate to be imposed on a country district, it is probable that, in the long run, it would come out of rent, for the profits of farming are already so low that a tenant might either seek a farm elsewhere, or betake himself to another employment, rather than submit to an abatement of income. But supposing a new rate to be imposed on the metropolis or any other growing

---

[1] Report on Local Taxation, pages 37-38.
[2] Report on Local Taxation, ib.

town, it would probably come, in the long run, out of the householder's pocket. The artisan must lodge within reach of his work, and will pay a famine-price for house-room, though he may put up with less of it, if rates be oppressive.

The fallacy of assuming that rates are exclusively paid by ground-landlords was ably exposed by Mr. John Stuart Mill in the debate on Local Taxation in May, 1868. He pointed out that "part of our local taxation was proportionate to the rent of land, and that fell upon real property; but part was proportionate to house-rent, was equivalent to house-tax, fell on the occupier, was one of the fairest of all taxes, and resembled the Income Tax—a house being probably a better measure of what a man could afford to spend than his actual income. The land-rent was a very small portion of the rent of a house, and the constant tendency of land to rise in value made its rent a kind of income which might with great justice be made a basis of taxation." The same distinction had been indicated long ago by Adam Smith and Ricardo, and it is one that has a material bearing upon the local taxation of London. The "building-rent," as Adam Smith called it, forms a much larger element in the gross rental of the metropolis than the ground-rent, enormous as this is; and so far as rates fall on building rents, they are paid by the occupants of the building, whether or not they be entered on the parish books as ratepayers. In other words, a great part of the local taxation supposed to fall on landlords really falls on tenants—and not only on ratepaying tenants, but on families, down to the very poorest, who rent lodgings.

The exhaustive returns procured by the Poor Law
Board in 1870 showed that Real Property, in its most
comprehensive sense, then contributed 79 per cent. o
the whole sum raised by Local Taxation, as against 21
per cent. levied indirectly in the form of tolls, dues,
and fees on shipping, and other descriptions of property.
The aggregate produce of Local Taxation in England,
including these items, was found to have increased from
£11,235,700 in 1826 to £20,640,000 in 1868—an increase which is described in Mr. Goschen's report as
"less than in other countries, but nevertheless so considerable as to justify the especial attention which it
has aroused." It was found that during the same
period the amount of direct local taxes levied on Real
Property had increased, in round numbers, by 100 per
cent. ; that is, from £8,000,000 to £16,000,000. The
greater part of this increase, however, amounting to at
least £6,500,000, had fallen upon urban and not upon
rural districts, and the whole evidence pointed to the
conclusion that house property in England bore an
exceptionally large proportion of Local Taxation.[1] Of
the whole £8,000,000, it was shown that £2,000,000
represented an increase in the Poor rates, £5,000,000
was due to Town-improvement rates, and £1,000,000 to
Police rates and miscellaneous purposes. The burden

---

[1] It was shown by a Parliamentary Return of 1870 that in the 512
Rural Unions of England and Wales, the "gross estimated rental" was,
in the year 1868, £64,045,322, the rateable value £55,024,624, and the
amount levied for rates £7,705,260; that is, 2s. 9¼d. in the pound. In
the 155 Town Unions of England and Wales, the "gross estimated rental"
was £54,339,377, the "rateable value" £45,001,968, and the amount levied
for rates £9,023,588; that is, 4s. in the pound. Thus the rate in the Town
Unions exceeded that in the Rural Unions by 1s. 2¾d. in the pound, or 44

on "lands" in respect of Poor Rate was found to have increased very slightly in the aggregate over the whole country, and the poundage rate had not increased at all; the rural district sin which the Poor Rate was very high being mostly those in which it had never been otherwise than very high. On the other hand, the large increase in urban Poor Rates had followed a more remarkable increase in rateable value, and appeared to have been caused not so much by an increase in pauperism, as by a more humane and liberal treatment of the helpless, the sick, and the insane. The £5,000,000 increase of urban rates for municipal expenditure represented "the lighting and paving of the streets, sanitary improvements of every kind, and public works of various descriptions, from vast enterprises like the Thames Embankment, the main drainage of the metropolis, and the many important works undertaken at a large outlay by Liverpool, Manchester, and the other large growing towns of the north of England, to the smaller but innumerable operations which have been instituted by the 700 Local Boards established during the last ten years" preceding 1869. Of course, much of the outlay on these purposes must be regarded as a more or less remunerative investment rather than as a burden on local resources. Even the comparatively insignificant

---

per cent.; and the contrast would have been still more remarkable but for the fact that, whenever a Union contained a town within it, it was classed with the Rural Unions. The same Return showed an increase of £594,753 in the expenditure of Rural Unions for Poor Relief between 1861 and 1869, and an increase of £1,299,404 in the expenditure of Town Unions for Poor-Relief during the same period; so that "in ratio of increase the Town Unions exceeded the Rural by 38·8 per cent."—*Parliamentary Paper* (437) *of* 1870.

increase on county rates must be subjected to some deductions of the same kind, for the maintenance of a county police, for the cost of Vaccination and Burial Boards, cannot be treated, like the Poor Rate, as a dead weight on the ratepayers, from which they receive no benefit themselves.

The Returns issued in 1879, and covering the decade ending with 1877–8, exhibit, as might be expected, a further increase in Local Taxation. The aggregate amount raised in England and Wales by rates falling on rateable property in 1877–8 was £26,375,600, of which sum £2,023,163 is classed as having been raised for Imperial purposes, being met by an equal sum from the Exchequer for the maintenance of county police and asylums. More than £4,715,000 was raised by tolls, dues, and rates falling on traffic,[1] and about £450,000 by duties falling on consumable articles, such as wine and coals. If we exclude these items, and compare the aggregate amount raised by rates on rateable property in 1877–8 with the amount raised in 1867–8, we find an increase of about £6,000,000, or 30 per cent. In the meantime, the increase in "gross estimated rental" exceeded £32,000,000, and that in "rateable value" exceeded 27,000,000, or about 27 per cent., respectively. The average rate in the pound, stated by Mr. Goschen in 1868 at 3s. 4d.,[2] seems to have remained almost stationary ever since, notwithstanding the steady growth of School Boards and the progressive

---

[1] Under this head are included Burial Board fees, School Board fees, and payments to "Urban Sanitary Authority."

[2] It is remarkable that Arthur Young estimated the average rate at 3s. 6d. in the pound.

outlay on sanitary improvements. This result is doubt-less largely due to a diminution of pauperism and a better administration of the Poor Law, as well as to a large increase of Treasury subventions. Here and there Sanitary and Education rates have pressed hardly on farmers, but, on the whole, the country has continued to be more lightly rated than urban unions.[1]

Lord Beaconsfield, replying to a memorial from Wiltshire landlords and tenants in February, 1880, was able to show a small decrease in the rates levied from the rural portion of that county during the six years ending 1878, especially since the increase of Imperial subsidies. Similar results are exhibited by a detailed Return for the County of Oxfordshire, compiled in 1880 from the Reports of the Local Government Board and of the Union Assessment Committees. It appears from this Return, covering the period from 1868 to 1879 inclusive, that in six out of the nine unions within the county the "Total Expenditure" had been considerably reduced within this period. In the remaining three, it had been very slightly in-

---

[1] A statement drawn up by an experienced statistician exhibits the amount of Poor Rate (including all other rates connected therewith), raised at various periods in various counties of England and Wales, selected as fair representatives of the agricultural districts. In these counties, the rateable value of land exceeds that of houses and other kinds of property in the proportion of about 27 to 33; and in order to show more correctly the amount of Poor Rate contributed by the land, the amount levied in the chief Town Unions has been subtracted. It appears that after the marked fall in the Poor Rate between 1833 and 1852, it rose in these agricultural districts by 37 per cent. between 1852 and 1868, but fell again by 4 per cent. in the decade 1868-78. The burden of the increase, of course, fell to some extent on houses, railways, and mines, but chiefly upon land. See Appendix VIII.

creased; but, for the whole county, it had declined
from £130,519 to £122,800. Of course, if the
Rural Unions had been distinguished from the Town
Unions, this decline would have been found to be proportionably greater.   Moreover, as the rateable value
of property had somewhat risen in every Union, the
rate in the pound had been diminished even more
appreciably than the total expenditure. Yet in most
cases, the Payments for Police Rate, Highway Rate,
Vaccination Fees, and Registration Costs, had become
heavier since 1868, while new rates had been imposed
for Sanitary purposes and Education.   On the other
hand, the expenditure for Poor Relief had been still
more largely reduced in every Union except one, doubtless owing, in part, to a simultaneous rise in agricultural wages.

Such being the present amount and distribution of
Local Taxation, we have next to inquire whether the
agricultural interest actually bears an undue proportion
of these burdens.   Here again we must resolutely put
aside several irrelevant considerations which have been
imported into the discussion.   One of these is the
amazing suggestion that by the inordinate pressure of
rates the price of land has been forced up, and small
landowners have been crushed out of rural society.[1]
It is obvious that if all the rates were taken off land
to-morrow, existing landowners would gain a very large
and undeserved windfall; but a purchaser would find
himself in the same position as before, and a yeoman
would have exactly the same inducement for selling his

---

[1] This argument was employed by more than one speaker in the debate
on Local Taxation in the House of Commons, May, 1869.

property. What prevents money laid out in land from yielding more than two or three per cent., unless under special conditions, is the fancy price which land commands: what causes land to command a fancy price is the extraordinary desire for the possession of it which now prevails: what gives rise to that desire is a combination of social and political motives beyond the province of economy; and the relief of land from rates would only increase its selling value. The best proof that landowners are not oppressed by exorbitant local taxation is, that so many shrewd men are anxious to become landowners. The indolent yeoman is not extirpated by the growth of rates; he is tempted to part with his patrimony by the agreeable discovery that he can make a larger income, and lead an easier life, on the interest of the purchase-money than on the profits of farming. He would make the same discovery, if there were no rates at all, for rate-free land would be all the more saleable. But the insatiable land-hunger which enables him to obtain a fancy price from some neighbouring proprietor or retired manufacturer does not seem to have been checked in any appreciable degree by the increase of rates; and, for aught that appears, rich men would continue to covet land, as they covet titles, even though its possession were absolutely unremunerative. It does not follow, however, that it would be right or politic for the State to raise the utmost possible amount of revenue out of this national passion. Other people, whose ambition takes a different—perhaps a less innocent—turn, and who spend their accumulations upon luxuries of which the enjoyment entails no public duties, have no moral claim to exemption from local taxation, whatever difficulties there may be in reaching them, or assessing their proper quota of contribution.

It is not only because land (including houses) was by far the most important kind of property in the reign of Queen Elizabeth, that it became the main, if not the sole, basis of assessment for Poor Law relief.[1] It was also because the feudal conception of peculiar obligations incident to its tenure still exercised a great influence; because very important powers and privileges were confided to its possessors; and because it, no doubt, invited taxation by its very quality of immobility. Of these reasons, the last two are by no means obsolete. Riches of many sorts may take to themselves wings and fly away, especially in these days, when capital has no abiding home; but land and houses are always there, and no vigilance can ever conceal them from the eye of the rate-collector. Now, we have already seen that, if every citizen were possessed of land or houses, and if his allotment of them always bore a definite proportion to his whole property, it would be perfectly fair, as well as highly convenient, to levy taxes, as well as rates, upon these alone. We have also seen, however, that any class of ratepayers would have reason to complain if their sense of security were disturbed by the sudden imposition of new burdens, and it is possible that farmers, having already to struggle with the uncertainty of seasons, may have

---

[1] In Appendix II., drawn up by Mr. A. C. Humphreys-Owen, some reasons are given for believing that personalty was intended to be charged with poor-rate, but that, in practice, it gradually ceased to be rated, until it was formally exempted by an Act of 1840.

suffered more from this real grievance than other classes of ratepayers. But this is not the ostensible grievance of the landed interest. Their ostensible grievance consists in the comparative immunity from local rates of thousands upon thousands of villa-residents in rural districts and of lodgers in towns, whose territorial stake and rateable income in the localities for which they are assessed represent but an infinitesimal part of their real fortunes.

Let us examine this ostensible grievance somewhat more closely. Let us suppose A to be a squire of limited means, with an estate rated at £2,000 a year, and B to be a neighbour living near the railway-station in a small house rated at £200 a year, but with a real income of £20,000 a year. At first sight it seems a monstrous injustice that A should pay, directly or indirectly, upwards of £300 a year in rates, while B escapes with a contribution of little more than £30 a year. But whence is B's income derived? It may be entirely derived from large business premises in the City or suburbs of London, on which he pays a far higher rate in the pound than A and himself are required to pay in a country parish. It may be entirely derived from shares in gas companies, or water companies, or railway companies, or mines, or from some other form of property, bearing its full share of rates, in other parts of the country. In either of these cases, and in many other cases that might be suggested, B is not enjoying the enviable immunity from local taxation which is so readily imputed to him, but contributing largely to it in the localities where his property is really situated. He is not a man of £20,000 a year in the parish of his residence, but only perhaps of a few hundreds a year, and it would be palpably inequitable that he should pay on the rest of his income twice over.

No doubt B's income may be wholly or partially derived from investments in the funds or in foreign loans, and in this case he will so far evade the burden of local rates, though not of the income tax. But even in this case, is his advantage over A absolutely unjust? and would it be absolutely just, on the other hand, to charge him with a liability to local rates on £20,000 a year? Surely not. If this rule were to be adopted, the settlement of a millionaire in a country parish would reduce the rates of all the other inhabitants to zero, and his departure would cause widespread distress, by virtually raising the rents of all the farms and cottages. Apart from all other questions respecting the basis of local taxation, it must be admitted that a ratepayer's liability should bear some proportion to the benefit which he may receive from the expenditure of rates.[1] If B, owning or renting a house and garden valued at £200 a year, used as many carriages and carts as A and his tenants, this would be a reason for his contributing as much towards a Highway rate; and it is certain that many brewers, millers, and others, occupying comparatively small premises, but employing

---

[1] Upon this principle, the expense of arterial works for Agricultural Drainage is charged on the landowners of the district in proportion to the advantage which they may receive. The same principle has been carried a step further in Ireland, by Acts such as that which authorises the Midland Great Western Railway to borrow £500,000 from the Public Works Loan Commissioners, and to charge the ratepayers of certain baronies with 1½ per cent. interest upon it, until they shall be repaid out of the profits upon a portion of the line.

numerous teams of horses, escape their fair share of this rate. Such persons, however, mostly live in towns, and if it be unreasonable that inhabitants of towns should wear down country roads to which they contribute nothing, it is not less unreasonable that country folk driving in to market should profit by the well-paved and well-lighted streets, bridges, and police, maintained exclusively out of town-rates. Again, if B's property required as much protection against contagious diseases and other nuisances, he could not complain of paying as heavy a Sanitary rate; while, if he employed as much low-priced labour, to be ultimately supplemented by parish relief, he might well be content to bear an equal share of the Poor Rates. On the other hand, if he gets no more benefit from the rates, under these and other heads, than any ordinary occupant of premises worth £200 a year, then, so far as rates are payment for value received, it is by no means self-evident that he should be rated on a higher scale by reason of his extrinsic wealth.

It must be remembered that B, as a tax-payer, already contributes largely, by means of Treasury subventions, to the cost of the County Police and County Lunatic Asylums, besides having to bear the whole cost of County Prisons; and it is quite possible that additional demands of the same kind may be made, and justly made, upon him. For instance, the Education rate may properly be considered a tax for national purposes, and it is somewhat hard that landowners and farmers, in common with other employers, should bear so large a proportion of it, while they are prohibited from employing the cheap labour of children, and compelled to pay a higher scale of wages to adults. But such demands cannot fairly be adjusted to B's income by strict arithmetical rules ; still less would it be fair to shift upon his shoulders a great part of A's burdens, without regard for vested interests. For it must not be forgotten that men's rights are to be measured, to some extent, by the expectations which the law has encouraged. A and B may have started in life with equal fortunes, but with different ambitions. The former, preferring the dignity of a landowner to a large income, may have bought a country place with a full appreciation of the privileges and liabilities attaching to it. The latter, preferring the consolations of wealth to a county position, may have gone into business and be satisfied to live in a villa, with the pleasing assurance that his gains will scarcely be touched by the rate-collector. The ambition of A may be the nobler and more generous, but that is no reason why, having realised the object of it, he should call upon B to share with him the pecuniary sacrifices which it entails.

This consideration brings into view that which is, in fact, one main justification for the " peculiar burdens of land." These burdens are, in reality, the price required by the nation, and willingly paid by the would-be proprietor, for its peculiar privileges—never, perhaps, more extensive or more eagerly coveted than at present. As English landlords, though released from many of their ancient liabilities, have been saddled with many new liabilities which do not fall on fundholders, so, having lost many of their ancient powers, they have been invested with many new powers, to which the mere fundholder, however wealthy, cannot aspire. To understand this, we must picture to ourselves the leading features of that rural government which is so familiar to us that we can hardly imagine it otherwise, yet which foreigners recognise as unique in modern Europe.

To an Englishman born and bred in the country, it appears the natural order of things, if not the fixed ordinance of Providence, that in each parish there should be a dominant resident landowner, called a squire, unless he should chance to be a peer, invested with an authority over its inhabitants, which neither the Saxon chief, nor the Norman lord, in the fulness of his power, ever had the right of exercising. This potentate, who, luckily for his dependants, is usually a kind-hearted and tolerably educated gentleman, concentrates in himself a variety of rights and prerogatives which, in the aggregate, amount to little short of patriarchal sovereignty. The clergyman, who is by far the greatest man in the parish next to himself, is usually his nominee, and often his kinsman. The farmers, who are almost the only employers of labour besides himself, are his tenants-at-will, and, possibly, his debtors. The petty tradespeople of the village community rent under him, and, if they did not, might be crushed by his displeasure at any moment. The labourers, of course, live in his cottages, unless, before the Union Chargeability Act, he should have managed to keep them on his neighbour's estate; but this is by no means his only hold upon them. They are

absolutely at his mercy for the privilege of hiring
allotments, generally at an "accommodation" rent;
they sometimes work on the home farm, and are
glad to get jobs from his bailiff, especially in the
winter; they look to him for advice in worldly
matters as they would consult the parson in spiritual
matters; they believe that his good word could
procure them any favour or advancement for their
children on which they may set their hearts, and they
know that his frown may bring ruin upon them and
theirs. Nothing passes in the parish without being
reported to him. If a girl should go wrong, or a young
man should consort with poachers, or a stranger of
doubtful repute should be admitted as a lodger, the
squire is sure to hear of it, and his decree, so far as his
labourers and cottage-tenants are concerned, is as good
as law. He is, in fact, the local representative of the
law itself, and, as a magistrate, has often the means of
legally enforcing the policy which, as landlord, he may
have adopted. Add to all this the influence which he
may and ought to acquire as the leading supporter and
manager of the parish school, as the most liberal
subscriber to parochial charities, as the patron of village
games and the dispenser of village treats, not to speak
of the motherly services which may be rendered by his
wife, or the boyish fellowship which may grow up
between the youth of the village and the young gentlemen at the Hall; and it is difficult to imagine a position
of greater real power and responsibility.

Yet even this does not exhaust the special advantages and prerogatives attached to the position of an
English country gentleman. Until very lately, he alone

was lawfully eligible to a seat in Parliament; and even now his class, which may be said to engross the Upper House, predominates conspicuously in the Lower. By this class the whole machinery of county taxation, county government, and county judicature, is regulated and worked. In those of them who may be magistrates is vested *ex-officio* a right of taking part in Poor Law administration; in their gift is a great variety of lucrative county offices, and the wealthiest magnate of the greatest manufacturing town is "nobody in the county" until he shall have secured their good opinion. That powers so vast and so arbitrary have not been more frequently abused is an honour to our national character; nor can we reflect without some feeling of pride on the admirable manner in which the "duties of property" are acknowledged and discharged on thousands of English estates. But this must not lead us to idealise this form of rural economy as our forefathers idealised the British Constitution, to ignore the grave defects and anomalies inherent in it, or lightly to dismiss the experience of other nations as inapplicable to our social condition.

It is, indeed, impossible to survey county administration in its entirety without being struck by the extraordinary absence of self-government in rural communities. We are wont to look back on Saxon times as barbarous, and on the feudal system as oppressive; but the simple truth is, that nine-tenths of the population in an English country parish have at this moment less share in local government than belonged to all classes of freemen for centuries before and for centuries after the Norman Conquest. Again, they have not only less share in local government than belongs to French peasants in the present day, but less than belonged to French peasants under the eighteenth-century monarchy—if not, than belonged to their own ancestors of the same age, as described by Fielding. For it must be observed that modern reforms of local administration, however beneficial in other respects, have tended, by the very enlargement of the administrative area, to destroy the old idea of the village commune. There was a time within living memory when each country village was still an unit of local administration, with no authority interposed between itself and Quarter Sessions—that non-elective body which has gradually absorbed so many powers formerly exercised by elective officers. The vestry meeting still represented those primitive gatherings of village elders on the banks of the Indus or the forests of Germany, to which representative government itself owed its origin. Its petty jurisdiction embraced not only the maintenance of the church fabric, but the parochial management of poor relief, and the repair of parish roads, as well as the appointment of a parish constable. The first of these functions is now superseded by voluntary assessment, and the last by the institution of County Police; the second and third are practically vested in Union authorities or Highway Boards. The sanitary control of villages has also been placed in the hands of Union authorities, and a host of inspectors, surveyors, registrars, and other officers (mostly appointed by the County, the Union, or the State), have relieved the parish householder of his time-honoured responsibilities.

But all these changes have by no means weakened the power of the squire, who, on the contrary, is a greater man than ever, relatively to other classes in the village community, since he is no longer jostled by independent yeomen, but surrounded by obsequious tenants and labourers. The Lord. Lieutenant of the county, always a great landowner, seldom places any but landowners in the commission of the peace; indeed, until lately, the possession of, or reversion to, landed property of considerable value was the necessary qualification of a magistrate; and though persons who have paid inhabited house duty to the amount of £100 for two years are now legally eligible, few of them are actually appointed. If a squire is also a magistrate, he not only helps to conduct the driving-wheel of county administration at Quarter Sessions, and of Union administration at the Board of Guardians, but is charged individually with multifarious public duties which, burdensome as they are, greatly enhance his personal influence. Even if he is not a magistrate, he can scarcely fail to be virtually the "headman" of the village, as lord of all the farms, cottages, and allotments round his own domain, as the chief employer of labour in the locality, and as the main supporter of all the village charities; so that, if the old "town-moot," or village assembly, could be revived, its unanimous resolutions would be outweighed by the expression of his own individual will. All this enters into the calculations of those who purchase country places, and might well reconcile those who inherit country places to "peculiar burdens on land" as heavy as are alleged to exist, and far heavier than actually exist. In short, the questions of Local Taxation, of Local Government, and of Land Tenure, must be treated, if at all, as a whole.   There is much to be said for transferring certain sources of Imperial revenue, such as the house-duty, to the disposition of local authorities ; and something to be said for the principle, though little for the feasibility, of a local income-tax.[1]   But the proposal to distribute rates uniformly over all the schedules of the existing income-tax is a proposal, by a few lines in an Act of Parliament, to confiscate so much income of the general taxpayers for the benefit of landowners, and to relieve the rental of eldest sons out of the scanty annuities of younger children.[2]   Such a proposal will never be entertained seriously by the Legislature, and we may safely predict that any comprehensive redistribution of local taxation in rural districts will be accompanied by a comprehensive redistribution of rural government and territorial power.

[1] It is remarked by M. Lavergne, in his " Economie Rurale de l'Angleterre," that, whereas in France two-thirds at least of the taxes raised locally are spent in Paris and the great towns, in England three-fourths are spent in the localities from which they are raised.

[2] See Mr. Giffen's Essays in Finance—"Taxes on Land," p. 247–8.

CHAPTER II.

The Agricultural Depression of 1879–80, and the Prospects of American Competition.

THE Agricultural Distress of the year 1879–80 will long be memorable in the economical records of the country, and may probably be remembered as marking a crisis in the history of the English Land System. Its most obvious and principal cause was the occurrence of several bad seasons in succession, culminating in the coldest, wettest, and least genial spring and summer that had been known within living memory. But this calamity was greatly aggravated, as regards the interest of farmers, though mitigated, as regards those of the public, by a singularly low range of agricultural prices, as well as by a general sense of insecurity, due to a vast expansion of foreign competition. It is only by a separate examination of all these conditions that we can fully realise the gravity of the question now pressing upon the agricultural interest.

Of the six years beginning with the year 1873, two only yielded more than an average crop of wheat per acre, while four yielded a crop far below the average.[1]

---

[1] Mr. Bear, reviewing the Grain-Crop Returns for ten years ending with 1878, points out that only one (1874) yielded an exceptionally good wheat crop, only three a good barley crop, and only two a good oat crop, while the crops of peas and beans were almost uniformly poor.—"Agricultural Depression," *Fortnightly Review*, February, 1879. Messrs. Lawes and Gilbert, in an elaborate paper on the "Home Produce, Imports, Con-

But the wheat crop of 1879 was not only worse than any in this series, but the worst that has been harvested since 1816.   Such is the conclusion of Mr. Lawes,[1] whose authority is second to none on the subject of wheat-growing, and whose opinion is amply supported by that of other competent witnesses.[2]   He calculated that, allowing for deficiency of weight, as well as for scantiness of quantity, the wheat crop of 1879 on his own land at Rothamsted fell short of the average for the last twenty-seven years in the proportion of $45\frac{1}{2}$ to 100, and fell short of the average for the first seventeen years of that period, in the proportion of $43\frac{1}{2}$ to 100.   Though he believed the deficiency to be somewhat less on lighter soils, he estimated the acreable produce for the whole United Kingdom at little more than half the average, and the whole produce as no more than 5,000,000 quarters, out of about 23,650,000 quarters required to feed the population.   The loss was naturally heaviest on highly farmed land, since the additional capital expended on it was almost thrown away.   Thus, whereas three artificially manured plots at Rothamsted had yielded, in 1863, 55 bushels per acre, at an average weight of $62\frac{3}{8}$ lbs. to a bushel, the same plots under the same manures yielded, in

---

sumption, and Price of Wheat, over the harvest years 1852-3 to 1879-80 inclusive," supply abundant evidence leading to a like conclusion. They show that, during the last eleven years of the period, the average produce of wheat per acre was but $27\frac{4}{5}$ bushels, against an average of $28\frac{1}{2}$ bushels during the previous sixteen years.

[1] "The Wheat Crop of 1879." By J. B. Lawes.—*Journal of the Bath and West of England Society*, 1879.

[2] See the opening address of Mr. Wm. Sturge, at the general meeting of the Institution of Surveyors, Nov. 10th, 1879.

1879, only $19\frac{1}{2}$ bushels per acre, at $53\frac{3}{8}$ lbs. per bushel, equal to only $16\frac{3}{4}$ bushels at the same weight per bushel as in 1863. This consideration helps to explain the fact that some of the best and most scientific farmers were among the greatest sufferers; for the profits of scientific farming are only to be obtained by a large outlay, and such is the levelling effect of bad seasons that he who has laid out most reaps the smallest proportionate return. If A, farming 300 acres, has £4,000 invested in his land, and B, with the same acreage, has but £2,000, A ought to obtain a profit of £100 in excess of B, in order to keep down the extra interest on his capital, whereas, in a bad season, his crops may be little, if at all, heavier. Happily, the whole area under wheat in the United Kingdom had decreased from 3,982,000 acres in 1869 to 3,056,428 in 1879, of which Scotland contributed but 76,613 acres, and Ireland but 157,508. Still a deficiency of nearly half the wheat crop on 3,000,000 acres, amounting to nearly 5,000,000 quarters, would represent a deduction of £10,000,000 or £12,000,000 from the profits of farmers, without allowing for the inferiority of quality.

This deduction was not, as in ordinary years, redeemed by a corresponding abundance in other crops. All cereals, except oats, are known to have been damaged, though in a less degree, by the excessive rainfall. In many low-lying districts the hay crop was carried away, or utterly spoiled, by floods, and, even on higher ground, the grass was found to be rank and almost void of "heart," or nutritive properties. Even root crops were injuriously affected by the same causes, both in quantity and in quality, so that it was impossible to keep an average head of stock during the winter, and store cattle purchased a few months before had to be sold off at a considerable loss. In the meantime the disease known as sheep-rot, engendered by the continuous saturation of pastures, devastated the flocks " not only in parts of the country which are liable to periodical outbreaks of the malady, but also in districts which are usually free."[1] The live stock on farms, therefore, fully shared the disasters which fell upon agriculture in all its branches, and no resource was left whereby farmers could recoup themselves for the poverty of the harvest. The aggregate deficiency in all kinds of agricultural produce was estimated at 25 per cent., that is, one-fourth of the materials out of which rent, wages, subsistence, and profit must be provided.

In former periods, however, bad harvests had generally brought with them an equivalent, and sometimes a more than equivalent, rise in prices. This natural law of compensation, as it once seemed to be, has ceased to operate of late, and a bad harvest now yields even a smaller return per quarter to an English farmer than a good one, inasmuch as the quality of the wheat is inferior, and fails to command the full price of foreign wheat in the market. It has been calculated that if the price of home-grown wheat during the six years beginning with 1873, had varied inversely with the deficiency of product, as of old, it would have fetched on the average 62s. 6d. per quarter ; whereas it actually fetched, on the average, but 49s. 6d. per quarter.[2] It

[1] Professor Brown on the " Effects of Excessive Rainfall."—*Journal of the Bath and West of England Society*, 1879.

[2] Address by Mr. G. Shaw-Lefevre, M.P., to the Statistical Section of the British Association, August, 1879.

has been calculated, further, that if the wheat crop of
1879 had been only equal in quantity to those of the
bad years 1871 and 1872, and sold at the same price, it
would have realised above £9 an acre; whereas it probably realised little more than £5 10s. per acre. But
this is not all. Though barley and oats had felt, to
some extent, the effect of several bad seasons preceding
1878, the price of these crops had been well maintained
up to the beginning of 1879.[1] During the year 1878
the mean price of barley was 40s. 2d. per quarter, or 25
per cent. above the tithe commutation average; and that
of oats 24s. 4d., or 10 per cent. above the average. This
great increase in the price of barley doubtless explains
the fact, shown by the Agricultural Returns of 1879,
that " barley has partly taken the place of wheat, being
this year sown on 2,932,000 acres, an increase of 209,000
acres, and nearly 8 per cent., over 1878, and the largest
area sown with that crop since the Agricultural Returns were first obtained in 1867." But in the course
of 1879 the fall in prices extended itself more or less to
all kinds of agricultural produce. " Wheat fell to 40s.
per quarter, barley to 28s. or 30s., oats to 18s. or 20s.,
whilst the fall in the price of cheese was extraordinary
—20 or 30 per cent.—and for some months the price
ruled lower than has been known for upwards of fifty
years."[2] The price of meat, which had increased by

---

[1] The Tables given in Appendix V. show that during the period 1849—
1879 the average price of barley was 2s. 2d., and that of oats 2s. lower
than it had been in the period 1800—1848, including many years of war.

[2] Address of Mr. William Sturge to the Institution of Surveyors,
November 10th, 1879. This extraordinary fall in the price of cheese,
however, produced a no less extraordinary effect in stimulating consumption, which, again, re-acted upon price. Prime American cheese soon rose

nearly one-half in the previous thirty years, at last fell about one penny a pound, and that of prime butter twopence per pound, while the price of English wool, which had exceeded 2s. in 1865, and reached 1s. 11d. in 1873,[1] was reduced to 9½d. or 10d.

Two causes are amply sufficient to account for this general fall in agricultural prices. The first is the depression of trade which prevailed throughout the year 1879, compelling the working classes to curtail their purchases of all articles, except the bare necessaries of life, and manifesting itself most remarkably in the diminished consumption of alcoholic liquors. The second is the enormous increase in the importation of wheat and other provisions from abroad. Since this cause must be regarded as permanent, while depressions of trade are naturally followed by corresponding revivals, it may be well to consider it more particularly.

The vast extension of the railway system in the United States, dating from the year 1869, brought the great corn-growing area of Central and Western America within easy reach of the English markets. The effect of this new supply first made itself felt on the price of wheat in England about the year 1873, but the increase of production in America had been truly extraordinary at a much earlier period. It was greatly stimulated by the westward emigration of the surplus population from the Eastern States, after 1873 ; by the

from 36s. to 56s. per cwt., and the best qualities of Cheddar and Cheshire reached a much higher maximum, fully maintaining their superiority in the English market.

[1] " Agricultural Returns for 1879," Table 26.

adoption of minimum traffic-rates on the railways and of minimum freights on the Atlantic steamers; and by a cycle of abundant harvests in America coinciding with a cycle of deficient harvests in this country. It appears from official tables that whereas the quantity of wheat grown on the Atlantic coast had risen but slightly, from about 6,500,000 quarters in 1849 to about 8,000,000 quarters in 1877, the quantity of wheat grown in the Central Belt had risen in the same period from about 5,500,000 quarters to about 18,500,000 quarters; and the quantity of wheat grown in the Trans-Mississippi States from about 660,000 quarters to upwards of 19,000,000 quarters. In 1868 a further increase of nearly 8,000,000 quarters took place in the production of the Western States; and the whole area under wheat in the United States was then stated at 30,000,000 quarters, and had reached 32,836,000 acres in 1879, being more than tenfold as great as the wheat-growing area of the whole United Kingdom.[1] But even this immense area is but a small part of that now in process of development for wheat growing on the American Continent. It is supposed that less than one-third of the cultivable land in the United States is already cultivated, and every year fresh districts, as large as English counties, are being allotted to settlers, on the " alternate block system," along the lines of railways.

It is stated that in the three months ending with November 30, 1877, above 1,000,000 acres were thus appropriated in Minnesota and Dakotah by Go-

---

[1] See the Addresses of Mr. William Sturge and Mr. G. Shaw-Lefevre, M.P., already cited.

vernment land offices and railway companies, while in
the first three months of 1879 nearly 500,000 additional
acres were sold in Western Minnesota alone. In the
meantime, no less than 3,000,000 acres of land suitable
for wheat growing were taken up during 1877 by
actual settlers in the adjoining province of Manitoba,
belonging to Canada. The area drained by the two
Saskatchewan rivers, and stretching north-west for 300
miles, is estimated at 90,000,000 acres, all capable of
growing the finest wheat, and the whole " fertile belt
of the North-West," stretching on both sides of the
frontier between Canada and the United States, is said
to embrace " at least 200,000,000 acres."[1]

The average production of American and Canadian
wheatfields per acre is, of course, far below that of
arable land in Great Britain.   But the first crops
obtained from the virgin prairie or pasture are often so
prodigious as to cover, and more than cover, the small
cost of purchase, and return the whole capital invested.
We read of 40 and 50 bushels per acre being sometimes
produced by land newly broken up in the north-western
provinces of Canada, and of the farmer realising £2 or
£3 per acre over and above his entire original outlay
and working expenses.[2]   A continuous succession of

---

[1] See a suggestive paper on " Our New Wheatfields in the North-
West," by Mr. T. T. Vernon Smith (*Nineteenth Century*, 1879). See
also an article by Mr. Atkinson, of Boston, on the Effects of Railways
and the Development of the West on the Agriculture of New England,
in the *Fortnightly Review* of July, 1880.

[2] In the article by Mr. T. T. Vernon Smith, above cited, a case is mentioned in which a great proprietor in Minnesota realised a clear profit of
£24,000 on 8,000 acres under wheat in the year 1877, since each acre cost
him less than £2 for seed, cultivation, harvesting, and threshing, and produced 25 bushels, valued at £5.

white crops, without a liberal application of manure, impoverishes even the fertility of virgin soil in the course of a few years, and the average wheat crop over the whole United States territory does not exceed 13 or 14 bushels, or 1¾ quarters, per acre.[1] Now, the average cost of growing wheat in the Western States has been reckoned at about £1 per quarter, and the average cost of exportation to England through New York, with insurance and all other extra charges, has been reckoned at about 17s. 6d.[2] It follows that each quarter of wheat imported by England from the Far West by this route has cost, on the average, 37s. 6d. out of pocket, exclusive of the grower's profit, which, if it be taken at 4s. 6d. per quarter, would raise the entire cost to 42s.[3]

[1] The acreable yield of wheat in the United States was officially stated at less than 11 bushels for 1875, 10 bushels for 1876, 13½ bushels for 1877, and rather less than 13 bushels for 1878.—Agricultural Returns for 1879. According to Messrs. Read and Pell's report on "American Agriculture," the yield for 1879 was 13·1 bushels, and the average yield over a long series of years has just exceeded 12 bushels. They estimate the whole cost of growing wheat on prairie-land at about £2 2s. per acre. On the famous Dalrymple farm, twenty-five miles west of Fargo, Dakota, which is probably the largest cultivated farm in the world, the estimated yield of 24,000 acres under wheat, in 1880, was 18 bushels per acre. In 1879, it averaged 20 bushels. The cost of production in that year was estimated at about 34s. per acre, or 1s. 9d. per bushel, while the wheat could be sold at the nearest railway station for at least 3s. per bushel.

[2] According to another estimate, the cost of freight may be taken at about 12s. per quarter, nearly representing the rent paid by an English farmer. But it is probable that in this estimate no account is taken of insurance and other charges.

[3] The sea-freight of Californian wheat from San Francisco to England was about 12s. per quarter in 1879. But, notwithstanding the vast increase in cultivation, its price at San Francisco was about 38s. per quarter, so that it could not be delivered at Liverpool under 50s. per quarter. The reason why the export price of wheat grown in California so greatly exceeds the average for the Western States is that most of the older farms near the

If this be so, and if the expense of carriage should not be increased —still more, if it should be diminished— it is difficult to see how English farmers can long continue to compete with their Western rivals in the cultivation of wheat, unless, indeed, the consumption of the Americans themselves should ever be large enough to overtake their production. Considering that enough wheat is already produced in the United States to feed at least 20,000,000 of people beyond their existing population of 50,000,000, that some two-thirds of their cultivable area remains to be reclaimed, and that of that already reclaimed but a small proportion is thoroughly cultivated, such a contingency as the exhaustion of Transatlantic corn-supplies is beyond the region of reasonable speculation. On the contrary, when the communications between Lake Winnipeg and Hudson's Bay have been completed, we may fairly expect a large increase of these supplies at a price which cannot yield a profit to English farmers.[1]

These conclusions are substantially confirmed by the official "Report of Messrs. Read and Pell on American Agriculture." After discussing the various factors which determine the cost of American wheat grown within 300 or 400 miles of Chicago in the English market, they give the following general estimate :—

Californian sea-coast have been already exhausted by over-cropping. This involves a heavy outlay in artificial manures, balancing the greater cost of carriage from the new farms in the interior.

[1] Mr. G. Shaw-Lefevre, M.P., in the Address already cited, arrives at a different conclusion, mainly relying on the probable increase of traffic rates, and on the fact that " every year the central line of wheat production is being carried further to the westward."

	£	s.	d.
Cost of growing a quarter of wheat (480 lbs.), in the West, including delivery to local depôt	1	8	0
Freight to Chicago	0	6	8
Thence to New York	0	5	2
New York to Liverpool	0	4	9½
Handling in America (which may be avoided on through rates)	0	1	1
Liverpool charges	0	2	1
	£2	7	9½

To bring the estimate up to English weight of five centals the quarter, one twenty-fourth, or nearly 2s., would have to be added.

The estimate may possibly ere long be affected by a reduction in the freights from the farms to Chicago to the extent of one-half, and special "through" contracts are said to defy any precise calculations. Allowing a deduction on this head of 3s. 9d., or about 6d. a bushel, the estimate would be brought down to 44s., or, without Liverpool charges, to 42s. the quarter.

At the same time Messrs. Read and Pell point out many circumstances which may help to redress the balance in favour of English agriculture. The Western farmer, it is true, has a virgin soil, which he buys at a nominal price and cultivates without manure, a level surface, clear of stones though not always of stumps, and abundance of unbroken sunshine. These are obviously great advantages, but the effect of them must not be overstated. Rent, formerly supposed to represent one-third of a farmer's expenditure, is now supposed to represent no more than one-fourth or one-fifth, so that a Western farmer does not gain more than 20 or 25 per cent. as compared with his English rival, by occupying land rent-free. His mode of husbandry is wonderfully simple and cheap, it is true, but, after all, his soil does not produce more per acre than Mr. Lawes has obtained at Rothamsted *from land con-*

tinuously unmanured upon an average of twenty-six years.[1] Moreover, he must contend against severe winters, suspending agricultural operations, frequent droughts, the ravages of destructive insects, and the scarcity of good water on the prairies. He uses labour-saving machinery, it is true, to an extent barely conceivable in the old country, so that, in one instance, we hear of only two labourers regularly employed on a farm of 5,000 acres. Nor does the labour which he employs probably cost him more than would be paid for the same amount of human toil in England, for labourers are there expected to be at work from sunrise to sunset, and are discharged without scruple after harvest.

But the Western farmer himself, aided by the members of his family, is his own chief labourer, and, for this reason, he is usually content with a farm of one-quarter section, or 160 acres. "He adds to all the mental cares of ownership the physical stress of manual labour of the severest description. No other class of men toil so unceasingly, enduring the life of savages for a while in order to conquer the backwood or civilise the prairie. Save in the harvest, certainly no agricultural labourer in England expends anything like the same time and strength in his day's work." Again, his present system of tillage is one which depends mainly for its economical success on the power of a natural seed-bed, never fallowed or manured, to produce successive crops of wheat. Even the accumu-

---

[1] It appears from Mr. Lawes' memoranda on his field experiments that on plots unmanured continuously from 1852 to 1877, the average produce of wheat was 13½ bushels per acre.

lated vegetable deposits of centuries must one day be exhausted by such a process, and the central valley of North America will ultimately lose its agricultural supremacy unless recuperative crops be introduced to renew its fertility. In this case, the cost of cultivation will be greater, while, if the corn-growing area should be advanced still further westward, the cost of transit will be greater. In the meantime, the inevitable development of American manufactures, stimulating afresh the marvellous growth of American population, yet withdrawing more and more hands from agriculture, cannot fail to increase the home consumption and raise the price of American wheat. The combined effect of these and other conflicting tendencies cannot, of course, be foreseen with certainty ; but the presumption must be that, for many generations at least, the Western States of America will be the chief granary of Great Britain. With at least equal energy and skill, with a climate and soil better adapted to wheat-growing, with an ever-increasing supply of labour, and with ever-multiplying channels of transport, Western farmers of English race can scarcely fail, ere long, to maintain the same lead in the markets of Europe, which English manufacturers, but for a protective tariff, would be able to maintain in those of America.

The report of Messrs. Read and Pell does not supply equally complete materials for an estimate of the extent to which American competition may be expected to affect the meat supply of Great Britain. It would appear from the facts stated in one part of this report that fat cattle, of $3\frac{1}{2}$ or 4 years old, reared on the vast plains about Cheyenne, in the Wyoming

territory, can be delivered and sold in the Chicago
market, at a large profit, for about £7 a head.   On the
other hand, according to the official return of the sales
of live stock in that market during 1879, the average
price of a bullock weighing 1,200 lbs., and sold in the
usual way by the 100 lbs. of live weight, would be
nearly £10.   The carriage from Chicago to New York,
including food, water, and attendance, is calculated by
Messrs. Read and Pell at £1 2s., and the freight to
England at not less than £5, exclusive of 30s. for
attendance, food, and insurance, and exclusive also of
dock charges, landing charges, and other dues incident
to delivery.   This would raise the value of a beast
worth £7 at Chicago to near £15 at Liverpool, and that
of a beast worth £10 at Chicago to near £18 at Liverpool.   As the cost of transit from Texas to Chicago is
greater by some 18s. or 19s. than from Wyoming, the
profit of fattening cattle in that State for the English
market ought to be proportionately less ; but, in fact,
cattle bred in Texas are mostly driven up to be fattened in the corn-growing Middle States.   Happily for
the British grazier, " the great mass of the bullocks
from the West, however well they are grazed, are not
good enough to export alive, especially as a beast of
inferior weight costs nearly as much for transport as a
prize animal."   It appears that none but the primest
American oxen find their way to England, and the
condition of these is sensibly injured by the voyage.
It is well known, however, that sea-freights of cattle
have often been much lower than £5, which is here
assumed as the natural standard, or even than £4, which
Mr. Caird, writing in 1878, had assumed to be the

natural standard. In the latter part of 1879, beasts were actually being conveyed from Boston to Liverpool for £2 10s. a head, and an appendix to Messrs. Read and Pell's report shows that during the first seven months of 1879 the average freight of cattle from New York to Liverpool was £3 10s. a head. Moreover, if we may trust this report, " it is generally acknowledged that the average profit of the stockowner (in the central plains) has been for years fully 33 per cent.," so that a considerable margin remains for a reduction upon the original selling price of American cattle.

It is to be regretted that Messrs. Read and Pell studiously forbear to draw inferences from the evidence which they have collected. While they recognise the " singular advantages " enjoyed by the American stockman in the Western States—"land for nothing and abundance of it "—they point out some countervailing disadvantages which are likely to enhance the price of American stock. The difficulty arising from a want of water must of course increase with the increase of stock, and especially of highly-bred stock. The appropriation of land and the loss of " free ranges," which must result from the progress of settlement, will raise the cost of rearing stock, and the demands of a growing population will enable the breeder to make a good profit at home, without incurring the manifold risks of exportation. On the whole, Messrs. Read and Pell do not seem to anticipate any very large expansion of the American trade in fat cattle, even when more effective precautions against pleuro-pneumonia in the United States may justify the British Government in removing all restrictions upon it. The cost of carrying a bullock

over some 4,000 miles by land and sea is a deduction
from the profit of the American grazier, which may
fairly be set off against the rent of land sufficient to
rear and fatten a bullock for some three years, which
he escapes, but which the English grazier must pay.
All other conditions are in favour of the latter, and
rent is more easily reduced than railway or ocean
freights.

Let us now glance at the official returns, which show
the extent to which Great Britain has become dependent
on foreign countries for other articles of food within a
period of twenty years.[1] In 1859 the number of live
cattle imported was 85,677 ; in 1878 it was 253,462.
Within the same period the number of sheep imported
had increased from 250,580 to 892,125, and that of pigs
from 11,086 to 55,911. The aggregate value of imported
salt beef and pork, bacon and hams, fish, butter, eggs,
cheese, &c., had mounted up, in the meantime, from
£5,182,426 to very nearly £34,000,000. The number of
eggs imported had risen from 148,631,000 to the astonishing total of 783,714,720 ; the importation of cheese had
increased from 406,547 cwts. to 1,968,859 cwts.; and that
of vegetables from a value of £189,870 to a value of
£3,064,732. Altogether, the aggregate value of agricultural imports, as distinct from groceries, liquors, and
luxuries for the table, had been quadrupled in twenty
years, rising from £24,359,598 in 1859 to £95,996,249

---

[1] In Appendix IV. will be found Tables showing the quantities of the
principal articles of food imported into the United Kingdom in each year
since 1820. These Tables have been compiled from official sources, and in
the case of wheat, barley, and oats, the statistics of yearly importation
have been given from 1800 onwards. In other cases, the yearly importation could not be traced further back than 1820.

in 1878, while the value per head of population had been more than trebled, rising from 17s. to £2 16s. 10d. Nor is there any ground to anticipate such an inflation of prices abroad as could alone check the development of this vast import trade. It may be true, perhaps, that American exporters half ruined themselves during 1878 in the desperate attempt to obtain command of foreign markets, and that when American cheese was sold at less than a third of what it had fetched a few years before, it was sold far below the cost price. But it is equally certain that machines for milking cows, and the extension of the co-operative principle to cheese-making, have enabled American dairymen to compete at an advantage with those of Cheshire and Somersetshire in the manufacture of all but the finest qualities of cheese. It is still more certain that scientific appliances and the acceleration of transit will facilitate more and more the importation of fresh meat, either "chitted" or "canned," from the vast pastures of America, and that it may become a common article of diet in Lancashire and Yorkshire.

For the present, however, the British grazier or sheep farmer has no right to complain. Though beef and mutton have declined in price from the maximum which they reached a few years ago, they are still much dearer than they were thirty years ago, and the price of good beef at New York during 1879 was much the same as it was in England before the Repeal of the Corn Laws. Nevertheless, in the winter of that year, American beef of excellent quality was sold retail by London butchers for a penny a pound less than English beef. It has been confidently predicted that in the course

of a few years it will be delivered to English consumers at less than 6d. a lb., which is considerably
below the current price of English beef forty years ago.
This prediction can hardly be realised unless the cost of
ice, upon which the whole American meat trade so
largely depends, should be very much reduced in this
country, and the elaborate arrangements for the conveyance of meat on American railways should be here
carried out with equal perfection.   Nor can it be
realised, in the opinion of Messrs. Read and Pell, unless
the rate of transit-charges be kept down to an unremunerative level.

For instance, though money is said to have been
made by exporters in 1878, when freights were low,
money is said to have been lost in 1879, when freights
were high.   "After balancing the various opinions of
the meat exporters, it appears that really prime beef can
be delivered in England and sold at a fair profit at 6½d.
per pound ; that 7d. gave a margin for a most lucrative trade ; but that 6d. per pound was barely sufficient
to pay the risks and outgoings, and would leave little
or no profit to the exporter."   But it is probable that
in this computation a minimum allowance is made for
the cost of distribution in England, which makes so
great a difference between the wholesale and retail price
of English meat.   Let the price of American meat at
the port of delivery be compared with the price of
English meat as sold by the grazier, or let an equal
allowance be made for the profits of middlemen on
both, and English farmers, with the prospect of a
constantly-increasing consumption, will find no reason
to despair of the future.

But, in the face of such facts, the conclusion appears inevitable that English farmers must in future study to reduce the price of those commodities which can easily be procured from abroad, and to meet the ever-growing demand for other commodities of which they ought to have an almost complete monopoly. "Nature," says Mr. Caird, "has given us a climate more favourable to the production of meat and milk, vegetables and grass, than that of any other European State. These, in proportion to their value, are the least costly in labour, and therefore the least affected by the rise of wages." This rise of wages, aggravated as it too often is by diminished efficiency in farm-labour, is often alleged as a principal cause of the agricultural distress. But it is largely compensated already, and might be far more largely compensated, by the use of steam-power and labour-saving machines, while the conversion of arable land into pasture reduces the effect of it to a minimum. On many farms the labour-bill is less, and the cost of working the land not greater, in the aggregate, than it was a generation ago, though fewer labourers are employed to do the same work, by the aid of machinery. Nor must it be forgotten that machinery gives the modern farmer an advantage beyond the mere economy of labour, for it greatly economises time, and enables him to seize on those golden moments the loss of which so often spoiled the harvest in olden times.

It may well be asked, indeed, why the farmer of 1879 or 1880, apart from bad seasons, is more to be pitied than his father or grandfather, after the decline of war prices. The price of wheat, it is true, has

ranged on the average about 7s. 6d. per quarter lower
during the ten years 1870–79 than during the ten
years 1840–49. On the other hand, barley has ranged
above 5s. per quarter higher, and oats above 3s. per
quarter higher. Meat costs the consumer nearly twice
as much as it did forty years ago ; poultry more than
twice as much ; wool, butter, eggs, vegetables, and
every kind of fancy-product supplied in old times by
farmers, have become much dearer within living
memory. When the Corn Laws were repealed, it was
never anticipated that agricultural prices could ever
rise to their present level, and many rents were then
fixed upon the assumption that wheat, in future, would
command an average price of 40s. per quarter; barley,
30s. ; oats, 20s. ; wool, 1s. per pound ; and butter,
10d. or 1s. per pound; no account being taken of
milk, for which the demand in great towns was then
infinitely less than it now is. Rents, it is true, were
very generally raised during and after the Crimean
War, and the remissions lately granted have probably
not more than compensated for that increase. Had
they remained stationary for the last thirty or forty
years, it would be extremely difficult for the farmer to
show in what respect his position has been altered for
the worse during this period. If the benefit of
machinery be set off against the higher price and
diminished efficiency of labour, the decrease in the poor-
rate against the addition of new rates, and the rise in
meat against the rise in tradesmen's bills, the profits of
farming ought to be quite as great as they were before
the Crimean War, especially as every improvement in the
breeds of cattle or sheep means earlier maturity, and

earlier maturity brings quicker returns. But then it is notorious that farmers are no longer content with the homely style of living common in the last generation, and this change of habits means far more than an ambitious and wasteful scale of household expenditure. It means, too often, aversion to manual labour on the part of the farmer himself, neglect of petty farm industries on the part of his wife and daughters, the purchase of hunters and pianos, the sacrifice of valuable days in unprofitable attendances at markets, and clandestine visits to bankers in the hope of procuring further accommodation. It is impossible, from the nature of the case, to ascertain the extent to which farming is now conducted on borrowed capital; still less can we compare the liabilities of modern farmers with those of their predecessors. But there is good reason to fear that a very large proportion of them have been living far more on credit than used to be possible, having indulged the passion for taking farms too large for their means, which Arthur Young so emphatically condemns, and never shaking off the load of debt. This is one explanation of the fact that so many tenants of the most respectable class proved unable to withstand one or two bad seasons. It is just such tenants who find it easiest to borrow money, and it is in bad seasons, when most landlords are willing to abate their strict rights, that less indulgent creditors not only refuse to make fresh advances, but also call in those already made. Then it turns out that a great part of the farm-stock really belongs to some one else, and that, after all, the British farmer may be as heavily indebted as the small French proprietor.

It must be admitted, moreover, that he is slow to discern the signs of the times, and to modify his old routine in accordance with new circumstances. Herein consists the elasticity of American agriculture, even in those Eastern States which have felt the pressure of Western competition almost as much as Great Britain. As the more important crops formerly grown in Massachusetts were gradually displaced by the influx of grain from more favoured districts, some estates were altogether deserted, and large numbers passed into the hands of new owners, while most of the few rented by tenants were purchased by the occupiers. The general result was that farmers were driven to a more thorough but more varied system of cultivation, leading to a reduction in the size of holdings, and to a considerable increase in the aggregate value of farm-produce in the State, as well as in the average yield of each acre. Thus, although only half as much barley was grown by Massachusetts farmers in 1875 as in 1865, and only one-third as much as in 1855, the "acreable yield" rose during this period from $19\frac{1}{2}$ to $25\frac{1}{2}$ bushels, and a similar increase was realised in the acreable yield of wheat, oats, Indian corn, beet-root, and potatoes. In the meantime, the production of milk was far more than trebled, and, upon the whole, more was extracted from the soil under the new method of farming, whether or not the farmer's profit was as great as before. Indeed, the aggregate value of the farm-products of Massachusetts in 1875 exceeded their aggregate value in 1865 by 8,000,000 dollars, notwithstanding the stress of Western competition, and the general reduction of currency prices.

It can hardly be said that an equal power of adaptation has been exhibited by English agriculturists, and it may well be doubted whether it could have been exhibited by rent-paying farmers, especially if encumbered by restrictive covenants.[1] But it is not only the dependence of tenancy or the conditions of restrictive covenants, dear to lawyers, which keep English rent-paying farmers in bondage to old routine. For instance, it has yet to be explained why the continuous rise in the price of milk for the last twenty years, and the steady growth of population at the rate of 1,000 a day, has not led to a corresponding extension of dairy farming. The dairy farmers of the Midland Counties, even when they live at some distance from a station, can well afford to deliver milk carriage-paid at a London terminus for 8d. or 9d. a gallon in summer, and 10d. or 11d. in winter. The same milk is sold to London consumers at a tolerably uniform price of 5d. a quart, or 20d. a gallon, so that the cost of distribution within the metropolis actually exceeds the joint cost of production and transit. It is truly marvellous that dairy farmers and town consumers should willingly submit to a system which robs both for the sole advantage of retail dealers, but it is no less marvellous that dairy farmers should be unwilling to sell milk to country neighbours, even at a profit of 40 or 50 per cent., until at last the very demand for it has died out in some districts, to the great injury of the rising generation. We are informed by eminent agricultural authorities that the consumption of milk in

---

[1] In Massachusetts, out of 44,549 separate farms 43,495 were cultivated by their owners in 1875.

England might well be multiplied tenfold,[1] and that where it is now sold by the spoonful it might be sold by the pint, if the mass of the people should recover the habit of drinking it, and could rely on obtaining a regular supply at a moderate price.   Yet, notwithstanding the fall in the price of cheese, there are many villages in which labourers cannot buy fresh milk for their children at any price, though it is often given to pigs, and Mr. Bear states that "even on farmhouse tables it is not uncommon to see condensed milk all the way from Switzerland." Here, then, is one branch of farming which seems capable of a very remunerative development, even though no changes should be made in the present English system of land-tenure or land-tenancy.   The London milk supply is, in fact, largely derived from dairy-farms conducted on a grand scale by joint-stock companies, or by enterprising farmers who supply the companies, and it is difficult to understand why far more farming capital should not be invested in so lucrative a business.

Unfortunately, the attractions of speculation combine with the influence of prejudice to fix the attention of English farmers on corn-growing, and to divert it from safer and more promising openings for his skill.   In the autumn of 1879 this besetting temptation of English agriculture received a fresh impulse from the publication of returns purporting to show the marvellous success of Mr. Prout's experiments in " continuous corn-growing"

---

[1] See the comprehensive speech of Mr. Clare Read on the appointment of an Agricultural Commission in July, 1879. Mr. Read says that "if you could only get 6d. a gallon for the milk that can be produced on a farm in the summer, or 8d. a gallon in the winter, that would pay the farmer better than grazing bullocks."

on a farm owned by himself near Sawbridgeworth. It was stated that on this farm, consisting of 450 acres, about six-sevenths of the whole acreage had been kept under white crops, and only one-seventh under clover or sainfoin hay, for a period of fourteen years from 1866 to 1879, all the crops—grain, straw, and hay—being sold off the farm by public auction. The loss of all this straw and hay, which ought naturally to have been consumed by cattle and to have found its way back into the soil, was compensated by wholesale purchases of artificial manures, averaging 50s. an acre annually. It was alleged, however, that selling off the straw was not an essential feature of the system, and that an equally good profit might have been obtained by feeding cattle, and using farmyard manure to some extent in the place of bones, guano, and nitrate of soda. The balance-sheet of receipts and expenditure for the fourteen years exhibited an average yearly profit of £600, after allowing 3½ per cent. on £16,000 purchase-money, and interest at 5 per cent. on landlord's and tenant's improvements. But it was explained that during the five years 1874-8, in which the seasons had been generally unfavourable, a still higher average profit had been realised, amounting to about £900, in consequence of the outlay for manures being smaller, and the return from produce greater.

The inferences suggested by these startling figures were vigorously challenged by Mr. Lawes, from whose example Mr. Prout had borrowed the idea of his system, as well as by Mr. Caird, whose researches into the conditions of British agriculture pointed to very different conclusions.[1] Mr. Lawes gave strong reasons for believ-

[2] See their letters in the *Times* of Aug. 27 and Sept. 1, 1879.

ing that Mr. Prout's system could not be permanently adopted with success, even if all the soil-ingredients removed by his crops were replaced by artificial manures, but that in fact, while certain of these ingredients were thus replaced, he was " drawing upon his soil-capital for both nitrogen and potash ;" in other words, that he must have been gradually exhausting his soil, though its natural richness, aided by deep and skilful tillage, might disguise this effect for a considerable period.   He warned landlords and farmers that greater freedom in the growth and sale of crops, though desirable in itself, would probably involve larger demands on the latent soil-capital, and declared his conviction, based on his own experiments, that although corn, and especially barley, might be grown with profit more frequently than is permitted by the received theory of rotation, farmers must learn to depend more and more on meat and other products derived from stock.[1]   Mr. Caird, fully concurring with these views, earnestly deprecated the extension of a system which, if generally followed, would convert six-sevenths of the cultivated land in England into one vast corn-field.   Without denying that, under favourable conditions, handsome (though not extraordinary) profits could be realised for a while on that system, he insisted

---

[1] In a pamphlet entitled " Is Higher Farming a Remedy for Lower Wages ? " Mr. Lawes states, as the general and uniform result of the Rothamsted experiments, " that, beyond a certain limit, the increase of crop is *not* in proportion to the amount of manure supplied," or the increased cost of cultivation.   " Whether we go from high to still higher farming, with an ordinary rotation of crops, with large amounts of farm-yard manure applied year after year for the growth of corn, or with artificial manures in gradually increasing amounts, less increase of produce is obtained for a given amount of manure applied, the greater the excess of it over what may be termed moderately high farming."

upon the impolicy of extending the wheat-growing area at home, at the very moment when the English markets are threatened with a glut of cheaper and better wheat from abroad. This argument appears to admit of no answer. If a progressive rise in the price of wheat and barley were to be expected, it might be wise to defy Mr. Lawes' warnings, and to ascertain how far the system of continuous cropping is really capable of being pushed without breaking down. It is asserted, on credible testimony, that land in Portugal, of no abnormal fertility, but abundantly manured every year in the old-fashioned manner, has regularly borne corn crops summer after summer for several generations.[1] Facts of this kind, however inconsistent with received doctrines of scientific rotation, are not unworthy of serious investigation ; but the lesson which they appear to convey is one of far greater importance to American than it is to English farmers. It may possibly be shown that, even without the use of artificial manures, the soil-capital of land may go on reproducing itself under the operation of laws hitherto imperfectly understood. But it never will be shown that, so long as free trade prevails, the highly-rented land and uncertain climate of Great Britain can produce wheat to compete in quality and cheapness with that grown on the boundless prairies of Western America.

[1] See an interesting letter from Mr. Oswald Craufurd, Her Majesty's Consul at Oporto, in the *Times* of Aug. 27, 1879. Mr. Craufurd attributes these results to the practice of stall-feeding large numbers of cattle on artificial grasses, mixed with the straw of wheat, barley, and oats, none of which is used for litter. The litter is composed of gorse, heather, ferns, and mosses, which are afterwards spread on the fields with the manure, and greatly increase its chemical value.

There is, however, one very obvious source of waste and loss in the economy of modern English farming which admits of being indefinitely reduced. In the olden times, however low might be the price of farm produce, the farmer got the whole, or nearly the whole, of it. The corn-dealer, no doubt, in spite of statutes, bought up most of his grain, and made an ample profit upon it, but there was scarcely any other intermediary between the agricultural producer and the consumer. The country being then more thickly peopled, and the whole organisation of trade far simpler than it now is, the farmer virtually undertook the entire cost of distribution, and received the full value of his commodities, buying and selling without the intervention of middlemen. He usually bred and often slaughtered his own cattle, thereby appropriating the breeder's, dealer's, and butcher's profit, as well as that of the grazier. His wife carried her own turkeys, poultry, butter, cheese, and eggs, to market, not without a considerable expenditure of time and trouble, but with the prospect of realising their retail, instead of their wholesale, price. All this is now changed: a whole army of middlemen has sprung up, and a toll is exacted at every stage in the process whereby the national food supplies are brought within the consumer's reach. The aggregate effect of these various tolls in lowering the farmer's profit on meat greatly exceeds the loss caused by American competition, and, in the case of butter, the deduction is still more inordinate. It is stated that butter produced in the pastures of Cork usually pays no less than six or seven profits before it is placed on a London householder's table,[1] and a like subdivision of the gains which might conceivably be reaped by the farmer alone might be found in other branches of agricultural manufacture.[2] Of course this subdivision of profit may possibly be more than compensated by a saving in labour or some other form of outlay, or it may possibly be inevitable under the circumstances actually existing. But these propositions cannot be taken for granted. It may be that, with a little effort, the farmers of one or more villages might combine to employ a salesman to dispose of their produce in London at the best market price, and thus increase their profit by a very large percentage, as it is certain that parties of fishermen on the coast might protect themselves by a like method against scandalous extortions on the part of middlemen. In short, an extensive application of the co-operative prin-

---

[1] I am indebted for this statement to Mr. W. Bence Jones, a land-owner and practical farmer of great experience in the county of Cork. He thus enumerates the recipients of the several profits : (1) the dairy farmer, (2) the local dealer in the nearest country town, (3) the Cork butter buyer, (4) the Cork export merchant, (5) the English import merchant or factor, (6) the wholesale cheesemonger, (7) the retail shop-keeper. Where one person combines two of these capacities he incurs a double risk, and takes a double profit.

[2] In the graphic description of agricultural life, by Mr. Richard Jefferies, entitled "Hodge and his Masters," an old-fashioned farmer is introduced, who declares, as the result of his life-long experience, that a modern farmer submits to eight or nine tolls instead of the single rent paid by his grandfather. The receivers of these several tolls are his landlord, the lawyer who advanced half of his original farm-capital, the banker to whom he is indebted for short loans under the seal of secrecy, the auctioneer through whom he sells his cattle and sheep, and who often keeps a depôt for horses, the railway company, the seedsman, the manure merchant, the manufacturer of agricultural implements, and the school-master who educates the farmer's own children, while he is rated to educate those of his labourers.

ciple to the distribution of farm produce, if not to agriculture itself, may prove to be one solution of the agricultural problem. Before the English farmer is driven by foreigners out of English markets, he will certainly strain every nerve to utilise all the advantage which proximity to English markets ought to secure for him.[1]

[1] Mr. Lawes, in reviewing " the Wheat-crop of 1880," furnishes some interesting statistics respecting the comparative yield of that and the previous year. He regards the wheat crop of 1879 as the worst of the present century, since it averaged only about 16 bushels per acre, of miserable quality. He estimates the wheat-crop of 1880 at about 30 bushels per acre, or slightly above the average. At this rate of production, the 3,057,784 acres harvested in 1880 would yield 11,466,690 quarters, which, after proper deductions for seed, would leave a little over 10,500,000 quarters available for consumption. The result is, that about 43 per cent. of the population would be fed on home-grown wheat in 1880—81, whereas it is probable that not 25 per cent. were fed on home-grown wheat in 1879—80. On Mr. Lawes' own experimental farm at Rothamsted, the yield of a plot continuously unmanured for 40 years was above the average of the last 10 years, though below that of the previous 18 years. A second plot, treated continuously with farm-yard manure, produced a crop somewhat above the average of previous years, while three other plots, treated continuously with various kinds of artificial manure, produced crops nearly corresponding with the average.

CHAPTER III.

Foreign Systems of Land Tenure.

No survey of the English Land System would be complete which should take no cognisance of the land systems inherited or adopted by other civilised nations. Since the famous inquiry of Arthur Young into the agrarian institutions and agricultural state of France, increasing attention has been paid by English economists to foreign customs of land-tenure and land-tenancy. The reports drawn up for the Foreign Office in the years 1869-70, by Her Majesty's Secretaries of Legation in the principal countries of Europe and the United States of America, contain a mine of precious materials on both these subjects. Though specially directed to points bearing immediately on the objects of the Irish Land Bill, they include a large mass of evidence on such questions as the descent of land on intestacy, and the general tendency of various codes to favour the accumulation or dispersion of landed property. Some extracts from the results thus obtained, supplemented by the testimony of independent authorities, may help us to appreciate the unique character of the English Land System, and to forecast the course of its future development.

1. In France, as is well known, "the land is chiefly occupied by small proprietors, who form the great majority throughout the country," so that of some 7,500,000 pro-

prietors, about 5,000,000 are estimated to average six acres each, while only 50,000 average 600 acres.[1]   This *morcellement* is the direct and foreseen consequence of the partible succession enforced by the Code Napoléon, under which all children inherit the bulk of their father's property equally, without distinction of age or sex, a testator with one child being allowed to dispose of half, a testator with two children of one-third only, and a testator with three children of one-quarter.[2]   The dismemberment of estates thus produced is stated to be progressive.   "With some rare exceptions, all the great properties have been gradually broken up, and even the first and second classes" (averaging 600 and 60 acres respectively) " are fast merging into the third."[3] This statement, however, must be taken with some qualification.   In France, as in England, the ostensible

[1] The distribution of landed property in France is somewhat differently stated by M. Lavergne.   Writing before the loss of Alsace and Lorraine, he estimated that 5,000,000 proprietors owned on the average 3 hectares, or 7½ acres, each; that 500,000 proprietors of a higher class owned on the average 30 hectares, or 75 acres, each; and that 50,000 great proprietors owned on the average 300 hectares, or 750 acres, each.   This classification is followed in the text as the more trustworthy.

[2] Under a salutary provision of the French Code, prodigals can be placed under an interdict, and trustees appointed to manage their estates.

[3] According to Mr. G. Gibson Richardson, "the estates that are disappearing are the medium-sized ones, of from 50 to 100 acres; they are eaten into on both sides.   A large landowner is glad to add to his estate a small adjoining one; and small owners will give almost any money to put another small bit to what they already possess."   He entirely denies that small French landowners must needs become poorer and poorer in each generation, as contrary to experience.   "The men make money and buy back land which has been divided, or they do so with the dowry of their wives; the law of succession divides, accumulated wealth unites; small properties increase a little at the expense of large ones, but very much at the expense of middle-sized ones."   (" Corn and Cattle-Producing Districts of France," pp. 40, 41).

number of very small properties is magnified by the inclusion of little plots surrounding dwelling-houses, of market-gardens, and of fields in which a cow or horse may be kept by persons either mainly supported by wages or engaged in non-agricultural callings. The number of proprietors is certainly not so great as the number of properties, several of which may belong to one owner; and many of the smaller proprietors are engaged in the cultivation of the vine—a very exceptional branch of agricultural industry, requiring minute attention and incessant manual labour. After all, only one-third of France, exclusive of State domains and communal property, is owned by peasants, with an average of 7½ acres each, and a very much smaller proportion is cultivated by this class, who appear to let their lands freely. Another third part is owned, and apparently cultivated for the most part, by yeomen proprietors averaging some 75 acres each. The remaining third is owned by landlords averaging some 750 acres—some, perhaps, descended from ancient *seigneurs*—whose estates are chiefly farmed by others, and sometimes approach in extent those of great English noblemen.[1] The average price of agricultural land in

---

[1] These conclusions have lately received a strong confirmation from the exhaustive researches of M. Gimel, *Directeur des Contributions Directes*, the chief results of which have been ably summarised by Mr. Barham Zincke. According to M. Gimel's estimate, founded on the communal assessment lists, the actual number of proprietors in France—including those below one-quarter of an acre—was, in the year 1858, no less than 8,264,795; and the increase between 1835 and 1858 had been 20·37 per cent. A more detailed examination of the statistics relative to four typical departments shows this increase to have been largely contributed by purchasers of sites for houses, with or without gardens, and proves that only one-twentieth of the soil passes into these minute parcels.

France is no less than forty years' purchase, and small capitalists on the whole outbid larger capitalists in the competition for it.   Indeed, such is the passion for landed property, that French peasant-owners, like English farmers, will often spend capital which they can ill spare, or borrow from usurers, to extend their little domains.   Yet the mortgages on the small properties of France, as stated by M. Lavergne, amount to no more than 10 per cent. on their aggregate value.

It is a very delusive, though very common, error to interpret the statistics which show the distribution of landed property in France as if they implied that nearly the whole of the soil is cultivated by peasant-owners. This error is apparently confirmed by the fact that, out of every hundred farms in France, seventy are cultivated on the " faire-valoir direct " system, against twenty-one on the " fermage " or tenancy system, and eight only on the " métayage " or co-operative system. But if we look at the acreage over which these systems prevail respectively, we find that more than one-third of France is cultivated under the system of tenancy, thirteen per cent. under that of co-operation, and about half on the farmer-proprietary system, which includes cultivation by yeomen as well

---

About one-third of these four departments is possessed by owners of less than 20 acres, one-third by owners of 20 to 100 acres, and one-third by owners of more than 100 acres.   It is observed that in one district adapted to cattle-breeding, there is a tendency for peasant-properties to rise to, and stop at, about 25 acres, that being the extent of land most conveniently worked by a single family.

It is curious that Arthur Young, so far back as 1787, supposed one-third of France to be occupied by " small properties," which, however, he does not define.

as cultivation by peasants.[1] It is interesting to observe that, as might be expected, most of the corn sent to market in France is produced under the system of tenancy, or métayage, and not under that of farmer-proprietorship. The late Mr. G. Gibson Richardson, one of the highest authorities on this subject, estimating the entire wheat-growing area of France at about 17,000,000 acres, explained why the acreable produce of this area should appear to be so far below the English standard, and so far below what it really is. This result arises from a strange inaccuracy in the official method of computation, whereby all the 87 departments, whatever their wheat-growing acreage, and whatever their acreable produce, are treated as units of equal value, and the general acreage is very unduly depressed by the shortcomings of districts wholly unsuitable for wheat. For instance, four departments, with 134,000 acres under wheat, yielding only eleven bushels per acre, count the same as four others with 1,213,000 acres, yielding twenty-five bushels per acre ; so that, whereas the average yield of the eight is twenty-three bushels per acre, it is reckoned at only eighteen. Mr. Richardson states that, in the great wheat-growing districts of France—Flanders, Artois, Picardy, Beaune, Brie, and Poitou—the average produce per acre probably exceeds that for the United

---

[1] Mr. G. Gibson Richardson gives the following statistics of farm occupations in France:—"The cultivated land is occupied by 3,225,877 farms, each under separate management; more than half the number, 56 per cent., are under 12½ acres; a fifth, from 12½ to 25 acres; so that three-fourths of them are less than 25 acres." ("Corn and Cattle Producing Districts of France," p. 30.)

Kingdom, and on some farms reaches forty bushels.[1]

There is, however, no doubt that on the whole the acreable produce of wheat in England is greater than in France; only it must be remembered that France has brought under cultivation a much larger extent of its whole area than England, that of this area it devotes five or six times as large an acreage to wheat-growing as England, and that, if this acreage is less productive than it might be made, the fault lies with French tenant-farmers, and not with French peasant-owners.

Volumes of controversy have not exhausted the arguments either for or against the French law of inheritance, but it is instructive to remark how entirely its opponents have shifted their ground. Mr. McCulloch, writing in 1823, predicted that, under its operation, France must certainly become, within fifty years, "the greatest pauper warren in the world," and share with Ireland the honour of furnishing hewers of wood and drawers of water to other countries. Arthur Young, writing in 1787, had condemned the voluntary subdivision of property on the same ground, and it was long a received opinion that compulsory subdivision of property stimulated the increase of population to a frightful extent. The same law is now attacked, with at least equal justice, as directly contributing to keep the population almost stationary. However this may be, it is a very significant fact that neither under the First Empire nor under the restored dynasty of the

---

[1] See his letters to the *Times* of September 15th and October 20th, 1879, elucidating the statistics furnished in Mr. G. Baden Powell's letter of September 6th.

Bourbons, nor under the Orleanist monarchy, nor under the Second Empire, nor under the new Republic, has any serious attempt been made to repeal this law, bequeathed to France by the authors of the Revolution. For, as we are truly informed in the report of Mr. Sackville West, drawn up shortly before the Franco-German War, "the prevalent public opinion as to the advantages of the tenure of land by small proprietors is that it has been advantageous to the production of the soil, and has tended to the improvement of the material condition of the agricultural population." It is believed, he continues, that subdivision "conduces to political as well as social order, because, the greater the number of the proprietors, the greater is the guarantee for the respect of property, and the less likely are the masses to nourish revolutionary and subversive designs." That it conduces to industry and thrift, is too well known to admit of argument; indeed, the proverbial reproach of the French peasantry is that, in their miserly frugality, they sacrifice all that makes life worth having. But, if they starve themselves, they do not starve the land. M. Lavergne, though fully alive to the possible evils of excessive subdivision, bore witness that, on the whole, the best cultivation in France was that of the peasant proprietors, and assuredly the richest provinces of France are those in which this class of landowners predominates.[1]

[1] Much valuable information on the effects of the French land laws has been collected by Mr. Kay, in his "Free Trade in Land," chap. x. See also an article on "La Situation Agricole de la France," in the *Revue des Deux Mondes*, Jan. 15, 1880, and Mr. James Howard's treatise on "Continental Farming." Mr. Howard's opinion is not favourable to small farms, the owners of which, he says, "work from sunrise to sunset,

2. The elaborate report on land tenure in Prussia and the North German Confederation, by Mr. Harriss Gastrell, attests the same preponderance of public opinion in favour of small proprietorship, which is encouraged by the law. "In cases of intestacy the law divides all property, including land, in certain proportions, among widow and children; or equally amongst the children, if there be no widow," and no disposition can deprive the "natural heirs" of their claim to a fixed allotment, sometimes amounting to as much as two-thirds of the whole. Though subject to these limitations, "the custom of making a will is almost universal:" but "the restrictions on land by settlements and the like are much less than in England." Entails are not absolutely prohibited, but the extent of land affected by them in Prussia is said not to exceed one-thirteenth of the whole kingdom, the rest of which is held in absolute ownership, with the amplest facilities of mortgage and sale. The consequence is that in Prussia, exclusive of the Rhine provinces and Westphalia, there were in 1858[1] 1,300,000 proprietors, of whom 108 only had estates large enough to be rated over £1,500, and only about 16,000 had estates of more than 400 acres, while about 350,000 had estates varying from 20 to 400 acres, and the rest, some 925,000 in number, owned less than 20 acres.[2] Of the smallest

doing double the work for themselves they would for an employer, and live far harder than the English peasants." He observes that "the size of farm considered necessary to support a family is about four hectares (ten acres)."

[1] The report of Mr. Harriss Gastrell was based on the Returns for that year.

[2] Mr. James Howard states that "in Prussia there are 900,000 farms under four acres in extent." Probably this estimate includes the Rhine Provinces and Westphalia.

proprietors, a large proportion were day-labourers, working occasionally for wages; and the minimum extent of land sufficient to support a man and his family was estimated at from 7 to 20 acres or more, according to fertility of soil and other local advantages. Many of these peasant proprietors, living wholly on the fruits of their own soil, have raised themselves from the rank of day-labourers into the class of yeomanry which, in modern Prussia, as in old England, constitutes the bone and sinew of the nation. Even the greatest proprietors seldom delegate the work of cultivation to mere tenants, but either farm themselves or manage their estates through bailiffs.[1] In the Rhine provinces and Westphalia, where the French laws were introduced at the beginning of the century, the subdivision of landed property is carried so far that each proprietor has but 10 acres on the average. The result is that, as we are told in the report of Mr. R. D. Morier, "the Palatinate peasant cultivates his land more with the passion of an artist than in the plodding spirit of a mere bread-winner."

The Prussian land system, established by a series of legislative acts extending over half a century, and expressly designed to favour the elevation of the peasantry into a body of independent proprietors, has been copied by other States of North Germany. Its effects on the agriculture of Saxony have been graphically described, from personal observation, by Mr. Barham Zincke, whose intimate acquaintance with the agriculture of Switzerland, Central France, and the Channel Islands,

[1] See Mr. Shaw-Lefevre's "Freedom of Land," chap. vi., and Mr. Kay's "Free Trade in Land," chap. xv.

gives an additional weight to his remarks. He found the district west and north of Dresden cultivated, for the most part, by yeomen owning farms of about 50 acres each. According to him, the land is kept infinitely cleaner than it is in England, since there are no hedges or ditches sheltering weeds or harbouring vermin. No space is wasted, for the heart of the owner is in the soil, tending every plant with parental care, and regarding every weed as an enemy. Comparatively little is expended in hired labour, and such labour is more efficient than in England, because the labourer works side by side with his employer, and is separated from him by no class distinction. The enormous influx of grain from the Western States of America having reduced the demand for German corn in the English market, the Saxon farmer, like the farmer of New England, has adapted himself to circumstances, and raises a far greater variety of produce than English farmers attempt to raise on a far better soil. Potatoes and other vegetables, poultry, milk, and butter, are exported in large quantities from these sandy plains; where agricultural plants could not live, forest-trees are skilfully planted, and fruit-trees, without the slightest protection, line the roads and footpaths, as they do in Switzerland and other parts of the Continent in which the ownership of land is widely diffused.[1]

3. "Wurtemberg is remarkable as the country where subdivision of land is carried to the greatest extreme," containing as it does some 280,000 peasant

---

[1] See an excellent letter on "Agriculture in Germany," by the Rev. F. Barham Zincke, published in the *Times* of August 27, 1879.

owners, with less than five acres each, and about
160,000 proprietors of estates above five acres.   Upon
intestacy, the land is equally divided among all the
children, male and female.   The father, however, seems
to be allowed full liberty of disposition over the property, so long as a certain moderate portion, defined by
law (*pflicht-theil*), is reserved for each child.   On the
smaller peasant farms, " when, in accordance with the
will of the father, one child becomes owner of all the
paternal land, an estimate is formed on a footing rather
favourable to him, and he compensates the brothers and
sisters by equal sums of money.   The daughters, however, are more frequently on their marriage allotted an
equal share of land ; and, as the husband is probably
the proprietor of a piece of land elsewhere in the commune, the intersection and subdivision of the land goes
on increasing."   On the largest farms the custom of
Primogeniture has encroached still further on that of
equal division.   Here the eldest son commonly succeeds to the whole property, " often in the father's
lifetime.   When the parent is incapacitated by age
from managing his farm, he retires to a small cottage,
generally on the property, and receives from the son in
possession contributions towards his support both in
money and kind.   The other children receive a sum o
money calculated according to the size of the property
and the number of children, but which, in any case, falls
far short of the sum which they would receive, if the
property were equally divided, or even were the law of
pflicht-theil acted on.   They have, however, their home
there until they establish themselves independently or
take service on another property."   Mr. Phipps, who

gives this account of the Wurtemberg land system, adds that political economists of that country are now " of opinion that small proprietors, who complete their means of livelihood by industrial pursuits, are the most desirable class to encourage, whereas formerly agriculture on a large scale was considered the most profitable." Precisely the same opinion is recorded by Mr. Bailie, writing on the " Land System of Baden," where property is much subdivided. He states that owners of small freeholds do not differ from the larger proprietors in respect of dwellings, clothing, mode of living, or education ; that they realise better returns from the same number of acres ; and that, in consequence, large estates and large farms are giving place to small estates and holdings. This change, he adds, is there regarded as tending " to promote the greater economical and moral prosperity of the people, to raise the average standard of education, and to increase the national standard of defence and taxation."

4. In Bavaria, where the land is very much subdivided, Mr. Fenton attests the general prevalence of a custom very similar to that which characterises the larger peasant farms in Wurtemberg. Except in the Bavarian Palatinate, where the Code Napoléon is in force, the descent and inheritance of land are governed throughout Bavaria by the principles, though not everywhere by the express provisions, of the common law. " A proprietor is bound to bequeath at his death a certain defined portion of his property, to be divided in equal shares among all his legitimate children. That portion must not be less than one-half, if the number of children be five, or more than five ; and not less than

one-third, if there be four, or less than four, children."
Where the property consists of land, and especially if
it be a peasant property, the eldest son may, and
usually does, retain the whole, paying the rest a pecuniary indemnity for their shares, if the father has not
already installed him in possession, as sometimes
happens, during his own lifetime. "Amongst that
class the almost invariable custom is for the testator to
leave the whole of the real property—farmhouse, farm
buildings, and land—in the possession of one member
of the family, commonly the widow or the eldest son,
and that person then becomes responsible to the children
for the payment to them of a sum of money corresponding to the value (as ascertained by official appraise-
ment) of their share of the property, the children's
share being generally fixed at one-half of the whole,
real as well as personal. It is further a universally-
understood condition of an arrangement of the nature
above described, that the person who remains in possession of the property and becomes its owner, is
bound during a certain number of years (after the
payment of their shares to all the children) to provide
any one or all of them with board and lodging at the
homestead, in the event of their falling into distress
from sickness, want of employment, &c." In short,
the peasant proprietors of Bavaria, who are admitted
to be a thriving class, appear to keep up their family
estates with as much tenacity as our own landed gentry,
but with a jealousy for the rights of younger children
which reminds us of the Irish peasant farmers.

5. In the Austrian Empire, on the contrary, the devolution of all property, real and personal, is regulated

by the Civil Code of 1869, by which "no preference is accorded to eldest sons," nor have sons any advantage over daughters; but "an exception exists in the case of family entails (*majorats*)." Of course, these entails are mainly created on large properties. Whatever be the instrument which constitutes such an entail, Mr. Lytton remarks that it has no legal validity without the special consent of the legislative power. Mr. James Howard notices the existence of a further exception applicable to "peasant-farms," the maximum size of which is 60 acres, and the minimum 15 acres; which exception, however, is no longer sanctioned by law in the Archduchy of Austria itself, though maintained in other parts of the Empire. "In the case of such farms, when a proprietor dies, his eldest son takes the land; and an assessor is called in, who fixes the amount to be paid to the other children." The result of Mr. Howard's inquiries showed that in the Austrian dominions "no class of tenant-farmers exists; all are proprietors, except in a few districts, and rare instances." Nevertheless, a larger amount of agricultural machinery had been exported from England to Austria and Hungary than to any other part of Europe, and it was estimated that in ten years, 1860—70, nearly 2,000 steam threshing-machines had been introduced into the Empire, chiefly for use in Hungary.

6. It is almost superfluous to state that Switzerland is a land of small proprietors, the law of equal division being heartily supported by custom. According to Mr. Mackenzie's report, "the quantity of land usually held by each varies from six to twelve acres, small lots held together, and the larger intersected by other properties,"

yet, instead of being pauperised by subdivision, the Swiss are proverbial for successful enterprise in trade both at home and abroad. It is, indeed, difficult to say whether the purely agricultural peasantry of Switzerland, and the operative classes living on their own little freeholds in the manufacturing districts, offer the more remarkable example of industry and thrift, intelligence and comfort, widely diffused through a whole community. The evidence of this is too overwhelming and too patent to escape the attention even of ordinary travellers, and it may safely be affirmed that if Swiss habits and institutions could be transplanted into England, agricultural distress would almost cease to be possible.

7. In Belgium, *morcellement* has notoriously been carried, under the Code Napoléon, to a greater extreme than in France itself; so that, according to official statistics and estimates cited in the Foreign Office Reports, the average size of estates, deducting woodlands and wastes, might be stated at seven acres; and four - fifths of them did not exceed twelve acres. "The dispersion of land is increased by the system which generally prevails at public sales of dividing real estate into small parcels or lots;" otherwise the properties of small families, sold for the purpose of effecting a more convenient distribution among children, would be constantly passing into the hands of rich families. The works of M. de Laveleye and others have so familiarised the minds of English economists with the effects of the Belgian land system on Belgian agriculture that it would be superfluous to recapitulate them. It is admitted that Belgian tenant-

farmers are ground down by rack-rents, and that even the small Belgian proprietors lead a harder life than many an English farm-labourer. Nevertheless, the fact remains that, under this land system, one of the poorest soils in Europe, fertilised by ten centuries of laborious husbandry, fetches a higher price, acre for acre, if it does not yield a larger produce in grain, vegetables, and meat, than any but the most favoured districts of Great Britain.[1]

8. In Holland, as we learn from the same Reports, " the law of succession requires the division in equal portions, amongst the children or next of kin, of a major part of every inheritance without regard to its nature or origin, and this is naturally calculated to favour to a great extent the division of landed property. But, on the other hand, there exists a very prevalent desire with individuals to avoid unnecessarily splitting up the paternal estates. It is a common thing for a farmer, whether proprietor or tenant, to have accumulated before his death sufficient movable property, frequently in the funds, to enable him to assign a

---

[1] See M. de Laveleye's Essay on the Land System of Belgium and Holland, in " Systems of Land Tenure," 1876; Mr. Kay's " Free Trade in Land," Mr. Shaw-Lefevre's " Freedom of Land," and Mr. Thornton's " Peasant Proprietors." See also the Report of Dr. Augustus Voelcker and Mr. H. M. Jenkins on Belgian agriculture, in which its alleged superiority in productiveness is combated. Mr. James Howard, in his treatise on " Continental Farming," adopts the same view. He observes that, in comparing the English with the Belgian stock of cattle, it is often forgotten that many of the Belgian oxen are employed for draught purposes, instead of horses, and that most of the rest are inferior in weight and size to English oxen. Even if draught-oxen be included, he reckons the total quantity of meat raised per acre to be only 98 lbs. in Belgium, against 148 lbs. in England and Wales.

portion therefrom to one or another of his children."
The policy of the law, however, is rather against family
arrangements whereby the eldest son may retain all the
land and the younger children may be compensated in
money, since it imposes an increased tax on successions
thus modified by agreement. A very attractive picture
of rural life under the Dutch land system is drawn by
M. de Laveleye :—"The farmers of Holland lead a
comfortable, well-to-do, and cheerful life. They are
well housed and excellently clothed. They have china-
ware and plate on their sideboards, tons of gold at their
notaries', public securities in their safes, and in their
stables excellent horses. Their wives are bedecked with
splendid corals and gold. They do not work themselves
to death. On the ice in winter, at the Kermesses in
summer, they enjoy themselves with the zest of men
whose minds are free from care." The chief reason
assigned by M. de Laveleye for the superior prosperity
of Dutch, as compared with Belgian, farmers, is that
in Holland landed property has remained almost
entirely in the hands of peasants, the savings
of townspeople being invested in public securities;
whereas in Belgium there is an eager competition
of capitalists for estates, forcing up the price and
rent of land to an abnormal extent. But M. de
Laveleye's ideal of agricultural felicity in Holland
is to be found in the province of Groningen, where
much of the land is cultivated under a species of
hereditary lease, known as Beklem-regt, at a moderate
and invariable rent. "This system," he says, "derived
from the Middle Ages, has created a class of semi-
proprietors, independent, proud, simple, but withal

eager for enlightenment, appreciating the advantages of education, practising husbandry not by blind routine and as a mean occupation, but as a noble profession by which they may acquire wealth, influence, and the consideration of their fellow-men."

This description of Dutch rural economy cannot be accepted without some qualification. No doubt the national habit of accumulation, with the aid of lucrative marriages, enables peasant-owners in Holland to keep their properties together. But the competition of capitalists is not wanting, and the passion for proprietorship often tempts the peasant-owner to invest on new purchases of land, at a ruinous price, capital which might be far more profitably invested in improving that which he already possesses. The leaseholders under the Beklem-regt system are practically owners, subject to a quit-rent, and, though usually excellent farmers, do not appear to enjoy any special advantage, in respect of tenure, over semi-proprietors, holding at fee-farm rents, in various parts of the United Kingdom, and especially in Scotland.

9. The same de-feudalising movement, dating from the French Revolution, and deriving a fresh impulse from the democratic revival of 1848, has profoundly modified the land systems of most other European countries. In Sweden and Denmark the creation of new entails has been prohibited, though some old entails survive, as in Prussia. In Norway the French law prevails, being in harmony with the ancient custom of the country. Yet subdivision has not yet been carried to extremes, very few estates being under 40 acres, and very many above 300 acres, besides a large

tract of mountain pasture.[1] In the Hanse Towns, as
well as in Schleswig-Holstein, primogeniture is more
countenanced by law; but even where, as in Bremen,
the real estate goes to the eldest son on intestacy, the
"co-heirs," or younger children, are entitled to be
portioned out of it. In Italy, says Mr. Bonham, "the
laws in force tend in every way to favour the dispersion
of land," and equal division, without distinction of sex,
is the rule of inheritance on intestacy; but a landowner,
having children, may leave one-half of his property by
will; the other half—*legitima portio*—"cannot be burdened with any conditions by the testator." But the
political union of Italy has not yet brought about an
assimilation of its various provincial land systems, and
it will probably be long before the peasant-ownership of
Lombardy displaces the old territorial economy of
Sicily. In Greece and Portugal the law of intestacy
and the restrictions on testamentary disposition are, in
all essential respects, the same as in Italy, producing in
both countries a large and increasing subdivision of
landed property. Mr. Finlay, speaking of the stationary condition of Greek agriculture, observes:—" It
is the almost universal rule that each small proprietor
possesses a *zevgari*" (or plot requiring two pair of oxen
to plough it), " and that each cultivator of national land
occupies no more." Mr. Merlin, in his report on
Greece, mentions the curious fact that " it is extremely
rare for the sons to marry till their sisters are provided
for; and this feeling pervades all classes." The active
jealousy of primogeniture and partiality for subdivision

---

[1] Mr. Thornton's "Peasant Proprietors," second edition, p. 82; quoted
by Mr. Kay, "Free Trade in Land," chap. xi.

exhibited in the recent legislation of Portugal contrasts strangely with the survival of great ancestral properties in Spain.   It has, indeed, been carried further than even M. de Laveleye approves in the abolition of a father's right to designate one child as his heir, under the ancient form of Portuguese land-tenure known as the Aforamento, which resembles the Beklem-regt of Groningen.   In Russia, where the land system has been complicated by political and social distinctions between classes, by serfdom, and by the communal organisation, Mr. Michell reports that local usage regulates the descent of peasant properties.   The law of intestacy for the rest of the community is based on equal division, giving males a preference over females.   "There is no general law of primogeniture, although, in a few great families, estates have been entailed under a special law passed in the reign of the Emperor Nicholas.   In 1713 Peter the Great attempted to introduce a general inheritance in fee of the eldest son ; but this was so much opposed to the spirit of the Russian landowners, that one of the first acts of Peter II. was to cancel the Ukase of 1713."

10. Under the land laws of most States in the American Union, an owner in fee-simple has nearly the same power of disposition as he would possess in this country, but the rule of equal division prevails in case of intestacy.   The results of this system, and the reason why they differ so widely from those produced by our own, are succinctly described in the following passages of Mr. Ford's report :

" The system of land occupation in the United States of America may be generally described as by small proprietors. The proprietary class throughout the country is, moreover, rapidly on the increase, whilst that of the tenancy is diminishing, and is principally supplied by immigration. The theory and practice of the country is for every man to own land as soon as possible. The term of landlord is an obnoxious one. The American people are very averse to being tenants, and are more anxious to be masters of the soil, and are content to own, if nothing else, a small homestead, a mechanic's home, a comfortable dwelling-house in compact towns, with a lot of land of from 50 feet by 100 feet about it. In the sparsely-peopled portions of the country, a tenancy for a term of years may be said to exist only in exceptional cases. Land is so cheap there that every provident man may own land in fee. The possession of land of itself does not bestow on a man, as it does in Europe, a title to consideration; indeed, its possession in large quantities frequently reacts prejudicially to his interests, as attaching to him a taint of aristocracy which is distasteful to the masses of the American people.

" The landowner in the United States has entire freedom to devise his property at will. He can leave it to one or more of his children, or he may leave it to a perfect stranger. In the event of his dying intestate, his real estate is equally divided amongst his children without distinction as to sex, subject, however, to a right of dower to his widow, should there be one. If there are no children or lineal descendants, the property goes to other relatives of the deceased. If the intestate leaves no kindred, his estate escheats to the State in which it is situated. The laws of the different States of the Union regulating the descent and division of landed property on death of owner harmonise to a great extent with each other.

"It may be asserted that the system of land-tenure by small proprietors is regarded in this country with great favour, and that the prevailing public opinion is that the possession of land should be within the reach of the most modest means. A proprietor of land, however small, acquires a stake in the country, and assumes responsibilities which guarantee his discharging faithfully his duties as a citizen. Whilst practically any one man may acquire as much land as he can pay for, yet the whole tendency and effect of the laws of this country are conducive to dispersion and multitudinous ownership of land. The several States and the Government of the United States grant their lands in limited quantities; and under the laws of descent lands descend to the children, irrespective of sex, in equal shares; and the laws of partition provide for a division of the lands into as many parts as there are interests, where it can be done without prejudice. In many European countries the sale and transfer of land are so hampered by legal complications, and entail such heavy expenses, as frequently to discourage such operations. In the United States, on the contrary, the sale and transfer of land are conducted with about the same ease as would be the sale of a watch. Very large quantities of land are seldom held in this country, undivided, by one family for more than one or two generations. It is worthy of remark that in this country the same reluctance is not felt, as in Europe, to parting with family lands."[1]

[1] For a general account of the land laws of the United States, and specimens of State legislation on the descent and distribution of land, see

11. No foreign land system, however, is so interesting or instructive to an English ·economist as the land system of the Channel Islands.[1] This land system, founded on ancient custom, is the same as that of France in its essential features, but modified by certain reservations in favour of Primogeniture. In Jersey, upon the death of a landowner, leaving a widow and children, the widow has an indefeasible right to one-third of the income during her life, while the eldest son is entitled to the dwelling-house and curtilage, with about two English acres of his own selection, and one-tenth of the remaining land. Where the estate is less than one acre and a half, the eldest son inherits the whole. In other cases, the residue is divided among all the children, including the eldest, the sons taking equal shares of two-thirds, and the daughters equal shares of one-third, but so that no daughter shall take a greater share than a younger son. In Guernsey the eldest son's right is more restricted, but the other rules of division are similar. Entails were unknown in Jersey, until they were partially legalized by the Crown in 1635, and the practice of entailing has ceased for the last thirty years. Devises of land are only permitted where there are no children. In fact, subdivision is generally prevented by the eldest son buying out the rest, who go into business, sometimes retaining a rent-charge on the family estate.

Mr. Fisher's article on the American land system in " Systems of Land Tenure."

[1] See the Report of the Commissioners appointed to inquire into the laws of Jersey, 1861 ; Mr. Kay's " Free Trade in Land," chapter xii. ; Mr. A. Arnold's " Free Land," chapter xvii. ; and Mr. Shaw-Lefevre's article on the Channel Islands in the *Fortnightly Review* of Oct., 1879.

The total area of all the Channel Islands is about 50,000 acres, but the area capable of cultivation scarcely exceeds 37,000 acres, of which more than one-half is in Jersey. The population of all the islands is about 90,000, and of Jersey about 56,000, being nearly thrice as dense, relatively to acreage, as that of England and Wales. The proportion of the population employed in agriculture is still larger, being estimated at one cultivator to every four acres in Jersey and Guernsey. The number of landowners in Jersey has been variously stated at 2,500 and 2,300, and the average size of properties is eight or nine acres, but many of the smallest, as in France and England, are market-gardens, or belonging to persons having other means of livelihood. The largest properties rarely exceed one hundred acres in Jersey and fifty acres in Guernsey. Most farms are cultivated by their owners, with an industry and skill which owes less than is supposed to special advantages of soil or climate. Whatever test be applied to it, the agriculture of the Channel Islands must rank above that of almost any country in Europe. If we take the price of land as a measure of its agricultural value, we find that £200 an acre is as commonly given in Jersey as £50 an acre in England — not for residential sites, but for ordinary farms. If we refer to average rent, we find that it ranges from £4 per acre for poor land to £10 or £12 for good land, being four times as high as in England. If we look to expenditure of capital in manure, we find that Jersey farmers do not grudge £20 or £30, or even £40, per acre, in preparing their little plots for crops of early potatoes, some £300,000 worth of which have been exported to London from this island

alone in one year.   If we judge of success in cultivation
by the produce, we find that a much larger quantity of
human food is raised in Jersey than is raised on an
equal area, by the same number of cultivators, in any
part of the United Kingdom.   Not only does it support
its own crowded population in much greater comfort
than is enjoyed by the mass of Englishmen, but it
supplies the London market, out of its surplus production, with shiploads of vegetables, fruit, butter, and cattle
for breeding.   Even wheat, for the growth of which the
climate is not very suitable, is so cultivated that it yields
much heavier crops per acre than in England; and the
number of live stock kept on a given area astonishes
travellers accustomed only to English farming.   Nor are
these only the results of spade husbandry, for machinery
is largely employed by the yeomen and peasant-proprietors of the Channel Islands, who have no difficulty
in arranging among themselves to hire it by turns.

Considering all these facts, and the absence of
any special conditions, such as the close proximity of
lucrative markets, to account for the marvellous agricultural prosperity of these islands, we cannot greatly err
in attributing it mainly to their cherished land system.
The price of land is three or four times as high as in
England, not because it is a " luxury " for the possession
of which the great nobleman or capitalist will outbid all
competitors, but, on the contrary, because it is more
valuable agriculturally to small proprietors than it could
be to any other class of purchasers, because there are
many such bidders for every lot that is sold, and because
the cost of transfer is small.   It pays a rent at least
four times as high as English land, because those who

hire it are themselves small proprietors, cultivate it with their own hands, and apply to it a much larger capital per acre than an English tenant-farmer would think remunerative. It yields an amount and variety of produce which seems fabulous to persons conversant only with tenant-farming on the grand scale, not merely because it is more liberally manured, but also because it is studded with orchards, vineries, and other profitable *hors d'œuvres* of agriculture, which nothing but the magic of property will call into existence. The same lesson is taught by the abundance of the markets, the substantial character of the dwellings even down to the humblest cottages, the magnitude of the public works, the dress and diet of the labouring class, the comparative rarity of pauperism, and other signs which betoken a happy and thriving community. It would be interesting, were it possible, to compare the 37,000 cultivated acres of the Channel Islands with the best specimen that could be selected of an equal area owned by a single proprietor in Great Britain. If the advantage should prove to be on the side of the former, morally and socially as well as economically, it would be for the advocates of the English land system to reconcile this result with their belief in a threefold agricultural hierarchy of landlords, tenant-farmers, and labourers. Perhaps it might come to be perceived that whatever benefit is thus derived from a division of duties is more than compensated by a separation of interests; that a farmer who is his own landlord and his own labourer can dispense with the incessant trouble of supervision and fear of an increased rent; that, upon the whole, three profits fructify most abundantly in one pocket; and that freedom of agriculture, like freedom of trade, must needs promote the greatest happiness of the greatest number.

The conclusions to be drawn from a comprehensive review of foreign land systems may be expressed in a few sentences. No other nation has adopted in its entirety the English right of Primogeniture—a right which could only have grown up in a thoroughly feudalised society, and which could only have been perpetuated in a country where the feudal structure of society has never undergone any violent disturbance. In those States which have remodelled their jurisprudence on the principles of the Code Napoléon, the eldest son is effectually debarred from engrossing the whole landed property of the family. In other States, which have developed their law of succession independently, parents are allowed to " make eldest sons," under greater or less restrictions. In no considerable State but our own does the law itself, in default of a will or settlement, constitute the eldest son the sole heir to all the realty, and in no other is the exclusive preference of the first-born, thus consecrated by law, carried to such extreme lengths in family government. No highly civilised people but the English tolerate the dominion of a by-gone generation over the greater part of the national soil, under settlements and entails designed to limit the ownership and control the action of living owners. In no other part of Europe, nor in the United States of America, nor in the British colonies, is the division of landed property so unequal, or the predominance of a landed aristocracy so firmly rooted. In no other is the free transfer of land, or the power of mortgaging, obstructed by so many legal impediments, by so great a risk of delay, or by the certainty of so exorbitant a cost. Nowhere else is the land habitually occupied by a class of tenants who hold only from year to year, and cultivated by a class of labourers divorced from the soil and working for weekly wages. It is hardly too much to say that the rural economy of Norway and that of Italy, that of Germany and that of the United States, that of France and that of Australia or New Zealand, differ less from each other than any one of them differs from the rural economy of Great Britain. For every one of these countries—however diverse in respect of their soil, their climate, their history, their population, or their political constitution—has cast off the old shell of feudal land laws, has adopted the principles of Free Trade in Land, and has practically fostered the creation of a farmer-proprietary superseding, more or less, the relation of landlord and tenant. Bearing these facts in mind, we are brought face to face with the question, whether the group of institutions and customs which form the unique land system of England deserve to be upheld by English statesmen and economists, either by virtue of their intrinsic merits, or by reason of their having become incorporated into our national character; and, if not, in what manner it may be proper to modify them by legislative enactment.

Part IV.

CHAPTER I.

Reforms to be Effected in the English System of Land Tenure.

It now becomes our duty to consider what modifications of the English Land System are necessary or expedient, either in the special interest of agriculture, or in the general interest of social and political well-being. In discussing this question, it may be convenient to recall the five distinctive features already described as characterising that system—the law and custom of Primogeniture, the prevalence of strict family entails, the consequent aggregation of landed property in the hands of a comparatively small territorial aristocracy, the prevalence of strict family entails, the dependence of farmers on landlords, and the dependence of labourers on both these classes.

We have already discussed the considerations which prove the expediency—not to say the necessity—of reforming the institution of Primogeniture, so far as it depends on law, and of limiting the dominion exercised over land through family settlements. Upon one principle to be embraced in any such reform public opinion has long pronounced itself so decisively that it may be taken as already conceded. This principle is the assimilation of real to personal property in respect of distribution on intestacy. Even the stoutest adherents of Primogeniture, as a custom, are beginning to allow that, in default of a will or settlement, the law should incline to equality, especially as intestacies are more likely to occur in poor than in wealthy families. To what extent a change in the law of succession on intestacy would affect the practice of testators and settlors, is a matter of mere speculation on which it would be rash to speak confidently. Many are of opinion that no legal presumption in favour of equal partition would avail in the least to counteract the rooted propensity of Englishmen, once possessed of land, to found and keep up a family, but that, on the contrary, people who are now content to die intestate would forthwith make wills disinheriting all their children but one. This opinion appears to derive some little weight from the history of landed property in Kent, where the presumption in favour of gavelkind still prevails, notwithstanding arbitrary and statutory disgavelments, but where it is not found that wills are more favourable to younger sons than in the rest of the island. It has been well observed, however, that if Kentish settlors and testators fail to adopt the principle of partibility, it is not because law does not mould opinion, but rather because all local rules are powerless against the influence of a general law, believed to represent the collective will of the State.[1] Others believe that a deliberate reversal of the policy hitherto sanctioned by the Legislature would exert a powerful influence on popular sentiment, and, coupled with the direct operation of the new law, would leave a very sensible impression on the

[1] Kenny's "Essay on Primogeniture," p. 64.

rural economy of England within two or three generations. In support of this belief, it may be urged that,
in a vast number of cases, the form of settlements and
wills is practically dictated by the solicitors who frame
them, and who themselves follow, more or less exactly
and more or less consciously, the course prescribed by
the law on intestacy. A man informs his solicitor that
he knows little of legal phrases, but that he wishes to
settle his property strictly in the usual and right manner ;
upon which the solicitor makes a will, giving all the
land to his eldest son, and dividing the personalty, if
any, among his widow and children, nearly in accordance
with the Statute of Distributions. So close is the
correspondence of the custom with the law, that, whereas
in default of sons the law vests the land in all the
daughters and not in the eldest daughter only, the same
rule is adopted, with very slight variation, in most wills
and settlements of realty. Were the law altered, however, and especially were it altered after a thorough discussion of the whole question, the uniformity of these
usages would be effectually broken. Solicitors would
feel bound to ask for more precise instructions from their
clients ; testators and settlors would more fully realise
their responsibility ; and the dispositions of landed property hitherto embodied in the common forms of conveyances would have to be reconsidered by the light of
modern ideas. Here and there an old property would
devolve to several children under the law of intestacy,
and yet would be kept in the family by means of such
fraternal arrangements as are made every day on the
Continent.[1] A few instances of this kind would go far

[1] Many examples of these are given in the Foreign Office Reports of 1870.

to dispel prejudices against equal partition, while, in the case of properties to which no family sentiment attaches, directions to sell and divide the proceeds in specified proportions could hardly fail to supersede, by their superior convenience, the plan of devising to one child and charging portions for all the rest. Indirectly, therefore, the mere assimilation of real to personal estate, on intestacy, would probably effect a considerable though gradual revolution in the English land system, even though not supplemented by any other enactment.

A far more serious and difficult issue arises upon the various proposals for amending the existing law of entail and settlement. These proposals usually assume one of two general forms, widely differing, in principle, from each other. Either they contemplate a reconstruction of our land system on the model of the Code Napoléon, or they are directed to a simple restriction of the power whereby estates can be tied up for a life or lives in being, and a period of twenty-one years afterwards. Both of these schemes purport to promote Free Trade in land, and to check its aggregation in the hands of an exclusive aristocracy: the former, by constantly and forcibly breaking up properties into fragments, easily saleable; the latter, by prohibiting or curtailing the limitations which prevent their coming into the market. Thus, both involve an abridgment of the liberty now enjoyed by English settlors and testators, but with this important difference, that whereas the one scheme would only abridge the liberty of a bygone generation to control the action of the living generation, the other is directly at variance with full individual proprietorship. Under the French system of enforced partible succession,

the property of each citizen is rigidly settled, with the
exception of a fixed disposable portion, but the settlement is made by the State, instead of by himself, and
therefore without regard to peculiar family circumstances.
The causes which facilitated the introduction of this
great legal revolution into France have been explained
by MM. de Tocqueville and Lavergne, and Mr. Cliffe
Leslie has done much to repel the objections, both
social and agricultural, which have been persistently
urged against it in this country. We must give due
weight to the fact, already noticed, that no French
Government, whether Legitimist, Orleanist, Imperial,
or Republican, has ever attempted to reverse it;
nor can we fail to be struck by the opinion so
generally expressed in the Foreign Office Reports of
1870 that in countries which have borrowed this article
of the Code Napoléon it is believed to work beneficially.
On the other hand, it is not less significant that no
practical English statesman has ever advocated its
adoption, and that even those English theorists who
have least sympathy with the rights of property have
apparently no great partiality for the agrarian constitution of France and Belgium. Their ideal is not the
infinite disintegration of landed property among peasant
owners, which they would regard as a retrograde measure,
but, on the contrary, its concentration in the hands of
one national land commission, or a number of municipal
land commissions, under whom private individuals, if
allowed to call any land their own, must be content to
hold leases. With that far larger and more important
class who are engaged in amassing wealth in the assured
hope of leaving it as they please, enforced partible

succession would assuredly find as little favour as with
the landed aristocracy ; and if there be a leaning in this
class towards any foreign land law, it is not towards that
of France, but towards those of the United States and
our own colonies.　As for the great mass of Englishmen, it may be taken as certain that a law placing the
State *in loco parentis*, and declaring that a father who
has made his own fortune shall not be free to deal with
it by will, or to disinherit a child, however worthless and
ungrateful, would be in the highest degree unpopular.
Upon these grounds, apart from all economical considerations, we must dismiss this proposal as an impossible
solution of the problem before us—impossible because it
would satisfy no class or school of thought in England,
because it has no foundation to support it in the organic
framework of English society, and because the very ideas
necessary to lay such a foundation are entirely wanting.
It would be rash to assert that so direct an interference
with personal rights will never be accepted by this
country, but we may safely assert that if the only
alternative to English Primogeniture were indefeasible
equal succession, that institution would probably fulfil
the prediction of Adam Smith, and survive for generations longer.

For different, but equally cogent, reasons, we must
reject as impracticable the bold suggestion of Mr. J. S.
Mill, who condemns both the English and French rules
of succession, that it would be expedient to restrict,
" not what any one may bequeath, but what any one
should be permitted to acquire by bequest or inheritance," so that it should not exceed a *maximum* " sufficiently high to afford the means of a comfortable

independence." A little reflection upon the practical application of this suggestion ought surely to convince us that, even if it were possible to make it the basis of a testamentary code, it would be hopeless to carry it out with any approach to real equity. A different rule would be required for the rich and for the poor; for men with small families, and for men with large families. But we may spare ourselves any detailed criticism of a plan, not so much designed to check the abuses of Primogeniture, as to realise a favourite idea of Bentham, by diverting the surplus of private accumulations into the public treasury—an object which may or may not be desirable in itself, but which is beyond the legitimate scope of our present inquiry.

By what means, then, can the vices inherent in the English system of entail and settlement be remedied, without impeaching the essential rights of proprietorship and disposition? According to some law reformers, nothing more is required for this purpose than a simple legislative prohibition of entails upon unborn children. There can be no doubt that such a measure, if so framed as to exclude the evasion of its principle by the creation of "powers" or otherwise, might reduce by twenty-one years the period for which land can be lawfully kept *extra commercium* by the force of a single instrument. But it would leave the mischief of limited ownership and contingent incumbrances wholly untouched within the allotted circle of a life or lives in being; or rather, it would stimulate family pride and legal ingenuity to devise new modes of settlement which should make up by their greater complexity for the brevity of their restrictive operation. Indeed, if the power of entailing were maintained, subject only to a prohibition of entails upon unborn children, and without any further change in the law, the actual effect would probably be much less than might be expected at first sight. There would be nothing to prevent the creation of any number of successive life-estates preceding the first estate-tail. The practice of making the first and other unborn sons of a marriage tenants-in-tail by an ante-nuptial settlement must, of course, be abandoned, but the same objects might be effected with tolerable certainty after the birth of one or more sons. Provision might be made that, in the event of a tenant-in-tail dying childless, without having barred the entail, the property should revert to the settlor, or vest in some other living person, and all the sons might thus be designated, in succession, as heirs-in-tail. If the eldest son, or any other heir-in-tail, should marry and have sons, without barring the entail, the property would practically descend, *per formam doni*, to an unborn heir in the second generation, upon whom it had never been, and could not be, expressly entailed.

For these and other reasons, sound policy seems to require the entire abolition of entails, in the legal sense, and not merely the abolition of entails upon unborn children. This reform, however important, would not involve the abolition of family settlements, for the power of entailing is one thing, the power of settling is another. If the legal creation known as an "estate-tail" were finally swept away, it would still be possible to settle property before a marriage so that it should vest in the first son attaining his majority—not as heir-in-tail, but as heir-for-life or in fee-simple, as the case

might be. Whether a landowner should be allowed to
control his own future liberty of action even to this
extent, is a different question, to be decided on its own
merits. If it should be decided in the affirmative, a
valid distinction might still be drawn between the
power of settling upon the unborn children of the
settlor himself, and the power of settling upon the
unborn children of some other person. It may possibly
be reasonable to allow a man in possession of his property, and about to marry, the right of providing for
his own unborn children by an ante-nuptial settlement,
and yet quite unreasonable to entrust the same power
to a stranger, perhaps animated with the senseless
ambition of immortalising an ignoble name.

A further distinction may properly be drawn between settlements made by will and settlements made
by deed *inter vivos*, especially upon marriage. Posthumous dispositions of all kinds are watched in these
days, on very sufficient grounds, with increasing
jealousy, and posthumous entails are liable to peculiar
objections which do not attach to others. When they
are derived from wills executed in prospect of death,
they are far more likely to be capricious and self-
defeating than if they had originated from the same
mind in the full vigour of life; if the will has been
executed long before the testator's death, from which it,
nevertheless, " speaks," it may not represent his final
intention, owing to circumstances which have occurred
since the date of its execution. In any case, the power
of entailing by will is exercised secretly, and with
much less security for deliberation than is afforded
by the negotiations that usually precede a marriage

settlement, which is manifestly, of all settlements, the one entitled to most indulgence.

But it may well be doubted whether it can serve any good end that a bachelor should be enabled to designate as his heir a child which may never be born, so irrevocably as to defeat his own power of choosing among his children, when they are born, or rather when their characters are sufficiently formed. This grand abuse, peculiar to modern settlements of land, is, of course, greatly aggravated when the settlor is not the expectant father of the unborn heir, but the grandfather, or great-uncle, or some more distant relative. Yet it might be rectified by a very simple enactment, founded on a principle already adopted in ordinary marriage settlements of personalty. These settlements usually provide that, after the death of the parents, the money shall be divided among the children in such proportions as the parents, or the surviving parent, shall appoint; failing which, it shall be divided equally. Let such a provision, reserving to each father his natural right of selection among his own children, be imported into every settlement by implication of law, and half the evils incident to the present system would vanish at once. The effect would be that a settled property might be preserved, as now, in the direct line of hereditary descent, so that none but the children (if any) of the intended marriage could inherit it; and the eldest son might still, if the settlor desired, be designated as heir. But that designation would not be indefeasible, for the father in each generation would be armed with a power of appointment, enabling him to set it aside, and devolve the inheritance, whole and undivided, upon some other child,

or divide it among all the children. This enactment
might properly be extended to personalty also, and,
being there in strict accordance with the prevailing
custom, would involve no violent encroachment on the
liberty now enjoyed—a liberty, be it remembered, which,
so far as it is exercised, is exercised by grandfathers to
override the free action of fathers. It might also be
provided that every tenant for life of landed property
under an ordinary family settlement should have the
power, by a like implication of law, to charge the estate
for the benefit of his wife or any of his children, to an
amount bearing a stated proportion to its annual value.[1]
The proportion so fixed would thenceforth constitute, so
to speak, a legal standard of family justice.   Though its
adoption would be permissive, and not compulsory, the
consciences of many would thus be awakened to a sense
of their parental obligations, till it should come to be
thought a disgraceful thing for a nobleman with £50,000
a year to cut off his daughters, either married or single,
with portions of £5,000 or £10,000.

A more effective blow might, however, be dealt at
the social and economical evils arising from settlements
of land, by a simple abolition of life-tenancy. Supposing
this to be done, it would signify little whether tenancy-
in-tail were or were not retained ; for the artfully-devised
mechanism whereby family properties are now kept
out of the market, and protected against the claims of

---

[1] By the Irish statute 2 Anne, cap. 6, s. 10, it was enacted that where
the eldest son of a Papist should become entitled to his real estate as a
conforming Protestant, the property should be chargeable, at the discretion
of the Court of Chancery, with portions for younger children, not exceeding
one-third of its annual value.

creditors, entirely depends on the interposition of life-estates before and between the various estates-tail limited in the settlement. If there were no such thing as a life-estate, either in law or in equity, a landowner wishing to settle his property on his eldest son, without giving up the possession of it during his own life, must leave it to him by will either in fee-simple or in tail. Even in the latter case, the eldest son, if of full age at his father's death, would become absolute master of the property, since an estate-tail is convertible into an estate in fee-simple at the will of its possessor. In other words, the settlement would be virtually no settlement, but a simple gift or devise. If the eldest son were a minor at his father's death, and died without issue before executing a disentailing deed, the property might of course be made to vest in the next brother, or some other person, but under like conditions. No doubt the ingenuity of lawyers might possibly contrive fresh methods of tying up property by means of trustees, but, if the Legislature were resolved to sweep away life-estates, these methods would be declared null and void. The consequence would be that, however persistently the custom of entailing might be maintained, each successive head of a family would be, or might become, the real owner, instead of a mere life-tenant, of the family property. The chief difference, from the family point of view, would be, that eldest sons, being entirely in the power of their fathers, who might exercise the right of disentailing at any moment, would be, as it were, bound over in heavy recognizances to good behaviour. The chief difference, from the economical point of view, would be, that by virtue of the same right, the ostensible owner of a property might charge it for his debts to its full value, instead of only to the value of his life-interest. It is, however, incredible that under such a law the passion for making eldest sons would remain unabated. Since younger children would be consigned to beggary, where the father's property consisted solely or mainly of land, unless they were given shares of it or charges upon it, a general custom of breaking entails for this purpose would probably spring up, and apportionments so made out of a fee-simple estate would almost inevitably be far less influenced by the spirit of Primogeniture than re-settlements of the prevailing type.

The manifest objection to such legislation is that it would strike at the root of all marriage settlements. The object of ante-nuptial settlements is mainly to secure the future wife against the risk of the joint capital being dissipated by the future husband, and the expected children against the risk of that capital, ultimately destined for their fortunes, being dissipated by either of their parents. If the settled funds or lands were always, or almost always, in possession of the future husband and wife before marriage, there might be little hardship in denying them a power of taking security, as it were, against their own improvidence. But, in nine cases out of ten, the settlors are the future husband's father and the future wife's father. It may be urged that if they were compelled to place the joint capital—whether personal or real—at the absolute disposal of the future husband or at the joint disposal of him and his wife, they might well decline to advance that capital at all, or might limit its amount to a minimum. In the United States, it is true, these difficulties are not found insuperable, and it is usual for parents to give their married children an allowance during their own lives, making a further provision for them by will. It is by no means self-evident that society would suffer in this country if a similar practice were to prevail, and if English marriage settlements were henceforth to assume a much simpler form. There are very strong reasons for restricting complicated reservations of future interests even in personalty, and for doubting whether the efforts of the dead to regulate the enjoyment of wealth by the living for the sake of the unborn are sufficiently repressed by the rule against perpetuities and the Thelusson Act. But it is important to realise that life estates in land rest on the same principle as trusts for the preservation of settled funds, during the lifetime of husband and wife, in settlements of personalty. Now, for the present, it must be assumed that public opinion is not prepared to suppress a custom so widespread as that of settling personalty for the benefit of a second generation. Upon this assumption, we cannot decline to grapple with the broad question whether a valid distinction can be drawn between realty and personalty as regards the power of settlement, or whether every rule laid down for the one must needs be applied to the other.

To such a question a controversialist might reply that personalty and realty have never been treated by the law on a footing of equality. Not only have they been subjected to a different course of descent on intestacy, and to different scales of taxation on inheritance, but very invidious liabilities were in times past cast upon owners of personalty in the interest of landowners. For instance, the heir, taking all the land on intestacy, was specially exempted from the rule that sums advanced to sons in their father's lifetime should be deducted from their shares at his death ; while, by a monstrous perversion of justice, a mortgage debt, contracted on the security and for the benefit of the land, was primarily chargeable on the personal estate, until Mr. Locke King's Act was passed in 1854. Nothing, however, could be gained by multiplying proofs of the partiality formerly shown to land by a Legislature principally composed of landowners, nor could it now be redressed by showing an equally irrational partiality to personalty.

The policy of prohibiting life-estates in land, without prohibiting the corresponding life-interests in personalty, must stand or fall by the peculiar nature, claims, and obligations of Real Property. Not a Session elapses in which Parliament does not affirm the principle that land is a thing *sui generis*, over which the State may and ought to assume a control far more stringent than it would be politic to assume, but not than it might rightfully assume, over other kinds of property. Whether it be for the construction of railways, canals, and waterworks, for the requirements of public health, or for any other legitimate purpose of local improvement, the Legislature freely confiscates land, though it usually gives its owners an exorbitant compensation. The familiar arguments in support of this interference are derived from the fact that land is strictly limited in quantity, at least within the borders of each kingdom, and that its resources in a virgin state are not the production of human industry. These arguments are so far valid as to rebut what does not need to be rebutted—the presumption of any binding analogy between land and money. If an additional argument were needed, it might be found in the consideration that landed property is a specific and concrete thing, carrying with it manifold privileges and duties, whereas personalty, for the most part, consists in an abstract right to receive dividends, which may belong to one man as well as to another. It may be an evil, in itself, that a perfectly worthless person should have a large fortune settled upon him by an ancestor quite ignorant of his future character, but this evil is far less, both in kind and degree, if the fortune consists of money, than if it consists of land. In short, the one decisive justification for treating land as an entirely exceptional subject of property is to be found in the entirely exceptional power which the possession of it confers. If we contemplate the supreme influence wielded by landowners collectively over the condition and especially over the dwellings of the people ; if we remember that upon their estate-management depend the productiveness of the soil and the internal food-supplies of the country ; if we realise that not only is the land in a physical sense "the leaf we feed on," but in a political sense the substratum of our whole administrative machinery ; we shall not fail to perceive the full absurdity of postulating that it should be exactly assimilated to stock in plasticity for the purposes of settlement—but not, forsooth, in facility of transfer, in the course of devolution on intestacy, or in liability to probate and succession duties.

The abolition of life estates in land is, therefore,

perfectly consistent with the maintenance or toleration of life-interests in personalty, if public opinion is not yet ripe for a radical alteration in the form of ordinary marriage settlements. It is also perfectly consistent with the practice of vesting a family property, whole and undivided, in the eldest son, and charging it for the benefit of a widow or younger children. It would even be consistent with the practice of directing a family-property to be sold, and settling the proceeds as personalty, yet allowing the sale to be postponed, so long as all the parties interested should be willing to accept interest out of the undivided property, in lieu of capital sums out of the proceeds. This practice would carry out the principle and purposes of family-settlements quite as faithfully as the alternative, and not less radical, plan of maintaining life-estates in land, but enabling tenants-for-life to convert the land into money, to be held on the same trusts. For, in that case, the heir of a great ancestral property might improve his own life-income at his own pleasure, and yet relieve himself of all family claims and territorial responsibilities, thus cutting away the main ground upon which the institution of Primogeniture is supposed to rest.

Nothing short of prohibiting "limited ownership," in the sense of life-tenancy followed by estates-tail, will fully effect the object of establishing Free Trade in land. The more thoroughly we appreciate the almost insuperable difficulty of partially reforming an institution so deeply rooted and widely ramified as the custom of entail and settlement, the more irresistible will appear the conclusion that it is better to reform it altogether, by abolishing all kinds of ownership except ownership in fee-simple, with all customary and copy-hold tenures, and by imposing proper restrictions on the length of leases. The conception of such a measure would demand an effort of constructive statesmanship quite as bold as the solution of the Irish Land Question, while its execution would affect still vaster interests, and must be spread over a longer period of time. Once carried, however, it would cut half the knots which together make up the English Land Question. One of these knots consists in the difficulty, expense, and delay attending the transfer of land, especially in small lots, and it is sometimes assumed, too hastily, that all this could be rectified by a good system of registration, such as exists in most Continental States, where a public court does what is here done by conveyancers. It should be remembered that, even where a transfer of stock is effected by a mere stroke of the pen, a long and costly investigation must often be previously undertaken on behalf of the trustees who authorise the sale. No system of registration could bring about Free Trade in land under settlement, but a register would become invaluable both to vendors and purchasers when every name in it would be that of an owner in fee. Trusts of land, with all their vexatious incidents, would soon be obsolete, when there were no reversionary interests to be pro-tected. Mortgages on old family properties would be rarer and more easily cleared off, when every acre of land could be turned into ready money at the owner's pleasure. They would, however, be more frequently contracted on new purchases by capitalist farmers, when it was discovered that it might be cheaper, in the long run, to pay interest to a mortgagee than rent to a landlord.

Other advantages might be secured by the gentler method, already suggested, of reserving a power of appointment among children, by force of law, to every life tenant in possession of a family property. What cannot be secured by that method, or by any other method consistent with the principle of modern entails, guarded by life estates, is, in one word, unity of proprietorship. A settled estate is an estate which has not, and may never have, a real proprietor. For the common family settlement is a contrivance whereby the land itself may be saved from *morcellement* at the expense of the proprietary interest, which is dissected, split up, and parcelled out into more shares than a French lawyer would think possible. This process is repeated, as we have seen, in each generation, by a family compact between father and eldest son, in which no other member of the family has any voice, yet neither of the parties is truly a free agent, or in a position to reverse the self-renewing dispensation of which they are little more than instruments, and no single person can be identified as the author. Now let us assume that, due provision being made for vested interests,[1] all this ingenious network of particular estates, as they are technically called, were swept away by law, and that every acre of English soil belonged absolutely to some assignable owner. Let us, further, picture to ourselves a case in which the operation of the change would be most severely tested— the case of an heir succeeding to a family property strictly entailed by its original purchaser and held

[1] See Appendix VII. on "Vested Interests in Settled Estates."

together for centuries by settlements in the eldest male line, but finding himself at perfect liberty to sell it or devise it as he pleases. This is a case, be it remarked, which, but for the practice of re-settlement, would occur daily under the present system, and does occur sometimes, when the eldest son obstinately refuses to commute his estate-tail for a life-estate. It will hardly be disputed that a landowner so circumstanced has a more enviable lot, with greater inducements and greater power to do his estate and all connected with it full justice, than if he were the mere creature of a settlement, but it may be imagined that his gain is more than counterbalanced by some loss elsewhere. Where, then, is this loss, and who is it that suffers by the substitution of ownership for life-tenancy in the case supposed ? Not, surely, his ancestors, who, having brought nothing into the world, could not carry anything out, and whose memory it would be superstitious to personify. Not his wife or younger children, whom he is now enabled to endow according to his own convictions of justice, instead of according to a standard, determined by the paramount claims of Primogeniture, before his marriage, if not before his birth.[1] Not his eldest son, who, by the hypothesis,

[1] Mr. G. Osborne Morgan, M.P., in his pamphlet on "Land Law Reform in England," urges that if none but fee-simple estates in land were permitted, a landowner could not give a life-interest on jointure to his widow, or make suitable provisions for his family. But the abolition of limited ownership does not involve the abolition of the right to charge land; while an absolute owner would always be able to sell the whole or a portion of his estate to provide for his widow or any other member of his family. Mr. Morgan himself would confer this power on a limited owner, enabling him "to sell the land out and out, subject only to two conditions: first, that the sale be an honest one ; and secondly, that the purchase-money be secured and applied for the benefit of all persons interested in the land itself."

must have come into the world, or at least emerged from childhood, after the alteration in the law, and would have been educated in the full knowledge that his birthright, if any, was at the disposal of his father. Not any more distant relatives, whose interest in family estates, unless vested, is usually most shadowy and delusive. Not unborn descendants, who might possibly inherit if the entail were perpetually renewed, under the present law, but who are equally with the dead beyond the reach of appreciable injury. In short, we strive in vain to discover any specific individual, either in *esse* or in *posse*, who could be aggrieved by the legal extinction of life-estates and estates-tail, under proper conditions of time. Still it may be said that " families," that is, territorial families, would sooner or later cease to exist without the artificial safeguard of complex settlements, and that such a result would prejudice not only the happiness of their members in all succeeding generations, but the welfare of all the rural communities grouped around them, and even of the nation at large. And thus we are led back to a point of view from which the actual results of family settlements have already been estimated, and from which it may now be useful to forecast the probable results of the alternative system.

The first, and not the least salutary, of these would be the strengthening of parental authority in those families where it is most needed. The father is, upon the whole, a wiser lawgiver and a more impartial judge within his own domestic circle than any providence of human institution, whether it be embodied in a lifeless deed or in a lifeless statute ; and, as Mr. Locke King justly remarks, "if such a disposer of property did not exist, we should only be too happy to discover such a being." Invested with full dominion over his landed estate, the head of each family would no longer have any cause to be jealous of his eldest son, or feel bound to maintain him in idleness during the best years of his life. Doubtless there would still be a strong disposition in most representatives of old hereditary properties to leave the eldest son, if not unworthy, the principal family domain, with the bulk of the land; but since he would depend, like his younger brothers, upon his father's award, and could not raise money upon his expectations, he would, like them, betake himself to some profession or business, and endeavour to increase, instead of diminishing, his future patrimony. In such cases, the position of the younger children would be very much what it is under the present system, during the parent's life; but even in such cases, and still more in cases where hereditary traditions were less powerful, the father would seldom think himself justified in leaving them a mere fraction of the property at his disposal, and would often direct his outlying estates to be divided among them or sold for their benefit. In these ways land would be constantly "passing out of the family," and though some might be left back to it by childless uncles, the unity of family properties would be greatly and progressively impaired. Moreover, now and then a spendthrift who ought to have been disinherited would be allowed to succeed by a too indulgent father, and might gamble away in a year the purchases and improvements of many generations. This being the contingency which settlements on the eldest son are specially designed to prevent, and the occurrence of which is represented by the friends of Primogeniture as an unmitigated calamity, it may be well to pause for a moment, and observe both what it does and what it does not involve.

That it does not involve any destruction or even any " dissipation " of the land itself, is so obvious that nothing but the persistent use of confused metaphors could have obscured it. Money, or money's worth, can be eaten, drunk, thrown into the sea, or otherwise literally consumed in unproductive expenditure; but a fortune consisting of land can only be squandered in the sense of being transferred from the dominion of one man into that of another or several others, which may happen to be the best thing which can befall the soil and all who live upon it. Considering the enormous injury done to any estate by the life incumbency of one insolvent—not to say one absentee—proprietor, as well as the well-known tendency of families to degenerate after one such disgraceful interregnum, the burden of proof certainly lies upon those who hold that, in such an event, the greatest happiness of the greatest number is promoted by keeping it undivided and inalienable, lest an ancient feudal name should perish out of the county. Mr. Arthur Arnold has drawn a striking picture of the public evils which may result from the financial difficulties of great landlords, whose estates cannot be sold :—" The nominal owners of several of the finest properties in England are now adjudicated bankrupts; their lands are racked and impoverished, but those broad acres cannot be made free without co-operation of the tenant-for-life with the next tenant-in-tail, who in some cases is a minor, and in others is unborn, and may never be called into existence. But for every one of the landed gentry who is bankrupt, there are scores who are hopelessly embarrassed. . . . The cottages upon many estates are fever-nests, and are few and far between ; the homesteads are insufficient, inconvenient, and in many cases in ruins; the land is undrained, and there is no one with the interest of a proprietor to look to the estate. The ostensible owner, the lord or the squire of the district, who is harassed for subscriptions, and supposed to contemplate with the benign interest of a seignioral lord the welfare of all around, who is the great man in the church and in the village, is in the dull reality of his own home merely a poor annuitant, with his eyes fixed, not upon the many fields and farms which in the rate-book bear his name, but upon the slender remnant of income which is all that charges or settlements have left him for the daily and hourly labour of providing for a family, for whom ten times his means would seem insufficient. He and his eldest son have but one pleasure in the world, and as it appears to cost nothing, they think themselves meritorious in that they are content with the sporting which the estate and the neighbourhood afford. The younger children languish at home, well knowing that upon their father's death they must find a new shelter, with very small fortunes." Such cases are by no means rare in those parts of the country which are least affected by the stir of commercial activity, and it is precisely in such cases that Free Trade in land would come into beneficial operation. It is not the best landlords, but the worst, that would be eliminated by natural selection from the roll of county families, if they were not disabled from selling by settlements, and the capitalists likely to succeed them would not be those with least aptitude, but those with most aptitude, for the duties of proprietorship.

But this, as we have seen, is a very inadequate view of the question. We must also take into account the probable effect of abolishing life-estates and entails upon the heirs-presumptive—for there could then be no heirs-apparent—of family estates. Might it not be expected that if each successive eldest son of an illustrious house were actuated at once by ancestral pride and the fear of forfeiting his birthright through misconduct or incompetency, a healthy kind of atavism would develop itself in the landed aristocracy, and the virtues manifested by the founders of families would be more frequently reproduced in their descendants? Nay, more, does not our knowledge of human nature, confirmed by the experience of Germany, America, and the Colonies, encourage us to hope that, in terminating all indefeasible rights of succession, we should be unlocking hidden springs of energy and genius, calling into action the mettle of that "lounging class" which is the reproach of English Primogeniture, infusing unwonted industry into our aristocratic public schools and universities, and making henceforth the antiquity of a family a true mark of hereditary strength? If so—if the substitution of free ownership for life-estates and entails would help to banish the idea of privileged idleness from English society, and to introduce the condition of personal merit into the unwritten code of family inheritance in England — the moral influence of so wholesome a reform would outweigh in value its economical effects.

Since the law of Primogeniture and the right of creating strict family entails are the keystone of the English Land System, we may properly treat other needful amendments of that system as natural results of the measures already contemplated. But for the exigencies of complicated settlements, designed to keep landed property tied up for generations, the abuses of English conveyancing must have been abated long ago, and the worst of them will assuredly not survive the abolition of limited ownership. When trusts for preserving contingent remainders, outstanding terms, and other incidents of entailing deeds, have become obsolete mysteries it will be discovered that English titles do not require to be enshrined in "a mausoleum of parchment," and that English soil can be transferred or mortgaged quite as easily and cheaply as that of France, America, or Australia. Most of the difficulties supposed to beset registration will then vanish of themselves, and the difference between an official record of title and an official record of assurances will be reduced to much smaller proportions. The object of the former is to register only absolute ownership and simple mortgages, leaving unregistered all equitable and partial interests. But if limited ownership, with all the equitable interests grafted upon it, were swept away, absolute ownership and simple mortgages would practically be the only important rights over land which could be put upon the register, and a record of title would be, in effect, a record of assurances. For the same reason, these assurances might be indefinitely simplified in form, and, even if transcribed in full, would occupy much less space on a register. But they would also be indefinitely increased in number, because, if land once became as saleable as ships or shares in companies, it would constantly be changing hands, in small lots, and generally passing from an embarrassed to a more affluent owner.

It is needless to point out that any method of land registration worthy of the name must be made compulsory, by means of an enactment that no instrument shall be valid without being registered, and that every instrument shall rank in priority according to the date of its registration. It is equally clear that, being compulsory, registration must be made as convenient and safe as possible. In securing this object, many questions of practical detail will of course have to be solved in this country, as they have been solved elsewhere. Such is the question whether many district registries should be preferred to one central registry, whether there shall be a staff of official searchers and whether their certificates shall be made legally conclusive, whether a cadastral map shall be made an integral part of the register for the purpose of governing the identification of disputed boundaries, and in what manner a compensation-fund should be provided to indemnify persons who may suffer from official errors. Much stress has been laid on these questions of detail by those who have little sympathy with the abolition of limited ownership, and the principle of Free Trade in land. But it would be idle to discuss them as if they could seriously affect the policy of emancipating the English Land System from its feudal servitude, or as if English statesmanship were unequal to an administrative reform which has been accomplished by most other civilised nations.   Even the question of cost would prove far less formidable than might appear at first sight.   The preposterous charges which are now made for the simplest conveyancing operation, and which amount to a prohibitive duty on small transactions in land, would then undergo a sweeping revision, and the saving thereby effected would amply cover the expense of working the new machinery.   But in order to clear the soil of England from past encumbrances, and to give the present generation of vendors the means of granting an indefeasible title, it would be necessary to establish a Landed Estates Court, upon the basis advocated by Lord Cairns so far back as the year 1859, but tacitly rejected as inconsistent with the unreformed English land system.

The equal division of land upon intestacy, the abolition of limited ownership, and the encouragement of Free Trade in land by perfect facility of transfer, could not fail to produce a profound and cumulative effect upon the distribution of landed property in this country. Where the law of intestacy operated, the shares of younger children would often find their way into the market.   Where the whole property was left to, or settled upon, the eldest son absolutely, but charged with portions, he would often find it profitable to sell off parts of it, so as to retain the rest unencumbered.   Since there would be no tenants for life, and no power of preserving the integrity of a family property beyond one life-time, landowners would often raise money in the same way for purposes of improvement, rather than borrow it on mortgage.   Similar causes and motives would diminish the anxiety of neighbouring great proprietors to annex these parcels of land at a fancy price, and would increase the competition for them among professional men and tradespeople, if not among prosperous tenant-farmers. The gravitation of landed property, so to speak, would thus be gradually altered, and set towards a rural *bourgeoisie*, instead of towards a territorial aristocracy. This process of transition, once commenced, would be vastly promoted and accelerated by the assimilation of land to personalty in respect of transfer. What deters so many people from investing their savings in land is not merely the cost, trouble, and risk of employing a solicitor to complete the purchase of it, but also the knowledge that, before it can be mortgaged or sold, the same cost, trouble, and risk must be incurred over again, as well as a wholesome dread of the risk attending the custody of title-deeds. Hence the prevalent idea that land-owning is the privilege of the few, except in the immediate suburbs of towns, and that it is safer to hire a country residence than to buy it—an idea which it may take some years to eradicate from the minds of the English middle-classes. But it must ultimately give way before the disintegrating influences of absolute ownership and Free Trade in land. These influences will be further strengthened by reforms of a different character, some of which are already in progress, while others must inevitably accompany or follow a reconstruction of the English land system.

One of these reforms, and not the least important in its probable results, is the relaxation of the Game Laws. It is true, no doubt, that undue obloquy has been heaped upon the Game Laws as destructive to agriculture, and embittering the relation between landlords and tenants. It is true, also, that very strict laws against trespassing in pursuit of game are enforced in France, America, and other countries, where landlordism cannot be said to rule.[1] Nevertheless, it is certain that the English Game Laws, coupled with the English practice of yearly tenancy, have powerfully contributed—not merely to discourage agricultural improvement, but to favour the maintenance of great estates. In the first place, the love of game-preserving attaches to his ancestral domain many a nobleman and squire for whom it has no other attraction, who never resides there except during the sporting season, and who is quite unfitted to discharge the duties of proprietorship or local government. In the next place, the desire to keep a large tract of country undisturbed for game, with continuous or contiguous belts of covert well distributed among the arable fields, often renders the lord of many acres averse to letting in a stranger, and even impels him to rectify his frontier by fresh acquisitions. On the other hand, the would-be purchaser of a small farm or plot is unwilling to find himself surrounded by the well-stocked preserves of a powerful neighbour, dreading the ravages of hares and rabbits on his crops, and knowing that disputes are sure to arise with the gamekeeper. The custom of game-preserving is, therefore, a reason why the great proprietor is less ready to sell or more ready to buy, and, moreover, why the capitalist wishing to settle in the country is not disposed to invest in land intersected by the woods of the great proprietor. It is this,

---

[1] See the evidence on this subject collected in Mr. James Howard's treatise on "Continental Farming."

amongst other considerations of the same kind, which frequently induces a great proprietor to outbid all competitors when land is sold by auction. To others the land is only worth its agricultural or residential value, apart from its possible bearing on social position. To him it is worth all this, and, besides all this, it may enable him to boast of having some of the finest shooting in the whole county.

But this is not all. The community of sporting tastes fostered by the custom of game-preserving in itself typifies, and does something to keep up, that exclusive freemasonry of county society which repels the intrusion of urban new-comers, too probably of plebeian extraction. When the self-extinction of yeomen had once commenced, owing to economical causes, it could not fail to proceed with progressive rapidity. Those who remained found themselves more and more isolated, occupying a rank appreciably above that of ordinary tenant-farmers, yet far below that of country gentlemen in the commission of the peace. Persons of the same class disposed to settle in the country are perfectly aware of this, and think many times before placing themselves in a position where they would find hardly any neighbours to associate with them upon terms of equality. But let us now assume that, with the repeal of the laws consecrating Primogeniture and Entail, and the introduction of Free Trade in land, the order of landed proprietors will yearly become less and less of a caste, since the properties of decayed families will be constantly breaking up, and the line between the privileged and the unprivileged landowner will almost cease to be perceptible. Let us further assume that reforms in the whole system of parochial and county administration, reviving the self-governing capacity of Saxon times, will redistribute the civil functions of Quarter Sessions among elective Boards, and open a new career to active and public-spirited men with a territorial status in the county, though still beneath the dignity of squires. Can we doubt that, released from the artificial bondage which has too long repressed it, and quickened afresh by social ambition, the instinctive passion of Englishmen for a home in the country would reassert itself, as it did at the close of the Middle Ages, when orderly government succeeded the organised barbarism of feudal society? Is it impossible that certain branches of manufacture, now concentrated in unhealthy towns, would then flourish among green fields, as they do in New England, and that the "pit-villages" of earlier times would be revived in settlements of operatives clustered round new mills in convenient proximity to railway stations? Might not a new communal life, half urban and half rural, spring up in districts thus repeopled, as it has in other lands, breaking up the ancient stagnation of rustic parishes, but purged from the vice and squalor of populous towns?

These, however, are speculations which concern the next generation. In the meantime, we may rest assured that no sudden or startling change would be wrought by so moderate a reform of the land system in the characteristic features of English country life. There would still be a squire occupying the great house in most of our villages, and this squire would generally be the eldest son of the last squire; though he would sometimes be a younger son of superior merit or capacity, and sometimes a wealthy and enterprising purchaser from the manufacturing districts. Only here and there would a noble park be deserted or neglected for want of means to keep it up and want of resolution to part with it ; but it is not impossible that deer might often be replaced by equally picturesque herds of cattle ; that landscape gardening and ornamental building might be carried on with less contempt for expense ; that hunting and shooting might be reduced within the limits which satisfied our sporting forefathers ; that some country gentlemen would be compelled to contract their speculations on the turf, and that others would have less to spare for yachting or for amusement at Continental watering-places. Indeed, it would not be surprising if greater simplicity of manners, and less exclusive notions of their own dignity, should come to prevail even among the higher landed gentry, leading to a revival of that free and kindly social intercourse which made rural neighbourhoods what they were in olden times. The peculiar agricultural system of England might remain intact, with its three-fold division of labour between the landlord charged with the public duties attaching to property, the farmer contributing most of the capital and all the skill, and the labourer relieved by the assurance of continuous wages from all risks except that of illness. But the landlords would be a larger body, containing fewer grandees and more practical agriculturists, living at their country homes all the year round, and putting their savings into land, instead of wasting them in the social competition of the metropolis. The majority of them would still be eldest sons, many of whom, however, would have learned to work hard till middle life, for the support of their families; and besides these, there would be not a few younger sons who had retired to pass the evening of their days on little properties near the place of their birth, either left them by will or bought out of their own acquisitions. With these would be mingled other elements in far larger measure and greater variety than at present—wealthy capitalists eager to enter the ranks of the landed gentry, merchants, traders, and professional men content with a country villa and a hundred freehold acres around it, yeomen farmers, who had purchased the fee simple of their holdings from embarrassed landlords, and even labourers of rare intelligence, who had seized favourable chances of investing in land. Under such conditions, it is not too much to expect that some links, now missing, between rich and poor, gentle and simple, might be supplied in country districts; that "plain living and high thinking" might again find a home in some of our ancient manor houses, once the abode of landowners, but now tenanted by mere occupiers; that, with less of dependence and subordination to a dominant will, there would be more of true neighbourly feeling, and even of clanship; and that posterity, reaping the beneficent fruits of greater social equality, would marvel, and not without cause, how the main obstacle to greater social equality—the Law and Custom of Primogeniture—escaped revision for more than two centuries after the final abolition of feudal tenures.

CHAPTER II.

In considering the defects of the English Land System in its agricultural aspect, with a view to its amendment, we must not shut our eyes to its characteristic merits, or fall into the error of comparing it with a mere ideal. When, for instance, we are told on the authority of Lord Derby or Lord Leicester that, if full justice were done to the soil, the agricultural produce of England might be doubled, we are bound to ask several preliminary questions. In the first place, can any country be mentioned, under any land system whatever, in which the utmost amount of produce which the soil could yield is actually extracted from it? In the next place, is not the average capital per acre applied to agriculture in England greater than in France, or than in any other considerable European State?[1] Thirdly, even in those cases where English landlords are absolute owners, and cultivate their own lands without either settlements or restrictive covenants to impede their free action, does experience show that their success in agriculture vastly exceeds that of their neighbours? Fourthly, though it be granted that an unlimited investment of capital and labour might double the yield of a given farm, does it follow that such an investment

---

[1] In the Channel Islands, and in certain provinces of Belgium, still larger quantities of manure are purchased by farmers, and the rate of production is higher.

would be remunerative? and, if not, would any reform of the English Land System induce a sensible farmer to make it? These are questions which must be fairly met and answered, before we can be justified in asserting that no Continental nation has suffered from war or revolution losses at all comparable with those inflicted upon England by its land laws, and that, had British agriculture been developed as it might have been, " unborn millions would have lived upon the good so created." [1]

We may go further, and admit that, with all its faults, the agricultural system of England is founded on what appears, at first sight, a beneficial division of labour between three classes. A great English landlord of the best type brings to bear, not merely on agriculture, but on the whole rural economy of his neighbourhood, a higher intelligence, larger views of estate-management, a more enlightened public spirit, and a deeper sense of responsibility, than could be expected of peasant-farmers, or even of yeomen. He performs the unpaid public services which demand independence, leisure, and education; duties, which in France are very imperfectly performed, and which in the United States are mainly performed by salaried officials. He spends money in agricultural experiments which professional farmers could ill afford.[2] He sets on foot measures of local

---

[1] " Free Land," by Mr. Arthur Arnold, M.P., chapter viii.

[2] Adam Smith observes that " after small proprietors, rich and great farmers are in all countries the principal improvers. There are more such, perhaps, in England than in any other European monarchy. In the Republican Governments of Holland, and of Berne, in Switzerland, the farmers are said to be not inferior to those of England." It is remarkable that he does not contemplate the case of costly agricultural improvements

improvement which in most foreign countries would have to be initiated and carried out by the State. Moreover, it may be urged with some force that it is the prestige and privileges attached to landlordism which, in this country, attract towards land the inexhaustible wealth accumulated in trade or commerce. Were our agricultural society composed of yeomen and peasant-proprietors, the land might, or might not, employ a greater amount of labour, but it would not be subsidised out of surplus capital derived from banking profits, or from the ground rents of metropolitan property, which has been so liberally expended in developing some of the finest estates in England.

Again, it has often been pointed out, and it cannot be denied, that a farmer with a given capital, say of £10,000, can make a far better profit out of it by hiring and stocking land belonging to another man than by purchasing land for himself. In the one case, he may cultivate 1,000 acres and derive from them a net yearly income of some £800; in the other case, he will be lord of 200 or 250 acres, and will be fortunate if he derives from them a net yearly income of £400. Moreover, it is natural to expect that farming in the hands of trained and skilled men, relieved by their landlords of the cares and duties incident to ownership, should be treated more as a business, and less as a dignified inheritance or profession. It has not been the enterprise

being made by great landlords. Burke, writing in 1780, observed : " Agriculture will not attain any perfection till commercial principles be applied to it, or, in other words, till country gentlemen be convinced that the expenditure of a small portion of their capital upon land is the true secret of securing a large capital by ensuring increased returns."

of farmer-proprietors, but of tenant-farmers, which has brought to perfection the shorthorn breed of cattle, or the Leicester and South Down breeds of sheep; and, notwithstanding the extraordinary advantages of France in soil and climate, the superiority of the English agricultural system in productive capacity is fully acknowledged by French economists.[1] The advocates of that system may further allege that, in bad seasons, the landlord's capital serves as a kind of reserve fund on which tenant-farmers may fall back, and that a farmer-proprietor owing rent to himself could not grant a large remission of it without the risk of ruin.

The condition of agricultural labourers, as such, would not appear to depend materially on the relations of the orders above them in the agricultural hierarchy. The demand for labour being equal, the wages of labour ought to be equal, whether the employers be gentlemen-farmers, leaseholders, or tenants-at-will. But it is contended that agricultural labourers in England are, in fact, protected against being ground down, by the influence of a landlord class, superior to purely commercial motives, and with a more benevolent regard for the poor than is to be found among struggling farmer-proprietors. The English labourer, in general, " is not his landlord's workman, and he is not his employer's tenant; the man who employs cannot house, and the man who could house does not employ him."[2] But this double relation of labourers to landlords

---

[1] See an article on "La Situation Agricole de la France," in the *Revue des Deux Mondes* of January 15th, 1880, and Lavergne's "Economie Rurale de l'Angleterre."

[2] See Mr. Wren Hoskyn's "Essay on the English Land System."

and employers, which is alleged as a disadvantage of the English agricultural system, may be regarded, with at least equal justice, as one of its redeeming features. The labourer holding a cottage directly from a good landlord, at a rent far below its value, is far more independent, and has far more security of tenure, than if he rented it from his employer. He is bound over to good behaviour, it is true, by the simple fact of having much to lose, but so long as he behaves well, he may regard his cottage as a home, and dispose of his labour as he pleases.

Without disparaging the weight of such arguments in favour of a tripartite system of agriculture, we are bound to recognise the very powerful considerations which may be adduced on the other side. It is self-evident that, in order to play the beneficent part attributed to him in the agricultural partnership between himself and his tenants, a landlord must own a considerable estate, and be constantly or generally resident. Now, there are some 15,000 parishes in England and Wales, and the number of landlords owning 1,000 acres and upwards, who may for this purpose be described as squires, is probably about 3,500.[1] It follows that, even if every one of these lived on his estate, above three-fourths of the parishes in England and Wales must needs dispense with the presence of a resident squire, and this inference corresponds with the result of a local enquiry respecting the eastern division of Nottinghamshire, whence it appeared that, out of 245

---

[1] It is nominally 5,408. But it has been shown above, in the chapter on the Distribution of Landed Property, that, owing to double entries and other errors, the real number has been vastly overstated.

parishes, only 65 had resident squires.[1] But it is notorious that many squires and noblemen seldom reside for long in any one of the parishes in which they have property, spending much of the year in London, on the Continent, or at some watering-place. Nor must it be assumed that every resident landowner is an active and public-spirited man, ever ready to sacrifice his own ease and amusements to serious work. In the home-counties, especially, a landowner steadily devoting himself to estate management and public duties in his own locality is an object of respect, rather than of envy, to his more indolent neighbours. The number of county magistrates, it is true, exceeds that of landowners with more than 1,000 acres, but it is to be feared that if a public record were kept of their average attendance at Petty Sessions, Quarter Sessions, and Boards of Guardians, the illusion that English landlordism represents actual value received would be rudely dispelled. If the unpaid services of squires were compared with those rendered by clergymen, over and above their official functions, as school managers, as guardians of the poor, as representatives of authority in their respective parishes, we might perhaps find reason to doubt whether, after all, territorial influences are a more powerful agent than clerical influences in the civilisation of rural communities. Why should it be imagined that if landlordism were suppressed or weakened by a radical change in the agrarian constitution of England, its place could not be supplied by the rise or revival of other social forces ? If there were fewer great landlords, there might be,

---

[1] Mr. Shaw-Lefevre's "Freedom of Land," p. 79.

and probably would be, a more vigorous and independent middle class to play the leading part in rural government, and sustain a corporate life in villages of the same kind as that which exists in towns. If farmers could no longer rely on the indulgence of their landlords for help in bad seasons, it is at least possible that agricultural education would receive a new impulse, and that an unremitting attention to details, which characterises the peasant owner of France, Belgium, and the Channel Islands, would be more generally practised in England.

For, whatever may be said for a system of tenancy, as an instrument of agricultural production, there are obvious disadvantages inseparable from it. Tenant farmers without leases may have very adequate motives for improving breeds of cattle and sheep, from which they may confidently expect a profit; but they have no motive for permanently improving the soil, and their landlords, if limited owners, are in a like position. Tenant-farmers holding on lease have more inducement to study a far-sighted cultivation at the beginning of their terms, but are inevitably tempted to exhaust the soil at the end of them. If we could ascertain the pure waste of capital involved in letting the land run down before the expiration of a lease, and restoring its fertility during the early years of the next term, we should perceive how far even the leasehold tenancy of Scotland falls short of a perfect agricultural tenure.

The yearly tenancy which prevails in England is, perhaps, open to less objection on this ground, but is even less conducive to agricultural enterprise. A modern English farmer, even more than a Scotch farmer, is essentially a middleman, having neither the instincts of an owner, nor those of a husbandman. If that be the most profitable form of agricultural occupation "which most resembles ownership," that must surely be the least profitable which least resembles ownership, yet relieves the occupier from the obligation of personal industry; and such is the condition of the English tenant-farmer, holding from year to year. Whether or not he is bound down by unduly restrictive covenants, and whatever confidence he may have in the honour of his landlord, he never can feel that he is his own master, or free to follow out his own plans for the development of his business. His rent may be somewhat lower than might be obtained by competition, but this is no real equivalent for the uncertain ravages of game preserved to excess, for the constant apprehension of the agents' interference, for the risk involved in putting up fixtures, and for the sense of dependence under which he never ceases to labour. In these respects, the condition of the English farmer holding from year to year compares unfavourably not only with that of Scotch farmers, holding under leases, but also with that of Irish farmers holding under the Ulster tenant-right now recognised by the Irish Land Act. A man liable to be turned out without compensation, at six months' or a year's notice, but relying on the custom of an ancestral estate, may feel as secure in his own mind as if he enjoyed a freehold tenure, or the right to claim heavy damages for disturbance. Indeed, his sense of security may even be strengthened by the very difficulties, in themselves to be condemned, which now impede the alienation of family properties. But he does not practically act on this inward assurance; still less can he induce others to do so. The difference between an imaginary and a legal security of tenure becomes apparent the very moment that it is necessary to borrow money for improvements. This is why farmers in Scotland and the North of Ireland find it so much easier to obtain advances from the banks, and though such facilities are often abused, it is impossible not to see how much they have conduced to promote the development of agriculture in both countries.[1]

The further question now arises, whether it is not for the interest of the State that security of tenure

---

[1] The form of lease adopted on the Norfolk farms of the Earl of Leicester is justly recommended by Mr. Caird as supplying the great defect of most leases, and giving the farmer entire freedom of cultivation up to four years preceding its termination. "The tenancy is for 20 years, from the 11th day of October. It is to be terminable at the end of 16 years, at the request of the tenant and with the consent of the landlord; the intention being that, if both parties desire it, a new lease may be granted from the end of the 16th year for another term of 20 years," at the old rent for the four remaining years of the original term, and thenceforth at a rent to be fixed by agreement. During the first sixteen years, the tenant may cultivate according to his own judgment; during the last four, if he should fail to renew, he must cultivate on the four course system. (Caird's "Landed Interest," p. 153.)

A very liberal modification of yearly tenancy is adopted on the estates of Lord Tollemache, of Helmingham, in the shape of a "Lease-note," binding the landlord to allow the tenant undisturbed possession of his farm, without any increase of rent, for twenty-one years, upon condition of his keeping the land in a good state of cultivation, and draining or boning a certain number of acres. Under such a lease-note, while the tenant remains free to throw up his farm, the landlord resigns the power of giving him notice to quit, unless upon a breach of the conditions.

These agreements may be taken as representing the most favourable types of leasehold and yearly tenancy, respectively. If the principle of either had been imported, by general custom, into contracts between landlords and tenants throughout England, it is probable that no widespread demand for indefeasible tenant-right would have arisen.

should be legally guaranteed to English farmers, at least to the extent of compulsory indemnity for "unexhausted improvements." This question is essentially distinct from those of the succession to land, of settlements, and of land-transfer, and would call for solution, even though no other reform of the English Land system were attempted. It is not a question to be decided, either by the precedent of the Irish Land Act, or by analogies drawn from legislative intervention in cases to which freedom of contract is inapplicable. The Irish Land Act was justified by the existence of agrarian relations, due to historical causes, which have no place in the English land system. It was chiefly designed for the protection of tenants who, though nominally holding at will, had virtually inherited their land, had erected homesteads upon it, had been permitted to deal with it, for many purposes, as if they were part owners, and held a position in some respects like that of copyholders. The compulsory intervention of the Legislature in favour of children is justified on the ground that, by reason of their tender age, they are not free to contract for themselves. Its compulsory intervention in favour of miners or sailors rests upon the assumption that, although men are free to make their own bargains for wages, they are not free to barter away the safety of their own lives. Its compulsory intervention, in a variety of other instances, may be warranted by paramount considerations of public health or morality. Compulsory tenant-right, if defensible at all, must be defended on widely different principles, and it is these principles which now demand a dispassionate examination.

One plea often advanced in support of compulsory tenant-right must at once be dismissed as untenable. It cannot be alleged, with any justice, that by virtue of their having "a monopoly of land," or of their superior wealth, or of their social ascendency, the landlords have the power to force extortionate agreements upon tenants. No doubt landed property is a monopoly in the sense that the surface of the soil is limited in extent, and such a monopoly is, of course, far more valuable in a small and crowded island, overflowing with spare capital, than on a vast and thinly-peopled continent, where capital is far scarcer than land. This fact constitutes a sound argument for claiming and exercising a dormant right on the part of the State to control the action of landowners, so far as public interests may be concerned. But it does not constitute an argument for treating the whole class of English tenant-farmers, numbering some hundreds of thousands, like infants, lunatics, or persons under duress, as personally incompetent to make contracts with their landlords on equal terms. No one is compelled to hire land at all, and very recent experience shows that, when agricultural depression sets in, tenants become masters of the market, as landlords are during periods of agricultural prosperity. As between landlord and tenant, landed property in England is not a monopoly, for it is barely possible to conceive any combination among landlords whereby persons desiring to hire land can be deprived of an ample choice, or even subjected to oppressive covenants, on pain of having to go without farms or seek them in the Colonies.

But there is another view of the question. It
is quite possible to conceive that under a land system
so highly artificial as that of England inveterate
customs may have grown up, inconsistent with the real
interests of landlords and tenants no less than with the
public welfare, and only to be counteracted by the
superior force of law. If this were so, it would be
perfectly legitimate to prohibit the operation of these
customs, just as contracts in restraint of trade are
declared to be null and void, not because they benefit
one party unduly at the expense of another, but simply
because they contravene an established rule of national
policy. In that case, too, it might be urged, and with
equal force, that what is for the interest of the community is also, in the long run, for the interest of the
contracting parties, who might therefore be safely left
to follow their own inclinations without legal interference. But the sufficient answer in that case is one
which is equally applicable to contracts which may be
justly described as " in restraint of agriculture." It
is that society cannot always afford to wait until
economical principles have vindicated themselves, perhaps at a ruinous cost to consumers, in the course of
generations. Many instances may be cited in which
freedom of contract has been deliberately postponed to
considerations of public interest. Such is the Act
which sets aside any agreements between consignors
and railway companies whereby the statutable liabilities
of the latter may be evaded, the Act which compels
the landlord to pay half the Cattle Plague Rate,
notwithstanding any agreement to the contrary, and
that which invalidates any agreement under which a

tenant may be made liable for the Property Tax.[1] Nor is it unworthy of notice that by sects. 55 and 56 of Lord Cairns' Settled Land Bill of 1880, any contract by a tenant-for-life not to exercise the powers thereby conferred, and any provision in a settlement purporting to forbid or restrain his exercise of those powers, was declared to be absolutely void. The sufficient justification of this provision was that the State cannot give effect to a family law at direct variance with a national law, and this justification applies, in principle, to contracts in restraint of agriculture. In this case, too, where the immediate effect of a long-established and prevalent custom is plainly mischievous, it is the right and may be the duty of the Legislature to break the spell of it by a prohibitory, and not merely permissive, enactment, for which all parties may well be grateful.

How, then, should the law deal with the farmer's claim of a statutable tenant-right, in the sense of a right to compensation for unexhausted improvements? Before we can settle this question, we must ask ourselves first whether a positive security for such compensation, as

[1] For other instances of legislative interference with the right of contract, see Mr. James Howard's pamphlet on "The Tenant Farmer, Land Laws, and Landlords." Mr. C. S. Read, arguing before the Game Laws Committee of 1872-3, submitted that the law already interferes with freedom of contract between parent and child, master and servant, solicitor and client, debtor and creditor, guardian and ward, agent and principal, carrier and consignor, doctor and patient, innkeeper and tippler, pawnbroker and pledger, patron and presentee, captain and seamen, sailors and shipowners, mortgagor and mortgagee, and even landlord and tenant, under the Irish Land Act. In some of these instances, however, the disabilities imposed by law cannot be properly described as an interference with freedom of contract.

distinct from "reasonable expectations," is essential to good agriculture. Here the evidence appears conclusive, and our reply cannot be doubtful. The best agriculture is found on farms whose tenants are protected by leases; the next best, on farms whose tenants are protected by the Lincolnshire or other customs; the worst of all, on farms whose tenants are not protected at all, but rely on the honour of their landlords.[1] And the reason is self-evident. The farmer who holds without a lease or legal security knows that a model landlord may at any moment be succeeded by a heartless spendthrift, or a liberal agent by one whose pride consists in rack-renting every farm on the estate. He is, therefore, deterred by a traditional instinct from incurring expenditure which may lead to a re-valuation, with an advance of rent, if not to an appropriation of his invested capital. Still, we must further ask ourselves whether the enlightened self-interest of landlords and tenants may not be trusted to provide an adequate system of tenant-right by means of voluntary agreements. Here again experience returns a decisive answer. It was precisely because enlightened self-interest, crippled by life-ownership, had failed to supply the want of a statutable tenant-right, that a statutable, but permissive, tenant-right was introduced and defined by the Agricultural Holdings Act. Had the majority of English landlords hastened to adopt these provisions of the Act, or even to make equivalent agreements with their tenants, it would have been a presumption that

[1] So far back as 1848, Mr. Pusey's "Agricultural Customs Committee" reported "that this wider system of compensation to the outgoing tenant seems to be highly beneficial to agriculture, to the landlord, and to the farmer, to lead to a great increase in the productiveness of the soil, and to extended employment of the rural population."

now, at least, the value of a positive security for tenant-right was generally appreciated. Unhappily, the reverse was the fact. The same motives which had brought about the disuse of leases caused a general anxiety to negative the operation of the Act, and we cannot venture to hope that, for many years to come, any adequate system of tenant-right will be substituted for it by voluntary agreement. Under these circumstances, we have to ask ourselves, lastly, whether the development of agriculture is a national object of such importance as to justify the imposition of tenant-right upon unwilling landlords and indifferent tenants by legislative authority, and, if so, in what form it should be imposed.

If these islands were now compelled by war, as they once were by a selfish and fatuous policy, to maintain their own population for several years in succession, the paramount necessity of stimulating home production to the utmost would be self-evident. The most stringent laws for encouraging the application of capital to land, and annulling every contract which could impede the development of agriculture, would then be cheerfully accepted as essential to national existence. Of course, such a condition is almost impossible to conceive, even in the event of a long war, and in time of peace Free Trade, followed by the marvellous acceleration of transit by land and sea, renders Great Britain comparatively independent of her own home-production. But this independence is only comparative. Even if wheat-growing should be abandoned in England, as it has so nearly been abandoned in Scotland and Ireland, our main supply of most other articles of food, and our whole supply of the most perishable, must still be drawn from our own soil.   The whole community, therefore, has a far more direct interest in agriculture than in any other branch of national industry, unless it be the production of coal.   A deficient home supply of meat or milk or vegetables, like a deficient home supply of coal, would be far more severely felt by the mass of the people than a deficient home supply of cotton or hardware, since these commodities are less necessary, and might be procured at a slightly increased price from abroad.   It follows that, if the home supply of agricultural produce is materially limited by the want of an indefeasible tenant-right, it is an object of high national importance to apply the appropriate remedy.   But would this involve injustice or injury to any individual or class ?   On the contrary, the evidence shows that a good tenant would be glad to pay a higher rent for a holding protected by tenant-right, and, the higher the rent, the more skilful and productive the farming is likely to be.   All parties, then, would apparently be the gainers by the general adoption of tenant-right, which can only be enforced by legislative authority, erecting into a national custom that which is now a local custom in the best-farmed counties.   No doubt freedom of contract is preferable, on principle, to legislative regulation ; but freedom of contract has been tried for many ages, and has failed to effect the object which almost all admit to be desirable. Moreover, freedom of contract, even if it operated in favour of tenant-right, could not give that universal sense of security which is here of paramount value, and which the law alone can guarantee.   Once established on a sound and reasonable basis, an indefeasible tenant-right would soon cease to be felt as an obligation imposed by an external power, and would be accepted, like other salutary restrictions of individual liberty, as a rule of natural justice, working for the common benefit of all.

But, in order that it should have this effect, it must needs rest upon a sound and reasonable basis. Now, it is obvious that no law establishing indefeasible tenant-right could be sound or reasonable which should make no distinction between various classes of improvements. Those which are recognised as improvements of the "first-class" under the Agricultural Holdings Act are, for the most part, of a durable character, and, for that reason, have been commonly executed by the landlord in this country. Thorough drainage, the erection of buildings, the conversion of arable land into permanent pasture, the construction of fences, the reclamation of waste land, and so forth, are agricultural operations beyond the sphere of ordinary husbandry, which ought not to be executed by a tenant without the express consent of his landlord, and to which the rule of indefeasible tenant-right could not justly be applied. A poor landlord might be ruined by the cost of drainage or reclamation, however profitable they might be to his successors, and even a rich landlord might fairly object to pay for buildings or fences, which might become worse than useless in the event of his choosing to subdivide or consolidate his farms. Many such improvements have been executed at the cost of tenants in Scotland and Ireland, with great advantage to landlords, and it may sometimes be convenient to adopt the same practice in England, where the tenant happens to be a man of large capital and energy. But this should be a matter of voluntary arrangement; otherwise the farmer would become the landlord, or, at least, the landlord would lose all effective control over his own property. Even improvements of the " second class," such as boning, chalking, claying, liming, and marling, are scarcely fit subjects for compensation under a rule of indefeasible tenant-right, however proper it may be that a tenant should be compensated for them, where they have been carried out after notice to the landlord, and without objection on his part. In this respect the provisions of the present Agricultural Holdings Act appear to require little amendment, being chiefly directed to promote the investment of tenants' capital in far-sighted ameliorations of the soil, under the landlord's supervision. On the other hand, it is essential to good husbandry, under the conditions of modern farming, that artificial manures should be applied to land, that purchased feeding-stuffs should be consumed by stock, especially on those holdings from which straw is allowed to be sold off, and that foul land should be well broken up by the steam-cultivator. It would be absurd to require any preliminary consent, or to encourage any preliminary objection, to outlay of this kind. If the farm should be thrown up, the full benefit of it will be reaped by the succeeding occupier, from whom the landlord may recover it in the form of an advanced rent, and the cases in which there could be any valid objection to it are too rare to be worthy of legal recognition. There can be little doubt that a new spirit would be infused into British agriculture by the certainty that no risk could be incurred by a good farmer through following a liberal system of ordinary husbandry, but that he might always look either to realising the profit of it, or to receiving the value of it.

Such being the true grounds and limits of indefeasible tenant-right, we have yet to determine the mode in which it should be secured. The Agricultural Holdings Act contains various restrictions upon claims for compensation in respect of " third-class improvements," which include the consumption of purchased feeding-stuffs and the use of purchased manures. For instance, no such claim holds good if an exhausting crop has been taken off the land since the manure was applied to it, or the stock fed upon it. It would obviously be impossible to embody these, or any other special reservations, in a general law establishing indefeasible tenant-right. As part of a permissive Act, they may serve an useful purpose in formulating a standard of agricultural equity to which voluntary agreements may approximate more or less closely. But in a compulsory Act they would be wholly out of place, for the Legislature cannot absolutely prescribe the proper system even of ordinary husbandry for all parts of the kingdom. The utmost that can be done is to lay down a broad principle, and enact either that it shall be imported by implication of law into all contracts of tenancy, or that all contracts whereby it may be contravened shall be null and void.[1] It would not be difficult to frame a positive clause defining the ordinary acts of good husbandry for which a tenant

[1] A Bill of this character was introduced by Sir Thomas D. Acland, Mr. Duckham (a tenant-farmer), and other members, in the Session of 1880, under the name of the Agricultural Tenant's Compensation Bill. A full explanation of its objects and limitations, drawn up by Sir Thomas Acland, is subjoined in Appendix III.

should have an indefeasible right to compensation on the determination of his tenancy, subject only to a landlord's right of pleading a set-off, or other sufficient answer in derogation of the claim. Nor would it be difficult to frame a negative clause invalidating every contract which should purport to set aside the right so defined. Either method would be effectual to defeat attempts on the part of landlords to contract themselves out of the legal principle, which might well be extended so as to give landlords an indefeasible right to compensation for waste and exhaustion of the soil. For tenant-right and landlord-right are reciprocal. Both must be justified, if at all, by the interests of the community, and these consist, not in a one-sided protection of a single agricultural class, but in a vigorous development of agriculture by all classes entrusted with the land. Such reciprocity was conspicuously wanting under the old Common Law, which empowered landlords to sue tenants for dilapidation, and to recover their rent by ·distress, independently of any express covenant, without enabling tenants to obtain compensation for improvements.

The statutable regulation of sporting rights over land is open to the same patent objections as indefeasible tenant-right, and must be justified, if at all, by the same arguments. It may be said that farmers are perfectly able to recoup themselves for the loss incident to game-preserving by insisting upon a "game-rent," or may decline altogether agreements of tenancy wherein the game is reserved to the landlord. It may be said that consumers have ceased to have much practical interest in the ravages of game, since the price of corn is mainly governed by the foreign supplies; and it may be asked whether, apart from the interest of consumers, the suppression of these ravages can be an object of such importance as to warrant legislative interference with freedom of contract. The fallacy latent in objections of this kind has already been exposed. The interest of the public in good husbandry is more than co-extensive with the joint interests of producers and consumers, and is not to be measured by a merely pecuniary standard. Let it be granted that an English tenant has no claim to be treated by the law as so hopelessly the weaker party that he cannot be trusted to make his own bargain for himself. The question for the public is not what he can do, but what he does and will do, under the constant pressure of custom; not whether he can be trusted to make his own bargain for himself, but whether he can be trusted to make it for the benefit of agriculture, and of interests still broader and higher than agricultural interests. For instance, if excessive game-preserving, under the ordinary covenants, has a palpably injurious effect on the relations between landlords and tenants, or discourages men of independence and public spirit from undertaking the business of farming, or perpetuates other evils of the existing land system, it may be perfectly legitimate to revise the Game Laws in a sense adverse to absolute freedom of contract. The case is obviously much stronger, if it can be shown, as it assuredly may be shown, that excessive game-preserving directly fosters poaching, and indirectly contributes to multiply other crimes.

But there are special reasons for a statutable regulation of sporting rights over land which do not equally apply to indefeasible tenant-right. Sporting rights, as understood in England, are essentially the creation of statute, and could not exist for a day without legal protection. The semi-wild, but semi-domestic, animals known as "game" have been well described as "privileged vermin," and would soon become extinct in many parts of the country but for the maintenance of the Game Laws. Even the Game Laws do not countenance, but only recognise, the peculiar custom which is so mischievous to good husbandry. The separation of sporting rights from the occupation of land is in itself an anomaly, at variance with the presumption of Common Law, no less than with that provision in the Game Act of 1831 which expressly vested the game in the tenant, and made the right of sporting run with the land, unless it should be reserved by deed or agreement. Under this last clause most English landlords took care to keep the game in their own hands, and prohibited their tenants from keeping it down, while many let the right thus reserved to strangers, who had no motive for exercising it with any regard for the interests of farmers or the public. The Game Laws Committee of 1872–3 unanimously declared their opinion that no tenant ought to enter upon his farm without due protection against over-preserving, and that no protection would be so efficient as the concession of the power to kill ground game on his own farm, either exclusively or concurrently with the landlord. The fact that such protection was practically seldom conceded, and that great injury was thereby caused to national interests, was a sound reason for re-considering the Act of 1831. It could not be contended for a moment that it would be a violation of individual liberty for the Legislature to sweep away this and other Game Laws altogether, to convert game into property, or to relegate it into the class of un-privileged vermin. If so, it is absurd to contend that it is inconsistent with individual liberty for the Legis-lature to impose strict conditions on the exclusive rights which have grown up under its patronage. Supposing these rights to conflict with the good of the com-munity, they must either be abolished or regulated, and the regulation of them must needs involve some inter-ference with freedom of contract.

Such a regulation has practically been effected by the Ground Game Act, 1880. This Act renders the presumptive right of an occupier to kill game on his land an inseparable incident of his occupation, so far as hares and rabbits are concerned. It confines the exercise of that right, however, to the occupier himself and one other person, to be duly authorised by him in writing. A concurrent right to kill ground-game on the land may be vested in the landlord, or any other person, but the occupier cannot wholly divest himself of his own right, nor can it be defeated by contract. Henceforth, therefore, it will be entirely the fault of English tenant-farmers, if their crops are annually decimated by ground-game, though it is probable that sporting instincts, common to most classes of English society, will preserve even hares and rabbits from wholesale extermination.

One thing is clear, and that is that, so far as inde-feasible tenant-right may have the effect of modifying the present agricultural system, it will probably tend, at least, to reduce the average size of holdings. Instead of spreading his capital thinly over too large an acreage, the British farmer will naturally be induced to concentrate it on a smaller area. Now, whatever theoretical superiority may belong to agriculture on a grand scale entirely depends on capital being duly proportioned to acreage, and superintendence being effectively maintained. Where these conditions are actually realised, there must needs be great economy in the management of farms extending over thousands of acres, though it may be doubted whether they are equally conducive to social well-being in rural communities. But experience shows how seldom these conditions are actually realised, while it attests the remarkable success of working farmers occupying holdings which can be cultivated by the members of one family, with one team of horses. Those who press the analogy between agriculture and manufactures to extremes, and believe that small farmers are doomed to retire before civilisation, are bound to explain how it comes to pass that small farmers manfully hold their own in the present struggle for existence, both at home and abroad. The authority of M. Lavergne is often cited in support of the allegation that English agriculture surpasses that of France as a whole, and that more produce is extracted from the land by the British capitalist farmer than by the French peasant. But though M. Lavergne, writing many years ago, makes this admission in emphatic terms,[1] he adds that no similar area in England is cultivated as well as the Département du

[1] He says that, notwithstanding the great superiority of France in soil and climate, it would be impossible to select any French departments containing an equal area with the cultivated portion of England, which could be favourably compared with it in respect of agricultural condition. (*Economie Rurale de l'Angleterre*, p. 3.)

Nord, which is essentially a district of small farms ; and there is overwhelming evidence to prove that scientific English agriculturists have yet many lessons to learn from the small farms of Belgium, Switzerland, the Channel Islands, and Germany.

In comparing one agricultural system with another, it is not enough to ascertain which of them employs the greater amount of capital per acre, or yields the greater amount of gross produce. In both these respects England is outstripped by the Channel Islands, and certain provinces of Belgium, and several other special districts of Europe, but it still ranks exceptionally high. There is so vast an accumulation of spare capital in England, that under any agricultural system, however bad, the land would absorb more of it than would be possible in a new or very poor country. So, again, however bad an agricultural system may be, a lavish application of capital will ensure a return of gross produce absolutely large, though perhaps relatively small. The more important question to solve is, what agricultural system yields the best return of produce to a given amount of capital ; in other words, what system calls forth most effectively the energy of the labourer as well as the skill of the farmer? The answer to this question may be such as to disturb many preconceived opinions founded on the assumption, too common among doctrinaire economists, that human industry is exclusively regulated by strict laws of supply and demand, whereas it is largely influenced by habits and sentiments beyond the province of economy. The English tenant-farmer has as strong a pecuniary inducement to work like a slave as the yeoman-farmer of Belgium and the Channel Islands, but he is not prompted to do so by the same traditional spirit of thrift, the same pride of ownership, or the same ambition to vie in money-making with the mercantile society of his neighbourhood. Such feelings and motives are the growth of many generations, and cannot be suddenly transfused into English, much less into Irish, tenants, by any legislative process. On the other hand, we learn from history that England was once the land of yeomen farmers, and that English agriculture once flourished under a land system very similar to that which still prevails in the best-cultivated portions of Europe and America. If, then, a revival of this system, under altered conditions, and in a modified form, should hereafter appear to open the best prospect of regenerating British agriculture, there is no reason for rejecting it as radically incompatible with the national character.

But this prospect, like that of an industrial migration from towns into country districts, is too remote to be practically entertained by the legislator. For the present, it must be taken for granted that British agriculture will be mainly conducted on the old footing of a partnership between landlord and tenant, whether the landlord be a large or a small proprietor, and whether the tenant's capital be measured by hundreds or thousands of pounds. If the experiment of yeoman farming is again to receive a fair and full trial in this country, it will probably be tried, in the first instance, by persons who have made little fortunes in business, who have a shrewd eye for buying cheap and selling dear, and who are not fettered by the orthodox rules of regular agriculture. The ordinary English tenant, accustomed to farm on the four-course system, and too old-fashioned to adopt the petty shifts and resources familiar to Continental peasant-farmers, has no wish to become his own landlord, and will often even refuse a lease on favourable terms.   But he already appreciates the advantage of indefeasible tenant-right, and, having obtained it, he must needs perceive the advantage of spreading his capital over a smaller number of acres, if by so doing he can make it yield nearly the same rate of interest, besides reducing his rent and labour-bill.   Hence, increased security of tenure will constantly operate to promote the subdivision of very large holdings, except so far as it may attract new capital from business into farming, or encourage the development of joint-stock agriculture on a grand scale.   The process of subdivision, however, is likely to be very gradual.   Like the landowner who measures his dignity by acreage rather than by income, the farmer will at first be unwilling to ride over a smaller number of fields or to superintend a smaller number of labourers.   Moreover, farm buildings are not so easily subdivided as farms, and the many thousands of expensive steadings erected during the last thirty or forty years will long continue as a material guarantee for the policy of consolidation to which they owe their origin.

In the meantime, acute observers have already been led to dispute the wisdom of this policy, even under the favourable conditions which so long prevailed after the Repeal of the Corn Laws.   This was not the least suggestive of the many agricultural questions forced upon public attention by the agricultural distress of 1878-9.   Though almost all farms suffered more or less from the combined effects of a bad season and low prices, farms of moderate size were often found to bear the strain better than farms of the first class. Several reasons may be suggested to explain this difference, which is the more remarkable when it is remembered that farms of moderate size usually pay a somewhat higher rent per acre, since there is greater competition for them. We learn from the Registrar-General's Report on the Census of 1871 that 152 acres is the average size of a farm in seventeen representative counties, and that more than half of all the farms in those counties were under 100 acres. Now, the occupier of such a farm is likely to possess less scientific knowledge, and certain to possess less aggregate capital, than a farmer occupying 1,000 acres and upwards.[1] But it does not follow that he possesses less practical capacity, or less capital in proportion to acreage. On the contrary, like his ancestors in Adam Smith's time, he is usually content to be his own overseer and foreman, knowing the value of the master's eye in all manual work, and will not be above occasionally putting his own hand to the plough. He may perhaps be too liable to err on the side of penny wisdom, but he thus avoids the risk of sinking money in costly experiments and the breeding of prize animals. His wife is not too fine a lady to look after the fowl-yard, or to superintend, at least, the making of cheese and butter. His farm-buildings and fences may not be as neatly kept as they might be, and many things which offend the eye of a gentleman farmer are tolerated on his land, but, at all events, he takes care to get money's worth for money, and is not ashamed to drive a hard bargain at the end of a market day. He does not allow middlemen to run

---

[1] There were 582 such farmers in the seventeen counties in 1871.

away with the lion's share of his legitimate profits, by
paying an exorbitant price for store-cattle, and selling
fat beasts to a butcher for a sum far below the retail
value of their meat. He keeps neither hunter nor dog-
cart; if there is a piano in his parlour, it is a cheap one,
and seldom used; his scale of household expenditure is
niggardly; and it is to be feared that his charitable
subscriptions come to very little in the course of the
year. In short, he is a keen man of business, with the
same turn for petty economies as a grocer or draper of
equal income. And thus, although he never realises
the handsome profits on corn-crops which in good years
may reward the *grande agriculture*, he never incurs the
crushing losses incident to a lavish outlay of capital
in bad seasons, and is better able than his scientific
neighbour to contract his working expenses according
to circumstances.

Apart, therefore, from the possible effect of indefeasible tenant-right, or any other organic change in
the agricultural system of England, it is by no means
improbable that subdivision rather than consolidation of
holdings may hereafter be dictated by the mutual interests of landlords and tenants. Nor will this change
always involve any considerable outlay in buildings, for,
in many cases, the homesteads of extinct farms remain
in good repair, surrounded by yards and sheds, though
now tenanted by farm-labourers. But the impulse thus
given towards subdivision of holdings will naturally be
accelerated by the subdivision of ownership already
anticipated. It is a trite saying that large farms
always go with large properties, but the reason of this
conjunction does not lie on the surface. There is

apparently nothing to prevent the owner of a few hundred acres from letting the whole of it to a single tenant, or the owner of many thousand acres from parcelling them out, as was the practice in Ireland, into a multitude of peasant-farms. In reality, however, the owner of many thousand acres is actuated, consciously or unconsciously, by many other motives besides that of increasing his rental, which lead him to prefer a few substantial tenants, and to eschew small holdings. He is almost sure to be more or less in the hands of his agent, and his agent is almost sure to be an advocate of consolidation, because it is much easier and pleasanter to deal with half-a-dozen men of capital and independence, than to be always receiving petty complaints and requisitions from struggling occupiers of farmhouses out of repair. The aggregate rent paid by the former may be smaller, but this is the landlord's affair, and the agent, who collects it with far less trouble, assures him that it is far less precarious than if it depended on the solvency of many small tenants. The proprietor of a few hundred acres does not come within the sphere of these influences. Having no agent, he acts for himself, and thereby saves not only a large percentage on his gross-rental, but the manifold risks of loss into which owners are led by persons who lose nothing by the unproductive expenditure on grand improvement schemes which they recommend. He is not, therefore, in a hurry to throw farms together, or to spend money in bricks and mortar, so as to satisfy any ideal of scientific agriculture. On the contrary, if he is resident and possesses the instincts of proprietorship, he would rather be lord of several tenants than of one, and will very soon discover that subdivision of holdings is more profitable to a landowner than consolidation, if the necessary farm buildings exist or can be put up cheaply.

The prevailing objections to small holdings will be further mitigated, though insensibly, by that moderate reform of the Game Laws, which has restored to occupiers the control of ground-game on their own farms. Small farmers, and still more squatters and cottagers with cultivated patches of land, have always been suspected of poaching or complicity with poachers. It is they, more than any other class, who have been tempted to snare hares and rabbits devouring their little crops or plots of vegetables, and it has been the settled policy of landlordism to discourage them in neighbourhoods devoted to game preserving. Now that all tenants have an equal and inalienable right to kill and take ground-game, the motive for this policy will be weakened, and if the " game " ' landlord should ultimately disappear, it will almost cease to operate. So far as game is concerned, it will then become a matter of comparative indifference whether the holdings on an estate are large or small, and whether labourers' allotments be near the coverts or not, while the fact that a higher rent can generally be obtained from petty occupiers will be more fully appreciated.

Other tendencies, moving in the same direction, will gradually force upon the English farmer a mode of culture more suitable to small holdings. When it is once realised that the whole value of the home wheat-crop is greatly exceeded by the value of live cattle, dead meat, butter, cheese, eggs and potatoes, brought in annually from America and the Continent,[1] it may cease to be regarded as an axiom of English agriculture that a certain proportion of each arable farm must needs be laid down in wheat. It is, indeed, marvellous that such a doctrine should have been maintained with such persistence, notwithstanding the fact that only $\frac{1}{50}$th part of Wales, only $\frac{1}{130}$th part of Ireland, and only $\frac{1}{250}$th part of Scotland, was under wheat crops in the year 1879. As the growth of wheat becomes less and less profitable, the English farmer will be compelled to study new sources of profit, hitherto neglected as beneath the notice of a scientific agriculturist. It will then be discovered that it is precisely these minor branches of agricultural industry which depend most for their success on a degree of minute personal attention which it is vain to expect from the refined and well-dressed tenant of 1,000 acres, even if he possessed the capital necessary to practise the arts of the *petite culture* over so vast an area.

We have already noticed the inadequate supply and inordinate cost of fresh milk both in towns and country districts as offering the strongest inducement to an increase of dairy-farming. There is no reason, however, why dairy-farming, conducted with a view to the sale of milk alone, should not flourish on large as well as on small holdings. It is otherwise when dairy-farming is conducted with a view to the sale of cheese or butter. Experience had long ago shown that cheese and butter were made of the best quality, and with the greatest

---

[1] The home production of wheat may be taken at about 11,000,000 quarters, which, at 50s. a quarter, would be worth £27,500,000, and, at 55s. a quarter, would be worth £30,250,000. But the value of imported live stock, dead meat and provisions (exclusive of corn), amounts to nearly £37,000,000. (Agricultural Returns for 1879, Table 29.)

economy, where the delicate processes of their manufacture, requiring above all the utmost cleanliness, were
superintended early and late by a skilful mistress, who
had the whole dairy, so to speak, under her own eye. It
is notorious that very few wives of wealthy farmers are
now either trained or disposed to undertake the incessant toil of dairy-management. Cheese-making is, therefore, carried on for the most part either on farms of
moderate size, where the farmer's wife is her own dairymaid, or in great factories, to which the neighbouring
dairy farmers can dispatch all their milk to be worked
up under skilled direction, and with the best aids of
machinery.[1] The same may be said of poultry-keeping
and the production of eggs. Seeing that fowls now
sell (1880) for about double what they fetched thirty or
forty years ago, while the expense of breeding and fattening them has in no respect increased, it may well be
asked why every farmer, with a capable wife, and a
proper soil for the purpose, should not bestow far more
care than he usually does on this most profitable accessory
of agricultural industry. The reply must be that poultry-

---

[1] On the Cheshire estate of Lord Tollemache of Helmingham, the
cheese-making farms, fifty-two in number, range between 150 and 250
acres, the average size being about 200 acres. It is found by experience,
in Somersetshire no less than in Cheshire, that farms of this size yield the
best results, since the farmer has enough milk to make a whole cheese
with proper dispatch at the proper time, while his wife is not too fine a
lady to superintend the process in person. On some farms of this class
no hired labour whatever is employed, all the necessary work being done
by the farmer's own family. In such an establishment it is easier to
practise economy than in a great cheese-factory, supplied with milk by
contributions from several distant farms. Cows are also kept on Lord
Tollemache's Cheshire estate by no less than 267 cottagers, each of whom
holds an allotment of two and a-half or three acres at an ordinary farm-
rent. Butter is made on these little cottage farms, but not cheese.

rearing, like cheese-making and butter-making, requires infinite pains and study of details. It prospers in the hands of French peasant-farmers, among whom thrift is the highest of family virtues, and it prospers in great establishments where artificial egg-hatching and the rapid nutrition of chickens is reduced to a scientific manufacture. But it is little fancied by English tenant-farmers of the higher class, whose wives never go to market, and who profess to believe that no price which they are likely to receive from the dealers will cover the cost of the corn which the fowls consume. A like explanation must be sought for the remarkable decline in the home supply of eggs. Since eggs are a specially brittle commodity, and depend for their value mainly upon their freshness, it is truly marvellous that English farmers should be content to see nearly 800,000,000 of them, worth above two millions and a-half sterling, imported from the Continent every year, instead of imitating the French method of egg-culture and egg-preservation. But then egg-culture and egg-preservation are as tiresome kinds of drudgery as watching and rearing chickens for the market, and so they are neglected as unworthy of attention by tenants occupying several hundred acres.[1]

[1] The following account of extra-produce, sold in one year by a farmer's wife, on a holding of 30 acres, appeared, under the signature of H. T. F., in the *Times* of Aug. 20, 1879:—

	£	s.
5 reared calves	25	0
32 pigs at 16s.	25	12
20 cade lambs (less cost at 5s. each) ,.. ...	43	0
18 turkeys at 10s. 6d.	9	9
220 couples of fowls and ducks, at 4s. ...	44	0
Total £147	0	

"All this besides the ordinary produce of the land, and with only the

There is another branch of agricultural industry which is perhaps capable of still greater development in England, but which is still more specially adapted to small holdings. Seeing that London, with a population of nearly 4,000,000, is so miserably supplied with vegetables, which, moreover, are so dear that many hundred thousands of its inhabitants seldom taste any green food but water-cresses, it remains to be explained why market-gardening should be confined to an area of 36,610 acres in all England,[1] and why £3,000,000 worth of vegetables, mostly potatoes, should be annually imported from abroad. Here, again, we light upon the besetting weakness of farming on the grand scale. The farmer himself is a mere overseer, with no idea beyond that of conducting the great operations of agriculture, and with a rooted aversion to everything which savours of horticulture, while his labourers have neither the skill nor the heart for the patient work of a gardener. But there is an additional reason, applicable also to hop cultivation, why market-gardening in all forms should be practised most successfully on small holdings. The capital required to make a hop-ground or market-garden thoroughly productive is infinitely greater, in proportion to acreage, than is demanded by the most scientific tillage of arable land. It has been computed that, for

drawback of a few quarters of maize, and a few bushels of linseed. I do not mention the produce of two cows, which nearly met the house expenses." It is difficult, however, to believe that a few quarters of maize, and a few bushels of linseed, would have sufficed to fatten so many animals, unless largely supplemented by "the ordinary produce of the land."

[1] Agricultural Returns for 1879, Table 3. It is stated by Mr. G. Gibson Richardson that about 1,250,000 acres in France are devoted to growing green vegetables.

each acre of hop-land, £45 of working capital is essential upon an average of all the districts; that the actual expenses of cultivation—inclusive of a rent which sometimes rises to £10 an acre—amount to at least £22 ; and that, if packing, drying, and other incidental expenses be added, the whole annual cost of hop-culture amounts, on the average, to £35 per acre. In the neighbourhood of Farnham, even this standard of rent and expenses is sometimes exceeded, but the risks are so great that, although the produce of a single acre may occasionally realise £100, the average profit upon each acre of English hop-land during thirty years ending with 1878 was found to have little exceeded £10. The natural consequence is that few tenants are wealthy enough to rent any very large extent of hop-land, and that the 70,000 acres devoted to this crop in England are very much subdivided among small occupiers. A hop-farm of 300 acres near Maidstone is mentioned as an exceptional curiosity; a few planters in Mid and East Kent are said to hold 100 or 200 acres, but the average even there is but 50 acres ; in the Weald of Kent and Sussex it is stated at 20 acres, and in the hop-growing district of Surrey it is probably still lower.[1]

The cost of growing vegetables for town markets is not less enormous, though it is repaid by corresponding profits. The rents of market-gardens and market-farms within twenty miles of London are said to range from £4 to £9 per acre. The expenses of labour come to from

[1] See the article on the Cultivation of Hops, Fruit, and Vegetables, by Mr. Charles Whitehead, in the Journal of the Royal Agricultural Society for 1878. Part II.

£6 to £9 per acre, and the whole annual outlay per acre averages considerably more than £20.[1] The same lavish scale of expenditure on vegetable-growing is maintained in France, where the *capital d'exploitation* supposed to be needed by a market-gardener is a hundredfold greater in proportion to acreage than would there satisfy an ordinary farmer. In order to produce a constant succession of crops, at the rate of two a year, 40 or 50 tons of farmyard manure are often applied, and nearly 100 tons are sometimes applied annually to a single acre by the market-gardeners in the neighbourhood of London. It is well known that broccoli and other vegetables are forced into early maturity in Cornwall by the same unsparing use of manure. Much of this produce is still raised by spade husbandry in the inner circle round London, whence it is conveyed to Covent Garden in carts, which come back loaded with the litter of stables and cow-houses. For the field-cultivation of vegetables a migratory class of labourers is largely employed, who are often hired as hop-pickers at a later period of the year. But the business of market-gardening and vegetable-farming is mainly conducted on small holdings of less than fifty acres, doubtless because each acre so worked demands a concentration of capital, labour, and individual supervision, which very few tenant-farmers would be capable of bringing to bear on a much larger area. Yet many a skilful agriculturist, barely able to pay his rent on a farm covering a quarter

---

[1] See Mr. Whitehead's article, above cited, in the *Journal of the Royal Agricultural Society* for 1878. Mr. G. Gibson Richardson states that the rent paid for market gardens round Paris varies from £36 to £48 per acre, according to situation.

of a parish, might well envy a humbler neighbour who may realise £40, £50, or even £100 and upwards per acre in one lucky year by the growth of onions, early potatoes, celery, or cauliflower. There can be little doubt that, as population and wages advance, the consumption of vegetables will be vastly increased. Some which are now considered luxuries will come to be regarded almost as necessaries even by the working classes, and others, too little known in England at present, but highly valuable as articles of diet, will come into common use. It is stated in Mr. Giffen's report on the Agricultural Returns for 1879 that many farmers have lately been induced by the improved facilities of railway-carriage to devote a small portion of their land to vegetables and bush fruits. But the production of vegetables and fruit is a special art—the fancy-work of agriculture— which must always be most profitable when it is practised by a special class of farmers. If it should be largely extended, it will inevitably be extended on the system which has been heretofore found most successful, and will, so far, contribute to promote the subdivision of holdings.[1]

[1] In the able articles of Mr. Charles Whitehead on "Market Gardening for Farmers," reprinted from the *Mark Lane Express* of Aug. 9, 1880, this subject is fully discussed. Mr. Whitehead points out that vegetable culture has been somewhat discredited among farmers by the occurrence of occasional gluts in the market, involving heavy losses, but that such gluts are mainly due to a defective organisation of distribution. Vegetables may be extremely cheap in the heart of the metropolis, yet extremely dear in the suburbs, or at watering-places. He says "there are too many middlemen in the trade," under the form of salesmen, greengrocers, and costermongers. He suggests the formation of emporium-markets, in which each grower's vegetables should be kept distinct, and which might also serve for the sale of milk, butter, eggs, fowls, cheese, fruit, and even hay, straw, and oats. His conclusion is that while the chief wheat

There is one boon, hitherto denied to British farmers, which it is in the power of the Legislature to bestow upon them, and which may exercise no slight effect on the agriculture of the future. The want of a cheap and good agricultural education has never been felt as a farmer's grievance in this country, yet it is a more substantial grievance than many which have become the subjects of vehement agitation. There is probably no business requiring so great a combination of theoretical with practical knowledge as that of farming, or, at least, of high farming, yet it is habitually practised by men who have never received the most rudimentary scientific training, or even served a regular apprenticeship. A farmer's son, destined to be a farmer, is usually educated in much the same fashion as the son of a shopkeeper, learning nothing at school that has any bearing on agriculture, and hardly anything at home which might not be picked up by any intelligent farm-labourer. He may, of course, glean much information by degrees from the practical advice of others and the use of his own senses, especially in regard to the management of sheep or cattle, and the various capacities of the various fields on a particular farm. But the science of breeding is probably an occult mystery to him: he chooses beasts simply by the eye and not by weight, and even in the art of fattening them for the market he seldom has any better guide

supplies of Great Britain will continue to be derived from America and other foreign countries, " all we who cultivate land must endeavour to obtain as much as possible of those funds which are spent upon delicacies, luxuries, and additions to diet, and to stimulate expenditure in this direction by placing them before the public cheaply, and well grown, or well prepared."

than routine. Being ignorant of agricultural chemistry, he must buy his own experience, when he comes to deal with a new soil, perhaps requiring a treatment wholly different from any to which he has been accustomed. If he dabbles with artificial manures, he may easily throw away money, for he probably "cannot tell the difference between soluble and insoluble phosphate, or between ammonia and nitrate of soda." He must be much above the level of his fellows, if he even appreciates the value of precious materials supplied by his own farm-yard, and does not allow the greater part of its liquid manure to drain away into ditches, instead of collecting it in tanks. Being equally ignorant of agricultural botany, he is at the mercy of the seedsman for the proper varieties of artificial grass, and sometimes finds himself cheated in this respect to a serious extent. As for the engines or other machines which he employs, he does not profess to understand their construction, and is therefore dependent on experts for checking the mode and cost of working them. In short, he is not only not a scientific agriculturist, but has a wholesome contempt for scientific agriculture, never having realised that in agriculture, as in other branches of industry, science means economy of power, and ignorance of science means waste of power. He is content to know that a scientific theorist, without practical experience, cannot be a successful farmer, and does not care to ask himself whether a farmer, with practical experience, could possibly be the worse for a competent knowledge of science.

It would be idle to argue against the notion that agriculture, alone of human arts, can be learned by rule of thumb, when all other European nations, except one or two of the most backward, have recognised the necessity of teaching it methodically. In France, Germany, Austro-Hungary, Belgium, Holland, Sweden and Norway, Denmark, Switzerland, and Italy, a more or less complete system of agricultural education has been established, and it is impossible not to connect this fact with the progress lately made by foreign agriculture. In Germany there are said to be seventeen high schools or institutes of agriculture, thirty middle schools, and forty-four lower schools, besides "winter agricultural schools," "meadow schools," and other cognate institutions. Many of these schools have experimental stations attached to them, being partly supported by the Government, and partly by the provinces in which they are situated. The principles of agriculture are also taught in rural primary schools. In England, on the contrary, State aid to agricultural education is represented by the lectures and examinations of the Science and Art Department, and a subsidy little exceeding £400 annually. A few prizes and scholarships are awarded by the Royal Agricultural Society, and there are now two self-supporting Agricultural Colleges, accessible to students who can afford to pay for a collegiate training. But it may be said that nothing has really been done to bring agricultural education within the reach of ordinary tenant-farmers in England, though a sum of several thousand pounds is annually granted to Ireland for this purpose, and above 15,000 candidates passed the Government examination in agriculture during the year 1879. It may be true that, in Great Britain, other subjects of Technical

Education are equally neglected, but the concentration of manufactures in towns, favouring the constant discovery and rapid communication of improved processes, makes this neglect less harmful in the case of such industries than in the case of agriculture. The same may be said, with little variation, of horticulture. Gardeners seldom receive a regular horticultural education, but they form a comparatively small and compact profession, and their invention is stimulated by eager competition, no less than by the assured prospect of quick returns for every successful experiment. The consequence is that English gardeners are as progressive as English farmers are stationary, and that, in the very practice of agriculture itself, the latter have much to learn from the former, as well as from their Continental rivals. When the elementary principles and facts of agricultural science are commonly taught in country schools, and a cheap agricultural education has been provided in State-aided Colleges, tenant-farmers in England will for the first time reap the full advantage of their superiority in capital over peasant-farmers in foreign countries.

But, even if State-aid should be withheld, it is not too much to expect that private enterprise will prove equal to supplying a demand none the less imperative because it is seldom publicly recognised. Every thousand pounds judiciously expended in extending a scientific knowledge of agriculture would assuredly repay itself tenfold in the increase of agricultural produce. Nor is it only farmers who might be expected to avail themselves of it. Land-agents, as a body, are lamentably deficient in this qualification, and the difficulty of finding skilled agriculturists to accept the position of agent too often throws the management of great estates into the hands of lawyers. If tenant-farmers could regard the agent as a wise adviser, rather than as an instrument for enforcing the landlord's rights, many heartburnings would be avoided, and a fresh impulse would be given to good farming. Some attempt has already been made in Scotland, both to afford students of farming the means of attending agricultural classes, and to aid practical farmers by the employment of public analysts. An extension of this system under the best scientific guidance may go far to make up for the want of a special training in agricultural schools, and to remove the standing reproach of our tripartite agricultural economy. For, since this form of agricultural economy requires nothing but general intelligence from the landlord, and nothing but manual skill from the labourer, it is above all things necessary that a scientific knowledge of agriculture should be secured in the class of farmers.[1]

[1] See a paper by Mr. J. Macdonald Cameron, on the relative position of Agricultural Education in this country and on the Continent, read before the British Association for the Advancement of Science, in 1880.

An interesting report has lately been published on the very complete system of Agricultural Education established in Sweden, under the general direction of the Minister of the Interior, but under the immediate supervision of the Royal Academy of Agriculture at Stockholm. It appears that, besides an experimental farm and four agriculturo-chemical colleges, there are two higher-grade agricultural institutes, and twenty-seven school-farms, in which theoretical and practical instruction was given, in 1876, to 565 students. There is also a staff of agricultural engineers, and travelling professors, employed by the State to advise and assist farmers in their improvements.

CHAPTER III.

ONE more aspect of the future English land system remains to be considered. So profound a change as we have seen reason to anticipate in the rural economy of England could not fail to involve an equally profound change in Rural Government. The present organisation of power in counties and country parishes, chaotic as it is, bears little trace of its historical connection with those local institutions, the precious legacy of primitive self-government in the forests of Germany, which our forefathers cherished so fondly and idealised so persistently, as the "Laws of Edward the Confessor." It is essentially a modern superstructure raised upon a feudal basis. As manors gradually extinguished townships, and freeholders passed into free tenants, both administration and jurisdiction became less and less democratic. The ancient town-moot of the village republic was transformed into the lord's court-baron; the hundred-court lost its authority, as the court-leet usurped its most important function; the county-courts themselves ceased, at last, to be the *forum plebeiæ justitiæ et theatrum comitivæ potestatis*. The Curia Regis alone was able to settle the disputes of great barons, and before the circuits of Royal Judges checked the worst abuses of baronial jurisdiction, this jurisdiction had been so extended by Saxon grants of *sac* and *soc*, or the creation of Norman "liberties" and "honours," that large tracts of country were practically outside the sphere of the ancient popular courts. The Royal forests were under a separate local government, more or less popular, indeed, in its theoretical constitution, but highly tyrannical in its actual operation.

With the decay of feudalism and the growth of constitutional freedom, Rural Government in England entered upon a new phase, but it never recovered the spirit, or even the form, of its Anglo-Saxon original. A regular Commission of the Peace was established in every county, and was doubtless a powerful safeguard of law and order, but the justices were appointed by the Crown, and not elected by the people. The Court of Quarter Sessions was gradually invested with a judicial and administrative control from which no estate was exempt, and which no private individual could defy, but it completed the destruction of the county court, for which no substitute was provided. The independent spirit of the English yeomanry, it is true, was vigorously displayed for centuries after the old habit and capacity of self-government had well-nigh perished in rural districts. But the mass of the people were fast sinking into day-labourers, excluded from the Parliamentary franchise, divorced from the soil, and encouraged to rely on parochial relief. It is only since the Reform Act of 1832 that attempts have been made to revive the lost art of popular administration, by the formation of Poor Law Unions, Highway Districts, and School Districts, whose affairs are managed wholly or partially by representatives of the ratepayers. These measures have not been without their effect in awakening the farmers and shopkeepers in county parishes to a sense of public responsibility. But they have fallen very far short of restoring the old political life of village-communities in Anglo-Saxon times, long since undermined by feudalism. The law of Primogeniture, the custom of Entail, and other causes favouring the accumulation of land in the hands of a territorial aristocracy, have constituted a permanent influence far too powerful to be counteracted by the legislative creation of a few elective boards with very limited duties. Until this influence is weakened by a thorough reform of the English land system, it is vain to attempt a thorough reform of Local Government in English counties.

No foreigner, and no Englishman who is not familiar with the interior working of county institutions, can possibly conceive the real ascendancy of "property" in this country, or the extent to which that ascendancy depends on the mere possession of a broad acreage. True it is that a *parvenu* settling in a good neighbourhood must pass through a certain period of probation before he and his family are received into the inner circle of county society, even though he may have purchased a princely estate. True it is also that an ancient title is a passport to county society, and may secure for its bearer a considerable amount of authority, even though his estate be small by comparison with those of other county potentates. But it is certain that no ability and no force of character, without the aid of a title, will place a small freeholder, or even a squire who owns but a few hundred acres, on a par with the members of the county oligarchy, either in the estimation of his neighbours or in actual power. If he be a magistrate at all, and should have the advantage of a legal training, it is possible that he may be invited to act as Chairman of Quarter Sessions, but more probable that he will be postponed to a neighbour of inferior age, capacity, and industry, but with a larger "stake" in the county and a more numerous tenantry.   Perhaps he may fill the less dignified but more laborious office of Chairman at the Board of Guardians of his own Union, and earn respect by his discharge of the various unpaid services which mainly devolve upon those English country gentlemen who are not too rich to reside at their country places for most of the year. But he would scarcely be considered eligible for the representation of his county, not only because he could not afford to pay several thousand pounds for the honour of a seat in Parliament, but also because some youth of shallower brains and far less inclination for politics, if not of frivolous tastes and dissipated habits, would receive a heartier support from the leading county gentry, and would appear to party agents a "stronger candidate," if recommended by the qualification of a far more imposing rental.   As for his being made Lord Lieutenant under any circumstances whatever, such an idea could never enter into the wildest dreams of his ambition; for a Lord Lieutenant without a park, as Mr. Arthur Arnold says, is a being of whom a country-bred Englishman can barely form a conception.   Nor is the overweening preponderance of great landowners in their own counties to be measured by any political or official test which can be applied.   At every public meeting, at every agricultural dinner, at every county-ball, on the race-ground, in the hunting-field, and at every social gathering of county people, the small landowner is made to feel that he is essentially a small man by the side of those whose acres are counted by thousands, however inferior they may be in all other respects. One very simple reason is almost sufficient to explain this curious trait of English county life. The law of Primogeniture and the custom of Entail have erected great landowners into a privileged caste, admission to which is the highest aspiration of the English plutocracy, while the disappearance of a true middle class from English counties has removed the main counterpoise to their undue weight. They hold in their gift that social promotion which is the most seductive of bribes to English minds of the common order, and they are treated with a deference out of all proportion to their merit by men, and still more by women, eagerly struggling for this promotion.

This inordinate respect for great landowners, as such, was not equally characteristic of rural England in earlier times, and would probably not long survive the modernised feudal land system to which it owes its origin. It is wholly distinct from the spirit of clanship . and military allegiance which attached the feudal retainer to his lord, and enabled the most powerful barons to impose their will on vast tracts of country. Even in those days, a sturdy undergrowth of independent yeomanry and freeholders continued to flourish under the vast shadow of baronial suzerainty. The greatest landowners of all were greater than any now to be found in the roll of the Peerage; but great landowners, as a class, did not tower, as they now do, above the smaller gentry, then a far more numerous body. So long as the old popular courts maintained their activity, all landowners would there meet their brother freeholders on equal terms, to

administer justice, to settle local claims and disputes, to
enforce the abatement of nuisances, to assess local taxes,
and to regulate all matters of common interest, such as
rights of pasturage, rights of way, and repairs of roads
or bridges. A few nobles of the very first rank, living
in fortified castles, might perhaps afford to hold aloof
from these assemblies, and disregard their decisions.
But other landlords were bound to personal attendance
by the necessity of protecting their own rights against
encroachment, and, in doing so, might often encounter
stubborn opposition from men of very inferior degree
and acreage. Even after the institution of the unpaid
magistracy had withered the spirit of self-government,
and consolidated the power of the landed aristocracy
within each county, it is clear that rural society in
England presented a much greater equality of fortunes
and conditions, with a much greater community of
habits and tastes, than it does in the present day.
This comparative equality within the landowning class
is reflected in the pictures drawn by Addison, Fielding,
and Goldsmith, as well as in the constitutional history
of the two last centuries. It was rapidly impaired, as
the English Land System matured itself under modern
conditions, and for the last hundred years the landed
aristocracy has approached more nearly to a social
oligarchy than it ever did before.

In considering how far rural government would be
modified by a thorough reform of this Land System, it
may be well to fix our attention on one or two of its
existing anomalies. Perhaps it would be difficult to
find a better illustration of the almost despotic power
confided to landowners, in their capacity of magistrates,

than is furnished by their absolute control over licenses for the sale of intoxicating liquors. In days when cottage brewing was common, and spirits unknown in country parishes, this control was of less importance; but cottage brewing has almost died out with cottage farming, and the village public-house is practically the only place where a farm labourer can obtain a supply of beer, or some less wholesome stimulant, whether he choose to drink it on or off the premises. In Saxon times we cannot doubt that, if public-houses had been recognised at all, the regulation of them would have been vested in the court of the township, the hundred, or the county, and " local option " would have been fully established. It is certainly a striking proof of the change which has passed over the system of local government in England that licenses should be granted and renewed at the peremptory discretion of non-representative lawgivers, and that so little discontent should be excited by the exercise of this prerogative. For it must be remembered that landowners, acting as magistrates, not only determine whether there shall be any public-house in a given locality, but also whether that public-house shall enjoy a local monopoly, or shall be subjected to indefinite depreciation by the competition of new public-houses within a short distance of it. Indeed, a landowner who happens to own a whole parish, thence called a " close parish," may entirely suppress the sale of liquor within it by simply refusing to let any house for that purpose, thereby assuming exactly the same control over the liberty of all the inhabitants which is claimed, under the Permissive Bill, for a majority of the ratepayers.

No doubt, this power is incident to the right of property, and is sometimes used for the benefit of the people, as, for instance, when the proprietor of a village allows no public-house within it, but lets a house for the sale of liquor to be drunk off the premises, and institutes a village club and reading-room as a place of social resort. Still, the fact remains that such a proprietor is virtually armed with the authority of a dictator over the conduct of a whole village community, and the smaller the number of land-owners becomes, the more close parishes there must be. It follows that a more equal division of property would liberate many parishes, for good or for evil, from a paternal despotism of this kind, as it would manifestly facilitate the constitution of new Licensing Boards out of more popular elements. The reason why the juris-diction of county magistrates over the licensing system has been accepted, almost as a matter of course, is that no other body, competent to deal judicially with a question so vitally affecting the interests of the people, has existed in rural districts for many genera-tions. If there were more freeholders and more leasehold farmers within each Union or petty sessional area, if land-lord influence counted for less, and the sense of citizen ship were aroused in the labouring-class by an extension of education and a diminution of pauperism, this dif-ficulty would be speedily overcome. The regulation of the drink-traffic, as well as many other matters now super-intended by Parliament or Quarter Sessions, would then be naturally entrusted to local courts or councils, more or less democratic in their constitution, and intimately acquainted with the wants of their respective localities.

A still more glaring anomaly in the rural government of England, and one still more directly resulting from the anomalies of the English Land System, is the exclusive management of county finance by the magistrates at Quarter Sessions. It may be granted that, with few exceptions—such as the practice of rating splendid mansions at a preposterously low valuation — the financial administration of county magistrates deserves the credit of impartiality and economy. Whatever may be their faults, there is more intelligence and public spirit among English country gentlemen willing to undertake such duties than is usually to be found among the elective delegates of ratepayers, and they rarely lay themselves open even to a suspicion of jobbery. It may be granted also that, whereas the County Rate is now of trifling amount, as compared with the Poor Rate, it is difficult to make a County Board, elected to dispose of the smaller revenue, superior in power or dignity to the Union Board, which habitually disposes of the larger. Nevertheless, it is contrary to every principle of self-government that persons nominated by the Lord Lieutenant or the Lord Chancellor to serve on the Commission of Peace should, by virtue of that commission, become at once a Committee of Ways and Means or a Committee of Supply for the whole county, especially as local rates are assessed, for the most part, not upon owners, but upon occupiers. So palpable an encroachment on popular rights would never have been tolerated by our Saxon forefathers, and is only tolerated by their descendants because the heads of county families with a certain acreage, created and protected by Primogeniture and Entail, have come to be regarded almost as the hereditary rulers of counties. They are not irresponsible, it is true; but it is the Local Government Board, and not the ratepayers of the county, to whom they must render an account; as it is the Home Office, or the House of Commons, and not any local assembly, to which any abuse of magisterial justice must be referred for redress. The ignorant notions which prevail among farmers about county taxation are, to a great extent, the consequence of their exclusion from all discussion of the county budget.

From this point of view, the formation of County Financial Boards is much to be desired, as an instrument of political education; but County Financial Boards, on a representative basis, will not be easy to reconcile with an aristocratic land system. Here, again, the elements of which the new boards ought to be composed have been well-nigh crushed out by causes already described, and their place cannot be adequately supplied by agricultural tenants and shopkeepers. It is the independence of their position which gives weight to the decisions of magistrates at Quarter Sessions, and it is only men of equally independent position who can hold their own in association with them. The erection of a real communal government in parishes, or a real county Parliament with extended legislative powers, must needs be preceded by a real agrarian reform, and will then be accomplished in Old England as easily as it was accomplished two centuries ago in the New England States.

In the meantime, the way might be paved for representative institutions in counties by a revival of

communal government in villages. The autonomy of
townships and parishes, it is true, has passed away,
never to return, and no parochial authority can henceforth be exempt from the control of the Union, the
County, or the Imperial Executive. But this is no
reason why there should be no parochial authority at
all, and why all the local affairs of villages should practically be administered, or neglected, as is too often the
case, by an Union Board, acting through inspectors,
relieving-officers, vaccination-officers, and school attendance officers, besides a host of superior officials appointed by the Quarter Sessions or some Department of
State. What is wanted is a simple power of initiation,
supervision, and regulation on the spot, and such
a power might be entrusted to a Village-Council,
whose Chairman, as proposed by Mr. Goschen in the
Bill of 1871, should represent the parish at the Union
Board. To this Board the Village-Council would of
course be responsible, being constituted, for many purposes, a local Committee of the Union, and exercising,
in this capacity, much of the jurisdiction now vested in
municipal corporations over lighting, drainage, public
recreation-grounds, and all other matters of purely local
concern.[1] Probably, in the first instance, a Village-
Council of this kind would be mainly guided by the will

---

[1] For a fuller discussion of the reforms necessary to revive self-government in countries, see Brodrick's Essay on Local Government in England,
published by the Cobden Club. See also an article on the " Decay of
Self-Government in Villages," by the Rev. T. W. Fowle, in the *Fortnightly
Review* of August, 1879. The obvious objection to any system of Local
Government, strictly founded on parochial representation, is that many
parishes are too minute to supply even one qualified representative. The
besetting weakness of elective Boards is a tendency to local jobbery, and,

of the squire, notified through his agent, and the counsels of the parish clergyman. With the gradual infusion of new elements into rural life, it would acquire greater independence, and in the course of a generation English country-parishes might recover a great part of the communal spirit which made them, in bygone ages, the very nurseries and schools of self-government.

the smaller the unit of representation, the stronger will such a tendency become. To meet this objection, it has been suggested that each electoral district shall contain, at least, an area of nine square miles, *or* a population of 2,000, *or* rateable property to the value of £10,000 a year.

CHAPTER IV.

Probable effect of these Reforms on Rural Economy and Rural Society in England.

In calculating the probable operation of such causes, favouring both a subdivision of properties and a subdivision of holdings, we must ever bear in mind their reciprocal action and progressive tendency. We have already considered the social changes which might be expected to result, in process of time, from the simple abolition of Primogeniture and Entail. These changes would, of course, be hastened and aided by simultaneous reforms in the system of land-transfer, of mortgaging, and of improvement loans, as well as by the speedy completion of cadastral maps under the Ordnance Survey. In proportion as land should thus be rendered more easily saleable, and more available for the purpose of borrowing, great estates would be more liable to disintegration, and their fragments would pass, in many cases, into the hands of a new class, largely composed of retired tradespeople and men of business. This class, not being animated by aristocratic traditions, or allied with county families, would not only form the nucleus of a new rural society, but would carry new principles into the management of land. Many of them, perhaps, would live in farmhouses a little enlarged and embellished, and practise agriculture for amusement or profit. Others, not finding suitable residences or a congenial neighbourhood around them, would take up their abode in country towns, a revival of which could hardly fail to follow closely on Free Trade in Land. Landowners of this order, like their prototypes of the Tudor period, would associate with the provincial *bourgeoisie*, and they would be reinforced by a contingent of tenant farmers who had bought the fee simple of their own holdings when rents were at the lowest. By degrees, the old middle-class life of rural England, as described in the "Vicar of Wakefield," might cease to be represented exclusively by the humbler country parsons and a few surviving families of hereditary yeomen. For, as each hereditary yeoman who sells his patrimony to a great proprietor helps to isolate those who remain, and to deter others from joining their ranks, so each new purchaser settling on a small property, or in the adjoining town, helps to increase the attractions of small proprietorship.

It is needless to point out the connection between measures facilitating the subdivision of properties and measures restricting the exceptional powers or privileges of proprietorship. The adoption of the Ballot, for instance, has already rescued tenants from political dependence, and thereby materially weakened both the motive for enlarging estates unprofitably, and the motive for refusing leases. The political influence of the landlord is no longer measured, even in England, by the extent of his territory, and in Ireland it has been almost extinguished by secret voting. There are no longer any reasons, unless they be economical reasons, why he should not grant leases, and a lease-holding tenant is a comparatively independent man, with a position and credit of his own. It is not impossible that as the evils of life-ownership sink into oblivion, the advantages of leases for life, as compared with leases for terms of years, may receive fresh consideration, and that a new kind of freehold interest in the soil may thus be introduced, resembling in some respects the most ancient form of agricultural tenancy, but without the abuses of fines on renewal. On the other hand, it is possible that indefeasible tenant-right, with an extended notice to quit, may prove more acceptable to modern farmers than a lease, which in olden times was the only effectual safeguard against capricious eviction.   It is equally possible, however, that leases may prove more acceptable to landlords than compulsory tenant-right, without the power of summary eviction; especially, as the heavy expenses of agency might be thereby materially reduced.[1] But, in any case, it is clear that, since tenants have ceased to owe their landlords political service, landlords have less temptation either to multiply them or to refuse them due security.

The effect of abolishing the right of Distress is more doubtful, though it could hardly fail to further the rise of a more independent tenantry. Whatever may be said in favour of this right, from other points of view, it is evident that it must needs encourage landlords to accept as tenants men of whose solvency and capacity

---

[1] These expenses are extremely variable. Upon one very large and well-managed property in the Midland Counties they do not greatly exceed 4 per cent. on the gross rental. Upon another property of still greater extent, and comprising estates in the metropolis and various southern and eastern counties, they exceed 20 per cent.

they have no sufficient evidence. Were landlords deprived of their preferential claim, and placed on the footing of other creditors, they might be expected to become less indulgent, indeed; but tenants would be men of more substance in proportion to acreage, would have less occasion to be obsequious, and would obtain advances more readily upon their crops or stock. The statutory reservation to occupiers of an inalienable right to shoot hares and rabbits on their farms must operate in the same way, for good or for evil, as a solvent of landlordism. At first, perhaps, it may render many landlords more unwilling than ever to grant leases, inasmuch as they may rely on threats of eviction to deter churlish tenants from a wholesale destruction of ground game. But in the end it will be found to promote more business-like agreements between the two parties, as well as to remove one inveterate objection to small holdings. It is even possible to conceive that, with the progressive subdivision of properties and holdings, another description of privileged vermin would cease to be regarded with superstitious veneration. In those hunting counties where the fox is preserved as a sacred animal, it is idle to expect that poultry, ducks, or geese, will be reared to reward his depredations, and there can be little doubt as to what his fate would be, if his influential patrons among great landlords and farmers were succeeded by "smaller" men, with more taste for profit than for sport.

Such minor reforms of the English Land Laws, and of the customs blended with them, would insensibly help to modify the semi-feudal relation between English landlords and tenants, and would accelerate the movement already setting towards a subdivision of properties and of holdings. As the race of embarrassed life-owners, burdened with estates too large for their capital, and family mansions too large for their estates, should gradually become an extinct species, their places would be filled by new comers probably twice or thrice as numerous, with much less pride but much greater aggregate wealth and enterprise. The least worthy representatives of the remaining landed gentry would most resent the intrusion of this plebeian element, and would be most disposed to part with their game-preserves and fox-coverts, after the right of sporting had been curtailed. The consequence would be a fresh immigration of new men into the old acres, and a fresh depreciation of landed property as a passport to county influence and social consideration. After a while, it would no longer command a fancy price on this ground, and would be sold, more and more profitably, in small lots. The " residential " estates of a few score or a few hundred acres characteristic of the home counties, and of the districts round great manufacturing towns, would now propagate themselves in the heart of the country. And thus, by the operation of new causes and conditions, the rural economy of England might come to assume an aspect very different from that which it has presented during the last two centuries, yet not so unlike that which it must have presented in still earlier times.

One marked feature of this new rural economy would probably be a great extension both of population and of trade in agricultural counties. The West End of London is largely peopled during the season by many thousand families of landed proprietors, who there lay out a great part of the rents which they derive from their country estates, and attract thither myriads of tradespeople and dependents who might otherwise make their living in the country. The withdrawal of all this wealth and custom from rural parishes is the direct consequence of a system which severs the ownership from the cultivation of land, and creates a landed aristocracy. The substitution of several middle-class households in a rural parish for one splendid mansion, too often empty, would, in most cases, largely increase the number of mouths to be fed, but it would have other and far more important effects. The heads of these households would be more constantly resident, because they would have less spare cash to spend in the metropolis or on the Continent, and less inducement to spend it. They would also be far more disposed to welcome the spread of manufactures upon their domains, because they would be more eager to increase their incomes by selling or letting sites for mills, and less jealous of admitting millowners and artisans into their immediate neighbourhood. For similar reasons, they would usually keep their accounts at the nearest town, if not at village shops, instead of importing all their stores from London. By such means, while their own rental would inevitably be raised, local trade would inevitably be stimulated. As secluded hamlets expanded into populous villages, or even into market towns, farmers would buy their implements, tiles, and manures at a lower cost, and find a ready sale for such farm produce as meat, fowls, eggs, milk, butter, vegetables, and fruit. The production of these commodities would thus be encouraged, and, as we have seen, would be carried on with the greatest success on small holdings, if not by peasant-owners. Hence the reaction in favour of small holdings and subdivision of ownership would derive fresh energy from the very advent of new settlers in rural districts—themselves the creatures of Free Trade in Land. The hierarchy of middle-men, who now live off the land without contributing to its cultivation, would have no place in thriving village communities of this kind, where the producer and consumer would be in close and daily contact with each other, and the spectacle of homely farmers' wives conveying their own baskets to market might again enliven our rural highways. For it would then be discovered that a farmer's best labourers are not hirelings, but himself and the members of his own family, and that his best customers are not dealers or contractors, but his own next-door neighbours. By degrees he would realise that it pays far better to deliver milk at 4d., or even 3d. a quart, within half a mile or a mile of his dairy, than to sell it wholesale at 2d. a quart, to be retailed in London at 5d.; and that by clubbing together with a few others to employ a salesman for his poultry, instead of supplying a poulterer, he might pocket at least 50 per cent. extra on the price of each couple. No doubt, as these elementary truths obtained currency, some economical theories might be rudely disturbed, and some important changes might ensue in the modern system of distribution, which now relieves the farmer of a little trouble and much profit. But, if the general result were to check the unhealthy centralisation, which is the bane of modern industry, to arrest that over-population of great towns which has caused a degeneracy in the national *physique*, if not in the national character, to bridge over the chasm and mitigate the social contrasts between urban and rural communities, to restore in some degree the independent spirit of the ancient English yeomanry, and at the same time to invigorate the most promising branches of modern English agriculture, the country would have no reason to deplore so beneficial a transition.

But, whatever form the rural economy of England may assume in future years, we cannot doubt that room will be found in it for a considerable extension of cottage-farming. To justify such an extension, it is superfluous to invoke Continental experience, and the arguments in its favour are too strong to require the aid of legislative intervention. For many years past the difficulty of retaining the best class of labourers in rural districts, and that of building cottages to pay a fair percentage on their cost price, have been among the standing complaints of landlords and farmers. Now, it is plain that both these difficulties may be mitigated, if not overcome, by a return towards the ancient practice of attaching plots of lands to labourers' dwellings. As the want of security discourages good farming, so the husbandman is reduced to a mere hireling by the want of stability in his relation to his employer on the one side, and his landlord on the other. It has long been observed that improvidence and pauperism are most prevalent among those classes of labourers who are engaged by the day, and least prevalent among those who are engaged by the year. When this is more fully realised by farmers, the advantage of giving labourers a more permanent and valuable stake in their native parishes will come to be more fully realised by landlords. We have seen that the value of good allotment ground to a cottager is estimated at no less than £16 an acre, above the ordinary farm rent, by the Commission on the Employment of Women and Children in Agriculture. Mr. Bailey Denton, in his treatise on the Agricultural Labourer, forms the same estimate. He states that a labourer, having a rood of land, "may grow vegetables sufficient to yield him a return, after payment of rent and purchase of seed, of at least £4 a year." If so, it would be more than worth a labourer's while to pay £8 rent for a cottage-garden of half an acre. Let us suppose, however, that he pays no more than £4, in addition to £4 a year for his cottage, the real value of which is perhaps £6 a year. Now, since no farmer would pay above £1 a year for half an acre of land, the landlord will gain more by the extra rent of the land than he loses by the under rent of the cottage, and will find that cottage property, with large gardens attached, is by no means an unremunerative investment.[1]

Another form of allotments, peculiarly suitable to pastoral districts, has been tried with admirable results on some estates in Cheshire and other parts of the country. Plots of land, sufficient to maintain one cow,

---

[1] On Lord Tollemache's estate at Helmingham, in Suffolk, it has long been the practice to attach an allotment garden of half an acre to each cottage. As these allotments are let at an ordinary farm-rent, the privilege of holding them is of course highly valued, and the effect of the system on the conduct of the labouring population is described as most salutary.

and ranging from two and a-half to three and a-half acres, according to the quality of the soil, are let with each cottage, at an ordinary farm-rent. This practice, after all, is but the revival of a custom once almost universal among the peasantry of England, and it is found to be fraught with manifold advantages. The most obvious of these is an abundant supply of milk for the farm-labourer's children, who in many districts grow up without tasting the natural diet of childhood. But the habits of thrift and forethought encouraged by cow-keeping and dairying, on however small a scale, constitute a moral advantage of great importance. The possession of a cow-pasture is at once a reward of good behaviour, a stimulus to exertion, and a source of profit, which sometimes enables the industrious labourer to rise into a small farmer, and prevents his drifting into the great towns. On Lord Tollemache's estate in Cheshire, where the system has been long established, and carefully managed, its results have been eminently beneficial, and attended by none of the drawbacks so often magnified into insuperable difficulties by the opponents of cottage-farming. The butter made by the cottagers' wives is collected and marketed by small dealers, themselves cowkeepers, and residing generally on the estate. Petitions for subscriptions from labourers who have lost a cow, though common elsewhere, are there unknown, since regular " cow-clubs," for purposes of mutual insurance, have been properly organised and are in full operation. Not less satisfactory has been the experience of other landlords who have given the system a fair trial, and the Second Report of the Women and Children's

Employment Commission is full of evidence in its favour. Yet such is the conservatism of agriculture that it continues to be a rare feature of English rural economy, and it is quite possible that generations will elapse before it is widely extended.[1]

Let us now go a step further, and suppose that in an ordinary village of some 2,000 acres, containing some seventy or eighty labourers (including boys), 100 acres were assigned as arable cottage-farms to ten labourers carefully selected for their skill, thrift, and sobriety.[2] These cottage-farms of ten acres each would, of course, be far above the scale of allotments, and, if cultivated with the spade, would demand the whole labour of the occupiers, with their families, as well as a good deal of occasional assistance from neighbours or strangers. Assuming the rent to be £30 a-year for each, or double that which an ordinary farmer would give, the landlord's rental would be increased by £150 a-year. But, even if the entire plot of ten acres were treated as a farm, and not as a market garden, its produce under spade-cultivation would amply suffice to pay this rent, with all incidental expenses, and to leave the holder a margin of profit far beyond the average wages of a farm labourer. If a simple alternation of wheat and potatoes

---

[1] See an interesting paper on " Cowkeeping by Farm Labourers," by Mr. Henry Evershed, republished from the *Royal Agricultural Society's Journal* of 1879. I am indebted to Lord Tollemache of Helmingham for personal confirmation of the facts there stated in reference to his own estate.

[2] Mr. Howard states, in his treatise on " Continental Farming," that in France a farm of ten acres is considered sufficient to support a family, and that little is grown on such farms except wheat, rye, oats, clover, and potatoes. Two cows, however, are commonly kept upon them.

were adopted, the land being equally divided between these crops, the five acres of potatoes ought to be worth £200, and the five acres of wheat, including straw, about £70 on a moderate computation.[1] Reserving to himself £120 a-year for the maintenance of himself and his household, which is certainly much above the average earnings of a farm-labourer's family, he would still have £150, or £15 an acre, to cover his rent and rates, wear and tear of tools, extra wages, and purchased manure, of which he would require all the less if he should keep a considerable stock of pigs. His risk would be materially diminished, though his average profit would not be so great, if five out of the ten acres should consist of good pasturage, capable of feeding two cows. The milk of these cows would be worth some £40 a-year, with a very small drawback for wages, and he might then be able to cultivate the remaining five acres without recourse to hired labour, and with a proportionate reduction of other expenses.

No account is here taken of the many little shifts and resources by which a clever man, under favourable conditions, might eke out the profits of a cottage farm. If he could afford to buy a horse, for instance, he might earn a considerable sum by hauling and carrying for his neighbours, in spare hours, and there are many parts of the country where a poor man's horse may pick up a good deal of his own fodder by the roadside or on a common. By looking after gardens, rough carpentering, and executing small jobs for others, many an honest

---

[1] It is here assumed that the yield of potatoes is about 8 tons per acre, and the price about £5 per ton. The yield of wheat is taken at 4 quarters per acre, and the price at 50s. per quarter.

penny may be earned by the cottage-farmer who is not above turning his hand to anything which brings in money. Some cottagers already pay their rent with the proceeds of their beehives or flower-gardens; others deal in fowls, eggs, or pork, and all these petty industries could be practised more successfully by the cottage-farmer than by a mere day labourer. Sometimes he might find it worth his while to go out for a week's harvesting at high wages, paying for help in getting in his own crops. But such expedients would not be open to every cottage-farmer, nor is it every cottage-farmer who could be trusted to avail himself of them, without neglecting his own proper business. It is, therefore, safer to exclude them from the calculation, and to regard the cottage-farm simply as an ordinary farm in miniature. On the other hand, it is not unreasonable to believe that the habits of thrift encouraged by cottage-farming would bear additional fruit in an extension of those domestic industries, such as glove-making, straw-plaiting, lace-making, and stocking-knitting, which can be carried on by the daughters of cottagers in spare hours. In old times, a working farmer had few dealings with shopkeepers, and the clothing, as well as the food, of the whole family was mostly produced at home. It may now be cheaper to buy cloth or linen than to weave them with a hand-loom, but only upon condition that a more profitable use is made of the hands that might otherwise be employed in weaving. This obvious truth seems to have been forgotten by modern housewives, and in many parts of the country, where girls do not work in the fields, they earn nothing for themselves until they marry or go into domestic service.

But the cottage farmer would be essentially a crofter or peasant, such as peopled English villages before the Poor Law of Elizabeth, and, if experience proves anything, it proves that a peasant's household is a far better school of economy than a tenant-farmer's or day-labourer's household.

The benefits to be derived from a few such cottage-farms in an English village cannot be measured by the direct pecuniary return that might be shared between the landlord and the occupiers. The successful example of a deserving labourer thus promoted to be a small farmer would tell upon the character of other labourers, and inspire many with the ambition to rise from the lower into the higher ranks of agricultural industry. It is often said that an irresistible attraction draws off the true descendants of the old English peasantry into manufacturing towns, and that a growing aversion to manual labour has been fostered by the spread of popular education. If this be so, and if no counteracting forces should manifest themselves, it bodes ill for the vigour, the happiness, and the virtue of coming generations. But it has yet to be seen whether the prosperity of English manufactures will long be maintained at such a pitch as to command the labour market, and whether the lot of an English husbandman must needs compare unfavourably with that of an English artisan. Not until the agricultural labourer is offered the prospect of bettering himself by toil and thrift, without deserting his own handicraft, will the industrial competition between town and country be conducted upon equal terms. Let the cottager, working for weekly wages, realise that he may earn the position of a cottage-farmer, and the flower of our village youth may cease to look for advancement everywhere except at home.

It may be said, however, that cottage-farming of this kind, even without cattle, machinery, or farm implements of any sort, would require a certain amount of capital, for the cottage-farmer must at least feed himself and those working under him until he can get in his crops. This is true, and therefore no sensible landlord would let a cottage-farm to any labourer who had not qualified himself by exceptional industry, and laid by money enough to subsist for a year without realising anything from the land. But it does not follow that if the cottage-farming system were extended beyond the proper sphere of spade-husbandry, as, for instance, to holdings of twenty or thirty acres, it would be necessary for the farmer to own a farm-capital of £200 or £300. It is quite possible, and by no means improbable, that if other circumstances should favour the growth of this system, and bring the landlord into immediate contact with a class of peasant-farmers, the old métayage tenure may be revived in a modified shape, and under new conditions. The essence of this ancient tenure, which seems to have once prevailed in many parts of England,[1] does not consist in the payment of rent in kind; still less, in an equal division of the profit between landlord and tenant. It consists in the provision of farming capital by the landlord, instead of

---

[1] Professor Rogers states that, in the leases granted by Merton College during the latter part of the fourteenth century, the stock was generally let with the land, in whole or in corn, the rents being made payable either in money or in corn. ("History of Prices," Vol. I., p. 24.)

by the tenant, whatever be the mode in which the rent is paid, or the share of profit allotted to the landlord. On the other hand, the admitted abuses of métayage as it exists in Lombardy and elsewhere arise from a want of security for the tenant's share of profit, which it is within the province of law to supply. At all events, this principle affords one solution of the agricultural question which has lately perplexed so many thoughtful minds—the question whether a continued fall of prices may not render it impossible to maintain a landed interest, consisting of three classes, on the less fertile soils of England. It is not all land that will yield rent to a landlord, profit to a farmer, and wages to labourers, but it is not to be assumed that land which cannot support a threefold burden will cease to be cultivated. One of these classes may be altogether merged in another. Here and there an active and capable landlord may take his farms permanently into his own hands, thus becoming his own farmer. Here and there a farmer may buy up the fee-simple of a depreciated farm, thus becoming his own landlord. But a still more promising experiment would be the occasional conversion of labourers into farmers, and this process would be greatly facilitated by the adoption of something like a métayage tenure.

The stock objection to this or any other system of cottage-farming is that a single bad season would ruin any but a capitalist farmer. But there is no reason why the landlord, before accepting any applicant as tenant of a cottage-farm, should not take security for his possessing the means to weather at least one bad season, or insist upon his crops being duly insured. It has been suggested that village-committees might be formed to make themselves responsible for the original rent, and re-let the land at an increased rent sufficient to cover risks, accumulating the surplus for the purpose of enabling the cottage-tenant, after reaching a certain age, to occupy his farm rent-free during the rest of his life. A similar machinery might be adapted to purposes of insurance, but the same object might be attained in many other ways, as it is practically attained in many parts of the Continent, by the simple practice of individual saving. To speak of cottage-farming as a chimerical ideal, and to regard with complacency the absolute dependence of English farm-labourers on weekly wages and Poor Law relief, as if it were an ordinance of Nature or Providence, is to ignore the lessons of foreign experience, no less than of our own agricultural history. In the production of corn and meat, indeed, the cottage-farmer is never likely to supersede the capitalist who can bring science and economy of labour to bear on a large acreage. But for the minor operations of agriculture he possesses many advantages over his wealthier rival, and, if the pressure of agricultural distress should be prolonged, he may find a niche ready-made to receive him in the rural economy of a no remote future.

The future transition from cottage-farming to peasant-ownership appears so natural and simple that many economists speak with confidence of it as the certain result of Free Trade in Land. There is much to be said for this belief, and many of the presumptions opposed to it are demonstrably fallacious. It may be conceded that Primogeniture and Entail · are constant obstacles to peasant-ownership, not only because they promote the aggregation and prevent the dispersion of land, but also because they maintain an organisation of rural society in which the peasant-owner is altogether out of place. It may be conceded that peasant-ownership would be tried under far more favourable conditions, if there were more properties of moderate extent and more small holdings, if greater social equality should come to prevail in country districts, and if the law should cease to impose an almost prohibitory tax on buying, selling, mortgaging, or improving estates of a few acres. It has been proved, over and over again, that in countries where these impediments do not exist such estates command the best price and the best rent, yield the best return on a given amount of capital, and are the best school of agricultural co-operation, as well as of domestic thrift. It has been well pointed out that no contrary inference can fairly be drawn from instances in which squatters of irregular habits, and without capital or previous training, having cleared patches of barren land and imitated the routine of agriculture on the grand scale, have barely succeeded in making a livelihood, and perhaps sunk into a condition below that of farm-labourers. It should also be remembered that, in proportion as cottage-farmers are able to pay a higher rent for land than capitalist farmers, the difference between the selling and letting value of land loses its cogency as an argument against peasant-ownership. A capitalist farmer who can hire land at thirty shillings an acre may be unwise to purchase it at £60 an acre, since he could make a better use of his capital by laying it out upon the farm, but a cottage-farmer paying £3 an acre might do wisely to relieve himself of rent altogether, if he could obtain the fee-simple at twenty years' purchase. Nor must it be taken for granted that cottagers are incapable of appreciating, or unwilling to pay for the "residential," as distinct from the agricultural, value of land. Even an Irish peasant-farmer, though he may be a mere tenant at will in the eye of the law, clings to his ancestral mud cabin as fondly as if it were a family mansion, and no less than 5,000 Irish tenants of this class eagerly seized the opportunity to buy up the fee-simple of their holdings under the provisions of the Irish Church Act. The same passionate desire for a home, strengthened by the pride of proprietorship, inspires the peasant-farmers of the Continent with the "slavish industry" of which they are so often accused, by way of reproach, and induces them to offer a fancy price for land, which defeats the competition of wealthier bidders.

All this is true, and yet it affords no adequate ground for anticipating that peasant-ownership will become a prevalent feature of rural economy in England within any appreciable time. The well-known passages in which Adam Smith describes the advantage of peasant-owners over tenant-farmers rests on the assumption that peasant-owners have either inherited their properties, or, at least, possess them unencumbered by debt.[1] The pictures of peasant-ownership

---

[1] "Wealth of Nations," Book III., ch. ii. He compares the farmer to one who trades with borrowed money, and the proprietor to one who

drawn by those who have studied it in France, Belgium, Switzerland, or the Channel Islands, represent the ripe fruit of social habits and moral sentiment cultivated for centuries in village communities bearing little resemblance to an English country parish. Before an English farm-labourer can be converted into a small freeholder, he must find a plot of land suitable for his purpose, and a landowner willing to sell it for that purpose. He must have shaken off the hereditary taint of pauperism, and, instead of looking to parochial relief as the natural provision for sickness and old age, he must have accumulated a small fortune of £400 or £500, equal to some ten years' earnings. There is no imprudence in his resolving to invest this money in land, for land, at all events, yields as good a return as the Savings Bank, but, having made up his mind to invest in land, he may well pause before investing in a few acres of English soil. For £100, he and his family might be conveyed to Upper Canada, or the Western States of America, where a quarter section, or 160 acres of land, may be had at the cost of a few pounds, the payment for it being spread, under the Homestead Law, over a period of five years. Herein consists, perhaps, the most serious obstacle to a system of peasant-ownership in England. The English farm-labourer with thrift enough to save the price of a small freehold, and with energy enough to break the spell of custom, which binds him to lifelong dependence,

trades with his own; and proceeds to argue that while, in the former case, a large share of the produce will be consumed by the rent, in the latter the whole produce will be at the disposal of the cultivator.

with the workhouse for his final resting-place, is not likely to rest content with the prospect of owning a ten-acre farm. His weaker and less intelligent fellows, indeed, shrink from the discomforts of a new settler's life, and prefer to work for others under the shadow of the parish church, within reach of the village charities, and in the midst of a thousand cherished associations. But these are not the people to lay by money for many years in the hope of living under their own vines or fig-trees. The English labourer who does this must be a man of more than ordinary education and character. The effort required to carry him so far will generally suffice to carry him further, and his territorial ambition, if roused at all, will take a wider range than that of a French or Belgian peasant. Once emancipated from the spirit of predial serfdom, he will aspire to be a landowner among landowners, breathing the free air of social independence, and this ambition he can scarcely hope to satisfy in his native country.

Upon these and like grounds, while it is highly probable that cottage-farming may be widely extended within the next generation, it is highly improbable that peasant-ownership, in its true sense, will be evolved out of it on a considerable scale. At the same time, we may confidently predict that if the sale of land should ever become easy and simple, a new race of small freeholders will rapidly spring up, possessing estates of five, ten, or twenty acres, and representing, so far, the peasant-owners of the Continent. These freeholders would not, in most instances, be derived from the class of farm-labourers, but rather from that miscellaneous class of tradespeople and petty capitalists who form so large an element in county constituencies. The village carrier, wanting a paddock for a horse or two, and employment for himself at odd times—the village bricklayer, carpenter, and blacksmith, now beginning to rise in the world, to employ several journeymen, and even to undertake contracts at some little distance—the village innkeeper, wishing to supply himself with milk and butter, eggs and bacon—the village butcher, already a judge of sheep and cattle, enriched with the enormous profits of his own trade, and thinking to increase them by turning grazier—the village greengrocer, with visions of market-gardening on his own account—the retired postmaster, schoolmaster, or shopkeeper from the nearest market town—such are the materials out of which a peasantry proprietary, if it be created at all in England, is probably destined to be first built up. The idea of buying their own homesteads is far more familiar to people who have lived in the suburbs of towns, where tempting chances often present themselves, and many of them would fully appreciate the dignity of a petty rural landlord, with a tenant under him. Instances are not wanting in which miners and other artisans working at high wages have purchased small freeholds, or obtained plots of wild land at nominal rents, erected their own houses, and exhibited a remarkable aptitude for agricultural improvement.[1] Similar examples of the " slavish industry " supposed to be peculiar to continental peasant-owners may be found among Scotch

[1] A little settlement of this kind is to be found on the property of Sir Thomas Acland, in Cornwall.

crofters, most of whom earn a part of their livelihood by fishing or some other non-agricultural
labour, and few of whom are actually proprietors of
the plots which they, nevertheless, treat as their
own.   The speculative and hopeful temper necessary
for such enterprises has yet to be developed among
English farm-labourers.   It may be developed with
the progress of education, and land may ultimately come to supersede the Post Office Savings
Bank as the favourite depository of surplus weekly
earnings in English rural villages.   But this revolution
in habit and sentiment will take long to accomplish.
and before it is accomplished the English farm-labourer
may have learned to regard emigration to America or
Australia with as little repugnance as emigration to a
neighbouring parish.

At the same time, it is quite within the bounds of
possibility that a new method of combination may be
adopted, under the stress of agricultural necessity,
among landowners of a higher order.   Whatever be the
merits of the English agricultural system, it certainly
involves very heavy outgoings for superintendence.   As
the profits of a lucrative commercial business may be
well-nigh absorbed by unduly high salaries and excessive office expenses, so the profits of farming may be
eaten up, if they are made to bear the charge of maintaining too many farmers' households.   So long as
farmers worked in their own fields, with their own
hands, and were assisted by their wives and daughters
in all the minor industries of the farm homestead, a
great part of their income represented the wages of
very efficient labour rendered by themselves and their

families, and another part represented interest on capital, leaving a comparatively small residue for the cost of superintendence. Now that a farmer occupying 200 or 300 acres is content to act as an overseer, while his wife too often disdains all out-door work, and his daughters know more of music than of poultry-keeping or dairy-management, the whole expense of his establishment, far higher than it would have been in former days, must be charged against the value of his superintendence, except so far as it represents interest on capital. Let us suppose this expense to be no more than £300 for each farm of 300 acres, the agricultural superintendence of 3,000 acres (including interest on capital) will then cost £3,000, and that of 10,000 acres will cost £10,000, besides all that may be spent on agency. But it may well be doubted whether one highly-trained agent-manager, at a salary of £1,000 a year, aided by a proper staff of ten foremen, at a salary of £100 each, would not superintend the tillage of 10,000 acres more effectively than thirty-three farmers of the modern school, especially as they would be able to employ machinery, buy wholesale, and execute large orders from London, far more economically. A further sum of some £4,000 must of course be set aside for interest on the farm-capital required to work 10,000 acres. But upon these assumptions, at least £4,000 might well be well saved out of £10,000, on the mere cost of superintendence.

No doubt the "master's eye" is usually more searching than that of a paid manager, but, on the other hand, a paid manager of 10,000 acres ought to possess a much higher degree of agricultural skill.

Whether English country gentlemen would be disposed
to enter into such a joint-stock partnership with each
other, and to substitute a quasi-mercantile organisation
for the familiar relations between landlord and tenant,
is a wholly different question. Probably few would
entertain the idea, unless many farms were thrown on
their hands, and they were driven, as a last resource,
into cultivating these farms through bailiffs. This was
the very practice which prevailed, not only on demesne-
lands, but on ecclesiastical and college-property in the
Middle Ages, and the revival of it in a modified form,
under modern conditions, would be a strange instance
of reversion to an ancient type in the development of
English agriculture. It was gradually superseded four
or five centuries ago by the introduction of farming
leases, but these leases were held by men who ploughed
their own lands, in days when machinery was unknown,
and the farmer was anything rather than a manufacturer of food-supplies for great towns. Now that
crop-raising and cattle-breeding are a science, that hand-
labour is fast giving place to machine-labour, and that
one large capital has prodigious advantages over many
small capitals, it is at least possible that a reaction may
set in towards landlord-farming, on the one side, as it
may set in, under the operation of different causes, towards
peasant-farming, on the other side. If this should come
to pass, it is equally possible that several landlords with
contiguous estates may find it profitable to employ the
same agent to superintend the cultivation of all. The
management of Crown property, Greenwich Hospital
property, and other property belonging to public bodies,
might probably furnish some instructive lessons, if not

actual precedents, for the working of such a system, which is, at least, one conceivable mode of relieving the land from the burden of supporting three agrarian classes.[1]

---

[1] An eminent practical farmer has lately published a calculation, showing that in his own parish, containing 2,500 acres (2,000 arable), and nine farms, a saving of nearly £2,000 a year might be effected on the working expenses of farming, by throwing all the nine farms into one, and organising all the labour of men, horses, and machinery, on co-operative principles.

CHAPTER V.

So comprehensive a reform of the English Land System as we have been led to contemplate, will assuredly not be fully accomplished within one generation. Nor is it to be desired that measures seriously affecting the Rural Economy and Rural Government of such a country as England should be carried out with the haste of revolutionary legislation. Time must be given, not merely to exhaust vested interests, and to overcome selfish opposition, but also to convince many enlightened minds that whatever is admirable in English character, or noble in English society, is not vitally connected with the maintenance of the English Land System in its distinctive features. Very few of such persons would venture to uphold Primogeniture and Entail, with the social and agricultural conditions which naturally result from them, as the perfect ideal of an agrarian constitution. But there is a very prevalent belief among English economists and practical statesmen that, however anomalous, this agrarian constitution, like the political constitution of which it forms an outwork, has grown with the growth and strengthened with the strength of the English people, until it would be highly perilous to disturb it. They admit that for other countries a more numerous proprietary, a more independent body of occupiers, and a peasantry worthy of the name may be preferable to English landlordism, yearly tenancy, and a semi-pauperised class of day-labourers. But for England they would deprecate any material change, regarding this organisation, with all its faults, as the best security for a high standard of culture in the landowning class, as well as for agricultural improvement and civilisation in rural districts.

Whatever else may be said in favour of this opinion, it is not recommended by any historical presumptions. We have seen that, in Saxon times, the agrarian constitution of England was essentially democratic; that, in Norman times, ecclesiastics rather than barons were the pioneers of agricultural improvement, and the models of territorial benevolence; that, in the England of Elizabeth, and for two centuries after the Reformation, the lesser gentry and yeomanry were the bone and sinew of the landed interest; that the dependent condition of English labourers dates from the Poor Law, and that of English farmers from a far more recent period; that, in fact, the English Land System is not a spontaneous growth, but an artificial creation of feudal lawyers, improved by their successors in the evil days after the Restoration, largely modified by such temporary causes as the high prices current during the Great War, and afterwards strengthened by a constant flow of population towards great towns, partly consequent on the operation of the Land System itself. We have observed the intimate connection between English landlordism and English pauperism, as well as the influence of the County Franchise, the Game Laws, the Law of Distress, the Law of Fixtures, and other legislative or judicial rules on the natural relations between landlord and tenant. We find that the existing agrarian constitution of England is out of harmony, not only with the rural economy of the most civilised and progressive countries in Europe, but with that of the great American nation, and of all the more flourishing British Colonies. No doubt it may, nevertheless, be the best possible agrarian constitution for the people of these islands, but this must not be accepted as a self-evident truth. Why should it be supposed that rural society in England has at last settled down into its most perfect and ultimate form—that, having assimilated and adapted itself to so many diverse conditions, it has lost the power of further assimilation or adaptation? Why should not law undo that which law has done? and why should custom, hitherto governed or guided by law, be stereotyped in the nineteenth century into an immutable ordinance of nature?

Equally untenable is the notion that a territorial aristocracy, and a tripartite system of agriculture, are the legitimate results of economical tendencies which cannot be reversed. It is a pure confusion of ideas to imagine that because organisation on a grand scale, with a minute subdivision of labour, are conducive to efficiency and profit in manufactures, they must needs be the one thing needful for agriculture. The experience of mankind encourages the belief that a sense of proprietorship is the most potent of all forces in extracting produce from the soil, and that no concentration of management is so fruitful of economy as the absolute unity of management and execution secured by the fusion of landlord, farmer, and labourer into one and the same person. Because the various parts of a complicated machine are best constructed by a number of separate artisans, or because an extensive commercial business is best divided into many separate departments, it does not follow that husbandry, the oldest and simplest of human arts, should be conducted on a like principle.   As a matter of fact, indeed, it is not so conducted even in England, and nothing can less resemble the administration of a great manufactory than the administration of a great estate.   The nominal owner of it is seldom the real owner, and hardly ever takes an active part in the every-day supervision of it; the agent who fills his place is not personally interested in it; the farmer who directs the labourer is seldom trained for his duties; and the labourer, upon whose skill everything depends, is barely animated at all by the effective hope of promotion.   May it not be that economical tendencies, deeper and more universal than are dreamed of in the philosophy of English landlordism, are ignored or counteracted under this peculiar system, that co-operation may be destined to replace subordination as a motive power in agriculture, and that, in the end, that method of cultivation will prove to be most productive into which the cultivator puts the greatest amount of heart and thought and energy?

Be this as it may, let it be remembered, again and again, that no legislative interference with free agency, in its true sense, is involved in the proposed reform of the English Land System.   If this reform should take effect, the new law of Gavelkind succession on intestacy will be as permissive as the existing law of Primogenitary succession.   The living head of the family in each generation, instead of being fettered by the will of a dead ancestor, will be free, as he is not free at present, to deal with his own property, and to regulate the inheritance of his own children. His power of mortgaging or of selling will be unrestricted, and these processes will be vastly simplified and cheapened by a proper system of land registration and land transfer, long since adopted by less advanced nations. Even his power of settling, though limited, will not be illusory; for not only will he be enabled to charge the estate for a widow, or younger children, but he will always have the option of directing it to be sold, and converted into money to be held on any trusts permitted in a settlement of personalty; in which case, with the consent of the parties interested, it may remain undivided in the hands of one, and subject only to rent charges for the benefit of others. The courts of law, it is true, will no longer enforce contracts which may prejudice good agriculture, or deprive a tenant of his presumptive right to keep down ground-game, but landlords and tenants will be perfectly free to make any agreement for their mutual benefit, and only debarred from claiming a legal guarantee of that which the law condemns. If the result should be that landed property is more frequently divided on death than heretofore, and that fathers do not always choose to aggrandise the eldest son exclusively, but sometimes leave an outlying estate to a younger son or even to a daughter —if attachment to family-places sometimes gives way to pecuniary exigencies—if small capitalists occasionally outbid noblemen and squires in the land-market, with the advantage of cheap transfer and secure titles—if large farms come to be usually let on lease, and cottage-farms, in the hands of industrious occupiers, should here and there be transformed into cottage properties; all this will prove, not that the rural economy of England is being forced into a strange and unnatural mould, but, on the contrary, that it has been too long left in a strange and unnatural mould, and is at last feeling the life-giving atmosphere of freedom.

Such legislation has nothing in common with the ignorant prejudice against landlords, as such, fomented by demagogues in Ireland, or with schemes of which the object is to limit the amount of landed property which any individual may own. To proscribe land-lordism, in the abstract, is to proscribe tenancy; and to extirpate the greater landlords, were that possible, without extirpating the smaller, would be to inflict a grievous injury on the whole class of tenants. In all states of rural society, it will often be found expedient for a man who owns land but has not the leisure, or the skill, or the means, or the inclination, for culti-vating it, to let it on hire to another, who perhaps could not afford to buy it. The relation of landlord and tenant is common among the small proprietors of France, Belgium, and other countries under the Code Napoléon itself, and, so far as the great English land-lords differ from these, they assuredly differ for the better, since they are in comparatively easy circum-stances, and are impelled by higher than commer-cial motives towards a generous treatment of their tenantry. These motives have probably never operated with so great force as at present, and, though great English landlords may reside less constantly on their estates than in former generations, they interpret their duties, on the whole, more liberally, and give more personal attention to estate-management. As for laying down a hard and fast maximum of acreage which no landlord shall be permitted to exceed, the slightest consideration will reveal its absurdity. The ground rental of a few score or hundred acres in London is not only far more valuable, but confers far more real power, than an absolute dominion over all Sutherlandshire. Cases might arise in which it might be necessary to check an inordinate thirst for territorial annexation, or an oppressive exercise of territorial rights. But these cases must be met by exceptional measures, and in the meantime, there is much less to be said against large tracts of barren soil being owned by a few great proprietors, than against the expansion of populous towns being absolutely at the mercy of "ground landlords," whether they be great or small. The rights of property, as well as the course of its descent on intestacy, are entirely within the control of the State, and if these be regulated by sound rules of policy, the extent of private estates may well be left to regulate itself.

Nor would the proposed reform of the English Land System tend, in the smallest degree, to weaken the idea of property, which is the birthright of civilised society. That idea is most liable to be weakened by causes which Free Trade in Land, with the abolition of Primogeniture and Entail, would go far to remove. Communistic sentiments are most readily propagated when the social contrast between the owner and cultivator of the soil is too flagrant, and when the former, enriched by the foresight and industry of others, is content to be a mere drone or absentee. Property which has been inherited excites far more jealousy than property which has been purchased, especially if it has been purchased by the hard earnings of labour. If the effect of Primogeniture were to create a complete monopoly of land, instead of merely to promote its aggregation, there would assuredly be a communistic agitation against landlordism, and the best safeguard for the universal recognition of proprietary rights is to make landed property savour of monopoly as little as possible by making it universally marketable. There is no room for agrarian communism where land is within reach of all who have saved enough to buy it, and nothing strengthens the idea of property so much as facility and frequency of transfer. For the act of selling is in itself the most direct assertion of ownership, and title by purchase is acknowledged to be the strongest of all possible titles. On the other hand, it is evident that ownership in fee-simple is the most perfect, as the " limited ownership " of English settlements is the least perfect type of ownership. To place a man in the ostensible position of an owner, and yet to deny him the ordinary powers of an owner, is not to uphold the rights of property, but to derogate from them, and to give occasion for questions which seldom arise in communities where land is held in fee-simple and much subdivided. Foreign experience teaches us that the instincts of proprietorship are cherished with the utmost intensity by peasant-owners, who show a mutual respect for the rights of property far beyond that which prevails in England. This is not merely true of Republican France and Switzerland, but of Imperial Russia and Austria—not merely of Latin races, but of Teutonic and Sclavonic races—not merely of Europe, but of America and the Colonies—not of civilised races only, but of barbarous tribes, once emancipated from communal ownership. That property is robbery, is an idea which has never taken root in any society of peasant-owners, nor indeed did the suggestion of it originate in the country. It is essentially the crude and wild conceit of a Parisian theorist, caught up as the watchword of a crusade against capital, rather than against property in land, which in France excites less envy than any other form of property.

No doubt, it may be truly said that "no man made the land," and this principle applies, more or less, to cultivated land, as well as to land in its natural state, inasmuch as even cultivated land depends largely for its value upon elements which no human industry *employed upon that land* has called into existence—such as the construction of towns, roads, bridges, harbours, and railways, on adjoining land, without the co-operation, or even against the will, of the fortunate landowner. Upon this ground, as well as upon others, the State has in all ages claimed a paramount dominion over land which has never been claimed over personalty. According to feudal law in England, the very highest order of landowners were but tenants of the Crown, and could not dispose of their estates by will for centuries after wills of personalty acquired legal validity. But, although landed property has always been regarded as peculiarly subject to State-regulation, there is no other kind of property so conse-

crated and protected by the common opinion of mankind.
The right to reap what a man has sown, and the right
to profit by what he had reclaimed, were amply recognised and enforced when the right of trading was
crippled by innumerable extortions, and that of lending
money on usury was placed under the ban of the law.
Whatever heresies respecting the rights incident to
landed property may now be afloat in England are
chiefly encouraged by the severance of interest between
the landlord, the farmer, and the labourer. Landlord-
right and tenant-right are thus brought into occasional
conflict with each other, and the modern champions of a
landless peasantry are sometimes led to echo the language
of John Ball and Jack Cade. Nothing would do so
much to dissipate such chimeras as a relaxation of the
caste-like barrier which now separates the three great
agricultural classes. If more landlords were farmers,
and more farmers were landlords, and more labourers
had the prospect of becoming farmers or landlords, or
landlord-farmers, there would be less disposition to
challenge the rights of landed property, though it is
to be feared that its duties might not be so liberally
interpreted.[1]

This consideration naturally suggests a wholly different question, and one which the advocates of agrarian
reform in England are bound to entertain impartially.
It may fairly be urged that English landlords, with all
their faults, possess the characteristic virtues of English

[1] In M. de Laveleye's Essay on the "Land System of Belgium and
Holland," published in "Systems of Land-Tenure," will be found some
interesting remarks on the effect of peasant-ownership in averting social-
istic dangers. He points out that, although Flemish tenants are far more
ground down than Irish tenants, agrarian outrage is unknown in Belgium.

gentlemen, and that a more democratic system of rural economy would involve a lower standard of public responsibility, as well as of culture and manners, in the most influential classes of rural society. Now, in estimating the force of this objection, it is material to bear in mind that, however admirable may be the ideal character of an English country gentleman, it is a character of recent growth. The rural civilisation of the Middle Ages was a civilisation not of castles but of monasteries, and more true refinement was to be found among the mercantile communities of towns than among the barons and knights, who looked down upon them. Even after feudalism gave way to a new order of social relations, and for at least two centuries after the Reformation itself, English noblemen and squires, with a few bright exceptions, seemed to have employed their leisure in rough sports and pastimes, rather than in literary and artistic pursuits, in agricultural experiments, or in the benevolent supervision of their dependents. Doubtless there were sometimes Falklands and Hampdens, as there were always Roger de Coverleys and Squire Allworthys, among the landed gentry of England, but the slow progress of social improvement in the sixteenth and seventeenth centuries is sufficient to show how little the " duties of property " were understood by the great mass of proprietors. The utter neglect of popular education, to which the Reformation had given a temporary impulse, and the gradual degradation of the agricultural labourer, into the condition from which he was partially rescued by the new Poor Law, are conclusive proofs of indifference or incapacity on the part of the class which exercised an almost despotic control

over rural districts, until a period within living memory.
It was the Nonconformist bodies, and notably the
Methodists, who first roused among the masses that
sentiment of self-respect and spiritual brotherhood
which is closely allied to a belief in the natural equality
of man. It was the parochial clergy who mainly
established schools for the people in the country, and
who long bore the main burden of their maintenance
out of their scanty incomes, while the squire too often
grudged a niggardly subscription. Happily, the last
and present generations have witnessed a wonderful
change for the better in the fulfilment of territorial
obligations. Few country gentlemen now look upon
themselves as mere receivers of rent; most are anxious
to make their cottagers and tenants comfortable; yet
how many reside long enough on their properties, or
devote themselves earnestly enough to estate management, local government, or county business to be greatly
missed, if they should give place to strangers? Certainly
the allegation that a partial restriction of the Game
Laws will drive away the landed aristocracy from their
country houses would, if true, constitute the most
damaging condemnation of the institution, and the
mere fact of its being frequently made proves how
lightly the more serious ties of property are regarded by
its most eager partisans.

But this allegation is not true. The best representatives of the landed aristocracy would be retained,
by a process of natural selection, under the new English Land System; it is only the worse that would
be eliminated. The love of power will always be
gratified by the possession of land. The man with a

real taste for county business, local government, and estate management will cling to his paternal acres, and will not be ashamed to economise for a while until his brothers' and sisters' portions are paid off. Country life will always have its attractions for those who love agriculture and those who love nature, for those who aspire to play a leading part in the little world of the parish or the county, and for those who seek a refuge from the feverish excitement of commercial, professional, and social competition, for the scholar and the gentleman, no less than for the retired statesman or colonist. The landlords who use their family-places as mere sporting villas, or pleasure-grounds for London friends, seldom inviting their country neighbours, or troubling themselves to attend the Board of Guardians and the Bench, may possibly find their position less enviable under the new Land System; but, if they would part with their estates, they are the very land-lords who can best be spared, and the loss of whose influence would be least regretted. Even if Free Trade in Land should uproot far more of the existing landed gentry than is at all probable, the social effect of such a change would be little perceived. The "landed aristocracy" of England is no longer an exclusive noblesse of ancient lineage, but rather a terri-torial plutocracy, largely recruited from the wealthiest class of traders; and this profound, though insen-sible, modification in its character appears to shock no ardent admirer of the existing Land System. Bankers, stockbrokers, and brewers, millowners, shipowners, Manchester warehousemen, and merchants of every degree, are already naturalised within the magic circle of county society, and even admitted freely to matrimonial alliances. In some counties near London, the number of long-settled families is extremely small, and parvenus are not only to be found among the most active county magistrates, but also among the most popular county members. The fact that such parvenus fall so easily into the duties of their new position is surely encouraging, for it shows that blood and breeding are not the only qualities that make a country gentleman. It may even be doubted whether men of this class are inferior in real culture to the heads - of old families around them, and whether, in particular, as large a proportion of the former as of the latter have not received a University education. Now, the extension of University education has done far more for national refinement, in England as in Germany, than any traditions of aristocratic breeding; and if modern English squires compare favourably with their hard-drinking ancestors, it is partly because more of them come under the spell of that humanising discipline. At all events, country gentlemen, as a body, are certainly more cultivated than at any former period, and if Free Trade in Land should introduce into their ranks a larger infusion of men with a varied experience of the world, it would not tend to deaden, but to quicken, the intellectual life of counties.

The days are past, however, when the inhabitants of rural districts were entirely dependent for their civilisation upon the influence of the hall or the parsonage. We may confidently expect that with the spread of popular education, and the steady growth of independence among farm-labourers under a less antiquated

Land System, the necessity for a patronising superintendence will become less and less, while gentleness and courtesy of manners will gradually penetrate, as it has in France, into rustic cottages.   There are already many villages in the north of England where a considerable degree of social equality prevails, and where the wage-earning classes have learned to act and think for themselves, with little guidance from their betters.   As village-clubs are substituted for public-houses, as voluntary schools pass under the management of School Boards, as the spirit of co-operative association gains strength, as household suffrage encourages a sense of personal dignity, and, above all, as the ever-increasing facilities of travelling promote emigration from one part of England to another, the patriarchal rule of country parishes must inevitably give way to a more democratic polity.   It is this last condition, more than any other, which distinguishes American from English villages, banishing the very idea of stagnation or repose, and compelling every citizen to rely on self-help rather than on charity.   It would be vain indeed, even if it were not unwise, to desire that Old England should assimilate her rural economy to that of New England, which, again, differs widely from that of the Western States; but it is not vain to regard the English farm-labourer as capable of being elevated to a far higher status than he now occupies.   Those who are best acquainted with country life know that every village already contains farm-labourers of high character and shrewd intelligence, who may be safely trusted with great responsibility on behalf of their employers.   If this be so, why should they be incapable of the duties attaching to citizenship and land-holding, and why should not the whole class to which they belong reach the same level, under far more favourable circumstances? Doubtless, before this ideal can be realised, new habits and traditions must be matured in minds eminently conservative by nature, but these habits and traditions have been matured among the peasantry of other countries, and were once the inheritance of the English peasantry.

Once more, let us ever bear in mind that no legislative reform of the English Land System can be either beneficial or lasting, if it be not wrought out in accordance with natural laws of evolution. We cannot revive the agrarian institutions of our ancestors, or borrow directly those of foreign nations. Nevermore, in these days of rapid locomotion and keen competition, shall the freeholders of a township, bound together by manifold family ties, be united in a political and agrarian partnership, wielding the powers of lawgivers and judges in their petty town-moots, with little thought of interference from the King's officers or Council. Nevermore shall we see, except in fancy, the Royal forests or the manorial wastes, the rude husbandry of the common fields, the indiscriminate hospitality of the feudal castle, or the distribution of alms at the Abbey gate, which formed such marked features in the rural life of mediæval England. The easy routine and immemorial customs of pre-scientific agriculture have been disturbed by causes of which the effects cannot be reversed, and little is to be learned by modern farmers, except thrift and simplicity of manners, from the practice of their predecessors before the beginning of the

present century. Even from the experience of the
Continent, the United States, and the Colonies, though
much can be learned, nothing can be copied without
the most careful adaptation. The new rural economy
of England must, above all, be essentially English. It
cannot be modelled upon that of France, where the
ground for a new Land System had been cleared and
levelled by a Revolution ; nor upon that of North
Germany, where the omnipotence of the Crown transformed feudal tenures into free ownership by a series of
Royal edicts ; nor upon that of Russia, where the same
means were employed to develop a pre-existing system
of communal property upon the ruins of serfdom ; nor
upon that of Switzerland, which Nature has subdivided
by mountain barriers into little village-republics ; nor
upon that of Belgium, where methods of agriculture
are largely determined by the density of population
massed together in its numerous towns. Still less can
it be made to resemble that of India, where agrarian
institutions of pre-historic antiquity have been re-
moulded into a land-settlement imposed by a conquer-
ing, though beneficent, Power. Even that of the
United States can furnish no precedent for its construction, for no Act of Parliament can divest an English
landscape of its historical features, or infuse the spirit
of new settlers into the inhabitants of an old country,
or endow England with the boundless prairies of
Western America. Whatever be the nature and degree
of the changes hereafter to be wrought out in the
English Land System, they will assuredly be governed
and moderated by the same happy peculiarities of
English national life which have enabled this country

to support a most unequal division of landed property, and a most precarious form of agricultural tenancy, with less injury or conflict of interests than foreigners are able to conceive. The distinctive virtues of the national character will assuredly not be undermined by the extension of Free Trade to land, the abolition of limited ownership, or the restoration of Gavelkind succession. The love of home, manifested now even by cottage-tenants holding at the will of a landlord, can hardly fail to be strengthened by security of tenure—still more by the pride of ownership. The respect for territorial families will not be diminished, when the hereditary possession of land for several generations has become a true sign of hereditary merit. Public spirit will not be abated, nor constitutional instincts quenched, when a greater activity of municipal self-government, with greater social equality, has found its way into country parishes. The sense of national unity will not be enfeebled, when the chasm between landlordism and pauperism has been narrowed from both sides, and when the distinctions between class and class no longer turn upon their relative positions in a three-fold agrarian hierarchy. The population of an English village-community will be less stationary and more fluctuating than heretofore, for the new race of English landlords will not be so deeply rooted in the soil, while tenants will transfer their capital more readily from one farm to another, and enterprising labourers will be constantly draughted off by emigration. But the motives for remaining, and for settling, in the country will also be stronger than ever, and England, already the Garden of Europe, will more fully deserve that title, if the charms of its picturesque scenery, and the supervision of its varied agriculture, shall come to be shared by a more numerous proprietary.   Land will not cease to be a luxury, when it becomes a luxury accessible to every rank of Englishmen; nor will the new order of English landlords be less enviable or less powerful, because it will embrace within itself a larger and more composite section of the English people.

APPENDIX I.

(*Contributed by* **A. C. HUMPHREYS-OWEN**, **Esq.**)

THE ABOLITION OF FEUDAL TENURES AND THE LAND TAX.

THE following statement may be taken as embodying a prevalent misconception respecting the origin and nature of the Land Tax in connection with the abolition of feudal tenures :—

"The landed interest . . . find it convenient to ignore such facts as the following :—That in the reign of Charles II. their ancestors in Parliament invented EXCISE DUTIES on the people, only as substitutes for their own RENTS previously paid to the STATE ; that the LAND TAX of four shillings in the pound, devised as a remedy for that gross legislative iniquity, has been frittered away to one of that amount on the value as it stood in 1692."—*Financial Reformers' Almanac for* 1880, p. 145.

The excise seems to have been an invention of the Long Parliament. It first occurs in 1643. The 14th Ordinance of that year (Scobell's Acts and Ordinance) is entitled "A new Impost on Several Commodities mentioned in a Schedule," and the 26th Ordinance of the same year is entitled "Additional Articles to the Ordinance of Excise." The names of the commodities are not printed in either case, but no doubt might be found on searching the original records. In 1643 (Ord. 29) an excise was imposed on flesh, victuals, and salt. By Ord. 41 of 1644 an excise was imposed on alum, copperas, hats, caps, &c. By Ord. 43 of the same year the excise of strong waters was mitigated. By Ords. 39 and 40 of 1649 moneys borrowed for the Commonwealth were charged on the excise. Ord. 50 of the same year contains elaborate provisions with regard both to public and private brewers. By Ord. 3 of 1650 an alteration was made in the way of collecting the excise on private brewing. In 1656 the whole system seems to have been re-arranged and regulated [by the 19th Ordinance of that year, which is printed in full in Scobell.

It is clear, therefore, that the excise was, in its origin, a popular, not a reactionary tax.

The history of the abolition of feudal tenures is admirably stated in Digby's History of the Law of Real Property, ch. IX. As early as Magna Charta the burden of the incidents of these tenures had been matter of bargain between the owner and the tenants. See extracts in Digby, ch. III., sec. 1. As the military organisation of society passed into the industrial, their irksomeness increased, though to some extent it was relieved by the operation of the old law of Uses. But the legislation of Henry VIII., and especially the creation of the Court of Wards, 32 Henry VIII. c. 46, greatly intensified their pressure and unpopularity. A proposal was made in the 18th James I., for their commutation into a perpetual rent to be paid to the Crown (Coke, 4th Inst., p. 303, para. 6), but this fell through, though much approved by Lord Coke.

The Court of Wards, however, and all feudal incidents, were abolished by both houses in February, 1645-6, and all tenures in chivalry and in capite of the king turned into free and common socage.

The resolutions effecting this are not printed in Scobell, but are stated by Digby, *ubi sup.*, to be entered in viii. Lords Journals p. 183. Their provisions, however, were repeated by the Parliament of 1656, chap. 4, and made retrospective to the 24th of February, 1645-6. The statute 12 Car. II. c. 24, is little more than an amplification of the Act of 1656, and the customs and excise imports of 1660 are in like manner substantially the same as those of 1656.

The suggestion, therefore, that the abolition of the tenures in chivalry was part of the retrograde legislation of the Restoration Parliament is absolutely groundless. Whatever the merits of the measure may be, they are imputable solely to the Long Parliament and the Lord Protector Cromwell. All that the Restoration Parliament (servile as it was) did was to confirm against the Crown rights which the subject had possessed for more than fourteen years.

With regard to the more substantial part of the allegation, viz., that burdens which had formerly been borne by landowners only, were transferred to the nation at large, it is not possible to speak with such perfect certainty. Several points, however, are overlooked by those who take the view adopted by the compilers of the *Financial Reformers' Almanac.*

First.—A considerable part of the national soil was never held in chivalry but in socage, or some analogous tenure, or in frankalmoigne. Whatever pretence of equity there may be against the present owners of land formerly held in chivalry, cannot obviously extend to these lands.

Secondly.—The extent of the burdens imposed on tenants in chivalry, though somewhat variable, only varied within limits strictly defined. Clearly the nation at large cannot even pretend to claim anything but a contribution bearing the same proportion to the present national income as the revenue from the Court of Wards bore to the national income (say) in 1645.

Thirdly.—The idea that the excise was substituted for the profits of the feudal tenures in the way suggested is shown to be erroneous from the fact that these duties were levied as early as 1643, while the feudal tenures were not abolished until 1645-6. The courtly flourishes of the Act of Charles II. ought not to disguise the fact that a mode of raising revenue originated by the Long Parliament and continued through the Commonwealth was adopted under the Restoration. The "assessments" of the Long Parliament and of the Commonwealth and the Land Tax Act of William and Mary were probably an effective substitute in the seventeenth century for the profits of the Feudal Tenures. At any rate, it is not an unfair inference that measures which approved themselves to Roundheads and Cavaliers in one generation, and to the Whig Parliament of the next, were in the circumstances equitable and politic, even though they may have lacked the complete precision which we expect in the financial legislation of our own day.

THE LAND TAX.

The statements on this subject at p. 145 of the *Almanac* are utterly misleading. The act referred to (4 W. and M. c. 1) is entitled "An Act for granting an Aid of four shillings in the pound." It enacts (sec. 2) "That their Majesties shall have and receive the rates and assessments hereinafter mentioned of and from every person . . . For every £100 of ready money and debts (due to him) and for every £100 worth of goods, wares, merchandises, or other chattels or other personal estate, the sum of 24s."

Sec. 3 imposes what we should call an income tax of four

shillings in the £ on the salaries, &c., of all servants of the Crown, except officers of the army and navy on actual service.

Sec. 4 imposes a similar tax on the yearly value of manors, lands, &c.

The charge on the capitalised value of personalty imposed by the 2nd section is arrived at by assuming the interest of money to be £6 per cent. per annum. Four shillings in the £ on that assumed income is of course 24s.

.The Act of 1692 was, in fact, an Income Tax Act with three modifications. (1.) The charge on incomes arising from mercantile capital was levied not on the actual income, but on that which it was assumed the capital would produce. (2.) All personalty, whether productive or not, was taxed. Thus, if a man had a picture worth £1,000, he would pay 4s. in the £ on £60, *i.e.*, £12 per annum. (3.) Professional earnings were not taxed at all.

Throughout the Long Parliament and under the Commonwealth "assessments," as they were called, were levied. These consisted of fixed sums payable monthly or at other short periods. No full text of any ordinance relating to these assessments is printed in Scobell until the 12th Ordinance of 1656. That Act provided for the raising in three monthly instalments of £180,000, to which every county (including counties of towns and cities) was to contribute a sum fixed by the Act. This contribution was to be levied from each district by commissioners (whose names are given in the Act), " By a pound rate on the several divisions, &c., aforesaid, for all and every their lands, tenements, hereditary annuities, rents, profits, parks, warrens, goods, chattels, stock, merchandise, offices, and other real or personal estate whatsoever, according to the value thereof, that is to say, so much upon every twenty shillings rent or yearly value of land and real estate, and so much upon money, stock, or other personal estate, by an equal rate (wherein every twenty pounds in money, stock, or other personal estate, shall bear the like charge as shall be laid upon every twenty shillings yearly rent or yearly value of land ").

The chief difference between these Commonwealth assessments and the "aid" of 4 W. and M. was that in the former case the interest on capital was assumed to be £5 per cent., not £6, and that the sum payable was decided on and apportioned between the different counties, &c., leaving the counties themselves to fix the rate of contribution of their inhabitants, while in the latter the rate at which contribution should be made was fixed without reference to the amount required. In both cases, however, personalty was taxed equally with land, and on the same principle, viz., that of taking its capital value and charging the rate on the income which that sum would produce at the legal rate of interest.

In fact, the statute of 1692 was the skilful development, by a seventeenth century Chancellor of the Exchequer, of the archaic subsidy and assessment into something closely resembling the modern income tax, affecting real and personal property alike.

To recapitulate. The excise was imposed by the Long Parliament, in 1643. The tenures in chivalry were abolished in 1645-6, two and a half years later. There can, therefore, be no question as to the two having been originally independent of each other. No doubt the excise was granted to Charles II. by the Act which confirms the abolition of the tenures in chivalry, and is stated to be a recompense for the profits arising from them. But both the abolition of these tenures, and the levying of the excise duties, were early Acts of the Long Parliament, and were confirmed under Cromwell. Whatever may now be thought of them, both measures were obviously then acceptable to the people.

Again, the tenures in chivalry only affected a portion of the soil of England. The loss of revenue from their abolition cannot, therefore, be alleged as a reason for taxing the whole of the land.

Further, the so-called Land Tax was not, nor were the earlier forms of taxation from which it was evolved, solely charged on land. On the contrary, they were universal charges on land and personalty ; and it may be remarked that it taxed a variety of the latter (moveable chattels not used for purposes of commerce), which nowadays only pay through the Probate and Legacy Duties.

Lastly.—The whole contention of the *Almanac* (p. 26), that landowners of the present day, even if they have acquired their property by purchase, may be charged with the same, or the like obligations as (it is alleged) were borne by their predecessors centuries ago, is one which ought not to enter into practical politics.

For more than 230 years, land in England has been bought, sold, mortgaged, settled, and dealt with in every possible way, on the faith that it shall bear certain burdens of rates, &c., variable in their amount, but applicable only to fixed objects, and that beyond those, all taxes which the exigencies of the State require, shall be borne by all the property of the country as equally as may be.   To impose a special tax on land at the present day, would disturb that sense of security upon which all property depends for its value.   The working of such legislation may be realised best by a single example.   Ten years ago, a self-made man invested the savings of his lifetime on mortgage of a farm on wheat land; shortly after, he died, leaving the mortgage money as the sole provision for his widow and children.   The farming panic of 1878-9 came.   The mortgagor is bankrupt.   The rents of the property just pay the interest on the mortgage.   Could it be proposed, with any show of justice, that in 1880 a tax of 20 per cent. should be levied on this, upon what is at the best a dubious assumption, that in 1646 the predecessors in title of the mortgagor got rid unfairly of some liabilities to the State?

The foregoing remarks have not been prompted by any hostility to the principle of direct taxation, supported with so much earnestness and ability by the *Financial Reform Almanac*.   They are intended solely to remove some misconceptions which, while they exist, must necessarily make it difficult, if not impossible, for a considerable number of Reformers to accept the *Almanac* as an exponent of their views.

APPENDIX II.

(*Contributed by A. C. HUMPHREYS-OWEN, Esq.*)

LIABILITY OF PERSONALTY TO POOR RATE.

IT is usually supposed that Poor Rates are, historically, a charge exclusively imposed on land, in consequence of the secularisation of Church lands at the Reformation; but this supposition is at least doubtful, if not positively erroneous.

The obligation rests on 43 Eliz. c. 2, sec. 1, enacting (*int. al.*) that certain persons therein mentioned shall "raise weekly, or otherwise (by taxation of every inhabitant, parson, vicar, and other, and of every occupier of lands, houses, tithe-impropriate, propriations of tithes, coal mines, or saleable underwoods, in the said parish, in such competent sum or sums of money as they shall think fit), a convenient stock of flax, hemp, wool, thread, iron, and other ware and stuff, to set the poor on work," &c., &c.

It will be seen that every *inhabitant* is to be taxed, as well as every *occupier*.

The earliest decision on the subject seems to be a case at Lincoln Assizes, in 1633, where Hutton and Croke, after hearing counsel, ordered the defendants, the overseers of Boston, to "make their assessments well and duly, and in an equal manner, according to the visible estates, real and personal, of such inhabitants within their town;" 2 Bulstrode, 354.

In 1698, a rate made by the overseers of St. Leonard, Shoreditch, was quashed by the Quarter Sessions, because it did not include personal property, and this order was confirmed by the Queen's Bench: 3 Salkeld, 483.

In 1706 it was laid down by the Queen's Bench that farmers were not rateable for their stock, but tradesmen were: 2 Lord Raymond, 1280.

No further decisions appear in the reports until the time of Lord Mansfield, whose judicial policy was evidently opposed to rating personalty. In 1769 it was held by the Queen's Bench that a superintendent of salt-works was not rateable on a salary payable monthly: 4 Burrowes, 2014.

In Rex *v.* Canterbury, ib. 2290, the judges made several remarks on the difficulty of rating personalty, and also spoke of its being unusual to do so.   •

In R. *v.* Witney, a rate which included stock-in-trade, was quashed on a point of form : 5 Burrowes, 2634.

The same thing was done in R. *v.* Ringwood, Cowp. 326, Mr. Justice Aston saying, " If the justices had amended the rate as they ought to have done, instead of quashing it, they would have found the difficulty of rating personal property.

Rex *v.* Andover, Cowp. 550, was a similar case. This was in 1770. It should be observed that in all of these cases before Lord Mansfield, the Court took care not to grapple with the general question whether personal property was rateable.

In 1787, the case of R. *v.* Hogg was decided in the Queen's Bench. The question of rating personal property was incidentally raised, and Mr. Justice Buller, in the course of his judgment, took occasion to dissent from Lord Mansfield's judicial policy. He said, " I have always been of opinion that it would be better to have given a direct opinion at once upon the construction of the 43rd of Eliz., than to state particular cases, to see whether they formed exceptions to the Act.* In the case of Atkins *v.* Davis, I stated the principle to be, that every man should pay according to his ability. . . . I then thought, and still do think, that as a general question, personal property is rateable." 1 Durnford and East's Reports, 721.

This was followed by a decision in 1792, that ships were rateable: R. *v.* White, 4 D. & E., 771. And in 1794, Lord Kenyon said, " There is no doubt that personal property is rateable." 4 D. & E., 755.

In 1807, Lord Ellenborough, deciding that a farmer's sub-tenant need not be separately rated, said, " It would be a different question if a farmer derived a profit from stock kept on his farm, but not connected with the management of it, as if he kept a large stock of cattle, which he fed with oil cake, for sale : there he would be separately rateable for it, as stock generally, from which he derived a separate and distinct profit." R. *v.* Brown, 8 East, 528.

---

* This was what Lord Mansfield had always insisted on doing.

It is not necessary to go into the more modern cases. The question was only finally set at rest by a statute passed in 1840. This statute (3 & 4 Vic. c. 89) enacted, " It shall not be lawful for the overseers of any parish, &c., to tax any inhabitant thereof, as such inhabitant, in respect of his ability derived from the profits of stock-in-trade, or any other property, for or towards the relief of the poor."

The fair inference seems to be that personalty was considered legally rateable for the relief of the poor long after the first Poor Law, but gradually ceased to be rated, by reason of the difficulties and inconveniences to which Lord Mansfield and his fellow-judges so constantly referred. It may be added, that in the argument of Rex *v.* Andover (Cowper, 550), many authorities are given for thinking that before the Reformation the charge of supporting the poor was primarily on the church, but also on the inhabitants, as exempted by 3 & 4 Vict. c. 89. A case is reported in the Year Book, 44 Edward III. (fo. 18), where the inhabitants of a parish decided to raise £10 for the repair of their church, and assessed a rate of 6d. upon every plow-land, $1\frac{1}{2}$d. upon every cow, and $1\frac{1}{2}$d. upon every ten sheep. Even if it were otherwise, and if the support of the poor was before the Reformation solely charged on church lands, that would be no reason for holding that all the land of the country, of whatever tenure, was exclusively chargeable since the Reformation.

APPENDIX III.

AGRICULTURAL HOLDINGS ACT AMENDMENT AND TENANTS' COMPENSATION.

THE Agricultural Tenants' Compensation (Sir T. Acland's) Bill applies to all Tenancies (whether for a term of years or for a shorter term) which are not under the Agricultural Holdings Act. It does not attempt to make the Holdings Act compulsory, nor to amend it in detail, nor to interfere in any way with those who voluntarily come under its operation.

It aims at providing as an alternative a simpler mode of proceeding, partly by direct or compulsory enactment of principles, partly by giving further effect to voluntary contract.

The Agricultural Tenants' Compensation Bill rests on a distinction between two different subjects :

    A. Outlay on the business of farming, with a view to immediate return.

    B. Outlay on the improvement of land, with a view to increase its productive capability and ultimate letting value.

Under the first head (A) it is assumed :

    1. That preparation for crops must be made by a Tenant on an average two years beforehand.

    2. That when a Tenant quits a farm before he has received the result of such preparation, he ought to have compensation for such preparation, and that such compensation ought to be secured to him by law. That to this extent legislation ought to be compulsory in principle.

Under the second head (B) it is assumed :

    1. That the lasting improvement of land is under ordinary circumstances a matter to be dealt with by the Owner. But that if a Tenant wishes to undertake such improvement it is desirable to define beforehand the outlay to be

made, the amount of compensation to be secured to the Tenant, and the duration of the claim.

2. That legislation is necessary to set many existing Owners of land free from the restrictions of settlement, and that such freedom (within moderate limits) may be granted by a simple enactment.

It is accordingly proposed as regards (A) Tenants' ordinary outlay:

1. That for acts of husbandry, manure, and manurial value of cattle food, compensation should be compulsory, notwithstanding any stipulation to the contrary (Clause 5 and Clause 13, line 19, 20).

2. That the measure of such compensation be the value to the succeeding occupier (Clause 6).

3. That the compensation may be recovered in the County Court, and that the Court be bound to recognise any *bonâ fide* agreement for such compensation (Clause 8). The Court will be able in case of need to call for evidence, and its proceedings will be public.

4. That as a further security to Tenants in the event of a change of ownership by sale or by death, no Tenant shall be disturbed in the terms of his occupation for two years after the transfer (Clause 12).

5. That as a security to the Landlord certain notice of claims shall be given by Tenants, and samples of manure, &c., may be called for by the Landlord (Clause 10).

It is further proposed as regards (B) the lasting improvement of land (held under settlement):

1. That the Legislature enable Life Tenants to charge on their estates an equitable compensation to Tenants for work done by agreement. The machinery of the Agricultural Holdings Act for this purpose is very cumbersome, and may in certain cases act very injuriously to a Tenant by introducing the addition to the letting value as a limit to the compensation for an outlay to which the Owner has consented.

2. That the Limited Owner be enabled to secure to the Tenant a compensation to the extent of one year's rent,

to run over seven or ten years; and that he be enabled to go further with the consent of his trustees or of the next heir.

By this plan the joint action of the Owner, Reversioner, and Occupier may be encouraged, with little room for litigation; and without the risk attendant on the customary conduct of arbitrations. It is also proposed in the Bill to provide for the appointment of a high class of umpires by public authority (Clause 9).[1]

It is submitted that it is more important for the Legislature to place the existing Tenants of farms, over 500,000 in number, in a position of equitable security for their share of the capital embarked in the business of agriculture (however limited that share may be), than to offer inducements to a new race of capitalists to supplant the present Tenants by enabling them to saddle the owners with heavy claims for outlay which may never be remunerative—in other words, to speculate with the Landlord's capital.

It has been suggested that the compulsory legislation of this Bill should apply to certain specified improvements of land by lime, chalk, clay, or otherwise. It seems to me better not to define particulars of improvements in an Act of Parliament; their effect and mode of application differ widely in different districts.

It has been recommended, on the other hand, that further safeguards should be introduced to protect the Landlord against the exhaustion of the soil. To this it may be replied that such matters are better left to written agreements, in which any covenants may be introduced which are not contrary to the broad principle of the Bill, namely, that manurial value, within certain limits, must be paid for by proper compensation. The whole question of manurial value is in its infancy. Parliament should not attempt to stereotype matters open to scientific inquiry.

T. D. ACLAND.

[1] The difficulty of securing an honest valuation is one of the main reasons which have deterred landlords from entering into voluntary contracts for due compensation.

APPENDIX IV.

TABLE I. A.

QUANTITIES OF THE UNDERMENTIONED ARTICLES OF FARM PRODUCE IMPORTED INTO THE UNITED KINGDOM, SO FAR AS CAN BE GIVEN, IN EACH YEAR, FROM 1800 TO 1879.

A.—CORN, &c.

Years.	Wheat.	Wheat Flour and Meal.	Oats.*	Barley.*	Maize.	Peas.	Beans.	Rice.	Potatoes.	Hops.	Years.
	Cwts.	Cwts.	Cwts.	Cwts.	Cwts.	Cwts.	Cwts.	Cwts.	Cwts.	Cwts.	
1800		1,232,557	1,425,724	468,054	—	—	—	—	—	—	1800
1801		5,995,332	1,531,107	407,186	—	—	—	—	—	—	1801
1802		2,277,958	635,486	29,057	—	—	—	—	—	—	1802
1803		1,319,661	669,223	3,939	—	—	—	—	—	—	1803
1804		1,643,309	1,313,337	32,400	—	—	—	—	—	—	1804
1805		3,517,689	719,659	98,729	—	—	—	—	—	—	1805
1806		873,940	481,028	7,350	—	—	—	—	—	—	1806
1807		1,526,784	1,118,011	10,600	—	—	—	—	—	—	1807
1808		176,022	90,069	15,375	—	—	—	—	—	—	1808
1809		1,657,072	777,879	47,021	—	—	—	—	—	—	1809
1810		6,047,903	303,733	63,243	—	—	—	—	—	—	1810
1811		792,901	30,702	143,289	—	—	—	—	—	—	1811
1812		552,783	38,637	142,443	—	—	—	—	—	—	1812
1813		1,428,760	158,655	70,389	—	—	—	—	—	—	1813
1814		2,619,792	651,131	104,929	—	—	—	—	—	—	1814
1815		804,854	316,247	7,264	—	—	—	—	—	—	1815
1816		880,551	197,602	53,089	—	—	—	—	—	—	1816
1817		4,468,930	1,269,676	478,075	—	—	—	—	—	—	1817
1818		6,694,044	2,591,949	2,486,607	—	—	—	—	—	—	1818
1819		1,983,253	1,537,389	1,333,561	—	—	—	—	—	—	1819
1820		2,536,841	1,874,892	102,396	—	38,034	46,114	282,068	—	—	1820
1821		561,652	278,704	48,378	—	2,601	600	130,551	—	—	1821
1822		186,823	153,455	68,028	—	1,913		120,259	—	—	1822

* For the years 1800 to 1820 the quantities of Barley Meal and of Oatmeal imported are included with the quantities of Barley and Oats imported.

TABLE I. A (continued).

QUANTITIES OF THE UNDERMENTIONED ARTICLES OF FARM PRODUCE IMPORTED INTO THE UNITED KINGDOM, SO FAR AS CAN BE GIVEN, IN EACH YEAR, FROM 1800 TO 1879.

A.—CORN, &c.

Years.	Wheat.	Wheat Flour and Meal.	Oats.*	Barley.*	Maize.	Peas.	Beans.	Rice.	Potatoes.	Hops.	Years.
	Cwts.	Cwts.	Cwts.	Cwts.	Cwts.	Cwts.	Cwts.	Cwts.	Cwts.	Cwts.	
1823		68,232	75,985	39	—	—	973	124,704	—	—	1823
1824		368,223	1,342,057	94,664	—	21,636	8,940	153,966	—	—	1824
1825		1,666,613	566,997	1,521,007	—	74,997	46,046	54,698	—	—	1825
1826		2,499,848	3,094,327	993,139	—	291,424	530,224	91,154	—	—	1826
1827		1,318,221	4,788,316	742,735	—	155,214	611,619	150,999	—	—	1827
1828	3,099,382	151,038	457,663	602,400	—	237,465	319,136	172,239	—	—	1828
1829	6,694,865	461,895	1,490,109	1,006,118	—	165,515	192,729	222,548	—	—	1829
1830	6,393,027	707,082	1,393,252	518,282	—	156,429	72,579	132,562	—	—	1830
1831	7,958,292	1,636,059	1,710,335	1,344,689	—	267,916	100,157	168,744	—	—	1831
1832	1,696,140	194,896	79,359	342,282	—	90,855	119,631	186,095	—	—	1832
1833	1,075,407	172,877	64,168	304,360	30	71,487	97,954	218,885	—	—	1833
1834	576,727	151,306	481,181	316,289	3,655	305,460	204,609	317,240	—	—	1834
1835	184,721	84,969	490,934	242,128	3,162	108,977	147,343	249,538	—	—	1835
1836	730,803	255,830	360,404	298,153	7,620	352,345	398,811	186,826	—	—	1836
1837	1,975,445	364,248	1,145,166	313,535	17,250	500,671	452,601	385,083	—	—	1837
1838	5,379,660	456,739	147,246	7,864	17,323	134,316	275,820	238,366	—	—	1838
1839	11,416,430	843,046	1,842,821	2,069,303	50,798	630,059	470,614	577,054	—	—	1839
1840	8,637,993	1,537,888	1,487,024	2,233,707	99,703	713,187	554,653	443,918	2,293	107	1840
1841	10,442,267	1,263,126	336,317	945,193	17,730	668,538	1,258,667	486,719	3,431	34	1841
1842	11,775,634	1,129,852	828,498	261,911	153,454	418,221	541,899	511,414	11,202	—	1842
1843	4,073,853	436,878	231,888	640,286	2,216	217,363	205,646	457,039	16,033	28	1843
1844	4,762,667	980,645	823,902	3,640,518	158,846	486,004	661,817	456,302	116,911	267	1844
1845	3,777,410	945,864	1,623,784	1,315,550	241,667	377,730	791,404	542,160	109,784	726	1845
1846	6,207,894	3,190,429	2,170,682	1,324,432	3,024,883	956,781	1,093,059	762,509	185,139	3,283	1846
1847	11,511,305	6,329,058	4,690,697	2,759,582	15,464,194	709,281	1,901,464	1,560,402	275,274	1,471	1847

Year											Year
1848	385	940,707	996,372	2,091,120	972,063	6,752,233	3,765,264	2,659,404	1,754,449	11,184,156	1848
1849	5,265	1,417,867	976,195	1,962,570	1,054,647	9,533,396	4,932,172	3,484,541	3,349,839	16,663,305	1849
1850	6,479	1,348,883	785,451	1,882,972	811,620	5,473,161	3,699,653	3,174,801	3,819,440	16,202,312	1850
1851	462	636,771	744,847	1,363,817	447,295	7,747,011	2,962,729	3,295,955	5,314,414	16,518,701	1851
1852	309	773,619	987,813	1,589,623	478,773	6,305,472	2,234,071	2,720,539	3,865,173	13,261,161	1852
1853	42,344	1,133,609	1,504,629	1,498,269	454,761	6,619,213	2,943,100	2,828,125	4,621,506	21,300,197	1853
1854	119,040	16,446	1,342,748	1,652,854	491,296	5,784,420	1,974,900	2,791,110	3,646,505	14,868,650	1854
1855	24,662	58,261	2,238,158	1,478,349	510,655	5,208,570	1,246,822	2,842,749	1,904,224	11,560,042	1855
1856	15,987	109,838	3,692,001	1,513,791	387,369	7,619,199	2,612,186	3,153,832	3,970,100	17,648,943	1856
1857	18,711	955,057	3,432,154	1,310,464	719,545	4,931,927	6,076,679	4,703,322	2,178,148	14,897,814	1857
1858	13,000	1,721,953	3,692,023	1,765,847	710,888	7,503,536	5,933,543	5,104,773	3,856,127	18,380,782	1858
1859	2,220	588,910	1,450,092	1,476,326	702,117	5,632,727	6,170,910	4,613,358	3,328,324	17,337,329	1859
1860	68,918	560,762	1,535,575	1,885,003	1,413,904	7,936,362	7,545,932	6,300,115	5,086,220	25,484,151	1860
1861	149,176	385,446	3,305,632	2,402,276	1,799,095	13,244,366	5,001,432	5,114,398	6,152,938	29,955,532	1861
1862	133,791	1,354,636	3,919,189	2,037,137	1,024,722	11,694,818	6,624,800	4,426,994	7,207,113	41,033,503	1862
1863	147,281	1,249,360	3,070,292	2,077,912	1,361,619	12,736,594	7,383,528	6,495,585	5,218,977	24,364,171	1863
1864	98,656	741,784	3,187,650	909,270	1,114,083	6,285,938	4,921,486	5,562,959	4,512,391	23,196,714	1864
1865	82,479	806,753	1,938,816	958,362	783,135	7,096,033	7,818,570	7,714,230	3,904,471	20,962,963	1865
1866	85,687	737,063	2,265,911	1,324,173	1,211,835	14,322,863	8,434,323	8,844,586	4,972,280	23,156,329	1866
1867	296,117	1,374,176	2,778,754	1,982,615	1,586,129	8,540,429	5,684,956	9,407,136	3,592,969	34,645,569	1867
1868	231,720	2,041,436	4,710,048	2,647,390	1,116,246	11,472,226	7,476,490	8,112,563	3,093,022	32,639,768	1868
1869	322,515	1,660,155	5,319,504	1,897,220	1,054,387	17,664,113	8,053,769	7,916,870	5,401,555	37,695,828	1869
1870	218,664	771,854	4,077,468	1,505,798	1,799,354	16,756,783	7,217,369	10,830,630	4,803,909	30,901,229	1870
1871	135,965	847,835	4,586,422	2,990,745	1,011,367	16,825,023	8,569,012	10,914,186	3,977,939	39,389,803	1871
1872	122,729	5,987,429	7,033,361	2,948,916	1,296,133	24,532,670	15,046,566	11,537,325	4,388,136	42,127,726	1872
1873	145,994	7,506,615	6,540,318	2,982,064	1,190,837	18,823,431	9,241,063	11,907,702	6,214,479	43,863,098	1873
1874	256,444	3,986,662	7,043,779	2,361,095	1,825,603	17,693,625	11,335,396	11,387,768	6,236,044	41,527,638	1874
1875	167,366	4,696,132	6,719,894	3,458,777	1,615,132	20,438,480	11,049,476	12,435,888	6,136,083	51,876,517	1875
1876	250,039	6,023,936	6,469,181	4,607,555	1,611,250	39,963,369	9,772,945	11,211,019	5,959,821	44,454,657	1876
1877	168,834	7,964,840	6,617,603	4,589,345	1,521,640	30,477,818	12,959,526	12,910,035	7,377,303	54,269,800	1877
1878	262,765	8,745,838	6,109,020	1,872,182	1,824,118	41,673,906	14,156,919	12,774,420	7,828,079	49,906,484	1878
1879		9,357,179	6,867,330	2,315,756	1,982,911	36,148,379	11,546,314	13,471,660	10,728,252	59,591,795	1879

* For the years 1800 to 1820 the quantities of Barley Meal and of Oatmeal imported are included with the quantities of Barley and Oats imported.

TABLE I. B.

QUANTITIES OF THE UNDERMENTIONED ARTICLES OF FARM PRODUCE IMPORTED INTO THE UNITED KINGDOM, SO FAR AS CAN BE GIVEN, IN EACH YEAR, FROM 1820 TO 1879.

B.—PROVISIONS, &c.

Years	Animals. Oxen, Bulls, Cows, and Calves. No.	Animals. Sheep and Lambs. No.	Bacon and Hams. Cwts.	Beef. Cwts.	Meat, Salted or Fresh. Cwts.	Meat, Preserved, other than Salted. Cwts.	Pork. Cwts.	Eggs. No.	Butter. Cwts.	Cheese. Cwts.	Lard. Cwts.	Years.
1820	—	—	1,166	—	—	—	—	31,893,019	68,292	83,179	—	1820
1821	—	—	1,453	—	—	—	—	40,544,648	115,649	84,077	—	1821
1822	—	—	1,626	—	—	—	—	50,644,025	118,204	72,952	—	1822
1823	—	—	2,316	—	—	—	—	49,878,847	121,945	94,489	—	1823
1824	—	—	3,390	—	—	—	—	51,829,756	160,355	158,435	—	1824
1825	—	—	4,709	—	—	—	—	64,503,790	279,067	220,474	—	1825
1826	—	—	5,261	450	—	—	—	62,542,641	196,086	175,148	—	1826
1827	—	—	5,922	8,339	—	—	—	66,429,330	210,788	189,885	—	1827
1828	—	—	5,191	6,509	—	—	—	65,843,843	201,796	217,986	—	1828
1829	—	—	3,340	1,458	—	—	—	63,494,037	147,737	168,888	—	1829
1830	—	—	2,975	976	—	—	—	52,933,408	108,264	109,742	—	1830
1831	—	—	2,034	503	—	—	—	58,464,690	123,169	134,459	—	1831
1832	—	—	3,233	2,592	—	—	—	61,936,588	130,925	133,446	—	1832
1833	—	—	3,735	4,732	—	—	—	67,603,114	136,986	134,073	—	1833
1834	—	—	3,727	4,155	—	—	3,730	69,588,589	133,871	146,594	—	1834
1835	—	—	3,554	4,095	—	—	3,507	59,964,496	146,784	140,852	—	1835
1836	—	—	5,879	10,072	—	—	9,462	69,082,480	240,738	211,169	—	1836
1837	—	—	4,360	9,090	—	—	20,924	74,733,037	282,947	237,732	—	1837
1838	—	—	6,548	13,108	—	—	19,138	83,749,743	256,193	227,877	—	1838
1839	—	—	8,149	16,227	—	—	31,843	95,291,844	213,504	210,436	—	1839
1840	Prohibited	Prohibited	6,181	29,779	—	—	29,632	96,149,190	252,661	226,462	92	1840
1841	Prohibited	Prohibited	5,194	42,960	—	—	44,579	91,880,187	277,428	270,219	6,226	1841
1842	4,264	644	8,355	30,022	—	—	54,164	89,548,747	175,197	179,748	28,998	1842

Year												Year
1843	76,503	179,389	151,996	70,415,931	27,118			60,724	7,368	217	1,521	1843
1844	69,547	213,850	185,511	67,565,167	30,844			106,768	6,768	2,817	4,889	1844
1845	46,070	267,824	253,723	75,627,362	39,700			87,815	5,483	15,957	16,833	1845
1846	109,899	341,682	257,385	72,252,159	72,789			177,172	14,203	94,624	45,043	1846
1847	128,719	354,802	314,125	77,485,487	235,899			117,695	107,732	142,720	75,717	1847
1848	312,040	441,635	294,427	88,012,585	254,132			121,980	219,033	130,583	62,738	1848
1849	186,373	390,147	281,969	97,745,849	348,275			149,962	396,447	129,266	53,449	1849
1850	229,614	347,803	330,579	105,689,060	211,254			135,414	352,461	143,498	66,520	1850
1851	120,409	338,659	353,718	115,526,245	154,800			117,384	192,118	201,859	86,520	1851
1852	63,340	289,458	285,497	108,281,233	95,555			124,693	81,436	230,037	93,061	1852
1853	118,851	396,404	403,289	123,450,678	152,731			183,285	205,667	289,420	125,253	1853
1854	274,595	388,714	482,514	121,946,801	160,898			192,274	423,510	183,436	114,338	1854
1855	118,109	384,192	447,266	99,732,800	204,326	2,155	382	230,755	241,494	162,642	97,527	1855
1856	136,650	406,323	513,392	117,230,600	156,266	23,899	1,170	187,838	372,793	145,059	83,306	1856
1857	182,860	393,323	441,606	126,818,600	88,752	6,134	327	151,174	366,934	177,207	92,963	1857
1858	121,367	364,087	387,566	134,685,000	89,765	575	632	168,558	196,685	184,482	89,001	1858
1859	93,597	406,547	425,663	148,631,000	163,330	1,758	2,690	219,589	107,251	250,580	85,677	1859
1860	198,030	583,283	840,112	167,695,400	173,325	6,131	15,007	262,194	326,106	312,219	104,569	1860
1861	324,691	706,395	992,772	203,313,360	136,416	2,784	1,101	152,635	515,953	312,923	107,096	1861
1862	530,090	703,909	1,037,371	232,321,200	227,758	725	695	189,761	1,345,694	299,472	97,387	1862
1863	530,512	756,285	986,708	266,929,680	170,751	2,310	973	288,369	1,877,813	430,788	150,898	1863
1864	217,275	834,844	1,054,617	335,298,240	228,015	1,474	1,474	346,821	1,069,390	496,243	231,733	1864
1865	136,898	853,277	1,083,717	364,013,040	222,419	8,083	3,480	244,431	713,346	914,170	283,271	1865
1866	228,459	872,342	1,165,081	438,878,880	205,282	2,318	151,820	232,948	635,782	790,880	237,739	1866
1867	246,839	905,476	1,142,262	397,934,520	150,285	15,539	97,916	246,767	537,114	539,716	177,948	1867
1868	237,260	873,377	1,097,539	383,969,040	151,362	20,118	38,343	245,120	638,127	341,155	136,688	1868
1869	255,964	979,189	1,259,089	442,172,640	190,874	32,214	50,247	229,223	740,193	709,843	220,190	1869
1870	217,696	1,041,281	1,159,210	430,842,240	257,014	80,636	34,300	215,748	567,164	669,905	202,172	1870
1871	477,568	1,216,400	1,334,783	400,473,000	296,144	254,833	42,340	302,079	1,093,838	917,076	248,611	1871
1872	579,056	1,057,883	1,138,081	531,591,720	218,260	350,729	55,354	228,912	2,001,855	809,382	172,993	1872
1873	626,090	1,356,728	1,279,566	660,474,000	289,695	260,749	79,841	260,554	2,987,229	851,116	200,802	1873
1874	676,328	1,485,265	1,619,808	680,552,280	322,574	265,223	119,403	261,721	2,542,095	758,915	193,862	1874
1875	540,244	1,627,748	1,467,870	741,223,560	266,663	171,373	144,954	215,581	2,638,875	985,652	263,684	1875
1876	562,174	1,531,204	1,659,492	753,026,040	378,607	283,066	92,556	413,351	3,181,569	1,041,329	271,576	1876
1877	592,264	1,653,920	1,637,403	751,185,600	303,734	469,003	130,178	678,505	2,820,482	874,055	201,193	1877
1878	908,605	1,968,859	1,796,517	783,714,720	389,439	439,900	145,981	729,123	4,295,151	892,125	253,462	1878
1879	840,819	1,789,721	2,045,399	766,707,840	441,209	567,877	153,284	812,237	4,917,631	944,888	247,768	1879

TABLE II. A.

QUANTITIES OF THE UNDERMENTIONED ARTICLES OF BRITISH AND IRISH FARM PRODUCE EXPORTED FROM THE UNITED KINGDOM, SO FAR AS CAN BE GIVEN, IN EACH YEAR, FROM 1828 TO 1879.

A.—CORN, &c.

Years.	Wheat.	Wheat Flour and Meal.	Oats.	Barley.	Peas.	Beans.	Malt.	Potatoes.	Hops.	Years.
	Cwts.	Cwts.	Cwts.	Cwts.	Cwts.	Cwts.	Qrs.	Cwts.	Cwts.	
1828	113	7,002	26,381	1,046	7,289		—	—	—	1828
1829	412	9,367	16,486	1,121	6,647		—	—	—	1829
1830	165	9,166	16,799	1,021	6,821		—	—	—	1830
1831	238	10,163	16,772	2,089	7,340		—	—	—	1831
1832	455	4,418	17,259	1,125	5,746		—	—	—	1832
1833	295	8,517	19,682	1,768	4,242		—	—	—	1833
1834	91	4,422	16,962	850	3,852		—	—	—	1834
1835	1,872	5,424	13,951	1,521	4,827		—	—	—	1835
1836	399	7,180	16,390	1,539	7,159		—	—	—	1836
1837	2,769	5,266	18,059	2,218	6,769		—	—	—	1837
1838	7,939	4,113	20,105	2,546	6,860		—	—	—	1838
1839	7,068	7,175	17,303	5,525	8,290		—	—	—	1839
1840	10,184	4,907	35,107	5,411	7,085		—	—	—	1840
1841	7,200	5,892	33,784	3,536	6,803		—	—	—	1841
1842	6,729	5,881	Not stated.	Not stated.	Not stated.	Not stated.	—	—	—	1842
1843	1,699	4,535	,,	,,	,,	,,	—	—	—	1843
1844	946	3,565	,,	,,	,,	,,	—	—	—	1844
1845	2,954	266	,,	,,	,,	,,	—	—	—	1845
1846	26,440	530	,,	,,	,,	,,	—	—	—	1846
1847	595,339	32,239	,,	,,	,,	,,	—	—	—	1847
1848	1,486	1,682	,,	,,	,,	,,	—	—	—	1848
1849	2,492	2,335	,,	,,	,,	,,	—	—	—	1849

Year			Cwts.	Cwts.	Quarters. / Cwts.	Cwts.		Not stated.	Not stated.
1850	3,237	7,610	,,		,,	,,	—	,,	
1851	47,502	21,477	,,		,,	,,	—	,,	
1852	124,770	19,241	,,		,,	,,	—	,,	
1853	155,276	67,371			119,988		—		6,066
1854	165,468	38,190			193,015		—		5,238
1855	459,836	71,999			251,207		—	51,014	8,904
1856	542,715	81,423			164,720		—	141,502	12,790
1857	509,929	75,458			171,687		—	63,354	12,250
1858	47,853	9,051			199,790		—	51,602	37,168
1859	178,217	20,513			162,282		—	53,617	10,696
1860	32,188	15,920			72,857		—	35,201	5,581
1861	1,512,554	104,314			93,521		—	128,663	4,679
1862	48,195	14,151			107,283		—	13,597	75,647
1863	167,245	14,405	150,373		Quarters. 6,284		62,799	22,411	17,833
1864	55,402	16,635	132,938		Cwts. 24,488		57,075	115,759	17,060
1865	51,925	15,684	84,524		22,749		61,655	40,271	21,012
1866	230,894	12,697	106,933		26,707		70,770	31,862	22,864
1867	339,335	15,375	360,787		37,841		45,080	28,081	12,050
1868	176,648	25,636	423,223		64,944		54,092	20,291	18,125
1869	60,541	15,089	105,425		48,316		68,305	42,555	13,733
1870	923,953	200,148	369,414		46,698		73,038	104,775	17,428
1871	3,293,406	657,297	902,430	Cwts. 83,876	Cwts. 22,086	Cwts. 6,631	70,694	Not stated.	10,208
1872	532,977	37,935	77,484	13,001	8,989	1,103	57,958	,,	31,215
1873	1,128,226	46,213	26,827	32,340	8,897	693	67,800	,,	33,892
1874	344,666	95,213	93,840	37,853	9,463	649	63,298	,,	9,508
1875	97,017	26,841	111,181	26,187	15,757	906	63,351	,,	13,140
1876	460,839	27,316	199,949	18,897	33,125	1,180	64,965	,,	20,305
1877	207,930	29,002	47,013	18,951	17,397	2,010	75,189	,,	13,508
1878	700,155	39,405	92,561	18,828	12,152	985	62,896	,,	12,620
1879	696,358	65,770	69,218	22,773	15,308	1,090	78,607	,,	7,153

TABLE II. B.

QUANTITIES OF THE UNDERMENTIONED ARTICLES OF BRITISH AND IRISH FARM PRODUCE EXPORTED FROM THE UNITED KINGDOM, AS FAR AS CAN BE GIVEN, IN EACH YEAR, FROM 1827 TO 1879.

B.—PROVISIONS, &c.

Years.	Animals.		Bacon and Hams.	Beef and Pork.	Butter.	Cheese.	Years.
	Oxen, Bulls, Cows, and Calves.	Sheep and Lambs.					
	No.	No.	Cwts.	Cwts.	Cwts.	Cwts.	
1827	Not stated	Not stated	11,072	107,037	84,300		1827
1828	,,	,,	8,333	58,540	94,623		1828
1829	,,	,,	10,039	98,127	89,875		1829
1830	,,	,,	12,197	108,178	73,124		1830
1831	,,	,,	7,564	72,175	63,260		1831
1832	,,	,,	5,972	45,764	72,349		1832
1833	,,	,,	11,114	86,752	76,105		1833
1834	,,	,,	18,583	108,658	88,396		1834
1835	,,	,,	12,434	106,667	88,508		1835
1836	,,	,,	14,536	85,456	75,243		1836
1837	,,	,,	12,312	85,057	60,054		1837
1838	,,	,,	17,009	60,281	69,554		1838
1839	,,	,,	31,519	115,889	73,760		1839
1840	,,	,,	27,172	102,352	52,972	11,653	1840
1841	,,	,,	14,787	38,298	46,450	9,255	1841
1842	,,	,,	16,446	31,941	53,077	8,526	1842
1843	,,	,,	18,140	26,698	61,042	10,088	1843
1844	,,	,,	14,998	18,744	46,142	9,535	1844
1845	,,	,,	15,509	20,193	46,592	7,113	1845
1846	,,	,,	10,694	19,503	46,601	6,466	1846
1847	,,	,,	11,164	10,865	35,844	7,509	1847
1848	,,	,,	6,586	9,209	45,649	5,645	1848
1849	,,	,,	7,926	15,216	64,831	6,759	1849
1850	,,	,,	9,962	16,759	60,639	8,643	1850
1851	,,	,,	12,727	25,081	67,028	9,493	1851
1852	,,	,,	14,546	20,140	95,039	17,164	1852
1853	,,	,,	33,368	25,789	93,724	32,650	1853
1854	,,	,,	23,935	52,745	92,269	16,987	1854
1855	410	2,030	40,012	75,587	120,098	22,318	1855
1856	694	2,689	51,023	49,040	139,548	39,545	1856
1857	357	1,497	68,351	44,910	110,974	28,278	1857
1858	812	1,499	45,089	32,802	112,296	23,488	1858
1859	323	1,199	65,256	57,999	139,768	34,428	1859
1860	662	2,755	69,993	40,360	125,352	28,700	1860
1861	490	5,470	40,708	16,917	96,969	31,724	1861
1862	636	5,554	64,710	20,097	80,594	32,320	1862
1863	541	2,876	73,679	24,506	102,607	41,031	1863
1864	437	2,627	67,292	28,908	.67,634	36,563	1864
1865	303	2,340	26,851	18,621	64,333	27,190	1865
1866	3	318	52,824	20,544	67,015	38,028	1866
1867	31	1,095	41,873	9,523	55,414	29,798	1867
1868	558	5,004	31,661	13,566	53,259	25,264	1868
1869	664	4,767	19,743	8,801	51,130	25,684	1869
1870	1,443	7,452	74,578	42,055	57,528	25,194	1870
1871	1,631	7,533	Not stated	Not stated	56,322	22,441	1871
1872	569	4,138	,,	,,	54,454	19,440	1872
1873	651	4,812	,,	,,	44,961	18,786	1873
1874	431	4,271	,,	,,	42,688	18,689	1874
1875	332	3,026	,,	,,	39,266	21,332	1875
1876	313	1,974	,,	,,	33,749	17,411	1876
1877	106	1,119	,,	,,	37,385	16,755	1877
1878	542	3,117	,,	,,	36,766	16,530	1878
1879	987	3,852	,,	,,	36,677	14,231	1879

TABLE III. A.

QUANTITIES OF THE UNDERMENTIONED ARTICLES OF FOREIGN AND COLONIAL FARM PRODUCE EXPORTED FROM THE UNITED KINGDOM, AS FAR SO CAN BE GIVEN, IN EACH YEAR, FROM 1800 TO 1879.

A.—CORN, &c.

Years.	Wheat. Cwts.	Wheat Flour and Meal. Cwts.	Oats. Cwts.	Barley. Cwts.	Maize. Cwts.	Pcas. Cwts.	Beans. Cwts.	Rice. Cwts.	Potatoes. Cwts.	Hops. Cwts.	Years.
1800		18,858	†525	—							1800
1801		30,471	†2,363	†14							1801
1802		550,574	†7,631	†4,800							1802
1803		228,501	†4,591	†1,196							1803
1804		133,984	†11,078	†286							1804
1805		237,548	—	†9,600							1805
1806		37,615	†1,995	†1,321							1806
1807		23,449	—	†11							1807
1808		66,835	†2,935	†871							1808
1809		11,495	†1,163	†3,800							1809
1810		264,533	†1,664	†12,907							1810
1811		299,523	†6,526	†83,896							1811
1812		76,457	†13,804	†103,364							1812
1813		* —	* —	* —							1813
1814		97,285	†2,431	†31,857							1814
1815		236,729	†312	†4,046							1815
1816		82,622	†4,544	†211							1816
1817		184,800	†1,470	†13,936							1817
1818		74,311	†94	†39							1818
1819		94,681	†5,620	†11,432							1819
1820		368,869	†10,379	†18,754				100,403			1820
1821		811,482	†35,771	†30,775				105,249			1821
1822		622,667	†39,084	†19,361				135,600			1822

* Records destroyed.   † Including the quantity of Barleymeal and Oatmeal re-exported.

TABLE III. A. (continued).

QUANTITIES OF THE UNDERMENTIONED ARTICLES OF FOREIGN AND COLONIAL FARM PRODUCE EXPORTED FROM THE UNITED KINGDOM, SO FAR AS CAN BE GIVEN, IN EACH YEAR, FROM 1800 TO 1879.

A.—CORN, &c.

Years.	Wheat.	Wheat Flour and Meal.	Oats.	Barley.	Maize.	Peas.	Beans.	Rice.	Potatoes.	Hops.	Years.
	Cwts.	Cwts.	Cwts.	Cwts.	Cwts.	Cwts.	Cwts.	Cwts.	wts.	Cwts.	
1823	502,887		†34,477	†19,554	—	—	—	79,370	—	—	1823
1824	227,014		†29,437	†9,136	—	—	—	93,514	—	—	1824
1825	138,995		†31,516	†14,704	—	—	—	53,181	—	—	1825
1826	59,745		†23,895	†16,700	—	—	—	40,881	—	—	1826
1827	116,961	76,982	3,377	67,193	—	—	4,949	52,691	—	—	1827
1828	254,133	58,846	18,409	14,704	—	—	12,900	51,615	—	—	1828
1829	226,157	70,652	161,246	36,775	—	—	10,162	95,584	—	—	1829
1830	108,550	33,768	71,886	4,589	—	—	2,934	50,946	—	—	1830
1831	188,305	68,664	15,320	2,293	—	—	2,587	88,886	—	—	1831
1832	1,022,160	183,073	230,431	27,936	—	—	13,048	82,550	—	—	1832
1833	149,413	207,508	53,600	11,464	—	—	5,984	64,994	—	—	1833
1834	492,163	160,731	36,977	35,232	—	—	2,912	121,199	—	—	1834
1835	368,299	165,309	84,678	158,446	—	—	16,432	244,343	—	—	1835
1836	753,714	283,862	154,506	65,068	—	—	10,309	180,585	—	—	1836
1837	935,294	323,244	129,022	37,875	—	—	20,856	212,245	—	—	1837
1838	413,409	212,461	148,666	70,775	—	—	23,352	232,241	—	—	1838
1839	33,670	108,920	110,564	2,214	—	—	10,599	245,467	—	—	1839
1840	133,003	174,871	100,336	15,639	—	—	8,905	288,510	—	—	1840
1841	5,464	76,773	64,581	7,554	—	—	9,767	229,017	—	—	1841
1842	193,795	60,502	151,126	49,125	—	—	68,597	311,015	—	—	1842
1843	198,286	68,428	115,495	15,874	—	—	89,943	207,225	—	—	1843
1844	199,806	117,567	68,788	3,721	—	—	15,648	184,301	—	—	1844
1845	204,390	70,334	79,043	83,286	—	—	40,070	352,515	—	—	1845
1846	481,624	83,881	47,429	12,925	—	—	14,967	328,720	—	—	1846
1847	545,744	207,659	25,165	54,289	—	—	53,846	588,708	—	—	1847

Year			Cwts.	Cwts.	Quarters. / Cwts.	Cwts.	Cwts.			
1848	24,904	17,873	20,562	11	—		12,610	213,125	—	—
1849	1,603	19,442	16,632	236	—		3,787	290,732	—	—
1850	19,760	25,443	16,596	47,357	—		11,774	248,135	—	—
1851	161,061	74,408	18,070	11,371	—		9,785	396,842	—	—
1852	67,262	67,839	20,072	5,500	1,620		13,368	450,979	—	—
1853	395,824	120,787	11,641	250	24,060			625,700	—	1,695
1854	368,013	61,067	21,973	1,923	37,195			804,490	352	6,824
1855	141,184	118,833	3,402	466	45,122			754,226	105	12,196
1856	390,732	96,337	15,015	49	36,433			1,090,819	37	2,305
1857	290,108	82,578	26,441	1,114	92,832			1,255,151		375
1858	21,038	16,376	6,197	20,679	17,476			1,199,714	773	2,963
1859	45,071	14,647	7,915	51,729	112,679			1,155,075	307	312
1860	21,645	8,167	890,662	80,134	3,446			1,173,090	693	1,935
1861	1,020,262	291,509	335,477	31,284	12,343			1,722,188	122	4,642
1862	46,332	33,571	19,580	509	10,103			1,272,049		14,280
1863	105,742	29,612	25,581	9,061	22,856	580	279	1,606,350	44	5,583
1864	37,869	42,759	53,546	290,464	12,286	2,927	77	1,679,325	347	8,831
1865	27,124	21,072	45,861	49,393	8,779	843	71	1,396,294	68	3,276
1866	46,813	18,365	110,221	5,982	5,471	195	220	1,298,649	270	13,224
1867	225,599	16,861	41,546	41,165	3,166	6,964	141	1,196,295	719	9,241
1868	291,547	15,085	86,455	71,300	9,109	18,778	1,193	2,041,420	635	8,065
1869	69,589	8,875	40,332	34,961	11,614	1,081	2,029	1,826,416	745	3,207
1870	1,093,498	372,187			43,151	30,283	2,600	2,221,520	1,223	4,665
1871	639,607	344,954			51,665	11,857	4,725	2,466,475	679	5,064
1872	213,179	11,119			27,007	211	3,119	3,138,701	1,285	6,564
1873	1,027,594	61,593			118,275	104	1,839	3,280,503	2,203	4,461
1874	719,998	110,710			98,448	4,927	1,512	4,095,751	807	1,726
1875	74,040	13,366			25,338	1,844	4,123	3,306,719	3,777	4,947
1876	822,107	14,316			242,144	14,433	18,117	3,434,575	5,880	17,307
1877	922,318	24,852			359,146	7,417	24,688	2,797,969	10,552	5,624
1878	853,321	59,085			305,054	3,945	13,502	3,844,975	7,502	4,804
1879	500,895	66,943			749,745	67,142	31,697	3,288,323	10,437	2,355

† Including the quantity of Barleymeal and Oatmeal re-exported.

TABLE III. B.

QUANTITIES OF THE UNDERMENTIONED ARTICLES OF FOREIGN AND COLONIAL FARM PRODUCE EXPORTED FROM THE UNITED KINGDOM, SO FAR AS CAN BE GIVEN, IN EACH YEAR, FROM 1820 TO 1879.

B.—PROVISIONS, &c.

Years.	Animals.		Bacon and Hams.	Beef.	Meat, Salted or Fresh.	Meat, Preserved, other than Salted.	Pork.	Eggs.	Butter.	Cheese.	Lard.	Years.
	Oxen, Bulls, Cows, and Calves.	Sheep and Lambs.										
	No.	No.	Cwts.	Cwts.	Cwts.	Cwts.	Cwts.	No.	Cwts.	Cwts.	Cwts.	
1820	—	—	858	—	—	—	—	—	—	700	—	1820
1821	—	—	848	—	—	—	—	—	—	724	—	1821
1822	—	—	1,329	—	—	—	—	—	—	1,876	—	1822
1823	—	—	1,456	—	—	—	—	—	139	2,041	—	1823
1824	—	—	2,889	—	—	—	—	—	6	2,200	—	1824
1825	—	—	3,142	—	—	—	—	—	31	3,152	—	1825
1826	—	—	1,951	227	—	—	—	—	1,085	3,152	—	1826
1827	—	—	2,618	4,061	—	—	—	—	734	2,160	—	1827
1828	—	—	2,921	4,047	—	—	—	—	1,813	2,621	—	1828
1829	—	—	1,762	2,098	—	—	—	—	2,771	4,762	—	1829
1830	—	—	1,114	1,075	—	—	—	—	1,053	3,544	—	1830
1831	—	—	1,099	331	—	—	—	—	1,443	2,678	—	1831
1832	—	—	1,816	842	—	—	—	—	1,664	2,617	—	1832
1833	—	—	1,693	4,182	—	—	—	2,000	2,721	5,884	—	1833
1834	—	—	2,120	3,048	—	—	3,331	—	2,304	6,784	—	1834
1835	—	—	2,366	1,738	—	—	3,321	3,600	2,789	5,670	—	1835
1836	—	—	3,882	4,969	—	—	8,972	6,240	1,646	7,157	—	1836
1837	—	—	3,040	7,840	—	—	19,660	4,000	2,031	5,285	—	1837
1838	—	—	4,673	9,531	—	—	15,980	3,000	4,640	6,818	—	1838
1839	—	—	5,321	11,351	—	—	31,101	1,800	2,534	8,340	—	1839
1840	—	—	5,006	19,880	—	—	28,238	2,400	4,313	8,620	—	1840
1841	—	—	3,473	32,306	—	—	29,367	—	3,834	9,321	—	1841
1842	—	—	2,361	18,902	—	—	23,864	—	7,660	6,123	—	1842

Year	(1)	(2)	(3)	(4)	(5)	(6)	(7)	(8)	(9)	(10)	(11)
1843		7,973	4,230		25,847			6,700	1,433		
1844		7,152	724		6,001			10,189	1,739		
1845		4,609	1,281	145	8,707			6,790	931		
1846		3,784	2,102	7,200	3,544			2,849	1,063		
1847		4,938	1,248	5,760	2,141			1,698	1,195		
1848		3,499	1,027		4,161			1,034	3,244		
1849		6,248	2,626		4,958			2,429	987		
1850		5,347	839		15,199			3,432	1,787		
1851		4,089	963		6,955			1,892	2,206		
1852		5,706	1,838		3,778			1,620	3,103		
1853		9,436	915		†5,149			*	6,372		
1854		5,605	1,348		†17,618			*	576		
1855	1,795	5,348	3,577		†14,450	17		*	2,621		
1856	1,298	7,112	1,845	6,500	†10,599	200		*	3,626		
1857	9,678	9,065	2,263	29,000	†13,318	1,451		*	23,368		
1858	103	7,088	1,670	22,080	†2,760	20			1,037		
1859	110	9,341	1,021		37,124	170	7	10,889	476	31	
1860	365	8,208	2,149	720,000	8,245	230	176	5,696	500	3	
1861	2,538	8,271	5,634	1,320	1,380	4		1,628	6,515		
1862	38,238	9,298	13,291		10,840	2,114		3,884	139,854	172	
1863	30,654	9,550	29,326		37,943	19	1,632	6,513	280,499	31	
1864	33,584	9,657	15,770		33,314	21	9	21,425	74,535	56	25
1865	2,158	10,733	14,868	1,680	5,557	80		9,959	4,569	138	3
1866	12,424	10,102	13,160		4,392	235	130	5,424	66,760	20	
1867	15,269	10,465	13,653	42,000	16,191	688	130	6,124	18,369	270	4
1868	9,776	11,454	14,981	1,920	8,432	735	99	5,056	8,396	82	
1869	792	12,999	17,994		2,029	991	97	9,777	5,196		
1870	536	30,743	16,084		41,011	25,976	1,105	38,515	22,952	20	124
1871	47,864	22,850	19,707	322,680	58,550	34,547	163	25,872	133,265	28	64
1872	121,977	21,066	30,118	1,512,120	20,869	19,946	293	20,982	454,310	46	
1873	69,428	26,041	22,256	79,200	11,677	18,242	177	16,352	397,579	235	6
1874	53,426	27,975	23,214	46,800	16,447	35,684	68	13,670	272,036	47	2
1875	22,812	31,287	31,024	484,080	7,165	41,228	15	16,844	224,893	84	15
1876	35,656	44,938	23,113	97,560	9,612	40,222	72	19,261	378,450	48	31
1877	38,330	50,201	41,993	390,240	17,441	27,431	257	16,743	430,089	97	23
1878	55,319	45,733	40,301	228,240	24,132	25,323	118	15,252	491,444	6	217
1879	64,925	40,146	41,969	275,040	30,274	16,134	683	19,110	391,764	18	88

* Included with Pork. † Including Pork.

TABLE IV.

TABLE SHOWING THE PERCENTAGE OF THE EXPORTS AS COMPARED
WITH THE IMPORTS OF THE UNDERMENTIONED ARTICLES, IN
THE PERIOD FROM 1828 TO 1848, AND IN EACH DECENNIAL
PERIOD FROM 1849 TO 1878.

(NOTE.—British and Irish produce is included in the Exports as well as Foreign
and Colonial.)

	1828 to 1848.	1849 to 1858.	1859 to 1868.	1869 to 1878.
Wheat	6·4	2·4	1·7	3·3
Wheat Flour	12·6	2·9	1·6	3·8
Barley	†5·0	Not known	Not known	*0·8
Oats	†23·6	,,	,,	*3·0
Maize	Not known	,,	,,	*0·8
Peas and Beans	†2·7	,,	,,	*0·9
Rice	47·2	36·7	51·6	50·3
Oxen	—	—	0·2	0·3
Sheep	—	—	0·6	0·5
Bacon and Hams	82·7	12·5	14·6	Not known
Beef and Pork	69·8	14·0	11·5	,,
Butter and Cheese	18·3	16·3	8·1	4·4

* For a period of 8 or 9 years only.
† For the period from 1828 to 1841 only.

APPENDIX V.

AVERAGE GAZETTE PRICES OF BRITISH WHEAT, BARLEY, AND OATS, PER IMPERIAL QUARTER, IN EACH YEAR FROM 1790 TO 1879.

Years.	Wheat.		Barley.		Oats.		Years.	Wheat.		Barley.		Oats.	
	s.	d.	s.	d.	s.	d.		s.	d.	s.	d.	s.	d.
1790	54	9	26	3	19	5	1835	39	4	29	11	22	0
1791	48	7	26	10	18	1	1836	48	6	32	10	23	1
1792	43	0	26	9	16	9	1837	55	10	30	4	23	1
1793	49	3	31	1	20	6	1838	64	7	31	5	22	5
1794	52	3	31	9	21	3	1839	70	8	39	6	25	11
1795	75	2	37	5	24	5	1840	66	4	36	5	25	8
1796	78	7	35	4	21	10	1841	64	4	32	10	22	5
1797	53	9	27	2	16	3	1842	57	3	27	6	19	3
1798	51	10	29	0	19	5	1843	50	1	29	6	18	4
1799	69	0	36	2	27	6	1844	51	3	33	8	20	7
1800	113	10	59	10	39	4	1845	50	10	31	8	22	6
1801	119	6	68	6	37	0	1846	54	8	32	8	23	8
1802	69	10	33	4	20	4	1847	69	9	44	2	28	8
1803	58	10	25	4	21	6	1848	50	6	31	6	20	6
1804	62	3	31	0	24	3	1849	44	3	27	9	17	6
1805	89	9	44	6	28	4	1850	40	3	23	5	16	5
1806	79	1	38	8	27	7	1851	38	6	24	9	18	7
1807	75	4	39	4	28	4	1852	40	10	28	6	19	1
1808	81	4	43	5	33	4	1853	53	3	33	2	21	0
1809	97	4	47	0	31	5	1854	72	5	36	0	27	11
1810	106	5	48	1	28	7	1855	74	8	34	9	27	5
1811	95	3	42	3	27	7	1856	69	2	41	1	25	2
1812	126	6	66	9	44	6	1857	56	4	42	1	25	0
1813	109	9	58	6	38	6	1858	44	2	34	8	24	6
1814	74	4	37	4	25	8	1859	43	9	33	6	23	2
1815	65	7	30	3	23	7	1860	53	3	36	7	24	5
1816	78	6	33	11	27	2	1861	55	4	36	1	23	9
1817	96	11	49	4	32	5	1862	55	5	35	1	22	7
1818	86	3	53	10	32	5	1863	44	9	33	11	21	2
1819	74	6	45	9	28	2	1864	40	2	29	11	20	1
1820	67	10	33	10	24	2	1865	41	10	29	9	21	10
1821	56	1	26	0	19	6	1866	49	11	37	5	24	7
1822	44	7	21	10	18	1	1867	64	5	40	0	26	0
1823	53	4	31	6	22	11	1868	63	9	43	0	28	1
1824	63	11	36	4	24	10	1869	48	2	39	5	26	0
1825	68	6	40	0	25	8	1870	46	10	34	7	22	11
1826	58	8	34	4	26	8	1871	56	8	36	2	25	2
1827	58	6	37	7	28	2	1872	57	0	37	5	23	2
1828	60	5	32	10	22	6	1873	58	8	40	5	25	5
1829	66	3	32	6	22	9	1874	55	8	44	11	28	10
1830	64	3	32	7	24	5	1875	45	2	38	5	28	8
1831	66	4	38	0	25	4	1876	46	2	35	2	26	3
1832	58	8	33	1	20	5	1877	56	9	39	8	25	11
1833	52	11	27	6	18	5	1878	46	5	40	2	24	4
1834	46	2	29	0	20	11	1879	43	11	34	0	21	10

AVERAGE GAZETTE PRICES OF BRITISH WHEAT, BARLEY, AND OATS PER IMPERIAL QUARTER, IN THE PERIOD FROM 1800 TO 1848, AND IN THE PERIOD FROM 1849 TO 1879.

Periods.	Wheat.		Decrease.		Barley.		Decrease.		Oats.		Decrease.	
	s.	d.	s.	d.	s.	d.	F.	d.	s.	d.	s.	d.
1800 to 1848	70	3			37	8			25	9		
			18	5			2	2			2	0
1849 to 1879	51	10			35	6			23	9		

APPENDIX VI.

STATEMENT RESPECTING THE OWNERSHIP OF LAND IN ENGLAND AND WALES (EXCLUSIVE OF THE METROPOLIS).

	Number of Entries in the Domesday Book.	Extent of Lands held.	Gross annual value at which the land is assessed.
		Acres.	£
Owners of land (Total) according to the Domesday Book	972,836	33,013,515	99,352,301
Owners of land of less than 1 acre in extent, according to the Domesday Book	703,289	151,172	29,127,679
Owners of land of more than 1 acre in extent, according to the Domesday Book	269,547	32,862,343	70,224,622
Owners of more than 3,000 acres of land assessed at more that £3,000 gross annual value, according to Bateman,* (1,704 persons)	† 3,873 (estimated.)	14,287,373	17,144,848 (estimated.)
Owners of land of between 2,000 and 3,000 acres in extent, assessed at not less than £2,000 gross annual value, and of more than 3,000 acres in extent, but assessed at between £2,000 and £3,000 gross annual value	† 1,311 (estimated.)	2,018,952	2,858,638
Public Authorities, Trustees of Charities, &c. &c. (which entries are printed in italics in the Domesday Book) ...	14,367	1,449,008	3,622,520 (estimated.)
Owners of more than 1 acre of land and of less than 2,000 acres assessed at less than £2,000 gross annual value ... [A few owners of estates of more than 2,000 acres may be included, but in all such cases the land must have been assessed on an average at less than £1 per acre.]	249,996	15,107,010	46,598,616 (estimated.)

* In Bateman's "Great Landowners," all persons are included whose estates in the *United Kingdom* exceed 2,000 acres in extent, and £2,000 in gross annual value. But as the above table refers to England and Wales only, a few persons may be included whose estates in that division of the Kingdom are below the limits mentioned.

† These estimates are founded on the figures in Bateman's "Great Landowners," with due allowance for those proprietors whose estates in England and Wales alone would fall below the standard indicated.

According to Mr. Arthur Arnold—

28 Dukes on an average own in the United Kingdom 142,500 acres each, and are repeated 5·6 times in the Domesday Book.

33 Marquesses on an average own in the United Kingdom 47,500 acres each, and are repeated 3·7 times in the Domesday Book.

194 Earls on an average own in the United Kingdom 30,200 acres each, and are repeated 3·3 times in the Domesday Book.

270 Viscounts and Barons on an average own in the United Kingdom 14,300 acres each, and are repeated 2·5 times in the Domesday Book.

And as the owners of between 2,000 and 3,000 acres in England and Wales on an average own 2,549 acres each, and are repeated 1·7 times in the Domesday Book, the number of owners of the 249,996 estates of above 1 acre and less than 2,000 acres given in the Table, assuming that they have been repeated as often, will be 147,657, and the total number of persons owning more than one acre of land in England and Wales will be about 150,153.

APPENDIX VII.

VESTED INTERESTS IN SETTLED ESTATES.

An important precedent for dealing with Vested Interests in Settled Estates is supplied by the Scotch Entail Amendment Act (Rutherfurd's Act) of 1848, and the subsequent Entail Amendment Acts.

By the Act of 1848, an heir of entail born *after* the date of any entail made on or after the 1st of August, 1848, was enabled to disentail on majority; and heirs of entail born *before* that date were enabled to disentail, with the consent of the heir-apparent born after the entail, and being twenty-five years of age. An heir of full age in possession of an estate entailed *prior to* that date, having been himself born after that date, was enabled to disentail at his own discretion; if born before that date, he was enabled to disentail with the consent of the heir-apparent born after that date, and being twenty-five years of age. An heir of full age in possession of an estate entailed *prior to* that date, whatever the date of his own birth, was enabled to disentail, if he were the only heir in existence and unmarried; otherwise, with the consent of the three next heirs in succession, the nearest being twenty-five years of age.

By the subsequent Act of 1875, the Court was enabled to dispense with any consents required in the last case except that of the heir next in succession, whose consent in all cases might be given at the age of twenty-one instead of twenty-five. The expectancies of the heirs thus passed over were directed to be valued, and the amount ascertained to be secured for their benefit. Moreover, in the event of the heir in possession being the sole heir of entail the disqualification of marriage was removed.

It will be observed that in these Acts no provision is made for protecting the interests of unborn children, though it has been held that "the emergence of a nearer heir" before the completion of the proceedings must put an end to the application. Subject to this risk, a Scotch tenant for life, as he would be called in English law, with the consent of his next brother, may disentail a family estate for his own benefit, compensating two other living heirs if they should object, but cutting off the contingent interests of his own unborn children.

Probably the principle of this legislation would be adopted in any English statute for the reform or abolition of entail, so far as the interests of unborn persons are concerned. Whether living remainder-men, having interests subsequent to those of unborn persons, are entitled to compensation, or whether no interest but that of an heir-apparent should be treated, for this purpose, as a vested interest, is a more difficult question. However it might be decided, a single generation would suffice to extinguish a large proportion of the interests arising under existing entails, and very remote expectations may usually be satisfied by the offer of a very moderate composition.

It is not unworthy of notice that Scotch Entail of the rigid type which has been reformed by the Acts of 1848 and 1875 is, after all, less than two centuries old. It was introduced by the Entail Act of 1685, a monument of the same degenerate period which produced the latest form of English family settlements.

APPENDIX VIII.

AMOUNT OF POOR RATE LEVIED IN THE UNDERMENTIONED UNION COUNTIES IN EACH OF THE YEARS ENDED LADY DAY, 1852, 1868, AND 1878.

UNION COUNTIES.	Poor Rate Levied (Years ended Lady Day).		
	1852.	1868.	1878.
	£	£	£
Bucks	82,958	101,010	84,727
Northampton	100,635	175,428	176,431
Huntingdon	29,573	43,135	40,313
Cambridge	101,412	123,126	114,857
Norfolk	203,681	246,169	220,864
Wilts...	147,816	189,948	174,793
Dorset	85,258	128,212	112,099
Cornwall	84,146	162,753	163,900
Hereford	51,854	78,209	112,523
Salop...	75,402	124,040	124,108
Rutland	9,655	15,823	14,006
Lincoln	157,644	212,928	203,181
York, N.R.	67,848	96,125	158,471
Westmoreland...	16,186	23,307	25,281
Wales, North	166,772	241,940	250,170
	1,380,840	1,962,153	1,975,724
Less for large town Unions, and corrections for change of areas...	245,252	403,073	464,667
	1,135,588	1,559,080	1,511,057
Increase over 1852	—	37 per cent.	33 per cent.

APPENDIX IX.

Average Extent of Land held by Small Proprietors between 1 and 100 Acres in groups of Counties.

MID-WALES.

	Acres.	
Montgomery	$31\frac{1}{10}$	
Brecon	$31\frac{3}{4}$	
Radnor	$33\frac{1}{2}$	Average about 35
Cardigan	$39\frac{1}{2}$	
Merioneth	$41\frac{1}{6}$	

EXTREME NORTHERN.

Cumberland	29	
Northumberland	$27\frac{2}{3}$	
Westmoreland	$25\frac{1}{2}$	Average about $30\frac{1}{2}$
Durham	$24\frac{3}{4}$	
N. York	$26\frac{3}{4}$	

SOUTH WALES.

Pembroke	26	
Glamorgan	$21\frac{1}{4}$	Average about 29
Carmarthen	$29\frac{1}{10}$	

WESTERN.

Devon	$27\frac{1}{4}$	Average about $26\frac{1}{2}$
Cornwall	$26\frac{1}{8}$	

EASTERN.

Cambs	$16\frac{1}{6}$	
Essex	$17\frac{1}{2}$	Average about 19
Norfolk	$19\frac{1}{4}$	
Suffolk	$22\frac{3}{4}$	

SOUTHERN.

Hants	$15\frac{4}{5}$	
Kent	$19\frac{1}{4}$	Average about $18\frac{1}{2}$
Sussex	$20\frac{1}{10}$	

NORTH WALES.

Flintshire (A Colliery County)	$12\frac{1}{8}$	
Carnarvon	$16\frac{2}{3}$	Average about 17
Denbigh	$17\frac{3}{4}$	
Anglesea	$21\frac{1}{3}$	

SOUTH MIDLAND.

	Acres.	
Huntingdon	17	
Oxon	$18\frac{1}{4}$	
Berks	$18\frac{1}{3}$	Average about $16\frac{1}{2}$
Bucks	20	
Northants	$20\frac{1}{2}$	
Beds	$21\frac{1}{3}$	

NORTH MIDLAND.

Staffordshire	$12\frac{1}{4}$	
Derby	$15\frac{1}{2}$	
Notts	$16\frac{2}{3}$	
Lincoln	$15\frac{1}{2}$	Average about 16
Leicester	$18\frac{1}{4}$	
Rutland	$14\frac{1}{4}$	
Warwick	$17\frac{2}{3}$	

NORTHERN.

E. York	$16\frac{3}{4}$	
W. York	$15\frac{1}{2}$	Average about $15\frac{1}{2}$
Lancashire	$15\frac{1}{2}$	
Cheshire	$14\frac{2}{3}$	

SOUTH WESTERN.

Dorset	14	
Wilts	$15\frac{2}{3}$	Average about 15
Somerset	16	

WEST MIDLAND.

Salop	15	
Worcester	$13\frac{3}{4}$	
Hereford	$13\frac{1}{3}$	Average about 15
Gloucester	$13\frac{1}{2}$	
Monmouth	$19\frac{5}{8}$	

HOME.

Surrey	13	
Middlesex	$14\frac{1}{10}$	Average about 14
Herts	$15\frac{3}{4}$	

APPENDIX X.

EXTRACTS FROM THE AGRICULTURAL RETURNS OF GREAT BRITAIN, 1880.

TABLE I.—TOTAL AREA AND ACREAGE UNDER EACH KIND OF CROP, BARE FALLOW, AND GRASS; AND NUMBER OF CATTLE, HORSES, SHEEP, AND PIGS, AS RETURNED UPON THE 4TH OF JUNE, 1880, AND 1879, IN ENGLAND AND WALES.

	ENGLAND.		WALES.	
	1880.	1879.	180	1879.
	TOTAL AREA AND ACREAGE UNDER CORN CROPS, GREEN CROPS, BARE FALLOW, GRASS, &c.			
	Acres.	Acres.	Acres.	Acres.
TOTAL AREA	32,597,398	32,597,398	4,721,823	4,721,823
TOTAL ACREAGE UNDER CROPS, BARE FALLOW, AND GRASS ...	24,596,266	24,503,882	2,767,516	2,758,743
CORN CROPS :,				
Wheat	2,745,733	2,718,992	89,729	94,639
Barley or Bere	2,060,807	2,236,101	142,514	152,491
Oats	1,520,125	1,425,126	239,526	226,967
Rye	31,683	39,808	1,765	1,464
Beans	404,071	419,504	2,619	3,031
Peas	231,280	273,591	1,963	2,985
TOTAL OF CORN CROPS ...	6,993,699	7,113,122	478,116	481,577
GREEN CROPS :				
Potatoes	324,931	323,992	38,940	42,609
Turnips and Swedes... ...	1,473,030	1,457,762	65,190	67,349
Mangold	333,609	352,671	7,685	8,410
Carrots	15,186	13,992	503	469
Cabbage, Kohl-Rabi, and Rape	155,001	162,296	1,096	1,237
Vetches and other Green Crops, except Clover or Grass	357,377	425,775	6,659	6,877
TOTAL OF GREEN CROPS...	2,659,134	2,736,488	120,073	126,951
CLOVER, SAINFOIN, AND GRASSES UNDER ROTATION	2,646,241	2,674,949	332,353	347,473
PERMANENT PASTURE OR GRASS NOT BROKEN UP IN ROTATION (exclusive of Heath or Mountain Land)	11,461,856	11,233,526	1,805,750	1,773,811
FLAX	8,788	6,970	15	12
HOPS	66,703	67,671	2	—
BARE FALLOW OR UNCROPPED ARABLE LAND	759,845	671,156	31,207	28,919

TABLE I.—*continued.*

	ENGLAND.		WALES.	
	1880.	1879.	1880.	1879.
	NUMBER OF LIVE STOCK, AS RETURNED UPON THE 4TH JUNE, 1880, AND 1879.			
	Acres.	Acres.	Acres.	Acres.
HORSES (including Ponies), AS RETURNED BY OCCUPIERS OF LAND :				
Used solely for purpose of Agriculture, &c.	766,527	769,590	72,605	73,130
Unbroken Horses and Mares kept solely for Breeding ...	325,745	331,117	62,290	63,261
TOTAL OF HORSES ...	1,092,272	1,100,707	134,895	136,391
CATTLE :				
Cows and Heifers in Milk or in Calf	1,593,157	1,604,550	261,356	262,000
Other Cattle :				
2 Years of Age and above	1,075,871	1,032,961	125,888	112,064
Under 2 Years of Age ...	1,489,018	1,491,429	267,470	269,751
TOTAL OF CATTLE ...	4,158,046	4,128,940	654,714	643,815
SHEEP :				
1 Year old and above ...	10,629,783	11,520,802	1,905,112	2,012,012
Under 1 Year old	6,198,863	6,924,720	813,204	861,448
TOTAL OF SHEEP ...	16,828,646	18,445,522	2,718,316	2,873,460
PIGS...	1,697,914	1,771,081	182,003	192,757

It is stated in the Prefatory Report that "in Great Britain the Area returned as under cultivation has increased by 126,000 acres since 1879, and the total increase in the ten years since 1870 is no less than 1,694,000 acres, or a greater Area than the whole of Devonshire. Of this increase about two-thirds or 1,187,000 acres were in England, 220,000 acres in Wales, and 287,000 acres in Scotland. As has been remarked several times in previous reports, a large share of this increased Acreage must be credited to the more correct Returns of late years, when errors from the use of local Acres, such as 'Scotch' or 'Lancashire' Acres, and also the omission of out of the way farms, have been discovered."

It appears from Table III. of the Agricultural Statistics that the acreage of orchards, &c., was 175,200 acres in England, and 2,834 in Wales; that of market gardens, 40,289 acres in England, and 596 in Wales; that of nursery grounds, 9,891 acres in England, and 316 in Wales; that of woods and plantations, 1,435,434 acres in England, and 162,135 in Wales.

From Table IV. it appears that the percentage of total cultivated acreage under various kinds of crops was as follows :—

—	ENGLAND.		WALES.	
	1880.	1879.	1880.	1879.
	PERCENTAGE OF TOTAL.			
Corn Crops (including Beans and Peas)	28·4	29·0	17·3	17·5
Green Crops	10·8	11·2	4·3	4·6
Bare Fallow	3·1	2·7	1·1	1·0
Grass :—				
Clover, &c., under rotation... ...	10·8	10·9	12·0	12·5
Permanent Pasture	46·6	45·9	65·3	64·4
Other Crops	0·3	0·3	0·0	0·0
TOTAL	100·0	100·0	100·0	100·0

Table VI. contains the following :—

STATEMENT OF THE NUMBER OF AGRICULTURAL HOLDINGS OF VARIOUS SIZES, AND OF THE ACREAGE OF EACH CLASS OF HOLDINGS, IN ENGLAND AND WALES, IN EACH OF THE YEARS 1880 AND 1875.

CLASSIFICATION OF HOLDINGS.	ENGLAND.		WALES.	
	1880.	1875.	1880.	1875.
	NUMBER OF AGRICULTURAL HOLDINGS OF EACH CLASS.			
50 Acres and under	295,313	293,469	40,836	40,161
From 50 to 100	44,602	44,842	9,767	9,656
„ 100 to 300	58,677	58,450	7,696	7,316
„ 300 to 500	11,617	11,245	454	433
„ 500 to 1,000	4,095	3,871	75	84
Above 1,000	500	463	6	10
TOTAL	414,804	412,340	58,834	57,660
	ACREAGE OF HOLDINGS OF EACH CLASS.			
50 Acres and under	3,528,840	3,550,405	647,587	631,941
From 50 to 100	3,233,053	3,259,110	707,743	698,879
„ 100 to 300	10,197,913	10,042,162	1,202,098	1,141,456
„ 300 to 500	4,359,794	4,202,402	155,993	157,725
„ 500 to 1,000	2,654,360	2,513,903	47,378	54,207
Above 1,000	637,311	571,994	7,176	12,941
TOTAL	24,611,271	24,139,976	2,767,975	2,697,149

The following explanation of the foregoing Table is given in the Prefatory Report :—

"On comparing the principal results with the figures of 1875, when the last Return of this kind was obtained, the proportionate Acreage of the large and small Holdings seems to have undergone little change. Thus for Great Britain the Area held in occupations of 50 acres and under is still 15 per cent. of the total ; that between 50 and 100 acres also 15 per cent. ; between 100 and 300, 42 per cent. ; from 300 to 500, 16 per cent. ; from 500 to 1,000, 10 per cent. ; and in farms over 1,000 acres, 2 per cent.

"In England alone a tendency to larger occupations may be noticed, the small farms of 50 acres and under being now 14 instead of 15 per cent. of the whole Acreage, and the moderate sized ones, between 50 and 300 acres, 54 per cent. against 56 per cent. in 1875, while farms over 300 acres amount to 32 per cent., or nearly a third of the cultivated area, as compared with 29 per cent. in 1875.

"In Scotland, however, the tendency is rather to an increase in occupations between 50 and 300 acres, which are now 59 per cent. against 58 per cent. in 1875, and the moderate sized farms in Wales have also somewhat increased ; so that, as before stated, the proportionate Acreage for the whole of Great Britain is almost the same."

INDEX.

A.

INDEX.